FEMINISM AND THE !

FEMINISM AND THE POLITICS OF READING

LYNNE PEARCE

Senior Lecturer, Lancaster University, UK

A member of the Hodder Headline Group
LONDON • NEW YORK • SYDNEY • AUCKLAND

First published in Great Britain in 1997 by
Arnold, a member of the Hodder Headline Group
338 Euston Road, London NW1 3BH
175 Fifth Avenue, New York, NY 10010

Distributed exclusively in the USA by
St Martin's Press, Inc.
175 Fifth Avenue, New York, NY 10010

British Library Cataloguing in Publication Data
A catalogue entry for this book is available from the British Library

Library of Congress Cataloging-in-Publication Data
A catalog entry for this book is available from the Library of Congress

ISBN 0 340 61413 7 (pb)
ISBN 0 340 70062 9 (hb)

Composition by Phoenix Photosetting, Chatham, Kent
Printed and bound in Great Britain by
J W Arrowsmith Ltd, Bristol

To Rowena Murray
and the Scottish Wilderness

Contents

List of Illustrations

Acknowledgements

The making of this book has been supported by a number of institutions, award-bodies, publishers and individuals to whom I should like to give thanks.

My first opportunity for extended research on the project occurred during my sabbatical leave in 1995, which I spent as a Visiting Scholar at the McGill Centre for Research and Teaching on Women in Montréal. This was an extremely welcome 'time-out' for me, and I should like to extend special thanks to all those who were working at MCRTW during this period and who gave me their friendship and support: in particular Nora Brown, Monica Hotter, Abby Lippmann, Blossom Schaffer and Sarah Baker.

I am also much indebted to the British Academy, whose Small Research Grant helped to finance this visit, and similarly to Lancaster University's own Research Travel Fund, which enabled me to visit different locations in Canada in connection with the research for Chapter 8.

My stay in Montréal also enabled me to make contact with the Art History department at Concordia University, whose students and faculty (in particular Janice Helland) have shown so much interest in my work, past and present: this has been greatly appreciated. I was also made very welcome at Concordia's Simone de Beauvoir Institute, and would like to thank Barbara Meadowcroft for introducing me to the Montréal women artists of the early twentieth century, especially the work of Prudence Heward, even if I was not able to include this in the final version of Chapter 8 due to the limits of space. Thanks, too, to all my good friends in Canada who made my stay there such an enjoyable one: in particular, Kathryn Campbell (Argyll, not Glencoe!) and Anne-Louise Howson.

The book's completion, meanwhile, has been made possible by my semester as an exchange professor at The University of Notre Dame, Indiana, and here I am especially grateful to both my Head of Department at Lancaster, Keith Hanley, and to Greg Kucich in the English Department at Notre Dame, for setting this up for me. Many of my colleagues at Notre

Dame showed a good deal of interest in the project, and I would like to thank them – and colleagues, friends and audiences on both sides of the Atlantic – for their comments on papers based on this research.

Moving on to the specifics of production, I should like to thank the following publishers for permission to reproduce the texts which appear here as Chapters 2, 3 and 4: Manchester University Press, for the essay '"I" the reader: text, context and the balance of power', which was first published in *Feminist Subjects, Multi-Media: New Approaches to Criticism and Creativity*, ed. Penny Florence and Dee Reynolds (1994), pp. 160–71; Harvester-Wheatsheaf, for the essay 'Pre-Raphaelite Painting and the Female Spectator: Sexual/Textual Positioning in Dante Gabriel Rossetti's *The Beloved*', which first appeared in *Gendering the Reader*, ed. Sara Mills (1994), pp. 155–72; and Falmer Press, for the essay 'Dialogic Theory and Women's Writing', which first appeared in *Working Out: New Directions for Women's Studies*, ed. Hilary Hinds, Ann Phoenix and Jackie Stacey (1992), pp. 184-93.

With respect to the book's illustrations and cover, I am *most* grateful to Angela Grauerholz for allowing me to reproduce a number of the photographs featured in her 1995 exhibition catalogue: their inclusion in the text will, I hope, greatly enhance my own readers' participation in the reading processes I describe. I should also like to thank the Tate Gallery, London, for permission to reproduce Dante Gabriel Rossetti's *Beata Beatrix* and *The Beloved*.

Ever since I first began working on this project, I was determined that the book should include the voices and texts of feminist readers other than myself, to give some context and perspective to its very self-reflexive central section. This would not have been possible without the co-operation of the groups of feminist readers who responded to my questionnaire for Chapter 8. While the individuals who comprise these groups are anonymized in the chapter itself, I would like to take the opportunity of thanking, personally, all those who contributed: Allyson Adley, Sarita Emelianna Ahouja, Melissa Branicky, Jan Carder, Sarah Franklin, Karen Grandy, Anne-Marie Grant, Jill LeBihan, Celia Lury, Jill McKenna, Maureen McNeil, Sara Mills, Ilya Parkins, Tessa Perkins, Jacqueline Reid-Walsh, Beverley Skeggs, Donald R. Spencer, Jackie Stacey, Adrienne Trucchi, Abbie Weinburg and Rhoda Zuk. I very much appreciate the time you took to do the reading for this exercise, and then to respond so fully, and with so much interest, to what was clearly a very demanding request; and I am especially grateful to those Canadian respondents whom I had not met before, and whose participation in the project was therefore an act of the utmost generosity.

In terms of the particular individuals who have contributed to the genesis, evolution and reworking of the project, especial thanks are due, first, to my colleagues at the Institute for Women's Studies at Lancaster (in particular Sarah Franklin, Celia Lury, Maureen McNeil, Beverley Skeggs, Jackie Stacey and Alison Young). It was at a research meeting of this group that

Acknowledgements

Sarah Franklin suggested, with typical decision (and vision!) that I should collect some of my existing work together in a volume called 'Feminism and the Politics of Reading', while 'the other Sarah' (Oatey) remains the ghost in the chinks of the whole machine.

As far as intervention in the new material is concerned, I am very greatly indebted to both Sara Mills and Jackie Stacey, who have taken a good deal of time to read and comment on the manuscript in draft form: their own research experience in the area of reading and spectator theory was *invaluable* to me, and I trust my acknowledgements throughout the text will mark their contribution. Thanks also to Deborah McVea for her assistance in typing up Chapters 2 to 4 with the eye of a skilled editor and scholar, and to my copy editor, Christina Malkowska Zaba, for all her excellent work.

Other friends, meanwhile (in particular, Carole Elliott, Michelle Nuttall, Karen Stanley and Viv Tabner) have accompanied me in many hundreds of miles (!) of recreation and challenge far away from the printed page, whilst Rowena Murray's presence is to be found in *all* the intertextual, extratextual, and techno/textual spaces from which this project takes its inspiration. And the best thing about the 'extratextual', of course – all the hills, mountains and wildernesses that now mean more to me than almost anything – is that though we might exploit them for metaphors, they can never be reduced to one.

Finally, my thanks go to Christopher Wheeler at Arnold for once again proving to be such an excellent publisher: your support of the project through all stages of its production is much appreciated.

Lynne Pearce
1996

Author's note

Please note that this volume employs two different type faces to signal different *acts of reading*, with the sans serif representing the preliminary engagements I made with the four texts that are the subject of my investigation in Chapters 5 and 6.

|1|

The Ghostly Romance: Towards a Theory of Implicated Reading

Before I begin mapping out the territory of this book – explaining its trajectory, detailing its boundaries, borders and limits – let me start by taking you straight to the wilderness at its heart: the space of greatest chaos and confusion in which I, 'the reader', am found floundering in the midst of a textual experience for which my training as a feminist/poststructuralist scholar is apparently of no assistance:

> [Olive Schreiner's] *Story of an African Farm* is a space/place I am compelled to haunt long after its central protagonists have been laid to rest.[1] In some sense, indeed, they exited after the first read when my act of narrative closure effected the end of their story. I, however,

Illustration 1.1   *'The dark forest of my own subjugated fears, desires and redemption'* (Chapter 5)

am left wandering amidst the deserted buildings they used to inhabit: a ghost among ghosts, caught up in a confusion of my own former reading-selves. This is the pain, assuredly, of deferral and difference: the pain attendant upon a desire for plenitude that can never be realized. As a reader, I am a ghost not only because I return, but because I am returning to a text. As a reader I am a voyeur of action in which I cannot participate or intervene. And this is sometimes experienced as a deep pain: to come so close to Lyndall, but to know that she will never see me; to be next to Waldo in his grief, but not be able to reach out and touch him. To this extent, engagement with any text we come to care about is potential agony. What we are experiencing is the loss of something that it was impossible for us to have from the outset. And so the textual deaths of Lyndall and Waldo enact what we already know, but didn't want to accept. Which is why it seems clear to me that it is we, as readers, who haunt texts; not they who haunt us. The reader-ghost is destined to continue her wanderings long after the actor-ghosts have gone. (Chapter 5)

This text, which is an extract from my 're-memorying' of Olive Schreiner's novel, *The Story of an African Farm* (1899), dramatizes some of the emotional disturbance of reading that has become my central concern, both as a feminist and a literary scholar.[2] As I moved from an interest in reading as an 'act of interpretation', with a particular concern for our agency and responsibility as feminist readers (see Chapters 2 to 4), towards a focus on textual positioning and text–reader interaction, so did the potential risk and trauma of reading become ever clearer. Reading was no longer something we 'did' to texts, either as scholarly textual-colonialists or as pleasure-seeking textual-tourists: reading was also something texts could 'do' to us whenever we took the leap into their uncharted territories.[3] Whilst previous reader-theory has dwelt on these questions of who/what is the source of a text's 'meaning' (author/reader/text or some combination thereof) as a largely philosophical issue, my own interest is thus, by contrast, motivated by care and concern for the reader. The unsurprising conclusion that reading is still best configured as a 'dialogic', if power-inscribed, *relationship* between text and reader (despite all the persuasive theorizing otherwise), is therefore the place my own investigations start from, not where they end.[4] The fact that this question of the textual 'balance of power' was a preoccupation of my own early work (see Chapter 2), and that the struggle for authority between text (and context) and reader (and addressee) continues to be central to much of my analysis, should not mislead the reader of this volume into thinking that this is what my project is 'about'.[5] In brief, my focus here is not the mechanics of interpretation (how meaning is made) but the *processes* of reading, which result in a text–reader relationship that I have described as *implicated*. My developing interest in reading/reception is, as it were, ontological rather than epistemological, although I have followed Elspeth Probyn's lead in seeing the value of each of these terms in its ability to explain, illuminate and perspectivize the other.[6] All this is not to suggest that I think we should discard interest in the professionalized *practices* of reading (i.e., what it means to 'make a reading'/effect an interpretation), but that we should look at these, too, 'from the inside', *vis-à-vis* the constitution and experience of such readers, and not simply the role they play in the interpretation itself. Chapters 7 and 8, for example, which consider how difference and disagreement come about *within* feminist reading communities, investigates what factors influence and constrain the reader engaged in professional critical practice and, in particular, those which block a more self-reflexive and interactive relationship with the text.

My mapping of this readerly wilderness has, of course, been based on personal experience, and the text which ensues is very much the story of my own anxious wanderings. This is made visible in certain chapters by the use of the personal pronoun in an autobiographical 'method' that I shall discuss below; but it is important to regard my 'reader's history' (see Chapter 2) as part of the more general cartography also, and to acknowledge that the professional 'maker of (feminist) readings' is myself as well as the readerly guinea-pig who is used to explore the more dialogic text–reader interactions which are the focus of Chapters 5 and 6 ('The Emotional Politics of Gendered Reading'). As far as feminist politics is concerned, moreover, the book travels from a concern with the opportunities, limitations and problems of using a feminist theoretical/ideological frame to wrest 'new' meanings out of recalcitrant texts (the professionalized 'feminist readings' to which I have just referred), to a questioning of what happens to those politics when the text–reader relationship becomes more interactive. Whilst, upon occasion, it appears that the feminism disappears, it is important to recognize that gender (despite reader-drives towards androgynous and/or transcendent modes of connection) never does.[7] The relationship between the reader and her 'textual other' (see below), even as it is power-inscribed, is also always already gendered in some way, making such *reading processes* of as much interest to feminist scholars as the *reading practices* which come waving the flag of their politics.[8] This book, then, looks at the politics of what it is to be a self-conscious feminist reader, and at the politics of what happens when that feminism is 'off-duty'. Whilst moving towards a new model of reading, by shifting attention from practice to process, it nevertheless avoids ideal scenarios, and grounds itself in the chaos and the confusion, the thrill and the anxiety, of *all* that it might mean to read as a feminist, allowing for the fact that the politics of any event is defined not only by what we do, but by what is done to us. If reading is an experience analogous to romance, as I hope to show, it is a predictably desperate one, in which the reader/lover must expect to be bewildered and lost as often as she is gladdened and saved.

In the remainder of this opening chapter I will situate this reconceptual-izaton of the text–reader relationship, and its implications for feminist read-ers, within the context of existing reader-theory in both literary studies and the visual arts (art history/film theory), as well as outlining the various pro-jects, methodologies and theoretical frameworks I have employed to enable me to engage and analyse the processes and practices of reading.

The Gendering of Reader Theory

Although not, perhaps, immediately apparent, the history of professional reading – why it evolved as a practice and not a process, why its character-ization has been cerebral rather than emotional – is strongly marked in terms of both gender and class politics. This also applies to the theories that have been used to analyse the practice. As Jonathan Culler observed some years ago in his book, *On Deconstruction* (1982), the reader-response the-ory associated with literary criticism has been 'generally cognitive rather than affective': 'not feeling shivers along the spine, weeping in sympathy or being transported with awe, but having one's expectations proved false, struggling with an irresolvable ambiguity, or questioning the assumptions on which one has relied' (p. 39). My own survey of twentieth-century recep-tion theory would confirm that this is true: and not only within literary crit-icism, but also with regard to film and media studies, and art history. Although a considerable amount of emotion has clearly attended the debates on the role(s) of author/text/reader in the production of textual meaning (witness the heated exchanges between Wolfgang Iser and Stanley Fish, for instance), few contemporary theorists have acknowledged the role of 'feeling' within the reading process itself.[9] So great has been the need to prove that text, reader, or some complex interaction of the two holds the 'balance of power' (see Chapter 2) that the commentators have been blind to those aspects of the reading process that appear to go beyond the ques-tion of meaning-production.

Although this obsession with interpretation can thus in itself be used to explain the lack of interest in the affective aspects of the reading process, it is worthwhile considering *why* the cognitive has come to dominate contem-porary textual theory and criticism in this way. As I have already indicated, gender and class – in as much as they are themselves the signifiers of power – are centrally implicated.

Within literary studies, the disregard for the emotions can first and fore-most be ascribed to the formalist/structuralist revolution. The trajectory connecting Russian Formalism with New Criticism and Structuralism demanded that the text become the autonomous object of study, and that all extratextual and contextual factors (authors, readers, historical discourses) were discounted in the practice of textual analysis. The most widely quoted rejection of the reader's role in the production of textual meaning came from W. K. Wimsatt and C. M. Beardsley in 1949. 'The Affective Fallacy', as they named it, 'is a confusion between the poem and its results . . . It begins by trying to derive the standard of criticism from the psychological effects [upon the reader] and ends up in impressionism and relativism'.[10] Implicit in this admonishment is, of course, a belief that the purpose of reading – at least professional reading – is not only the interpretation, but also the *evaluation* of the text; what it is blind to is the fact that such value does not reside in the 'verbal icon' itself, but in an external framework of taste and discrimination mediated by the reader. In writing off the effect of the text on the reader as a legitimate site for analysis, these early theorists also denied the role of the reader in their apparently text-centred analysis.

It is not difficult to see, even after one example, both how this rejection of the affective dimension of the reading process is predicated on a model of text–reader relations in which the text, for all its apparent iconicity, is 'mastered' by the reader, and how such a power-inscription can be analysed in terms of class and gender politics. Whilst Wimsatt and Beardsley reject so-called affective criticism, on the grounds that it 'ends in impressionism and relativism', we can speculate that their real anxiety is with the fact that such indeterminacy signals the reader's lack of control over both the text and the reading process; and such lack of control is, in modern Western culture, a mark of both the feminine and the un(der)educated, working class.

Whilst subsequent theorists, such as Wolfgang Iser, Stanley Fish, Jonathan Culler and Roland Barthes, have shown considerably more interest in the role and significance of the reader, it has still tended to be in the context of interpretation and meaning-production.[11] For example, in the following extract from Iser's celebrated *The Act of Reading* (1978), it is clear that although the reader has become the locus of the 'aesthetic response', our interest in him [*sic*] is limited to his role as 'actualizer' of the text, an interest as abstract and professional as the reader 'himself':

> It is generally recognised that literary texts take on their reality by being read, and this in turn means that texts must already contain certain conditions of actualization that will allow their meaning to be assembled in the responsive mind of the recipient. The concept of the implied reader is therefore a textual structure anticipating the presence of a recipient without necessarily defining him: this concept prestructures the role to be assumed by each recipient, and this holds true even when texts appear to ignore their possible recipient or actively exclude him. Thus the concept of the implied reader designates a network of response-inviting structures, which impel the reader to grasp the text. (p. 34)

Although the text–reader relationship described here is superficially interactive – each term depends upon the other – the simple fact that the reader exists to *interpret* the text means that his [*sic*] identity can never exceed his agency. According to Jonathan Culler, this failure to sustain a fully reciprocal model of text–reader relations is philosophically inevitable. Writing with respect to both Iser and Fish, he concludes, 'There must always be dualisms: an interpreter and something to interpret, a subject and an object, an actor and something he acts upon or that acts upon him' (*On Deconstruction*, p. 74). In most instances, moreover (as in Iser's), the term which tends to win out is the text, because 'reader-oriented critics have themselves found it makes a better story to talk of texts inviting or promoting responses than to describe readers creating texts' (p. 78). Whilst I agree with this analysis as far as it goes, my own feeling is that the the other reason the text triumphs is that, in most of these models, the reader's relationship is ultimately not with the text but *with the act of interpretation itself*. The practice Iser and Fish are describing, albeit from apparently opposite corners, conceives of the reader's 'textual other' (see below) in purely instrumental terms. The text dominates, in other words, not only because it 'makes for a better story', or represents a more secure object of study, but because reading is itself conceived as a primarily *hermeneutic* exercise. The truth of this seems to me to be reinforced, moreover, by the fact that even those critics who are ostensibly championing the reader over the text (such as Fish in his 'interpretive communities' phase) nevertheless make that reader into a sleuth: a 'reader-in-search-of-a-text-to-interpret':

> As soon as my students were aware that it was poetry they were seeing, they began to look with poetry-seeing eyes, that is, with eyes that saw everything in relation to properties they knew poems to possess. They knew, for example (because they were told by their teachers), that poems are (or are supposed to be) more densely and and intricately organised than ordinary communications; and that knowledge translated itself into a willingness – one might even say a determination – to see connections between one word and another and between every word and the poem's central insight. Moreover, the assumption that there *is* a central insight is itself poetry-specific, and presided over its own realization.
>
> (Fish, 1980: p. 326)

Whilst I agree with much of what this says about how interpretive communities work (see below and my own analyses in Chapters 7 and 8), it seems to me that Fish is blind to his own narrowly academic conception of the reader (even the student reader!) as one who is in search of something to interpret or explain. This is starkly in contrast with my own presentation of the reader as a lover, whose object is not to understand the text but to engage (with) it.

This leads us directly onto the even bigger question (and the one most reception theorists have stopped short of) which is *why* the reader, and the act of reading, continue to be conceptualized in these terms? As has already been indicated, the gendering of knowledge – in as much as reading is understood as an articulation of knowledge – plays a key role here, as does the class politics which has made 'the ability to interpret' the sign (and site) of bourgeois status.

It is because interpretive power is generally understood in terms of intellectual *cognition*, moreover, that the emotional aspects of reading continue to be kept at bay. 'Interpretation', even when seen as being dependent on the individual reader's psyche (as in the work of Norman Holland: see note 9) or his/her intepretive frameworks (as in the work of Stanley Fish), is nevertheless 'made respectable' by being figured as an act (voluntary or involuntary) of *reason*. The reader's role *appears* to be less subjective in this context because, as we are all aware, in the history of Western thought the discourse of rationality is diametrically opposed to that of emotionality: a binarism which is also profoundly gendered. Consciously or unconsciously, reception theorists thus seem to have been at pains to distinguish their criticism based on the concept of an 'intellectual reader' ('the ideal reader' is always highly educated) from Wimsatt and Beardsley's caricature of the reader as (to quote Virginia Woolf) 'a sponge sopped through with human emotions', simultaneously setting up a whole sequence of gendered oppositions which associate affective criticism with female/less well-educated readers (as epitomized by the reading practices associated with classic and popular romance).[12] What is crucial here, then, is the way that reading has been conceptualized as an act(ivity) of interpretation, and interpretation as mode of cognitive intellectual application; and the way in which both these concepts are classed and gendered to make sure that 'the reader', whether omnipotent, impotent or somewhere in between, is, at least, well-educated, respectable and (if only symbolically) *male*. Despite their superficial disagreements on the extent of his status, it seems to me that Iser, Fish and many other of the major reception theorists (see discussion of Barthes, Holland and more recent media-critics below) have had a broadly similar photofit in mind: a reader whose professionalism secures their own respectability, and whose capacity for interpretation translates into a capacity for *discrimination*.

This connection between the act of interpretation and the art of discrimination has been dealt with in Lynda Nead's work on obscenity and connoisseurship.[13] Here she has argued that, since the last century (at least) a reader/viewer's capacity for critical judgement has depended crucially upon his/her 'disinterestedness': and such judgement (or 'taste') is itself a mark of education, refinement – and *class*.[14]

In her work in this area, Nead cites a long chain of philosophers and art historians who have argued for the necessity of remaining *fully in control of one's feelings* during the act of aesthetic 'contemplation'.[15] Whilst Nead attends to the centrality of this discourse of repression and containment specifically in the context of erotic art, it clearly has a much wider application. 'Involvement' in a work of art/act of reading has historically been regarded as an indication that the reader/viewer lacks the education that enables him/her to distinguish between art (as 'representation') and 'real

Illustration 1.2   'For me . . . there can be *no* comfortable space from which to view art' (Chapter 5)

life'.[16] The bottom line of connoisseurship, then, is that *any* display of feeling (or declaration of personal involvement) in a text equals 'bad taste', and that – at the other end of the spectrum – the studious (and *visible*) control of such feelings assures one's place in the critical élite. The display of such 'distinction' (Bourdieu: see note 14 above), moreover, is not confined to the vestibule of the Royal Academy or the lobby of Covent Garden: it is also very vigorously at work in the feminist reading groups I interviewed for Chapter 8. Regardless of their own class backgrounds, most of the participants in my study were all too aware of the gap between declarations of textual involvement and the supposed disinterestedness of 'good taste'.

With respect to my own work, this focus on the gendering of meaning-production is addressed most directly in Chapters 2 to 4. Although the feminism of these chapters rests ostensibly with how the reader responds to her positioning by a text, circling around the issue of to what extent the female/feminist reader can resist, or embrace, her gendered positioning by a text, they also illustrate the way in which this hermeneutic model of text–reader relations is itself classed and gendered.[17] In line with my preceding discussion, Chapter 3 especially demonstrates the way in which the portrait of the reader as an interpreter of the text – even if she *is* a feminist one – inscribes her in the discourses of rationality and connoisseurship, and thus inhibits a more fully interactive and dialogic (that is, 'implicated': see below) response to the text, in which the emotional politics of reading are able to come to the fore and be explained. This misalignment of feminist politics and *reading practice* can thus be seen as an unformulated complication at the heart of each of these essays, and one which I address in the preface to this section of the book.

Reading and Pleasure

Once something of the ideological roots of the 'taboo' surrounding emotion in critical discourse is understood, the fact that reader and viewer *pleasure* is also evaluated in largely cognitive rather than affective terms is less of a surprise and paradox. Whilst pleasure is, indeed, the *only* emotion (or emotional framework) that has been given substantive treatment in the various schools of reader-theory, it is linked, in almost every case, with attempts to explain how and why people read and view texts, concluding that it is because interpretation itself is pleasurable.

Roland Barthes's writings are probably the most celebrated case in point. Although both *S/Z* (1974) and *Le Plaisir du Texte* (1975); (see note 11) engage a psychoanalytic vocabulary which abounds in the rhetoric of desire, the 'pleasure' analysed – be it *plaisir* or *jouissance* – is associated principally with the hermeneutics of reading. The pleasure attendant upon reading, in other words, is predicated upon interpretation (through the engagement, for example, of various textual codes) and is thus construed as cognitive rather than affective.[18] How Barthes describes this pleasure – as a process of deferred gratification dependent upon the various 'discontinuities' of the reading process – is interesting, to be sure ('It is the very rhythm of what is read and what is not read that creates the pleasure of the great narratives', *Pleasure of the Text*, p. 11), but his analysis misses the issue of how the (extratextual) emotions that are engaged as the reader pauses to look out of the window are *also* integral to a pleasure that is not wholly hermeneutic. The pleasure, in other words, is not simply a reflex of the interruption *per se*, but is crucially dependent upon what causes the break in concentration. As will be seen in the analysis of my own readings in Chapters 5 and 6, and in the analysis of the feminist reading groups in Chapter 8, the emotional fabric of the reading process depends very much on an interweaving of textual and extra-textual associations, as some cue in the text prompts us to the scripting of a *parallel* text based on some aspect of our personal or intertextual experience.[19]

Barthes's characterization of reading as primarily an interpretive and cognitive act also impacts upon his conception of the reader's 'textual other' (see note 8 above). As will be discussed in greater detail below, my own model of reading 'as romance' requires that we identify exactly who, or what, aspect of the text/(con)textual experience the reader engages in her interaction with it. Whilst this 'other' is most obviously posited as a character in the text, it can also be radically dehumanized into a 'collection of semes'. This last conceit, which derives from Barthes, proved very useful to me when I was looking for ways of explaining our involvement with texts in terms other than straightforward/humanist character-identification. In *S/Z*, for example, he writes:

> The person is no more than a collection of semes (inversely, however, semes can migrate from one figure in the text to another, if we descend

to a certain symbolic depth where there is no longer any respect of persons: Sarrasine and the narrator have semes in common). (p. 191)

For Barthes, however, this 'dehumanizing' of the textual character is part and parcel of his hermeneutic model of text–reader relations: 'reduced' to semes, the character is more easily incorporated into the total 'code' waiting to be cracked.

A similarly instrumental approach to pleasure may also be found in a good deal of psychoanalytic film-theory where it subtends the work on cinematic identification. As I will indicate later in this chapter, it is important to recognize that, in much of this work, too, 'pleasure' becomes the *object of study* at the expense of it being considered the site of emotional engagements with the text *per se*. The focus is on the psychic mechanisms which cause spectators to be positioned by texts in terms of a complex interaction of gendered and sexualized desires, *and not on the emotional follow-through of that engagement*. Despite the fact that theorists like Teresa de Lauretis and Mary Ann Doane instituted a more *active* model of spectatorship, pleasure thus continues to be discussed within the context of meaning production as the achievement of identity/identification.[20] A key point to observe here – and one that I will be developing below – is that reader-*activity* is not an automatic sign of reader-*interactivity*; and it is the latter which is, according to my own model, the prerequisite for a more complex and sustained emotional engagement with the text. As will be seen below, this lack of clarification around the active and the interactive in the designation of reader/viewer pleasure also complicates and muddles the work of much of the best audience-based research which otherwise – one might even say simultaneously – is tremendously helpful in moving us towards new, non-hermeneutic models of reading and spectatorship.[21] The intersection of pleasure and reader/viewer activity must, indeed, be thought of as one of the most contested sites of reception theory, with a good deal of confusion and disagreement resulting from the fact that the various theorists are differently invested in the concept of pleasure. As Jackie Stacey (see note 19) has observed:

> Within much cultural studies work, pleasure and activity have been further conflated. The resulting assumption has been that women's pleasure in a text can be equated with their activity as audiences, and activity is necessarily resistant, being the opposite of inactivity, which is assumed to mean collusion. It may be that this is wishful thinking on the part of the feminist critic who wishes to justify her own pleasure in texts which might be considered politically conservative or patriarchal. Indeed, one could take the opposite view and argue that, in fact, being an active female spectator of Hollywood stars, one is colluding more deeply with patriarchal cinema than a passive spectator would be. Or, alternatively, the activity of the female spectator may involve 'displeasure' and rejection or derision of the popular text she has viewed. (p. 46)

My own concern, following through from this political questioning, is that the overdetermination of pleasure has been concomitant with a tendency for the theorists concerned to focus on the reader-viewer's first-stage engagement with the text (the moment of recognition, identification and, perhaps, *interpretation*), and not on the emotional hinterland beyond. This narrow focus on the point of entry also helps to explain why the *displeasure* alluded to at the end of Stacey's quote, whose source is *not* simply hermeneutic, rarely gets mentioned.

The overdetermination of pleasure within reader/spectator theory, then, has resulted in a lack of interest in a whole range of emotional affects that hide behind its generic shop-front, including many negative ones. While, to be fair, Barthes's model of the reader's relationship to readerly and/or writerly texts does not conceptualize pleasure (either *plaisir* or *jouissance*) as an anodyne or 'comfortable' emotion, it is, nevertheless, resolutely *positive*: in as much as reading is fuelled by the same psychoanalytic chain that underpins our sexual relations, so must even our defences and denials be interpreted as part of a greater (and therefore good) 'desire'. As I have found in my own research, this implicit or explicit sexualizing/eroticizing of the act of reading is a huge (metaphorical) temptation; and, in as far as we continue to conceive of the engagement of text and reader as some sort of 'relationship', it is somewhat inevitable. However, as I will suggest later in this chapter, there also exist models of romance and desire which go beyond the Freudian 'pleasure principle', and which allow for a fuller range of emotional experience (and hence emotional *reader*-experience) than one based on a strictly Oedipal economy.

Textual Positioning

In the story of reception theory I have sketched thus far, the characterization of reading as an activity productive of emotional pleasure has depended upon a conceptualization of the reader as a hermeneutic intepreter of the text: the one who – in the last analysis at least – has the power to 'make the meaning', even if, as in Iser's formula (see note 9 above) it is simply a matter of joining up the dots. Not surprisingly, it is when this power shifts from the reader and back towards the text that we see the emotional skies begin to darken; and whilst a good deal of the work on what I shall refer to broadly as 'textual positioning' is still focused on meaning-production *per se*, other, non-pleasurable adjectives accompany descriptions of the reading/viewing event. It is important to recognize, however, that although the text becomes a more active agent in the models/theories I am about to discuss, the text–reader relationship falls short of becoming fully *interactive*, on account of the fact that reading/spectatorship is still characterized as a predominantly interpretive activity: that is to say, the interest is still focused on emotion in the context of meaning-production rather than through engagement of a textual, or contextual, 'other'.

Within the narrative of my own reader's history, the belief that texts *were* capable of 'positioning' their readers in terms of gender, class, sexuality, ethnicity and so on, emerged as a fresh anxiety at the end of my book on the Pre-Raphaelites.[22] As I record in Chapter 2, this crisis-moment in my feminist-reader's career turned on the question of how ethically legitimate it was for twentieth-century feminists to 'read against the grain' of the circumstances of a text's historical production and consumption.[23] To what extent was it 'good politics' to appropriate a text against its dominant reader-positioning? This qualm, moreover, becomes the context in which the stubbornly *unrecuperative* reading of Dante Gabriel Rossetti's *The Beloved* is made in Chapter 3, and is also in line with the conclusions of many of the other chapters of Sara Mills's *Gendering the Reader* (1994), in which this essay first appeared.[24]

A similar recognition of the text's ability to create dominant reader/viewer positionings is, of course, integral to contemporary feminist film-theory, begining with Laura Mulvey's groundbreaking 'Visual Pleasure and Narrative Cinema'.[25] Despite the many brilliant and persuasive arguments put forward in the 1970s and 1980s which challenged Mulvey's conclusions on the monolithically 'masculine' positioning of the spectator, it is interesting to discover, in the 1990s, how many feminists have returned to a covert acknowledgement of the power of the dominant reader/viewer positioning, and have expressed concomitant doubts about the political efficacy of more sophisticated models of gendered participation. Even Teresa de Lauretis who, as I have observed (see note 20), radically re-empowered the female reader/spectator with the concept of *double-identification*, has since argued that our scholarly interests are better directed towards the work of the alternative feminist film-makers who have striven to offer the female viewer *new* spectator positions.[26] This sentiment also appears to be shared by Annette Kuhn, who, in the second edition of *Women's Pictures* (1994), writes about Yvonne Rainer's ('experimental') *Lives of Performers* in these terms:

> None of the subject positions posed by classic narrative is at work here: identification with characters is impossible and there is no narrative closure. The narrative processes of *ellipsis* and *accretion* offer, on the contrary, the possibility of pleasures other than those of completion. First, in moments of accretion . . . the spectator has the option of pleasurable and open-ended contemplation of an image which constructs no particularly privileged viewpoint. The ellipses offer the possibility of a rather different pleasure, that of piecing together the fragments of the story – the active pleasure, that is, of working on a puzzle.[27]

What is interesting about this comment, of course, is not only that it is implicitly advocating a feminist investment in texts which, themselves, offer 'alternative' rather than 'dominant' reader/viewer positionings, but that once again the reader's activity (and her pleasure) are characterized as resolutely hermeneutic and cerebral. Despite the fact, indeed, that the history of the spectator-theory I have just sketched out has its roots in psychoanalytic models of desire and identification as unconscious processes, the presentation of the relationship between text and reader remains largely cognitive. The power-struggle that is engaged in by text and reader, or the negotiations they are seen to perform in terms of shifting reader-positionings, are nevertheless discussed within the same context of interpretation and meaning-production. Indeed, the line of thought Kuhn appears to pursue in the above quotation actively depends on shifting readerly activity *away* from a more interactive engagement with the text based on the problematic engagement of a 'textual other' (such as a character in the text). At this point we can thus see the logic of the interpretive model of readership come full circle once again: by making the act of reading predominantly hermeneutic, the problems of textual positioning and readerly disempowerment can be solved at a cognitive level, thus avoiding the complications of the reader's more messy, and more ostensibly 'naïve', participation in the text. Therefore, although many of the theorists mentioned here *do* appear to deal with questions of reader-involvement head-on (how readers engage and negotiate their relationship with textual characters, for example), they are questions which tend to be solved in terms of theoretical rationalizations: a riddle which, for all the struggle, is commensurate with the reader-pleasure discussed in the previous section.

From Positioning to Participation

If we follow through the implications of this observation, it becomes no surprise to discover that the areas of spectator theory which *have* explored a more genuinely interactive model of text–reader relations are those which have attempted to bridge the epistemological divide between universalist, psychoanalytic models of self–other relations (all focused, incidentally, on a 'textual other' who is in some way commensurate with a character in the text), and the material conditions of spectatorship through various kinds of audience-research. This has proven an Olympian task for all those involved, since the 'textual' and the 'empirical' spectator belong to such different sites of knowledge-production. The extent of the struggle is summed up by Jackie Stacey in *Star Gazing* (1994), which must be considered one of the most successful attempts at a synthesis of the two positions. She writes:

> The dichotomy of the 'textual' versus the 'empirical' spectator, or the 'diegetic' versus the 'cinematic' spectator is often used as a shorthand to characterise the difference between the psychoanalytic model in film studies and ethnographic approaches to female spectatorship which have characterised cultural studies work . . . Much of the ethnographic

work has remained within the study of television and, more recently, video. This work has drawn primarily on the field of cultural studies which has a long-standing concern with audiences and questions of cultural consumption. In contrast, film audiences have been of remarkably little interest to feminist film critics, who have remained sceptical about the empiricism of such studies. Such scepticism has resulted in a rather crude, blanket dismissal of women in the cinema audience, as if any study whch involves people who attend cinemas must necessarily fall into the traps of empiricism. (p. 23)

Stacey follows this summary of the 'great divide' with a diagram schematizing the differences between the two spectator-models, including the characterization of the 'film studies' spectator as 'passive' and of the 'cultural studies' one as 'active'. Whilst I would agree that the film studies spectator is characterized as *passive* in as much as her relationship to the text is 'production-led' (that is, the text is seen as the *dominant* partner in meaning-production), I would also argue that the fact that the activity in which she is engaged *is* meaning-production (that is, interpretation of the text) makes her only notionally passive since, as in the case of the reader-theories I have just examined, her presence is instrumental in *realizing* (releasing/'actualizing') the meaning of the text. It thus seems to me what makes her *appear* passive is the fact that, restricted to a readerly experience which is purely interpretive (her relationship to her 'textual other' is commensurate with her analysis of the text), she is prevented from *interacting* with the text in any less instrumental way. Her apparent passivity is, in effect, a symptom of her lack of *inter*-activity. By the same token, it is clear that what makes the cultural-studies spectator seem more active is that she belongs to a different model of text–reader relations: one which allows a range of possible interactive relationships with the text beyond the narrowly hermeneutic. The tension between these two models of readership is especially evident in my work with the feminist reading groups in Chapter 8, which shows individual readers oscillating between an interpretive and a more interactive function.

According to the thesis I have been pursuing here, then, there is a need to move away from the polarization of texts and readers as 'active' and 'passive' within a narrowly hermeneutic model of text–reader relations, and to recognize instead an alternative model of reading, which goes 'beyond interpretation' and characterizes the text–reader relationship as non-instrumental and *implicated*. A number of reception theorists, particularly those involved in media and cultural studies, have already contributed to the development of this alternative model of text–reader relations, although most of them have not, I feel, been fully aware of the nature of their epistemological shift. If we consider some of the ground-breaking work done in television studies in the 1970s and 1980s, for example, attention was still *ostensibly* focused on the 'balance of power' between text and reader/viewer in 'meaning production'. This is true of both Stuart Hall's work on 'encoding and decoding' in TV audiences and David Morley's work in *The 'Nationwide' Audience* (1980).[28] These authors were concerned, first and foremost, to correct the version of the reader/spectator as a passive 'dupe' of popular culture, a mission that was concurrently taken up by literary theorists such as Tania Modleski (1982) and Janice Radway (1984) on female romance readers.[29] Their interest, in other words, was in rescuing the reader/viewer from the site of her 'textual positioning' and the universalist psychoanalytic (or Marxist) models deployed to explain that inscription (see above), and to reveal, instead, the different ways she might *actively* negotiate, contest and renegotiate her relationship with the text, drawing on a wide range of textual and social/cultural 'experience'.[30] As this interest in audience-power grew, moroever, through a fascinating accumulation of ethnographic studies, so the emphasis on the role of the extratextual *contexts* of viewing increased. David Morley's later work was exemplary in its attention to the 'social relations of television watching', for example, as was Ann Gray's study of women's use of the VCR; whilst Janice Radway's *Reading the Romance* (see note 29) argued that the value of romance reading for women depended as much on the 'time-out' provided by the *act* of reading as upon the readers' relationship with the texts themselves.[31] What this shift from text to context also signals, however, is a new characterization of the reader and her investments. Although, as I have already indicated, most of the theorists I have just cited are still primarily concerned with the reader's role in meaning-production to a greater or lesser extent, the juxtaposition of textual and contextual experience also exposes the fantastic range of *non-interpretive* functions, both cognitive and affective, in which reading involves us. As Stacey (note 19) summarizes *vis-à-vis* David Morley's *Family Television* (see note 31):

> Television, then, is analysed here as an integral part of the patriarchal social relations of the family; it is used to produce conflict, as well as to avoid it, to start conversations, as well as to kill them. The viewers are seen not only to play an active role in producing the meaning of a media text, but also to *use* the television in their familial interactions, thus extending the 'meaning' of television beyond the actual representations it produces. (p. 39)

By recognizing the hugely significant role played by context in reading/viewing, these theorists were thus instrumental in reconfiguring reading as an *interactive and implicated process* rather than a *hermeneutic practice*. And this, needless to say, also has the effect of radically extending our conception of the reader/viewer's 'textual other' (see discussion following). Instead of being limited to a 'character in the text', as in the case of most of the text-based film theory discussed above, the 'other' may become a member of the reader/viewer's social circle (that is, her own 'audience' and 'interpretive community': see Chapters 7 and 8).

One media theorist who deserves special mention for her interactive model of text–reader/viewer relations is Ien Ang.[32] Her study, *Watching Dallas* (1985), defines a host of contextual factors that 'prepared' the Dallas audience for its weekly fix, whilst her utilization of Raymond Williams's 'structures of feeling' helps to explain why viewers can become involved with certain texts *despite* their different point of cultural reference, the apparent inauthenticity of the action or the fact that viewers don't especially 'like' or identify with any of the characters.[33]

> The realist experience of the Dallas fans quoted bears no relation to this cognitive level – it is situated at the emotional level: what is recognised as real is not knowledge of the world, but a subjective experience of the world: a 'structure of feeling'. (p. 45)

Ang's own work then goes on to focus on the paradoxical 'pleasure' viewers appear to take in what she identifies as the *'tragic* structure of feeling' characteristic of the serial or soap: 'the notion that in life emotions are always being stirred up, i.e. that life is characterized by an endless fluctuation between happiness and unhappiness, that life is a question of falling down and getting up again' (p. 46).

The notion of readers relating to texts via a mediating 'structure of feeling' which, according to Williams's own (notoriously expansive) definition, links the personal to specific historical and cultural moments (see note 33), is certainly useful in helping to explain why texts and stories which appear to bear no obvious connection to our own lives nevertheless make such a major emotional impact. The reassurance implicit in a cycle of disaster and recovery (Ang's own *tragic* structure of feeling), meanwhile, points to the explicitly cathartic function of such texts. There is a danger, however, that this focus on 'recognition' within the context of Ang's wider purpose of *explaining* pleasure will once again lead us away from a more detailed micro-analysis of the reading/viewing experience and the wide range of emotions contained therein. My own feeling (based on the evidence of Chapters 5, 6 and 8) is that whilst interpellation by a tragic structure of feeling might be *ultimately* reassuring, certain phases of the cycle will be distressing for certain viewers; and sometimes this distress will be *in excess* of the recovery that ensues. Excellent as Ang's analysis is, the subjugation of her data to the 'big question' of *why* some women get so much pleasure out of Dallas tends to lose sight of the full range of emotional response experienced along the way. The fact, moreover, that she explains this pleasure through the reflex of 'recognition' forestalls a more extended investigation of Williams's structure of feeling as a 'textual other'. In my own readings, indeed, recognition is simply the *beginning* of the relationship between the reader/viewer and this highly significant site of contact. And while recognition might in itself be 'pleasurable', the reader's subsequent involvement with the structure of feeling is likely to be far more emotionally complex.

The Textual Other

There has been much allusion throughout this chapter to 'the textual other', and the reader hopefully will already have inferred that I see the precise naming, and identification, of this 'other' as absolutely central to a full appreciation of how we come to interact and dialogize with texts in a non-instrumental way.[34] It is the existence of this other, indeed, that has enabled me to conceptualize the text–reader relationship *as a relationship* – and as a romance – and to equip it with an emotional vocabulary that has been noticeably absent from existing reader and spectator theory. As I have also already indicated (see note 8), the textual other can be represented by many things as well as by a character in the text: it might also take the form of a 'structure of feeling' (as above), an interlocutory subject position (how a character in the text positions *us*), an author-function, an interpretive community, or the (covert/overt) audience/addressee of our own reading. It can even, as I have already speculated, subsume the last two categories into an other which is the 'act of interpretation' itself. The textual other can, in other words, be both a textual and a *contextual* point of contact for the reader, and individual reading-events might well move *between* others.

When we turn to existing audience and reception theory, however, it is very clear that the textual other *has* predominantly been thought of as a character in the text, that is, as a humanistically defined, representational subject. Whilst the *con*textual focus of a good deal of media theory implies the existence of significant extradiegetic 'others' in the form of a mutual audience or interpretive community, such as the family members who share a particular TV viewing experience (see discussion above), the point of connection with the text itself has still tended, with the notable exception of Ang, to be thought of as the characters. Characters are thus also the *only* medium through which the reader/viewer's emotional involvement in the text gets discussed; and this, in turn, helps to explain why the affective conditions of spectatorship have proven even more problematic in the discussion on non-representational or non-figurative works within the visual arts.

Yet within the recent history of literary criticism, outside the focus of reception theory, any consideration of there existing a 'relationship' between the reader and a textual character has been regarded as symptomatic of an outdated, and theoretically suspect, 'authentic realist' approach to textual analysis.[35] Such involvement is immediately seen as a sign of the reader losing sight of the 'textuality' of the reading experience and identifying/evaluating the characters as though they were real people. To what extent it is useful, necessary or dangerous to break down the boundaries between the textual and the 'real' in the analysis of this dimension of the reading process remains a moot point, and one that certainly hangs heavily over my own readings in Chapters 5 and 6. While all those of us who have been poststructurally trained undoubtedly begin from a position that the textual character can never be responded to or analysed as though s/he were a 'real person', it seems to be equally problematic to deny that this is – on occasion – part of the *reading fantasy*. Culturally based research on spectators, which has emphasized the interaction between the reading/viewing subject and the textual character in the process of identity formation, has also shown how this binary between 'textual character' and 'real self' might be inherently problematic, whilst the analysis of my own readings cannot disguise the fact that I have repeatedly projected aspects of 'significant others' in the material world onto my textual subjects.[36] All this is not to suggest that interdiegetic characters are, in the last analysis, any less, or any other, than 'textual' (and therefore subject to all the laws of textuality); but it does acknowledge that *the readerly process* is sometimes strategically blind to this.[37]

It is clear, moreover, that most of the existing reception theory that has considered the emotional conditions of reading/spectatorship via interdiegetic characters has been predicated upon models deriving from the theorization of our interpersonal relationships in psychology and psychoanalysis. Thus whilst the best and most sophisticated film theory has endeavoured to keep the textuality of its subjects to the fore at all times, its analysis nevertheless replicates many of the processes, procedures and conceptualizations present in psychotherapy. The relationship between the reader/viewer and the character in the text is analysed in terms of the classic models of subject development as they are applied to 'living' subjects.

As Jackie Stacey has detailed in chapter 5 of *Star Gazing* (see note 19), 'Feminine Fascinations', the key point of focus for these psychoanalytic applications has been *identification*: indeed, we might go as far as to say that the relationship between the reader/viewer and her textual other has been thought of almost exclusively in those terms. Because identification, especially its specular manifestation, plays such a key role in the Lacanian model of subject development, this obsession is easy to understand; but I would like to consider some of its limitations as far as my own project is concerned. The first of these (which I have already alluded to) is that it focuses attention quite narrowly on *how* the reader-viewer first gets involved with a textual character, at the expense of the *development* of that relationship. Apart from looking at the different ways in which readers/viewers *enter* texts (see the first part of Chapter 5) we need also to explore more fully what happens once they have arrived there: how their 'identifications' shift and change; how they mutate and perish. The second problem is that, in most instances (and Stacey's own study is an exception to this), the processes of identification are dealt with in such abstract terms that the emotional components of the procedure never get named. Indeed, as I suggested earlier, it would be fair to say that a good deal of the criticism following Mulvey, de Lauretis and Doane, whilst notionally concerned with an interactive text–reader relationship, is frequently hermeneutic in character: that is to say, it sees the processes of identification as an aspect of meaning-production.

When we move beyond the mechanisms of identification *per se*, therefore, it is noticeable that theorists have still been reluctant (or perhaps
unable) to offer *details* of the relationship between reader/viewer and character. A classic case in point here is Murray Smith's *Engaging Characters:
Fiction, Emotion and the Cinema* (1995), which, first, locates viewers' emotional interest in filmic texts *entirely* within the realm of their response to (as
opposed to their 'relationship with') textual characters, and, second, which
limits the emotional range of this connection to expressions of 'sympathy'
and 'antipathy'.[38] As Susan Feagin has observed in another book (see note 8)
which deals explicitly with the role of emotion in the reading process,
'affects' such as 'empathy' and 'sympathy' cannot really be thought of as
emotions *per se*, but are rather 'more generic ways of grouping types of
responses' (p. 129). What this excellent observation reveals is the way that
a project like Smith's, which focuses so heavily on *the conditions of read-
ing/viewing* that make an emotional response possible (and he ranges from
structuralist features such as narrative and textual alignment/positioning to
behaviourist theories of 'motor and affective mimicry'), will almost
inevitably fail to get *inside* the process itself. We may be able to recognize
some of the mechanisms that draw us into a text/character, but the precise
and *changing* details of our engagement remain obscure.

Despite an evident desire to go beyond this point in her own philosophical investigation into the subject, Feagin encounters a similar problem. After
a whole book clearing the ground, she finds herself no closer to *naming* the
emotions that are involved in reading: 'There's no vocabulary to name
responses; it's difficult if not impossible to name them within the limited
vocabulary one does have unless one is a poet or an agile critic oneself' (p.
199). Whilst Feagin's obstacle is, admittedly, a little different to Smith's in
that – at this point of her text – she is once again thinking of the reading
process in the most abstract of terms (and not simply via reader–character
engagement), it seems to me that both theorists fail to gain access to this
next level of investigation precisely because they refuse to conceive of text
and reader in terms of what it most obviously is: a *relationship*. In an effort,
one presumes, to preserve the self-conscious textuality of their research,
they have resisted a model of human interaction drawn from 'real life', over-
looking the fact that the vocabularies of 'real-life experience' – or, indeed,
the models of relationship which are inscribed by such languages – are *not*
'real-life', but themselves a sign of life's discursive construction. As will
become clear in the next section of this chapter, it was only by using a set of
discourses saturated in emotional vocabulary to engage my texts, and by
using a model of human interaction predicated upon emotion (that is,
romance) to conceptualize the text–reader relationship, that I was able to
uncover/discover the full emotional range of the reading process. A language of emotion was needed, in other words, to make the emotion visible.
What critics like Smith and Feagin seem to believe, mistakenly, is that our
affective responses to texts can somehow be objectively or scientifically

revealed and analysed. In as much as emotions have precise discursive or ideological origins, of course they cannot. What we 'feel' in relation to a text, or with regard to a character in a text, will depend upon the discourses we bring to it. It is clear, for example, that it is the *language* of romantic desire associated with *ravissement* (see below) that has enabled me to name my emotional engagement with the characters of my chosen texts with such precision. This would also appear to be true of the cinema spectators in Jackie Stacey's survey, whose own inscription by the discourses of romance (and religion) enabled *them* to name their 'relationship' to the stars in terms of specific emotional experiences such as 'devotion', 'adoration' and 'worship'.[39] It is impossible, in other words, to conceptualize – or name – emotion outside its discursive origins and/or attendant relational models.

In this section, then, I have shown how it is through an identification of the 'textual other', and a remodelling of the reader's engagement of that textual other through a discursively inscribed concept of 'relationship', that we can begin to articulate the affective dimension of the reading process. Once the significance of the textual other is understood in terms of this newly defined relational model of text–reader relations, moreover, the fact that it may be represented by something *other* than a textual character becomes easy to understand. Once we accept that 'the will-to-relationship' is the fuel of text–reader interaction, we may expect readers to discover their textual others wherever they can, both inside and outside the text. What my own readings in Chapters 5 and 6 show is the remarkable lengths to which the reader is prepared to go in order to discover, define and defend her textual other – and how that desire/anxiety may, indeed, manifest itself in a transformation or substitution of the textual other (from textual character to interlocutory reader-positioning, for example).[40] The textual other, then, is whoever or whatever causes us to engage with a text in a manner that is *beyond the will-to-interpretation*. It is what, in terms of my own metaphorical conceit, causes us to both 'fall in love', and endure the sequel of our falling, in what is often an incredibly intense roller-coaster of emotional experience.

Reading as Romance

During the writing of this book I have had some interesting conversations with friends and colleagues about whether my utilization of 'romance' as both a structuring and discursive device to 'make visible' the emotional dimension to the reading process constitutes a method, a theory or something else. My feeling now is that it is possibly best explained as a *framework*, incorporating both theory and method: an agent which both provided me with the means to identify and define my object of study (to 'stake the wilderness') and the maps and equipment with which to begin my explorations. As we have already seen, it was my reconceptualization of the text–reader engagement as a romantic 'relationship' (in the fullest sense of the word) that enabled me to break away from existing, more instrumental models in which a full interaction betweeen text and reader is denied, whilst romantic discourse – the language(s) of love – has enabled me to name and specify some of the emotional consequences of reading. Without such a framework and its attendant vocabularies, these emotions, as I argued in the last section, would not have become visible; indeed, they could not have existed.

The section of the book where the romance framework is engaged most directly and explicitly is the central section on 'The Emotional Politics of Gendered Reading'. In the two chapters entitled '*Ravissement*' and 'The Sequel' I employ both the narrative trajectory and emotional 'dictionary' of Roland Barthes's *A Lover's Discourse* (1978) to identify and name the broad spectrum of emotions produced by my encounter with four texts: Olive Schreiner's *The Story of an African Farm* (1889) (see note 1); Jeanette Winterson's *Written on the Body* (1992); Jane Campion's film of *The Piano* (1993); and a photographic exhibition by Angela Grauerholz (1995).[41]

What Barthes's text provides, above all else, is a wonderfully rich taxonomy of the subtle, ever-shifting nuances of emotion suffered by lovers on their journey from the moment of first enamoration (*ravissement*) through to the sequel which Barthes describes as 'the long train of sufferings, wounds, anxieties, distresses, resentments, despairs, embarrassments and deceptions' (pp. 197–8). Through a 'method' which combines my autobiographical/first-person readings and 're-memories' of these texts with a retrospective commentary, I explore my involvement with their various 'textual others' under headings as various as 'enchantment', 'devotion', 'anxiety', 'jealousy' and 'disillusionment' – terms that, to the best of my knowledge, have rarely found their way into textual criticism.[42]

Apart from providing me with a means of naming and making visible aspects of the reading process that have never before been spoken, the discourse of romance is, I believe, better suited to the model of text–reader relations I have theorized than a *narrowly* psychoanalytic articulation of reading-as-desire.[43] Its socio-cultural inscription helps, for example, to make sense of some of the self–other dynamics which fall outside a strictly Oedipal economy. While psychoanalytic theorists may well argue that our patterns of behaviour in adolescence and adulthood simply mirror and replicate those of childhood, I would argue, along with theorists like Stevi Jackson, that they mutate into new, culturally sensitive forms.[44] The social groupings inhabited by teenagers, for example, are likely to make their experience of romance as a drama with more than two (or even three!) participants, and the tensions and jealousies that these large and complex interpersonal networks produce come much closer to the complex web of emotions that frequently inform the reader's relations with her various textual, and contextual, others.

The second major advantage to the romance trope is that its history of mythic and cultural inscription provides us with a richer and more extensive *narrative* base than the 'stories' of Freud *et al.* Regardless of where one draws the line – after the first enchantment? the first kiss? the moment of consummation (however defined)? – romance always involves a sequel (see above) and, in retrospect at least, takes on the illusion of *temporality* and *sequence*, two factors also apparently integral to the 'act of reading'. As Barthes writes:

> Though the lover's discourse is no more than a dust of figures stirring according to unpredictable order, like a fly buzzing in a room, I can assign to love, at least retrospectively, according to my Image-repetoire, a settled course: it is by means of this *historical* hallucination that I sometimes make love into a romance, an adventure. This would appear to assume three stages (or three acts): first comes the instantaneous capture (I am ravished by an image); then a series of encounters (dates, telephone calls, letters, brief trips), during which I ecstatically 'explore' the perfection of the loved being, i.e., the unhoped-for correspondence between an object and my desire: this is the sweetness of the beginning, the interval proper to the idyll. This happy period acquires its identity (its limits) from its opposition (at least in memory) to the 'sequel': the sequel is the long chain of sufferings, wounds, anxieties, resentments, despairs, embarrassments, and deceptions to which I fall prey, ceaselessly living under the threat of a downfall which would envelop once the other, myself, and the glamorous encounter that revealed us to each other.
>
> (*A Lover's Discourse*, pp. 197–8)

Although, following through Barthes's own inference, more recent work on the discourses of love and romance indicate that the *sequence* in which this classic trajectory is experienced is becoming increasingly uncertain, and although my own readings reveal constant contradictions and paradoxes within that chronology, the most important thing about this narrativization of romance is the way in which it identifies a long string of delicately distinguished emotional affects.[45] The fact that the *majority* of these pertain to the sequel is also of significance, since, as the earlier discussions in this chapter have shown, the emphasis of so much existing reception and spectator-theory has been on the reader/viewer's point of entry into the text: the moment of their first engagement or (to invoke the Barthesian vocabulary) their first 'enamoration'. In terms of new territory, indeed, I feel that one of the major contributions of this project is likely to be in its opening-up – perhaps, indeed, its 'outing' – of the readerly emotions associated with the sequel. So much theoretical energy has gone into explaining reading (why we read/how we read) in terms of pleasure that the attendant discomforts and distresses have repeatedly been pushed aside. Whilst Ien Ang discussed the role of 'the tragic structure of feeling' as part of the paradoxical 'pleasure' of reading, there has been a distinct reluctance to address the *tragic structure of reading* itself.

Although the concept of 'reading as romance' is highlighted in the central section of this book, its implications are also crucial to discussions in Part III. In these two chapters, which question the reasons for disagreements between readers both within the feminist community and outside it, I follow through my perception of the tension between the 'hermeneutic' and 'implicated' models of reading to account for the way in which 'professional readers', both journalists and academics, attempt to reconcile their experience of the *practices* and the *processes* of reading. The striking, though perhaps unsurprising, conclusion of these chapters is that the professionalized techniques of reading ('as interpretation') are a definite inhibition to a more implicated, non-instrumental relationship between text and reader: which is not to say that 'romance' is entirely repressed, either in a covert engagement with the text *or* (a possibility I have alluded to throughout this chapter) through a refocusing of that desire/anxiety onto an alternative, (extra)textual 'other' (such as a member of the reader's actual or imagined readerly community).

This reinscription of the reader's 'other' in the material world leads us back, after a noticeable silence, to the question of gender. Why is it that politics so often appears to walk out of the door when feminists fall in love?[46] Although, as the following chapters show, I do have an answer to this, I think the enormity of the problem is better served by my coming clean and admitting that, at every level I have attempted to deal with them, the discourses of emotion and the discourses of politics have pulled asunder – just as they did for the readers participating in my exercise for Chapter 8. This is another instance, then, in which I feel strongly that 'the fact of the matter' is *in excess* of the rationalizations I have brought forward to explain it. Whilst it does seem to me apparent that readers cannot hold emotion and politics together because they belong to two different systems, or models, or reading, the fact remains somehow more striking and consequential than this relatively small conclusion. Another way of understanding the schism is, of course, to look at it in terms of discursive rather than structural positioning – which was my initial choice of theory. According to this rationale readers cannot respond to a text as feminists at the same time as registering their emotional involvement with it because these are experienced as activities coming from different – and mutually incompatible – discursive sites.[47] Feminism requires that we read a text with attention to its gender, whilst an emotional engagement drives us back under the covers of Humanism and eternal, transcendent values that are gender-blind. This, again, is a fair explanation of the problem, and it fits comfortably with the more structural theory based on incompatible reading models ('hermeneutic' and 'implicated'). What neither 'explanation' does justice to, however, is the massive *discomfort* of those of us who, as feminist readers, regularly 'commute' between these two discourses/models of reading; and this is what my readings in Chapters 5 and 6 will hopefully *demonstrate* better than any theory will explain.

For in the (apparently inevitable) slippage between our enamorations and our consciousness of ourselves as feminist readers, there is a good deal of anxiety and guilt. With our professional clothes on, we cannot help but frown at the blind, gullible wanderings of our off-duty selves. My plea here, then, is for tolerance; and perhaps, too, imagination. Because, for all her apparent gaucheness, it could be argued that it is our scruffy, unsophisticated sister – bush-thwacking her way through the readerly wilderness – who is, even now, doing the really ground-breaking (or path-finding) work, which it is then up to our professional selves to chart.

The Ghostly Reader

Despite the physicality of the image with which I ended the last section, the most suggestive and enduring characterization of the reader that has formed in the course of this book is the one with which I began this chapter: her ghostly *insubstantiality*. Whilst the ostensible focus of that opening quotation was the intransitivity of the reader's role that stems directly from the textuality of the reading process, a concurrent concern, to which I have already alluded, and which will be explored in some detail in Chapter 5, is the question of the reader's *articulation within the text*: how she is logistically situated in relation to her textual other(s). For whereas the text's characters are fixed in the historical moment of their first inscription – performing the same roles, living the same lives, over and over again – the reader is free (if not actually compelled) to wander: to make her repeated

Illustration 1.3 'I think that at any moment I may see her, recognize her . . .' (Chapter 5)

journey through their landscape without *ever* being able to make herself seen or heard, without ever being able to make the connection between her life and theirs.[48] And this scenario pertains even when (perhaps especially when) the textual other exists in non-human, non-representational form. In such instances, as in my readings of *The Piano* and Angela Grauerholz's photographs, it is the sublimated form of that which I seek – 'the scene' (Barthes) of my own (extra)textual narrative fantasies – which makes the wanderings of my own ghostly persona even more poignant. Thus, although with effort and imagination the story of our readerly romance *can* be written to include moments of connection and fulfilment, and my own text discovers them, I concede that a narrative of insatiable despair/unsupportable loss will inevitably continue to be the trope most befitting the *conditions* of reading/viewing, in as much as it 'describes', perhaps too perfectly, a quintessentially unresolvable self–other relation.[49]

Whilst this admittedly sentimental dramatization of the reader's lot, her ghostly sufferings, has a very obvious resonance in psychoanalytic theories of desire/identification being predicated upon the loss of a primary 'Other' whom we will seek to replace or 'restore', repeatedly, though unsuccessfully, my *methodological* purpose was merely to find a conceit which would help us to imagine the reading experience 'from the inside'.[50] By conceptualizing our participation in texts in these spatialized, three-dimensional terms one gets closer, I feel, to the way we do indeed *move about texts*; how we voyeuristically explore our textual others from all angles, desperately looking for ways in which we may make them respond to us and include us in their script. It is the intimacy and intensity, then, of the reader's experience that I wish to emphasize, *alongside* its haunting and taunting reminders of the other's textuality (and the text's otherness): components that together do, indeed, constitute a 'ghostly romance'. On this point I should also observe that, for all the problems of producing models of reading that are cross-disciplinary (something I will address in the Prefaces to Parts I and II), it was undoubtedly my readings in the visual arts that prompted me towards this spatialized (re)conceptualization of the text–reader relationship, and a better understanding of what form our 'active participation' in a text actually takes.

In as much as it has provided me with a metaphoric framework through which to reconceptualize the text–reader relationship, and then to explore the reader's participation within the text, romance has indeed become a 'method'. Another aspect of my textual practice which was similarly strategic was my use of the autobiographical 'I' in the (re)readings and re-memories of Chapters 5 and 6. The first thing to observe here is that the purpose of the four readings I perform in that section of the book is *not* simply to provide a more accessible account of the reading process, although part of me does support the theoretical and pedagogic principles of what is now sometimes known as 'personalist' criticism.[51] In the context of the model of reading I have been advancing here, however, the use of the personal pronoun is better understood as the linguistic sign of my attempt to explore the processes of reading as a dialogic/implicated 'I–thou' relationship: a grammatical recognition that each and every act of reading is the site of potential intimacy and engagement. My practice here has also been usefully supported, on a methodological level, by the work of theorists like Elspeth Probyn (see note 6), who has argued cleverly for the strategic use of both 'experience' and 'autobiography' as an *enunciative practice*, strategic in function. In contrast to seeing such writing, especially within scholarly texts, as a 'reaction to theory', Probyn sees the 'I' performing a vital role in connecting the epistemological and the ontological levels of cultural enquiry. Drawing heavily on Raymond Williams's writings both in his theorization of ideology and 'structure of feelings' (see note 33 above) and in his own 'autobiographical' critical practices, Probyn argues that we need forms of enunciation that will enable us to conceptualize key aspects of culture (such as gender and sexuality) not only as they are discursively produced, but also as they are 'experienced from the inside' or 'lived'.

> At an ontological level, the concept of experience posits a separate realm of existence – it testifies to the gendered, sexual and racial facticity of being in the social; it can be called the immediate experiential self. At an epistemological level, the self is revealed in its conditions of possibility; here experience is recognised as more obviously discursive and can be used overtly to politicize the ontological. Both these levels – the experiential self and the politicization of experience – are necessary as the conditions of possibility for alternative speaking positions within cultural theory. (p. 16)

This 'mission statement' is perfectly in accord with my own desire to explore and chart the *processes* of reading as a 'felt facticity' (Probyn, p. 5) *at the same time as* evaluating the politics of reading *practice* at an epistemological level. Despite the fact that I began this section, then, by recalling some of the pain of the ghostly reader's intransitivity as regards the act of reading, the use of the first-person pronoun can be seen as part of an attempt to ensure that she is, at least, represented within my own textual analysis. While there are obvious issues here around the use of 'myself' becoming a model of the 'typical' or 'ideal' reader, I have struggled hard against such generalizations, keeping both the idiosyncrasy of my readings (and my conditions of reading) *and* the romance framework I have used to produce and analyse them self-consciously to the fore at all times. It is also my hope – and this again follows on from a point made in Probyn's book – that my use of the personal pronoun will work dialogically, as opposed to solipsistically, for readers of this particular text.[52] For autobiographical or 'personalist' criticism to be useful to feminism, in other words, it must dialogically include the other (woman) within its positioning: a condition that seems in some ways easy to fulfil (in as much as the 'I' cannot exist *without* a reciprocating 'you') and in others impossible (in as much as all dialogues are power-inscribed, and one can never guarantee the effect of one's address).[53] Unlike Probyn, I am not sure that is something that *can* be controlled by a conscientious and/or politically anxious author. What my own previous work with dialogics has shown me is that all acts of communication are power-inscribed, and that any address may, at any time, alienate some or all of its addressees (see Chapter 2). This is not to say we cannot strive to make our autobiographical practices accessible to as wide an audience as possible, but to acknowledge that we will sometimes fail. I am very aware that the readings which follow, for example, will include and exclude other feminists in turn. In this respect, however, I very much *did not* expect my texts to function as examples of universal (feminist) experience, but hoped merely that they would, at times, set up the 'shock of recognition' (Williams: see above) that itself helps to explain how communities/cultures can come to share a common 'structure of feeling'.

A further dialogization of the 'I' is structured into this book, moreover, by my representation of the first-person 'reader-stories' told by the groups of feminists interviewed in Chapter 8. As will be seen, there are many points of contact and exchange between their reading experiences and my own, and, whilst striving again against the universalizing of personal experience, I would like to suggest that this is another way in which my own 'I' becomes, on occasion, a 'we'; or, more to the point, is defined, contextualized and *productively challenged* through the reciprocating presence of another 'thou' (Bakhtin: see note 53).

This re-inscription of 'the reader' *as a feminist* now leads me to some final observations on the different forms the spectre takes in this volume, her politics slipping in and out of vision as easily as she herself.

In the first section of the book, 'The Politics of Gendered Reading', the feminism of the reader is, as we have seen, produced, sustained and guaranteed by an *interpretive* role which is self-consciously defined as feminist in purpose. The reader I present and investigate in these chapters does not become 'implicated' in her texts because she does not let herself become seduced, or led astray, by the textual others she nevertheless glimpses out of the corner of her eye. Because she is a professional reader, and because her professional training has been in literary criticism/textual analysis, her relationship both to the text and to the practice of reading is resolutely hermeneutic. Indeed, it is the hermeneutic inscription of reading that *makes* it a practice and not a process, so that even when she is debating the relative power of text and reader she locates the site of power as 'meaning-production'. Staying within this model of readership, meanwhile, her feminist politics remain clearly visible and methodologically unproblematic: in as much as she is reading 'for meaning', she is also reading for 'feminist meaning'. Feminism is a consciousness she brings to each and every act of interpretation.

While the notion of the 'feminist reader' survives more or less intact in these first chapters, which represent my early investigations into the politics of gendered reading, its roots are clearly shaken. It is noticeable, moreover, that it is the moment when emotions as apparently 'unprofessional' as jealousy present theselves that the concept of reading *as a feminist* begins to flounder. This decentring of the feminist project thus becomes the *context* in which the whole of the book's middle section, 'The Emotional Politics of Gendered Reading', was produced. As has been observed repeatedly throughout this introduction, the reader I track through these chapters is totally unreliable as far as her feminist politics are concerned: sometimes she has her wits about her, often she does not. As she plunges in and out of the emotional undergrowth of her textual encounters, she loses all sight of her *purpose*; and although (as I have also emphasized) her encounters are always gendered, making some of them notionally 'lesbian', they are rarely self-consciously feminist. As a result, the feminism of these chapters must be sought in my meta-commentary, or (such is the vastness of this particular wilderness) in *your* readings of both levels of mine.

In the final section of the book, 'The Politics of Feminist/s Reading', the feminist content of my discussion becomes explicit once again. In so far as both Chapters 7 and 8 deal with readers whose own texts favour 'reading as interpretation', both their politics and mine are clearly on the table. Part of my project in these chapters, however, is to create a mirror for my own 'professional' readings in Part I, and to show that the *implicated processes* undercut the *hermeneutic practices* of reading for these readers as much as for myself. Although the 'differences' between readers, and within reading communities, may therefore be very efficiently 'explained' through an analysis of all those contextual factors (such as audience and 'interpretive community') which compel and constrain readers to certain points of view, another, more profound site of discord is to be found in the way in which they have engaged (or not engaged) with the text according to an alternative model of implicated reading. For although the latter is less easily defined in terms of its feminism than the former, it is precisely the slippage between the two models of reading that alerts us to the conjunction of ideological and structural factors which lie behind our official reasons for 'liking' or 'not liking' a text, as well as helping to explain *why* the visible sign of our politics sometimes gets lost.

I feel I should conclude this chapter, meanwhile, by making it absolutely clear that the alternative model of 'implicated reading' I advance is assuredly *not* the only 'alternative' to the 'hermeneutic' one I also describe and define. Indeed, the very fact that its existence depends upon a combination of *metaphorical* conceits (wilderness/romance/ghosts) should indicate the facility with which other 'models' could be invented and 'tested'. For my own purposes, however, and in my own experiences as a gendered reader, I feel the tropes I seized upon have served me well, both in opening up the wilderness (a place, indeed, of beauty and of fear) and in showing me some pathways through it.

Notes

1 Olive Schreiner, *The Story of an African Farm* (1899; New York: Bantam, 1993). Further references to this volume will be given after quotations in the text.

2 'Re-memory': a reference to my practice of writing down my 'memory' of the texts I had read/viewed previously in advance of my re-reading of them. The item of vocabulary, of course, derives from Toni Morrison's novel, *Beloved* (London: Picador, 1988), where it possesses a broad range of connotations, *some* of which are implicit in my own use of the term.

3 Only recently have literary critics begun to speak candidly about their experiences as readers in this respect. Two books which bear an obvious relation to my own project, whilst conceptualizing the processes of reading somewhat differently, are Suzanne Juhasz's *Reading from the Heart: Women, Literature and the Search for True Love* (London and New York: Viking, 1994) and Lynne Sharon Schwartz's *Ruined by Reading: A Life in Books* (Boston: Beacon Press, 1996).

4 'Dialogic': a model of self–other relations deriving from the work of Mikhail Bakhtin, but much extended and developed by his followers. See Lynne Pearce, *Reading Dialogics* (London: Edward Arnold, 1994). The principle at the heart of Bakhtin's work is that no utterance (either written or spoken) is made in isolation, but is always dependent upon the anticipated response of another (actual or implicit) addressee.

In *On Deconstruction: Theory and Criticism after Structuralism* (Ithaca, NY: Cornell University Press, 1982), Johnathan Culler argues that reader-theorists have never – and will never – be able to present the relationship between text and reader as a proper relationship (implying mutual participation), because one term (text or reader) will always dominate (see discussion following). Further references to Culler's volume will be given after quotations in the text.

5 The role of 'context' and 'addressee' in my theorization of the reading process will be clarified below.

6 See Elspeth Probyn, *Sexing the Self: Gendered Positions in Cultural Studies* (London and New York: Routledge, 1993), pp. 1–31. Further page references to this volume will be given after quotations in the text, and the details of Probyn's reconceptualization of 'experience' and 'autobiography' will be discussed below.

7 As the readings presented in Chapters 5 and 6 will make clear, the reader's desire to engage with a text's 'eternal values' (the Humanist preoccupation with love, loss, death etc.) will often cause her to 'transcend' consciousness of herself as a gendered and historical subject. My point here is that the apparent transcendence is an illusion.

8 'Textual other': as I will go on to explain below, the reader's 'textual other' is whoever, or whatever, becomes the focus of her dialogic connection in the process of reading, and is not restricted to humanistically conceived characters/subjects in the text.

9 Wolfgang Iser and Stanley Fish have established themselves as two of the leading exponents of literary reader-theory, producing a whole series of texts on the subject (see Bibliography), many of which contest and dialogize with one another. See e.g. Iser, *The Act of Reading: A Theory of Aesthetic Response* (Baltimore and London: Johns Hopkins University Press, 1978), pp. 30–2, and Stanley Fish, *Is there a Text in this Class? The Authority of Interpretive Communities* (Cambridge, MA and London: Harvard University Press, 1980), pp. 221–3. Further page references to both these works will be given after quotations in the text. An early exception to this focus on the cognitive was Norman Holland's formulation of reading as a psychoanalytically inscribed, subjective experience: see Holland, *The Dynamics of Literary Response* (New York: Oxford University

Press, 1968). Although many theorists lambasted Holland's work because of its inference that a text's meaning lay entirely in the consciously negotiated ('defended'), unconscious responses of its reader, it is significant that he – of all the reader-theorists – has come closest to establishing a full *vocabulary* of reader-emotions (see especially pp. 290–3). It should be noted however that, in common with the other leading reader-theorists, Holland is more interested in *how* readers become engaged with texts than what the engagement entails.

More recently, the affective dimension to the reading/viewing process has been addressed by Susan L. Feagin in a work entitled *Reading with Feeling: The Aesthetics of Appreciation* (Ithaca and London: Cornell University Press, 1996) and Murray Smith in *Engaging Characters: Fiction, Emotion and the Cinema* (Oxford: Clarendon Press, 1995). Further page references to both these volumes will be given after quotations in the text, and both will be referred to in more detail in the discussion which follows.

10 See William K. Wimsatt and C. Monroe Beardsley, *The Verbal Icon: Studies in the Meaning of Poetry* (1954; London: Methuen, 1970), p. 21.

11 See nn. 4 and 9 above, and Bibliography. See also Roland Barthes, *S/Z*, trans. Richard Miller (New York: Hill and Wang, 1974), and *The Pleasure of the Text*, trans. Richard Miller (New York: Hill and Wang, 1975).

12 Virginia Woolf, *To the Lighthouse* (1927; Oxford: Oxford University Press, World's Classics Series, 1992).

13 I refer here specifically to a paper which Lynda Nead gave in the Art History Department of the University of McGill in March 1995 entitled: 'Troubled Bodies: Art, Obscenity and the Connoisseur'. See also her *The Female Nude: Art, Obscenity, and Sexuality* (London and New York: Routledge, 1992).

14 Nead here draws explicitly on the work of Pierre Bourdieu. See *Distinction: A Social Critique of the Judgement of Taste*, trans. R. Nice (Cambridge, MA: Harvard University Press, 1984). In *The Female Nude* (see n. 13) she observes: 'Legitimate, or high, culture is . . . constituted through the denial of the lower, vulgar and venal enjoyment and assertion of the sublimated, refined and disin-terested pleasure . . . Bourdieu provides us with an example of cultural distinc-tion based on the separation of the aesthetic ("pleasure purified of pleasure") and the venal ("pleasure reduced to the pleasure of the senses")'(p. 84).

15 Nead's references include Immanuel Kant; Kenneth Clark, *The Nude: A Study of Ideal Art* (1956; Harmondsworth: Penguin, 1985), Jacques Derrida, *The Truth in Painting* (Chicago: University of Chicago Press, 1987), and Steven Marcus, *The Other Victorians: A Study of Pornography and Sexuality in Mid Nineteenth-Century England* (London: Weidenfeld and Nicolson, 1966).

16 This point has been observed by many theorists dealing with popular culture such as romance fiction and soap operas. See Janice Radway's *Reading the Romance: Women, Patriarchy and Popular Literature* (Chapel Hill and London: University of North Carolina Press, 1984); Tania Modleski, *Loving with a Vengeance: Mass-Produced Fantasies for Women* (London: Methuen, 1982); and Ien Ang, *Watching Dallas: Soap Opera and the Melodramatic Imagination* (London and New York: Methuen, 1985). Page references to all these volumes will be given after quotations in the text.

17 I should also observe a point which will quickly become obvious to readers of Chapters 2 to 4 (and which I will discuss in the Preface to that section), which is that the particular hermeneutic model I was working with at this time was a (post)structuralist Marxist one drawing, in particular, on the work of Louis Althusser and Pierre Macherey (see Bibliography)

18 See Barthes's celebrated use of 'five codes' in his analysis of Balzac's *Sarrasine* in *S/Z*, pp. 18–20 (see n. 11 above).

19 The importance of the 'extratextual' in the production of reader/viewer pleasure has been rather better attended to in film theory. See e.g. Jackie Stacey's *Star Gazing: Hollywood Cinema and Female Spectatorship* (London and New York: Routledge, 1994), esp. chaps. 4 and 5. Further page references to this volume, which will be referred to in more detail below, will be given after quotations in the text.

20 I am thinking here in particular of the work of Teresa de Lauretis, *Alice Doesn't: Feminism, Semiotics, Cinema* (London: Macmillan, 1984), and Mary Ann Doane, *The Desire to Desire: The Woman's Film of the 1940s* (Bloomington and Indianapolis: Indiana University Press, 1987), both of whom produced extremely persuasive arguments for the complex processes of identification *across gender* that enable women to take pleasure in dominant cinema.

21 See n. 9 on Norman Holland above.

22 Lynne Pearce, *Woman/Image/Text: Readings in Pre-Raphaelite Art and Literature* (Hemel Hempstead: Harvester-Wheatsheaf, 1991).

23 'Reading against the grain': the critical practice which, for example, involves reading ostensibly sexist/misogynistic texts against the grain of their dominant discourse and using the ideological contradictions and inconsistencies to read them 'on behalf of feminism'. See e.g. Catherine Belsey's reading of John Milton in *John Milton: Language, Gender, Power* (Oxford: Basil Blackwell, 1988). See also my discussion of this in *Woman/Image/Text* (n. 22), pp. 5–11.

24 Sara Mills (ed.), *Gendering the Reader* (Hemel Hempstead: Harvester-Wheatsheaf, 1994).

25 Laura Mulvey, 'Visual Pleasure and Narrative Cinema', *Screen*, 16(3) (1975), pp. 6-18. Reproduced in Laura Mulvey, *Visual and Other Pleasures* (London: Macmillan, 1989).

26 See Teresa de Lauretis, 'Guerilla in the Midst: Women's Cinema in the 80s', *Screen*, 31(1) (Spring 1990), pp. 6–25.

27 Annette Kuhn, *Women's Pictures: Feminism and Cinema* (2nd edn, London and New York: Verso, 1994), p. 165.

28 See Stuart Hall, 'Encoding/Decoding', in Stuart Hall (ed.), *Culture/Media/Language* (London: Hutchinson, 1980), and also David Morley, *The 'Nationwide' Audience: Structure and Decoding* (London: British Film Institute, 1980).

29 See Tania Modleski and Janice Radway (n. 16 above).

30 Marxist models: although post-Althusserian Marxism (which is central to my own readings, especially in Part I) has qualified the determinism once associated with 'ideology' by regarding it as a contested, and contestable, site, there has still been a tendency to conceptualize the subject as the 'victim' of her various social/cultural inscriptions. See pp. 5–15 of *Woman/Image/Text* (n. 22) for further discussion of this.

31 See David Morley, *Family Television: Cultural Power and Domestic Leisure* (London: Comedia, 1986) and Ann Gray, *Video Playtime: The Gendering of a Leisure Technology* (London: Routledge, 1992). See also Stacey, *Star Gazing* (n. 19), p. 39 for discussion of this.

32 Ien Ang, *Watching Dallas* (see n. 16 above).

33 Raymond Williams coined the term 'structures of feeling' as part of his general overhaul of Marxist models of ideology: see e.g. *Politics and Letters* (London: Verso, 1979). Although the complexity of his argument cannot really be summed up in a few lines, Williams's insistence that we need to find a way of speaking about how individuals experience ideology 'from the inside' (as a 'structure of feeling' common to particular cultures/historical moments) helps to make sense of how some aspects of our social selves can be revealed to us through an 'act of

recognition' (e.g. we might discover the mark of our own class insecurity in the behaviour of another).

34 'other': it is important to distinguish my use of 'other' (as in 'textual other') from the 'Other' of Lacanian psychoanalytic theory. Whilst my 'textual others' do often bear the mark of this particular discursive formation, their otherness should also be understood in more general terms and/or in the context of my Bakhtinian frame of reference (see n. 4 above) as 'dialogic others'.

35 'Authentic realism': a view of texts which sees them relating closely to experience, both of the author and the reader. See ch. 2 of *Feminist Readings/Feminists Reading*, 2nd edn, by Sara Mills and Lynne Pearce (Hemel Hempstead: Harvester-Wheatsheaf, 1996).

36 See Jackie Stacey's work in chs. 5 and 6 of *Star Gazing* (n. 19) which analyses the way in which spectators move between the contextual and the textual, self and other, in the processes/practices of desire and identification.

37 'Interdiegetic/Extradiegetic': the terms employed by film theorists to describe characters and events situated inside and outside the text/narrative action.

38 Murray Smith, *Engaging Emotion*. For further details of Smith's analysis of the conditions of reading/viewing see my review in *Screen*, 37(4) (Winter, 1996) pp. 415-18.

39 See Stacey, *Star Gazing* (n. 19), pp. 138–45.

40 In the course of my readerly romance with Schreiner's *Story of an African Farm* (n. 1), for example, my initial positing of Lyndall as my 'textual other' has to be renegotiated when her heroic properties are compromised. My readerly manoeuvre here, as I detail in Chapter 5, is to re-designate as the textual other the space/place in which Lyndall places me as her own inter-locutory addressee. Her address, rather than 'herself', thus becomes the site of my interest and involvement.

41 Roland Barthes, *A Lover's Discourse: Fragments*, trans. Richard Howard (Harmondsworth: Penguin, 1978); Jeanette Winterson, *Written on the Body* (London: Johnathan Cape, 1992); Jane Campion (dir.), *The Piano* (Mirimax Pictures, 1993); Angela Grauerholz, exhibition hosted by Musée d'Art Contemporain de Montréal, 27 Jan.–23 Apr. 1995. Page references to all these volumes will be given after quotations in the text.

42 'Re-memory' (see n. 2 above). With respect to the use of an 'emotional vocabulary', I should refer the reader to my earlier observations on Norman Holland's work in n. 9, and also Jackie Stacey's *Star Gazing* (n. 19), which are significant exceptions to this.

43 Which is not to say, of course, that the contemporary discourse of romance does not owe a good deal to the discourse of psychoanalysis. This is especially true of Barthes's *A Lover's Discourse* (n. 41), which is saturated in the rhetoric of Freud and Lacan, and from which a good deal of my own 'reading' and analysis takes its cue. My point is simply that the discourse of romance is also predicated upon other cultural inscriptions, as the following discussion will hopefully explain.

44 See Stevi Jackson, 'Women and Heterosexual Love: Complicity, Resistance and Change', in *Romance Revisited*, ed. Lynne Pearce and Jackie Stacey (London: Lawrence and Wishart, 1995), pp. 49–62.

45 See the Introduction to *Romance Revisted* (n. 44 above) which discusses the whole business of narrative in romance in some detail, including contemporary variations on the chronology of events.

46 See Stevi Jackson, 'Even Sociologists Fall in Love: An Exploration in the Sociology of Emotions', *Sociology*, 27 (2) (May 1993), pp. 201–20.

47 The feminism of the 1970s, which operated out of the premiss that 'the personal is political', and struggled to ground politics in personal (including emotional)

experience, seems at first to contradict this separation, although the problems these feminists had in *realizing* their ideal goes some way to validating this point. I am grateful to Sara Mills for helping me clarify this.

48 I feel I should refer here to Wim Wenders's film *Wings of Desire* (1987), which I saw many years ago but whose central conceit – the pain of dying, becoming an angel, and wandering invisibly through the lives and places we once touched, inhabited – haunted me continually during the writing of this book.

49 This psychoanalytic (Lacanian) characterization of the text–reader relationship is, of course, explicit in much of Barthes's writing and builds a very obvious bridge between *The Pleasure of the Text* (see especially pp. 52 and 63) and *A Lover's Discourse* (see nn. 11 and 41).

Although working within a different (object-relations) framework, Suzanne Juhasz (see n. 3) also presents the act of reading in terms of the 'archaic' modalities of desire and the 'fear of abandonment'; see especially pp. 40–1.

50 While the theorists of the previous reference (Barthes and Juhasz) have their points of psychoanalytic reference in the work of Lacan and Winnicott respectively, the most suggestive source-text for this particular trope of reading has to be Freud's own 'Mourning and Melancholia': see *Standard Edition of the Complete Psychological Works of Sigmund Freud*, vol. 14, trans. and ed. by James Strachey (London: Hogarth Press and the Institute of Psychoanalysis, 1953–73), pp. 237–58.

51 For a well-balanced assessment of the usefulness of 'personalist criticism', see Janet Woolf, *Resident Alien: Feminist Cultural Criticism* (New Haven and London: Yale University Press, 1995), pp. 14–17.

52 Probyn (n. 6 above) writes: 'I am convinced that there are ways to talk about individuation without going through the individual and that I can talk about my experiences of being in the social without subsuming hers. Here I want to explore and theorize those processes in which I am and you are implicated . . . Of course, I am far from alone in recognizing that somehow we have to construct ways of thinking that are marked by "me" but that do not efface actively or through an omission the ways in which "she" may see differently.' (pp. 3–4).

53 See my *Reading Dialogics* (n. 4) for a discussion of the power-inscribed nature of all dialogic relations (pp. 201–2). The point here is that dialogism does not mean both partners 'being equal'.

PART

I

THE POLITICS OF GENDERED READING

Preface to Part I

The first section of this book reproduces three of my early essays on the politics of gendered reading. Despite the fact that the subsequent chapters, and the theoretical architecture of the book as a whole, now challenge the reasoning and conclusions of these preliminary investigations, I felt it important to include them: not only because they explain the 'origins' of what follows – the 'hermeneutic' model of reading, against which the 'implicated' alternative develops itself – but because I believe there is a residual value in some of the theorizing, even if its parameters have since been redefined. This is especially true of my feelings about Chapter 4, which I considered dropping from the book on a number of occasions on account of the very obvious flaws of its reasoning. In retrospect it seems clear to me, however, that these flaws – predicated upon my somewhat 'foolhardy' attempt to define 'women's writing' (or, to be more precise, contemporary feminist fiction) – are concomitant with the more utopian aspects of feminist thought, and with a *desire for* certain readerly/writerly identities, which should be respected, no matter how problematic or naïve. In revising the essay for this book, I made such changes and additions as I thought would improve the sense and strength of the original argument, but without changing the terms of the argument itself. This also applies to Chapters 2 and 3, although here I have intervened much less, trusting that the discussion in Chapter 1 will be sufficient to contextualize their position(s) within my advancing reader's history as a whole. In this respect, it should also be noted that Chapter 2 is in itself an overview of my reader-autobiography up to a certain point, for which the rest of this book serves as a coda.

In line with their focus on 'reading as interpretation' (see Chapter 1), all the chapters included in this section deal with our performances as professional or 'trained' feminist readers. This means that the 'politics' of the discussions should be very explicit. Both Chapters 3 and 4 are concerned – though from the polarized perspectives of 'male-authored' and 'female-authored' texts – with the contending power of reader and text in the production of meaning at that point in my career (following the publication of *Woman/Image/Text* in 1991) when I had begun to yield power back to the text and to analyse textual positioning in gendered terms.[1] At the time my questioning of the relative power of text and reader was still very much within the context of existing reception-theory debates on *interpretation*; but the subtext to *all* the chapters is a growing concern with the 'processes' of reading *in excess* of this. The essay '"I" the Reader' (Chapter 2) is, after all, the place where my first reader-emotion ('jealousy') was named, which caused me to reflect upon the processes of reading that are 'outside' both interpretation and (ostensibly) the reader's professional control. Even whilst they are notionally preoccupied with *reading as practice*, therefore, all these essays are also covertly and unwittingly concerned with *reading as process*; and Chapter 4 especially is well on the way to recognizing that the dialogic model of text–reader interaction I ascribe to feminist *writing* also presupposes a new model of (feminist) *reading*.

The other story these early chapters tell is one relating to my own professional training as a feminist/poststructuralist critic. In retrospect, it is easy to date my textual practices of the late 1980s quite precisely, with the Marxist-feminist/'symptomatic' readings of *Woman/Image/Text* showing the influence of Terry Eagleton *et al.*[2] Despite my increasing political disquiet with the practice of 'reading against the grain', recorded in some way in each of the following chapters, I do not wish to diminish the importance of this training to me as a scholar.[3] For all the problems I have since articulated, I feel there is still much to be said for the politics of a reading practice which self-consciously reveals the ideological construction of texts in this way, and which, through the 'gaps and silences' of the same texts, finds a way to read them 'on behalf of feminism'. My problem with such a model now, indeed, is perhaps less to do with *the type of reading* it produces in political terms, and more with the fact that it does not account for the *whole* of the reading process.

Another interesting paradox to emerge in these chapters concerns my own relationship to the gendering of textual production/consumption and connoisseurship (see discussion in Chapter 1). Although the central argument of Chapter 3, in particular, rests on my critique and analysis of the combination of textual and contextual factors which produce and sustain a text's 'dominant' reader-positioning, and whilst so many of those factors are class-inscribed, I fail to observe that my own analytic discourse still reproduces many of the rhetorical strategies of academic connoisseurship. Because at this point in my reader-history I am concerned only with my exclusion in terms of textual *interpretation*, I fail to see the highly conventional and discriminatory frameworks of my own hypothesis, or to recognize that my focus on 'textual positioning' is really a call for an new model of text–reader relations.

Another way of understanding this temporary blindspot in my reader-development is through the conceit of the reader's 'textual other' as introduced in Chapter 1. The fact is that, as a Marxist-feminist reader acutely aware of the importance of the circumstances of production and consumption in the reception of literary and visual texts, I have in Chapter 3 ceded all attempts to relate to any identifiable 'other' *in the text*. Although such 'contact' *is* made in some of the readings in *Woman/Image/Text* (mostly via a 'reconstructed' textual character or subject), here my focus on the mechanisms of exclusionary *address* pre-empt such a possibility. Like many of the 'professional' readers whom I analyse in Chapters 7 and 8, my 'textual other' is better understood as the views and opinions of my own Marxist/feminist interpretive community (and the like-minded audience I seek to address) rather than anything in the text itself. The same may also be said of my position in Chapter 4, except that here my (overt) dialogue with other feminist readers and theorists does not disguise the fact that my main argument is also a (covert) expression of my desire to find a new way of connecting with/*participating in* the texts in question. Although no 'textual others' get named in the very brief discussions of the texts concerned, we can assume that what excites me about the 'I–thou' relations I have discovered in them is the way in which they stand to connect me with structures, identities or 'presences' within the texts.

Chapter 4, for all the theoretical distraction caused by its attempt to engage dialogic theory in a new definition of 'women's writing', also goes some way to recognizing the essentially *structural* nature of the model of 'implicated' reading towards which it is covertly straining. It is clear from the conclusion to the chapter, for example, that in my struggle to extricate myself from the 'essentialist trap' of my argument I had glimpsed the possibility of arguing for a gender-specific model of textual positioning, which nevertheless allowed for the existence of many *differently/discursively positioned* addressers and addressees. Although a vast spectrum of black, white, straight, lesbian or differently classed 'speakers' might address an equally mixed spectrum of 'addressees' (both intratextual and extratextual), and although there might be struggles and 'exclusions' between these identities, I could still maintain that the dialogic 'I–thou' relation (the way in which all these speakers very self-consciously marked out and identified their addressees as recognizable *allies*) was a pervasive feature of contemporary feminist writing, whatever the *specifics* of the text's identity. Behind my imperfect, or imperfectly articulated, reasoning is the implication that the repressive and excluding forces of dominant patriarchal culture and discourse that have forced women into oppositional rhetorical strategies (such as the use of their own 'coded' languages) are, by necessity, more self-consciously dialogic. The reason that such signs of intimacy are absent in much male-authored work is precisely because men have traditionally assumed a universal male readership: all the world, as it were, is 'his' ally.

One final point to observe is that Chapters 2 to 4 also register the emergence of an autobiographical 'method' in my writing. Chapter 2, of course, represents the moment when I first took a metacritical and narrative stance on my own reading practice/process, but it would be fair to say that 'the autobiographical' has been a feature of all my writing from *Woman/Image/Text* onwards. From that point on it seemed that it was only through the use of the 'I' persona that I could adequately signal the tension between my reading practice, my politics and what I now perceive to be the broader *processes* of reading. In terms of method, I feel I should also point out the way in which these early essays demonstrate the slippage between 'reading' and 'writing' which becomes a central feature of my practice and analysis in Part II. In Chapter 3 especially, my 'reading' of a visual text is effectively my writing, or rewriting, of it. Raised to a new level of self-consciousness, such 're-scripting' is, I believe, one of the ways in which we might choose to transform, and re-evaluate, our practices as textual critics.

Notes

1 Lynne Pearce, *Woman/Image/Text* (see n. 22 to Ch. 1).
2 Terry Eagleton *et al.*: see the Introduction to *Woman/Image/Text* (n. 1), pp. 5–15, for an account/description of my inscription by this particular brand of literary criticism. A number of Eagleton's works are listed in the Bibliography to the present volume.
3 'Reading against the grain': the critical practice of reading/recuperating texts against their dominant ideological position or reader-positioning. See the Introduction to *Woman/Image/Text* (pp. 5–15) for further discussion of this also (as n. 2 above).

2

'I' the Reader: Text, Context and the Balance of Power

This chapter takes the form of an autobiographical account of my own history as a 'gendered reader', and the sexual/textual politics involved in each of my many readerly incarnations or 'positionings'. My method here is to utilize the perspectives of critical hindsight to reveal how each new self-positioning arose in reaction to the inadequacies of the former, but was then itself abandoned as a new set of textual and political pressures closed in. The visual metaphor that springs to mind is of someone trying to cross a river by leaping from slippery stone to slippery stone; of being propelled precariously onwards, only to find each new footing no more secure than the last. This recognition – that the rocks on which we stand as readers are ever liable to be swept away from under us – also accounts for the ironic cast of my perspective. It seems to me that this picaresque journey of ideological and ethical scrapes, of (inter)textual twists and turns, is not one that *could* be told 'straight'; that it is predicated upon the recognition that none of us will ever make it to the (politically) safe ground on the other side of the river.

To reflect upon the constraints, conditions and expectations imposed upon each and every one of us when we undertake to read a text as a woman/as a feminist is in itself a profoundly political act, and however much we are forced to laugh at our efforts to protect our ethical integrity it is, in my opinion, a useful form of intellectual narcissism. The particular focus of my self-scrutiny here – the relative power of *text* and *context* in the production of textual meaning – derives directly from the methodological issues raised by my book on Pre-Raphaelite art and literature, *Woman/Image/Text*, and also from my involvement with Sara Mills's edited collection of essays, *Gendering the Reader*.[1] However, as the following narrative will attest, there have been many embarrassments and misadventures *en route* to these more mature reflections.

In the beginning, which in my case lasted until at least halfway through my first degree, the thing that shall henceforth be known as 'the text' had one sure source of meaning, the author's; and one sure reader: me. As a student of literature, my role was to attempt to reach the author through his words (and, of course, I use the masculine pronoun advisedly), and to reconstruct his meanings and intentions through a process of polite and sensitive probing. The most curious thing I now remember about this time was my fondness for the pronoun 'we'. Despite the élitism of my 'sensitive' engagement with the text, I was always happy to share my responses with a group of anonymous but like-minded readers: as in the instance of my brave attempt to empathize with Stephen Daedalus in James Joyce's *A Portrait of the Artist as a Young Man*.[2] My senior school essays on *A Portrait* abound with sentences like: 'Chapter two is essentially a period of transition with regard to *our feelings* towards Stephen' and 'Unless the reader has himself reached the age of cynicism, bitterness is not an attractive quality' (!). Looking back over the essays, it is evident that I had to work extremely hard to empathize with Joyce's representative of male adolescence, but the 'anonymous' 'we' clearly gave me the means to grit my teeth and try. The fact that I was also sublimating my own gendered identity never occurred to me: English Literature as it was taught at school meant becoming a transvestite-reader on a permanent basis. No matter how complex the reader-positioning of the texts concerned, we were trained to respond as universalized male (though supposedly 'asexual') subjects.

It is also a significant comment on the limitations of English Literature as it was taught to me at university that my perception of the existence of a balance of power between author, text and reader only really became clear when I began my doctoral research. My Ph.D., on the nineteenth-century peasant poet John Clare, was undertaken at Birmingham University, where the sudden blast of critical theory offered by the staff–postgraduate seminar (then led by David Lodge) turned me from a passive reader into a textual activist. It was the early 1980s, the time when the British academic system was desperately scrambling to catch up with Roland Barthes, Jacques Derrida, Michel Foucault, and, to my own particular peril, Mikhail Bakhtin (see Bibliography). Suddenly the author was dead, the text 'untied', its meaning multiple, and the reader in a position of unprecedented power. With reckless confidence I set about releasing all the hidden voices from John Clare's now manifestly 'polyphonic' texts, employing deconstructive strategies to reveal their loss of faith in Romantic theories of language and the imagination.[3]

Powerful as I now was as a reader, however, I had yet to catch up with a sense of my gendered identity. Although I was teaching overtly feminist courses by this time, the material I was working with elsewhere failed to seem relevant to my work as a reader of John Clare. In terms of the text–reader equation, I can now explain this as the direct result of the 'false consciousness' of my readerly supremacy. These were the years when I subscribed to the (Stanley) Fishian maxim that it is the method that the reader brings to bear upon the text that enables it to be heard and seen, which meant that I was entirely oblivious to the fact that the text might in any way be positioning *me*.[4] Hence I achieved the strange feat of talking extensively about the polyphonic and heteroglossic coexistence of different voices in Clare's poems, without considering the fact that they were all *male* voices, which, although frequently addressed to a female subject *within the text*, nevertheless assumed a male reader. Because I thought it was I, the reader, who had made these voices audible, by bringing my Bakhtinian theory to bear upon the text, both their gender and mine were irrelevant. It did not bother me that these texts were excluding of a female reader in terms of their positioning, because I (as an existential female critic) had already bent them to my will. Looking back, this was the period of both my greatest power and my greatest blindness.

Thankfully, the megalomania did not last. At the same time that I, the postgraduate reader, was playing Faustus, another self was in the throes of a belated radical feminism. A generation removed from the revolutionary events of the early 1970s, I am one of those who read Kate Millett and Germaine Greer alongside Catherine Belsey, Cora Kaplan and Terry Eagleton; who caught up with the theory of WLM ('Women's Liberation Movement') feminism at the same time that its followers were charting its demise.[5] Looking back, I can see that what this produced was a peculiarly anarchic form of reader-schizophrenia. I, the reader, would read differently in different situations. Thus during the same period that I was completing my Bakhtinian reading of Clare, I had also begun a fairly crude 'images of women' assault on Pre-Raphaelite painting. While one self was oblivious to the gendered positioning of a text because she thought herself free to do what she liked with it, another was steaming through the exhibition rooms of the Tate Gallery furious at the blatant exclusiveness of these male-authored icons. In one context I felt so powerful; in the other, so powerless.

My earliest work with the Pre-Raphaelites, then, centring on a number of adult education courses I taught on Victorian Art and Literature, was very much an attempt to expose and vilify the 'negative representation' of women in such texts. It is interesting to reflect how unproblematically 'the author' crept back into the equation at this point: 'John Clare' might have been consigned to permanent quotation marks, but the most reprehensible authorial intentions were ascribed to Dante Gabriel Rossetti. I, the reader, meanwhile assumed the role of heckler, instigating groups of cultured, middle-class, female adult-education students to mock and despise the texts that they were only permitted to view from the margins. It was a readerly scenario exemplified by Lucy Snowe's visit to the art gallery in Charlotte Brontë's *Villette;* the Pre-Raphaelite images of women, like Lucy Snowe's *Cleopatra*, were rejected on the grounds that they had been wrought for the salacious pleasure of a male audience.[6] My most memorable reader's statement from this period was a reference to the Pre-Raphaelite Brotherhood's 'penchant for sick and dying women'. Satire, I confess, had become a rather enjoyable reading strategy, and as it spread its seeds amongst my students, it inculcated in us a sense of dissident group-power.

With the trashing and ridiculing of sexist and/or misogynist texts having noticeably declined in recent years, I am sometimes overwhelmed with nostalgia for the pleasure of such ribald malice. In an academic context it has disappeared, of course, because we are no longer so sure about who or what to ridicule: discourses, not authors, are now responsible for the anti-feminist world in which we live, and patriarchy is no longer the monolithic white elephant we can blame for all our ills. For today's feminist reader everything, everywhere, is almost oppressively subtle, complex and contradictory. Things (perhaps regrettably) have gone beyond a joke.

As it happens, the book that finally came out of my work on the Pre-Raphaelites, *Woman/Image/Text*, is not entirely without jokes or the occasional flippant aside. However, any feminist aspiring to scholarly credibility in the late 1980s could not afford to be too cavalier. I, the reader, finally got round to putting pen to paper just as the paranoia over 'essentialist thinking' really began to set in: the term 'woman' had by now become an epistemological minefield and, as all certainty over gendered identity fell apart, so too did the anxieties around reading increase. If it was no longer tenable to represent women as a group, where did that leave the woman reader, or, indeed, the feminist reader? Could there be any such thing as a reading position that was simplistically gendered, male or female? How could a text direct itself to a male or female audience when those terms in themselves are inclusive of so many differences and contradictions as to render them meaningless?

The grim burden of these questions caused me, like many of my contemporaries, to abandon satire and polemic, and to develop a new style of writing predicated upon the caveat. It is a style characterized by lengthy sentences with sub-clauses, parentheses and extensive footnotes. Theses, now, proceed with infinite caution: one step forward is followed by two steps back. Entire books are likely to end with a sentence which puts into question all that had gone before. We, as a community of feminist readers and critics, have found ourselves within a cleft stick, which requires us to advance new theories (which are always demanding of *some kind* of generalization) at the same time as recognizing that the thing we are theorizing – in my case 'gendered reading' – is impossible to generalize about. The skill that we all most aspire to is therefore circumspection: how to succeed in getting through a book or article without tripping oneself up: a second's lapse of concentration and the essentialist assumption will be out, and you, the guilty party, will be shot down.[7]

In many ways *Woman/Image/Text* may therefore be seen as the moment when I, the reader, lost my nerve. Its readings of eight poem–painting combinations are a strange mixture of textual dexterity (reflecting the confidence I had gained through my poststructuralist training), methodological and linguistic angst of the kind I've just described, and, most importantly, an increasing uneasiness about whether my readerly practices could be ethically and politically justified. I shall explain.

Alongside the growing demand for ever-greater critical complexity, 1980s feminist theory also required 'a positive approach' to textual analysis. Here, I have memories of publishers asking for a more 'up-beat' ending to books or chapters of books. Practising feminist criticism might be getting increasingly hard, but it must still be seen to be fun. Through the work of poststructuralist critics in literary and cultural studies, the fashion had been set for making the most recalcitrant of texts complex, exciting, and, of course, politically redeemable. Terry Eagleton's attempt to read Richardson's *Clarissa* 'on behalf of feminism' is a classic case in point, while in Kate Belsey's hands the manifest misogyny of Milton's *Paradise Lost* is blasted away to reveal exquisite points of doubt and contradiction.[8]

Thus by the time I actually came to write *Woman/Image/Text* in the summer of 1989 I was obliged to put aside the feelings of gendered exclusion that many of the texts inspired and set about seeing how they could be positively re-read. The question I posed myself, and which for a long time functioned as the working title for my introduction, was 'what can the twentieth-century feminist reader/viewer do with nineteenth-century male-produced images of women?'. Drawing upon the full range of 'deconstructive' reading strategies by then available to the feminist reader (for example, post-Althusserian Marxism, discourse theory and recent work on spectatorship and pleasure in film and media studies), I found ways of undermining the dominant ideologies of the texts concerned, and of inserting myself, the feminist reader, into their 'gaps and silences'.[9] By this means a radical collusion could be wrought between myself and the women represented in the texts. Beata Beatrix (see Illustration 2.1) might be dying (or, as Rossetti put it, 'rapt visibly towards heaven'), but her ghostliness and two-dimensionality are, in the last analysis, part of the discourse of masculine fear and impotence. The erotic threat presented by women in Pre-Raphaelite painting is circumscribed only by a formal and symbolic denial of their existential reality. Beatrice, as I suggest in my chapter, exults in her own ghostliness; she smiles in our direction.[10]

Yet even as I used my poststructuralist reader-power to prise apart these texts and reappropriate them, I began to have grave doubts about the ethics and politics of doing so. To redeem the images concerned meant, more often than not, to read them out of context: to extract the text from the circumstances of its historical production and consumption. On the one hand, this was reader-power being put to the most subversive of feminist uses; but, on the other, it completely ignored the dominant reading position offered by the text itself.

Although *Woman/Image/Text* brought this dilemma to consciousness and made it part of its central thesis, the whole book was predicated upon the assumption that as long as we, as readers, are aware of what we are doing, such breaking of the rules is acceptable. In retrospect, I am less sure.

Illustration 2.1   *'Beatrice. . . exults in her own ghostliness; she smiles in our direction'*
(Chapter 2)

When I come back to the paintings again now it is my sense of gendered
exclusion which prevails. That I can, and indeed have, read them against the
grain of their historical production does not alter the fact that they have a
preferred reader who is not me. The text I pretended was mine was all the
time in dialogue with someone else.

The consequence of this loss of confidence in my readerly power was to

turn away from male-authored texts altogether; and whenever I get lost in
the sophistications of whether there is such a thing as 'women's writing', I
hold on to this 'readerly response' as evidence that there must be. Indeed, as
I thought more about the force of my own reaction I concluded that here, if
anywhere, must be the definition of what we mean by women's writing: not
writing by women, or about women, but, more especially, writing *for* them.
However complex the categories 'male' and 'female' have become, texts *do*
gender their readers, either explicitly or implicitly. While there will, of
course, be some texts that are less specific in their address than others, at the
two extremes there are many texts produced fairly exclusively for men or
for women. Thus, having spent so long attempting to redeem the former, I
turned with joy and relief to the pages of the latter.

My attempts to formulate a theory for the specificity of address in contemporary women's fiction took me back once again to the work of Mikhail
Bakhtin. In an essay entitled 'Dialogic Theory and Women's Writing' I have
argued that recent work on Bakhtin's theories of dialogic activity can be
used to support the notion of a gendered exclusivity within certain female-
authored texts.[11] Through linguistic strategies of direct and indirect address,
through intonation and extra-literary context, it is evident that several
women writers have successfully defined their audience as both female *and*
feminist. Thus, once again, albeit for a short time, everything seemed very
simple. There may be millions of texts from which I, as a woman reader, am
excluded, but with an ever-increasing library of contemporary feminist writing it seemed obvious where my energies should be directed. I resolved only
to trouble myself with texts which spoke to me as a woman and as a feminist.

Unfortunately, this second wave of readerly euphoria lasted little longer
than the first. The texts I thought to be addressed exclusively to me turned
out not to be so. What I had experienced as an intimate relationship
between the chosen text and myself turned out to be but one of many. I soon
saw that I could only ever occupy but *one* of the multiple positionings
denoted by the category 'woman reader'. The text I had thought of as 'mine'
was talking to others as easily as it talked to me. All the time I was reading,
I kept overhearing scraps of conversation between the text and readers differently situated from myself. I became jealous and suspicious. I wanted to
know that the text was saying to *them*: to the black women, the heterosexual women, the working-class women; to the women who were ten years
older, or ten years younger, than myself. Once again I, the reader, felt
excluded and unwanted. With so many *different* readers jostling for the
position of 'preferred reader', I found it difficult to accept my own insignif-
icance. De-essentializing the category 'woman', as I knew I must, had de-
essentialized me.

I have since discovered a number of texts which have helped explain the
nature of this 'reader-jealousy' to me, as well as suggesting a possible way
forward. One of these is Martin Montgomery's 'DJ Talk' (first published in

Media, Culture and Society in 1986).[12] Part of Montgomery's analysis is concerned with the way in which the radio DJ's monologue is continually addressing different segments of the audience through 'identifiers' which include or exclude particular groups. For example, horoscope features identify and privilege the different star-signs in turn. The effect of this, as Montgomery explains, is that any individual listener will be positioned differently at different times, and that 'it is quite common for an audience to be in a position of the overhearing recipient of a discourse that is being directly addressed to someone else' (p. 428).

While Montgomery welcomed this constant realignment of address as evidence that no discourse 'speaks from a single authoritative position' (p. 438), I, the erstwhile privileged reader, received the evidence with gloom. It was clearly true that none of my favoured feminist texts could exist in an exclusive relationship with any one reader-positioning, and my status as addressee was as tenuous as it had always been.

Since this 'second splitting of the reader's ego' I have, however, come to realize that my jealousy was somewhat misplaced. While it may be true that my favoured feminist texts have more readers than I originally thought, this does not irredeemably alter my special relationship to them. Indeed, after reflecting some more on Montgomery's model of shifting address, I realized that mutability does not necessarily equal promiscuity. 'Polyphony', which, in the Bakhtinian sense, demands that a text be comprised of a 'plurality of consciousnesses with equal rights', is not my *reader's* experience of contemporary feminist writing any more than it is my experience of the male literary canon.[13] The text may be comprised of many voices; it may effect multiple text–reader positionings; but this does not mean that it does so without preference or discrimination. As Stuart Hall observed in his work on encoding and decoding in television discourse as long ago as 1973, 'polysemy must not, however, be confused with pluralism'.[14]

Therefore, even as I showed in my work on John Clare that the voices *within* the polyphonic text can be hierarchized according to the balance of power between speaker and addressee within the text, so, too, do I now propose a (mutable) hierarchy of reader-positionings.[15] Viewed in this way, a text like Alice Walker's *The Color Purple* becomes the site of a struggle for reader-privilege. Readers of different classes, races and sexual orientations may turn hungrily from page to page for a sign of their own preferment. Sometimes their desire will be appeased; sometimes it will be disappointed. But either way, by the time they finish reading, a judgement will have been cast and they will know their place in the schema of the text's reader-positionings.

While, on the one hand, the existence of such textual preferment helps to explain why reading books, watching films or looking at paintings continues to be such an exciting but nerve-racking occupation, it also offered me, the jealous reader, perverse consolation. Realizing that one text might privilege me even if another did not confirmed that the dialogue between text and reader was, after all, a 'real' relationship; that it was subject to the same laws of selection, rejection, and reciprocity as our interpersonal relations. If I, as a reader, have to learn to live with the continual possibility of rejection then I may also enjoy the possibility of preferment. Acknowledging that the relationship between text and reader is inscribed by a volatile power-dynamic in this way permits desire even as it engenders fear. We may look forward to opening a new book, even as we are apprehensive of it. Moreover, by recognizing this emotional dimension within the reading process, we may come to a new understanding of its politics.

At the time of writing, this is where my story ends, though I do not pretend to have reached a rock any less slippery than those I have perched on before. In terms of the thesis I have been pursuing – the question of whether, in the production of textual meaning, it is text or reader who holds the balance of power – it is clear that I have now conceded renewed authority to the text. While I, the reader, exist in dialogic relationship with the text (any text), I am nevertheless *positioned by it,* and the challenge and excitement of the reading process depends upon my not knowing, in advance, if it will embrace me or reject me, position me as an ally or as an antagonist.[16] Yet to acknowledge that all texts operate codes of address in this way, that they make selections among their readership in terms of age, race, gender, class, education, is not to say that the reader is entirely disempowered. While hers may be a *reactive* position (it is the text which initiates the relationship), she has a degree of choice in how she may respond to her positioning; and this is where the *politics* of reading may ultimately be located. The feminist reader like myself, for example, must consider whether or not to pick up the gauntlet a male-oriented text throws at me; must decide whether or not to engage in a struggle for its 'meaning', either 'with' or 'against the grain'. Similarly, I must decide how to conduct my relationship with texts which position me as their 'ally': do I accept their intimacy at face value, or do I take the risk of probing deeper, and establishing a more complex, more uncomfortable dialogue? For while I would now acknowledge that it is the text that initiates the relationship, I also believe that it is I, the reader, who must take responsibility for negotiating the terms upon which we are to proceed. Even as the text positions me, so may I (re)position my relationship to it.

Notes

1 See Lynne Pearce, *Woman/Image/Text* (see n. 22, Ch. 1); *Gendering the Reader* (n. 24, Ch. 1).

2 James Joyce, *A Portrait of the Artist as a Young Man* (London: The Egoist, 1917).

3 See Lynne Pearce, 'John Clare and Mikhail Bakhtin: The Dialogic Principle', unpublished Ph.D. thesis, University of Birmingham, 1987. Part of my thesis focused on the polyphonic nature of Clare's asylum poem 'Child Harold'

(written as a continuation of Byron's poem of the same name). In the Bakhtinian vocabulary 'polyphony' means simply 'many voices', and my reading of this text analysed the many different personae adopted by the narrator and his fluctuating power *vis-à-vis* his 'addressees' within the text. A shortened version of this analysis was published as an article, entitled 'John Clare's "Child Harold": A Polyphonic Reading', *Criticism*, 31(2) (1989), pp. 139–57.

4 See Stanley Fish's *Is there a Text in this Class?* (n. 9, Ch. 1) and the Introduction to *Gendering the Reader* (n. 24, Ch. 1) for further discussion of Fish's critical influence.

5 Kate Millett's *Sexual Politics* (London: Virago, 1977; originally published in the United States in 1969) and Germaine Greer's *The Female Eunuch* (London: Paladin, 1971) were two of the key texts which helped launch the modern Women's Liberation Movement. Catherine Belsey's influential *Critical Practice* (London: Methuen) appeared in 1980, and Cora Kaplan wrote an important critical response to Millett's *Sexual Politics* which is reproduced in her collection of essays, *Sea Changes: Culture and Feminism* (London: Verso, 1986). Terry Eagleton's work, from the 1970s onwards, has provided a model for much Marxist and feminist criticism: see in particular his *Literary Theory* (Oxford: Basil Blackwell, 1983).

6 See Charlotte Brontë, *Villette* (Oxford: Clarendon Press, 1984), pp. 278–93.

7 For an account of how anxious feminists have become about committing the 'sin' of essentialism see the 'round table discussion' between Marianne Hirsch, Jane Gallop and Nancy K. Miller ('Criticizing Feminist Criticism') in *Conflicts in Feminism*, ed. Marianne Hirsch and Evelyn Fox Keller (London: Routledge, 1990).

8 See Terry Eagleton, *The Rape of Clarissa: Writing, Sexuality and Class Struggle in Samuel Richardson* (Oxford: Basil Blackwell, 1986) and Catherine Belsey, *John Milton: Language, Gender and Power* (n. 23, Ch. 1).

9 The reference to 'gaps' and 'silences' here is an allusion to Pierre Macherey's model of 'symptomatic reading' as outlined in his *Theory of Literary Production*, trans. Geoffrey Wall (London: Routledge, 1978). For a brief account of what this type of reading practice involves see my *Woman/Image/Text* (n. 22, Ch. 1), pp. 5–15.

10 See Pearce, *Woman/Image/Text* (n. 22, Ch. 1), pp. 46–58.

11 Reproduced here as Chapter 4.

12 See Martin Montgomery, 'DJ Talk', *Media, Culture and Society*, 8(4) (1986), pp. 421–40. Further page references are given after quotations in the text.

13 'A plurality of independent and unmerged voices and consciousnesses': see Mikhail Bakhtin, *Problems of Dostoevsky's Poetics*, ed. and trans. Caryl Emerson (Manchester: Manchester University Press, 1984). See Chapter 4 for further discussion of how I developed these ideas in relation to contemporary feminist writing.

14 See Stuart Hall, 'Encoding/decoding' (n. 28, Ch. 1).

15 For my discussion of the power relationship existing between speaker and addressee in John Clare's 'Child Harold', see the article in *Criticism* cited in n. 2 above.

16 See Anne Herrmann, *The Dialogic and Difference: 'An/Other Woman' in Virginia Woolf and Christa Wolf* (New York: Columbia University Press, 1989). In this fascinating application of Bakhtin's dialogic theory Herrmann compares the way in which Wolf's texts position their reader as a female 'ally', and Woolf's as a male 'antagonist'.

3

Positioning Pre-Raphaelite Painting

This chapter addresses the question of how twentieth-century feminist readers and viewers are positioned by texts from an earlier historical period. To what extent are they able to challenge the conditions of production and consumption by which such texts are historically inscribed? To what extent can they create an 'alternative' reading position? My conclusion, based on my earlier work with the Pre-Raphaelites and reviewed and revised in the reading of the Dante Gabriel Rossetti painting which follows, is that such recuperation is extremely problematic.[1] While it might be possible for feminists to be active in writing and rewriting the 'scripts' of contemporary art-works, there are more theoretical and political obstacles to reading nineteenth-century texts 'against the grain'. While we are the historically specified audience of the one (even allowing for our exclusion/marginalization on the grounds of gender), we cannot intervene in the meaning-production of the other without overriding the particular set of historical circumstances in which that work was first received. Such constraints would seem especially important when dealing with 'high art', moreover, since the cultural values of the institutions in which such texts first circulated are not easily displaced; indeed, they persist, very visibly, in the nineteenth-century art galleries in which Rossetti's and other paintings continue to be viewed. Therefore, while as twentieth-century feminist viewers we may *desire* to 'usurp' the reading position originally authorized by Rossetti and his patrons, we are seriously circumscribed. The reading which follows instances a number of ways in which the ropes (metaphorical as well as literal) drawn round the nineteenth-century art-work are effective at keeping feminists out.

Dante Gabriel Rossetti's *The Beloved* is probably not a painting that most of you would want to own (see Illustration 3.1). I remember that once, when the Tate Gallery was selling off copies of this particular print for 25p, I bought two, for myself and a friend. Yet while assorted other Pre-Raphaelite images found their way onto our walls, this one never did. Looking at it again now, I can understand why: aesthetic considerations

Illustration 3.1 'Rossetti's work at its worst . . . its most *unfascinating'* (Chapter 3)

aside, what has this image to say to the twentieth-century feminist viewer that is at all salutary? A century of ideological self-consciousness has wedged itself between ourselves and this text's production so successfully that a canvas representing six female subjects (the most Rossetti ever included on a single canvas) must now be seen as excluding the female viewer. Our education as feminist readers/viewers will have enabled us to recognize, in a moment, that the gaze of these six pairs of eyes is *not for us*, but for some nineteenth-century male voyeur. Exactly who he is, and exactly how we (as twentieth-century female/feminist spectators) are positioned outside this text will be the subject of the following chapter.

Before I engage with these questions directly, however, I should perhaps say something about the theoretical and political reasons for my choice of such a recalcitrant text.

First, it was a choice made somewhat wearily and cynically, soon after the completion of my book *Woman/Image/Text* (1991; see note 1). After many years of probing Pre-Raphaelite representations of women for the Machereyan 'gaps and silences' that would allow us, as feminist readers and viewers, to intervene in a text's 're-production' and appropriate a meaning and/or pleasure 'against the grain', I had concluded that such reading strategies, while theoretically possible, were politically dubious.[2] I ended my book with the rather depressing qualm that to read *against* the historical context of a text's production and reception was, in many cases, to excuse the inexcusable. How could I justify the revelation of a painting's 'competing discourses' or 'hidden subtexts' if the dominant discourse, the one exchanged between the historical producer and consumer (that is, the male patron/purchaser or nineteenth-century viewing public) was as distressingly demeaning and misogynistic as these often were? My book concluded that only two of the eight poem–painting combinations I had considered were of 'sufficient ideological complexity' to allow for a *positive* feminist appropriation. In all other instances, I found the dominant discourses which overlaid the text too securely dominant: reclaiming these representations as subversive and/or 'heroic' was certainly possible, but was it ethically legitimate?[3]

And so, in writing this chapter, I decided to put all pretensions of feminist appropriation behind me. I picked up the Tate Gallery catalogue with an eye not for complexity, but for cliché. After reclaiming Pre-Raphaelite paintings against the odds I would attend, once more, to their surfaces: to their predominant ideologies. The focus of the volume for which the chapter was originally commissioned was, after all, 'positioning the reader'; and, no matter how dexterous the feminist reader/viewer might be in usurping that role, it was clear she was not meant to be there. Pre-Raphaelite painting is, by and large, a canon of art made by men, for men: or, to phrase the point a little less essentially, these are texts which were inscribed by, and are re-productive of, patriarchal discourse. With these cynical criteria in mind, *The Beloved* selected itself without too much difficulty. This is Rossetti's work at its worst, I thought: at its most parodic, its most *unfascinating*.[4]

Positioning and Context

Perhaps the first thing to observe about the 'art history' of this painting is that my criticisms would probably go unchallenged by even the most devoted Rossetti scholars. Painted in 1865–6, it is a canvas from Rossetti's 'decadent' middle period: the decade in which, following Elizabeth Siddal's death in 1862, he took up his paintbrush once more (during the 1850s he worked almost exclusively in pen and watercolour), and began manufacturing a series of bust-length 'portraits' of beautiful women which are variously described as 'sensuous', 'decorative' and 'degrading'.[5] The appearance of these paintings – including such titles as *Venus Verticordia* (1864–8), *The Blue Bower* (1865), *Regina Cordium* (1866) and *Monna Vanna* (1866) – has traditionally been explained in biographical terms as part of Rossetti's reaction to Siddal's death.[6] Siddal, who mythologically has always represented the virginal/spiritual pole of Rossettian womanhood, had become, during the early 1850s, virtually his only model. Her face figures again and again in the drawings from this period, frequently as a representation of Dante's Beatrice.[7] Although Rossetti had, in fact, already begun to use other models before Siddal's death, the popular story-line is that his 'descent' into the 'fleshly' was an emotive response to Siddal's loss.[8] With his icon of purity gone, the despairing artist turned (both personally and professionally) to the pleasures and comforts of the flesh: Fanny Cornforth, Alex Wilding and Marie Ford (sitter for the bride in *The Beloved*) became his new models, while Jane Morris, muse of his later years, waited in the wings. Closer attention to Rossetti's output during these years will reveal that this chronology is wrong (see note 8); but the narrative is an appealing one. Read in this way, the new eroticism of the portraits from the 1860s is seen as a confrontation not only with carnality, but also with *mortality*. Instead of mere degeneration into the 'fleshly', we see a preoccupation with the *carpe diem* motif.

This biographical context has subsequently 'permitted' aesthetic criticism of paintings like *The Beloved*: they are seen to represent a period of technical experiment and emotional readjustment, in which the lack of anything to say is noted but excused.[9] This assessment nevertheless conceals two important facts about the paintings: first, Rossetti's own high esteem of them, and second, their market success.

Rossetti's own pleasure in his successful return to oil painting is most triumphantly expressed in his comments on one of his 'Venetian' subjects from 1866. Of this painting he wrote:

> I have a picture close on completion – one of my best, I believe, and probably the most effective as a room decoration which I have ever painted. It is called 'Venus Veneta', and represents a Venetian lady in a rich dress of white and gold, – in short the Venetian ideal of female beauty.[10]

Notable in this proud self-assessment is, of course, the conjunction of 'success' with 'decorative quality'. Read cynically, the statement could be taken as tacit acknowledgement that the function of 'art' is ultimately no more than 'decoration': a criterion that most artists and art-historians would reject as profoundly heretical. For the feminist reader, however, this bald reduction of art to decoration is made disturbing by the fact that the decorative commodity is 'woman': 'the Venetian ideal of female beauty'. With art reduced to its material function, the representation of the female body is similarly demystified: the woman/art/commodity nexus gives 'female beauty' an unambiguous market value.

The actual market price of *The Beloved* was £300.[11] As with many of the paintings from this period, it was a commissioned piece, and its price was negotiated in advance by one of Rossetti's principal patrons, George Rae. In 1863, when this picture was first started, £300 was a considerable fee for a canvas of these modest dimensions (32½″ x 30″), as comparative pricings show; but its market value is probably best understood in terms of the *demand* that arose for Rossetti's paintings of this kind. The exhibition 'The Pre-Raphaelites: Painters and Patrons in the North East', held in the Laing Art Gallery, Newcastle in 1989–90, revealed the vogue Rossetti's work had gained with collectors (in this case, mostly wealthy industrialists) by the mid-1860s. Alexander Stevenson, for example, partner in the Jarrow chemical company, paid 150 guineas for the small watercolour of *Lady Lilith,* being unable to afford the 500 guineas being asked for the oil painting of the same subject.[12]

While the collectors of Pre-Raphaelite art were not *exclusively* male, it is hardly surprising to discover that they were predominantly so. Although Rossetti, during this middle period, undertook a number of commissions for family portraits, and although the wives of his patrons (for example, Margaret Smith of Newcastle) sometimes played a prominent role in the selection process, it was usually the male heads of the households who held the purse-strings.[13] The relationship between the wives of these collectors and the images of women that found their way into their households is, indeed, a curious one: positioned, on the one hand, to share in their husbands' pleasure in acquiring the desired purchase, they were, at the same time, excluded by their economic superfluity to the transaction. Thus, while we may never *know* if and what George Rae's wife thought when she saw *The Beloved* being mounted on her wall, we do know that she had no material means of intervening in a transaction that was between her husband and the artist or his dealer. Whether the painting delighted or offended her, whether she received it as an image commensurate with her husband's feelings for her or of his dissatisfaction, it hardly matters, since his *ownership* of the canvas meant that it was ultimately his to do what he liked with. George Rae might have been a generous and discriminating man who, like Thomas Smith, consulted with his wife on all such purchases. If, on the other hand, he was not, his wife's moral/aesthetic preferences would not necessarily be taken into account.

Positioning and Text

I want to move now from the man who may be positioned as the historical legatee of the painting to his hypothetical brother, the 'implied' reader/viewer. My thesis here, as I expressed in my opening remarks, is that this is a text which unequivocally addresses itself to a male audience. Even were *The Beloved* painted by a woman (and, as noted below, there were several woman artists producing similar images by the end of the century), and even were it bought by George Rae's wife with her own money, I would argue that the semiotics of the text position the reader as a white, heterosexual, middle-class male. To this extent I am therefore allowing that, in matters of address, text and context may be at variance; that the expectations raised by our information about the historical producers and consumers of a text might not be realized by our examination of the text itself. Such deviance is possible, I believe, because the ideological discourses of any society, and at any historical moment, cut across the biological sex of its producers and consumers. As we see in the case of the *fin-de-siècle* women followers of the Pre-Raphaelites, such as Henrietta Rae and Evelyn de Morgan, it is quite possible for a woman artist to position a male viewer as the audience of her painting, to reproduce images of women that are the objects of the male gaze.[14] In the case of *The Beloved,* however, text and context concur: the patriarchal hegemony of the painting's production and consumption are replicated in its textual politics. In the second half of this chapter, I am therefore going to deal with four of this text's positioning devices: first, the verbal text inscribed on the frame of the painting; second, the gazes and gestures of the women in the painting; third, the painting's formal properties; and fourth, the inscription of ethnicity and class.

The Verbal Text

As I argue in *Woman/Image/Text*, the appending of verbal texts to a painting is clearly the most explicit of the ways in which its potential 'meaning' is directed and circumscribed.[15] Although the interaction of the visual and the verbal is often a suggestive interface, there is little doubt that the Victorian artists' penchant for this device was part of an attempt to prevent ambiguity. The addition of a literary inscription (in Rossetti's case, frequently one of his own poems) to the frame of the canvas has the effect of pre-empting the viewers' own attempts at interpretation; it also positions the reader, as we shall see, in terms of class, education and gender.

As is the case with many of Rossetti's paintings, the inscription for *The Beloved* was added some time after the completion of the actual painting, when a new frame (dated *c*.1873) was supplied.[16] The text itself is a conflation of the Song of Solomon 1: 2 and 2: 16, and Psalm 45: 14:

> My Beloved is mine and I am his,
> Let him kiss me with the kisses of his mouth:
> for thy love is better than wine.
> She shall be brought unto the King
> in raiment of needlework: the virgins
> that be her fellows shall bear her
> company, and shall be brought unto thee.

These lines, which focus on the bride's dedication of herself and her attendant virgins to her future husband, are an exemplary instance of reader
positioning. First, and most dramatic, is the opening invocation in the first
person. Here, a statement of sexual abandonment ('My Beloved is mine and
I am his') is followed by the erotic appeal, 'Let him kiss me with the kisses
of his mouth' (but not, significantly, 'let *me* kiss *him*'). Freed from their biblical context, the invitations of Solomon's future wife address themselves
provocatively to the viewer of the painting. This, of course, positions 'him'
as a heterosexual male, and offers anyone in that category an immediate
rapprochement with the woman represented in the painting. Those of us
who are not heterosexual/males are simultaneously excluded or marginalized: we are consigned merely to *overhear* what is being said. As with the
verbal texts which accompany visual representations in today's popular
pornographic magazines, the reader/viewer is made to feel wanted: he is
positioned in such a way that he 'believes' himself and the woman represented in the picture to have formed a 'special' relationship. Her use of the
first-person pronoun constitutes *him* as the second-person singular
addressee, and the success of the provocation depends very much on how
'exclusive' the reader/viewer feels this relationship to be.

But Rossetti's text – cleverly culled from different biblical sources –
underwrites this invocation/provocation with another dynamic. The five
lines from Psalms, which represent a movement from the first-person to the
third-person pronoun ('She'), also register the commodity status of the
'Beloved'; an impotence further endorsed by the passive verbal construction:
'shall be brought'. In this way, the reciprocity of power implicit in the opening invocation ('My Beloved is mine and I am his') is neatly circumscribed,
and the addressee is positioned not only as 'desired object' but also as 'master'. Needless to say, this 'mastery' is enhanced by the fact that the bride is
attended by virgins who 'shall be brought' in the same manner. Meanwhile,
the reappearance of the second-person singular pronoun in the final word of
the inscription ('thee') re-establishes the intimacy formed in the opening
line.

Gesture and Gaze

The positioning of the reader/viewer effected by the verse inscription is replicated and reinforced in the gestures and gaze of the bride and her attendants
in the painting itself. In common with the other bust-length 'portraits' painted
during the 1860s, the subject of *The Beloved* looks directly out of the canvas
to engage the viewer. This 'eye-contact' is very much in contrast with
Rossetti's drawings and watercolours of the 1850s, where the women are
nearly always represented with their eyes averted, and for which Siddal's
Beata Beatrix ('rapt' towards death with her eyes closed) may be seen as the
culminating symbol (see illustration 2.1).[17] The sexual politics of eye-contact

are however, no straightforward matter. Although we might read the direct gaze of the woman in *The Beloved* as more sexually provocative simply because she is engaging her viewer, the 'unconsciousness' implicit in the averted gaze (implying that this woman does not know she is being looked at) permits the voyeuristic pleasure that is denied by direct eye-to-eye confrontation.[18] Direct eye-contact, then, is ambiguous in its sexual import: it betokens challenge at the same time as registering the classic 'come-on'. Both these messages are, I would suggest, present in Rossetti's representation of King Solomon's bride. Her *faux-naïve* invitation is mixed with artful selfconsciousness. As she unveils herself for her viewer, so is she exercising a degree of power over him; the element of confrontation mitigates her passivity.

The sexual-political significance of the act of veiling/unveiling has also been probed by Ludmilla Jordanova in her book, *Sexual Visions* (1990). With reference to its representation in the history of Western art, Jordanova shows the 'powerful moral ambivalence' attached to the actions of veiling/unveiling to be commensurate with 'the absence of any stable value attached to the female body and hence its visibility or concealment'.[19] The veil is the paradoxical signifier of both innocence and corruption, both vulnerability and (sexual) threat. Although ostensibly there to protect the wearer, the veil also protects the viewer. Removing the veil removes the protection. It is a profoundly risky act. Jordanova writes:

> Why, then, must we ask, is it the *female* in particular that is to be (un)veiled? Un/covering women's bodies has two implications that may be pertinent here. First, covering them implies shame and modesty. . . . Secondly, veiling implies secrecy. Women's bodies, and by extension feminine attributes, cannot be treated as fully public, something dangerous might happen, secrets be let out, if they were open to view. (pp. 92–3)

The gender-specific nature of veiling is further explained by Jordanova as an indication of the massively overdetermined symbolic significance of the female body, and the fact that 'by contrast, the idea of unveiling men is comic, implausible and unthreatening, presumably because their bodies are not the symbolic carriers in modern society of either creative or destructive forces' (p. 96). While un/veiling, then, is an action which discloses the disturbing connotative ambivalence of the female body in modern Western culture, it also signifies the way in which the threat has been contained.

One way in which this particular painting is exceptional in Rossetti's *œuvre* is, as I indicated at the beginning of the chapter, in the presence of the supporting cast. The bride's attendants consist of four dark-haired women and a black (African) child. The sex of the latter is a matter of uncertainty for most viewers, although Virginia Surtees reveals that late improvements to the painting in 1865 included the replacement of a mulatto slave girl with a black slave boy.[20] Like the bride, all these attendants (with the possible exception of the one on the far right) look *out* of the canvas, although the 'directions' of their gazes (both literal and metaphorical) are different. They are, in effect, *mirrors* for the impression of her beauty upon its recipient. The fact that they are looking at him from slightly different angles helps to distinguish the import of their looks from hers; it also lends a certain sense of movement to an otherwise static composition. While the bride's gaze fixes her husband/viewer in space, those of her attendants register the fact that he has just appeared and is walking towards them.

Returning to the sexual politics of these positioning devices, it may consequently be argued that where the directness of the bride's gaze replicates the invocation/provocation of the literary text ('Let him kiss me'), those of her attendants preserve her passive role as the third-person *object* of the (male) viewer's gaze. Her commodity status is, moreover, reinforced by the slave child's 'offering' of the vase of roses which, in semiotic terms, functions as her 'supplementary signifier'.[21] According to the system of exchange expounded by Judith Williamson in her work on advertisements (see note 21), the face and flowers in this text, would, indeed, become interchangeable signifiers revealing a mutual signifier that might be translated, without too much trouble, as 'beautiful gift'. According to these hermeneutics, the position of the husband is equally simple: if she is the gift, he is its honoured *recipient*.

The Formal Properties

It may be argued, however, that the sexual provocativeness of paintings like *The Beloved* risk threatening their male audience. Notwithstanding the various strategies to undermine the threat by emphasizing the female subject's essential passivity, there remains the danger of the eroticism being in excess of the means of controlling it. Sex and sexuality are so overdetermined in these paintings (Rossetti's series from the 1860s is arguably 'about' nothing else) that the positioning described above may not be sufficient to keep the male viewer in a position of power. It is for this reason that the formal properties of such paintings become as important as their representational content. As I argue in *Woman/Image/Text*, the viewpoint, surface detail, two-dimensional flatness, colour and decorative symbolism of Pre-Raphaelite art can all be seen as devices to undermine the *material presence* of the female subject and hence neutralize her (sexual) threat.[22] In this respect, as in so many others, *The Beloved* is a prototypical text. As in all these 'portraits' from the 1860s, the 'subject' of the painting (the representation of a beautiful woman) vies aesthetically with the decorative appeal of the composition. In line with Rossetti's own comment on *Monna Vanna* as a successful 'room decoration', paintings like *The Beloved* can, one feels, be 'enjoyed' purely in terms of their rhythm of colour and line. They work, on one level, as little more than successful 'patterns'. *The Beloved* is especially conservative and formulaic in this respect. With the palette reduced to two contrasting spectrums of red and green, the composition is structured according to a predictable system of chromatic counterpoint: an area of green here necessitates an incidence of red there. Hence the green sleeves of the bride's dress are balanced by the red roses and lilies held by her attendant, and the red brocade of their dresses (which form the background to the bride's own) are complemented by the greenery that floats gratuitously in the space at the top of the picture. In sexual-political terms it is also interesting to observe that, while the reds of the flowers, the jewels hung about the slave child's neck and the bride's own coral head-dress all, on one level, serve to draw attention to her mouth (which is the same colour), they simultaneously diffuse its sexual connotations by making it part of the pattern. In terms of the hypothesis I am proposing, this can be read as a protective device for the male viewer, whereby the most erotic constituent of the painting is thus safely fetishized. The careful balance of colour is also underwritten, in this particular painting, by its almost square dimensions ($32\frac{1}{2}'' \times 30''$) and the 'mirror-image' distribution of forms. Indeed, it is only the slight tilt of the bride's head, and the fact that it is situated a little high, which prevents this from becoming the dead-centre axis around which all the other forms and colours are arranged.

Concomitant with the aesthetics of decoration is the tendency of these paintings towards two-dimensionality. As I argue in *Woman/Image/Text* with regard to Burne-Jones's *Laus Veneris,* the attention to surface detail is correspondent with a lack of perspective: a feature usually explained technically by the fact that the Pre-Raphaelite artists used to work in a 'fresco' manner, applying small patches of colour to a wet, white background.[23] Building up a painting in this 'patchwork' manner invariably made it difficult to create a sense of depth successfully, and paintings like *The Beloved* avoid the problem by cramming everything into what is virtually a single plane. Although the painting represents three rows of figures (slave child, bride and rear attendants) they are all distributed within a single dimension. The politics of this two-dimensional representation of space is similar to the decorative distribution of colour: like the latter, it effectively undermines the (three-dimensional) materiality of the women represented, and hence mitigates their sexual 'presence'.[24]

A similar mechanism, moreover, can be inferred in the painting's use of symbolism. As in many of the portraits from the 1860s, *The Beloved* juxtaposes its female subject with flowers that are representative of her sexuality. Honeysuckle and roses (*Venus Verticordia*) and passion flowers (*The Blue Bower*) are symbols of sexual seduction; and it is, of course, significant that the lily included in *The Beloved* is not 'virginal' white, but red. Like the formal devices, such symbols have the effect of converting the female subject's pretensions to a material reality 'beyond the canvas' back into abstract signification. The male viewer is thus once again granted a means of controlling the sexual potency of an image which he simultaneously desires and fears.

Ethnicity and Class

I want, finally, to move from discussion of how the text positions its reader in terms of gender and sexuality to its positioning in terms of ethnicity and class.

Although most Pre-Raphaelite paintings are notable for the *absence* of racial groups except the white European, *The Beloved* registers both an implicit and an explicit politics of colour. An important hidden subtext to the representation is, first of all, its biblical source, in which the bride claims beauty in spite of her 'blackness':

> 5. I am black but comely, O ye daughters of Jerusalem, as the tents of Kedar, as the curtains of Solomon.

> 6. Look not upon me, because I *am* black, because the sun hath looked upon me: my mother's children were angry with me: they made me the keeper of the vineyards, *but* mine own vineyard I have not kept.

Despite the fact that 'blackness' in this biblical context might well refer to a dark or sallow complexion rather than an ethnic identity *per se*, Rossetti's portrayal of the bride as unequivocally white and *blonde* places the painting firmly in the tradition of white, Aryan representations of biblical subjects: the textual evidence that King Solomon and his bride were black is set against the contrary expectations of the white audience.[25] In this instance, a particular prejudice revolves around the ambiguous meaning of the word 'fairness', used repeatedly to describe the bride. In the Bible, the epithet clearly means 'beautiful':

> 4: 1. Song of Solomon: Behold, thou *art* fair, my love, behold, thou *art* fair: thou hast doves' eyes within thy locks: thy hair is as a flock of goats, that appear from mount Gilead.

Rossetti, however, has clearly inferred the secondary, Western European sense of 'blondness'. The irony of his misreading is enhanced by the information that the painting began life as a 'Beatrice' subject, which was changed to the Song of Solomon when Rossetti found the model's complexion *too bright* for his conception of Dante's Beatrice.[26] Her 'ultra-fairness' is, moreover, compounded in the painting by her juxtaposition to the slave child and the attendants. The latter, presumably of Mediterranean or Middle-Eastern birth, are all dark-haired and darker-skinned in comparison with the bride.

This disturbing conflation of sexual and racial politics (the 'whiter' the woman is, the more desirable) positions the reader/viewer most revealingly. While on a textual level we may still infer that the bride's husband, King Solomon, is black (as he is in the Bible), the Eurocentric logic which led Rossetti to paint a white bride clearly presupposes a like-minded and like-skinned nineteenth-century audience. It is possible, then, for the subject of *The Beloved* to have two implied viewers in this respect: the narrative subject, King Solomon, who is black, and the contemporary nineteenth-century viewer, who is white. Although positioned differently in terms of their own skin colour, both viewers are therefore assumed to concur in their racial politics ('white is beautiful'), especially since blackness (in this text) so clearly equals inferiority and servitude.

Where this racial positioning leaves the contemporary feminist is rather more complex. While the explicit gendering of the painting might have excluded or marginalized the female spectator, both black and white, it is important to recognize that the issue of colour represents a counter-politics, inviting new processes of identification and alienation. While for the white feminist this might take the form of an invisible/unconscious alignment with the bride, and a short-sighted assumption that the text's colour politics are concentrated in the representation of the black slave, the black feminist is likely to experience the explicit privileging of whiteness much more consciously: perhaps, indeed, to the extent that this, and not gender, represents the painting's most overt exclusionary practice. Recent work in the area of white racism has revealed that, for too long, white feminists have considered colour politics to be simply an issue of black representation, and in their discussion of such matters have failed to register the significance of their own whiteness.[27]

The implied social class of the viewer of this painting is probably the least remarkable aspect of its positioning. All nineteenth-century painting presumed a largely middle- to upper-class audience; as I noted earlier, the Pre-Raphaelites distinguished themselves only by the high proportion of *nouveau riche* industrialists amongst their patrons. Extratextually, the class of *The Beloved's* viewers would have been determined by its market value (discussed at the beginning of this chapter) and the places of its exhibition: in this case, the Arundel Club, London, where it was shown for one day only on 21 February 1866. Intratextually, class positioning is implicit in the 'cultural capital' necessary to interpret most of Rossetti's works, whose textual referents range from the Bible, as here, to classical mythology and early European literature (for example, Dante).[28]

Conclusion

Were we to construct an ideological photo-fit of the 'ideal'/'preferred' reader/viewer of Rossetti's painting, these readings seem to leave little doubt that he would be the prototypical white, middle- or upper-class, heterosexual male that I hypothesized at the beginning of the chapter. Both textually and contextually, everything we as twentieth-century feminist readers and viewers are able to deduce supports this conclusion.

Nor is this a text which can easily be read 'against the grain'. As I noted in my opening remarks, it is now my feeling that feminist attempts to appropriate texts like *The Beloved* – to usurp the male reader/viewer, and insert ourselves in his place – are in many instances misguided. *The Beloved* is, for me, one such instance. While it could be argued that the sexual threat posed by the bride means that her gaze is directed ironically at us, her feminist sisters, *as well as* at her male admirers, it is a dubious intervention.[29] The reader positioning of Rossetti's painting is so grossly caricatured in terms of gender that I see few feminists *wanting* to stake a claim.

To construct an alternative woman-to-woman relationship between this text and a feminist audience necessarily overrides the politics of its production and consumption, and suspends (albeit temporarily) knowledge of the patriarchal/heterosexist ideologies by which it is so blatantly informed. To this extent I would propose that it is more problematic to intervene in the meaning-production of a nineteenth-century text than of a contemporary one: the discourses by which it is inscribed are not 'open' to us in the same way.

At the beginning of my work on the Pre-Raphaelites, the fact that a text (any text?) could elicit a range of contradictory reading positions seemed to me exciting and politically liberatory. I believed it was quite possible to make a pro-feminist reading of a text without losing sight of its gendered specificity or historical context. Like many poststructuralist critics, I thought the days of making those sort of 'either/or' choices were long past; that it was truly radical critical practice to extend and multiply the range of possible meanings/reader positionings in whatever texts we dealt with. Now I am not so sure. While it is hypothetically true that no text is restricted to a single readership any more than it is restricted to a single meaning, it is surely difficult to foster multiplicity at the same time as retaining a proper sense of a text's controlling discourses and address.

For this reason I find myself coming back to a position which advocates feminist intervention in such texts as 'critique' rather than 'appropriation'. This is a subtle difference of methodology which for a long time was confused in my own work, but which may be explained as the difference between privileging the 'alternative' and 'oppositional' ideological inscriptions of a text ('appropriation'), and deconstructing the dominant ones ('critique').[30] This means in practice that although it would be quite possible to read Rossetti's as a pro-feminist celebration of female sexuality addressed to a female audience, it remains more politically urgent that we intervene to expose its dominant ideologies and gendered specificity of address. This is the sort of transgressive intervention that Cindy Sherman's photographic montages achieve so superbly, and that Zoe Wicomb advocates in her article on advertising in the volume edited by Sara Mills, *Gendering the Reader.*[31]

Many critics, I am aware, will insist that this sort of radical critique can be performed alongside a more positive appropriation of the texts concerned. They might be right; but for me the fact remains that these alternative readings demand that we *transcend* our positioning as historical and/or gendered readers. To read *The Beloved* as a call for female sexual liberation we must, albeit temporarily, oust the historical male audience, and assume that the text is indeed speaking to (and for) us. Poststructuralist theory has led us to believe that this is precisely the sort of mutability we can, and should, aspire to. I still aspire, but I cannot quite believe.

Notes

1 See Lynne Pearce, *Woman/Image/Text* (see n. 22, Ch. 1).

2 'Gaps and silences': see n. 9, Ch. 2.

3 See Sara Mills's 'Reading as/like a Feminist', in *Gendering the Reader* (n. 24, Ch. 1), pp. 25–46, and also Chris Christie, 'Theories of Textual Determination and Audience Agency: An Empirical Contribution to the Debate' in the same volume, pp. 47–66, for further discussion of these political problems.

4 See Jackie Stacey's groundbreaking essay on what female spectators have found compelling about women stars in Hollywood cinema, 'Desperately Seeking Difference', in *The Female Gaze: Women as Viewers of Popular Culture*, ed. Lorraine Gamman and Margaret Marshment (London: Women's Press, 1986), pp. 112–29.

5 The first two adjectives are used extensively in texts describing Rossetti's paintings from this period (e.g. the 1984 Tate Gallery exhibition catalogue, *The Pre-Raphaelites*, hereafter TGC), while it was John Ruskin who found them 'degrading' and 'coarse': Edward T. Cook and Alexander Wedderburn (eds.), *The Works of John Ruskin*, vol. 36: *Letters* (London: Allen, 1909), p. 491.

6 See e.g. John Dixon-Hunt, *The Pre-Raphaelite Imagination* (London: Routledge and Kegan Paul, 1968) and Jan Marsh, *The Pre-Raphaelite Sisterhood* (London: Quartet, 1984).

7 See my chapter 'Beatrice: Hazy Outlines', in *Woman/Image/Text* (n. 22, Ch. 1) for a full account of Rossetti's treatment of this subject.

8 Marsh (n. 6) corrects the chronology of these events in *The Pre-Raphaelite Sisterhood*, chs. 9–12. She notes that Rossetti 'never really lost touch' with Fanny Cornforth during the years of his marriage, and that she modelled for a number of figure drawings in 1861–2 (i.e. before Siddal's death). Jane Morris, whom Rossetti first met in 1857 before her marriage to William Morris, also sat for Rossetti in 1860, although she did not become his principal model until 1867.

9 Stephens, writing in the *Athenaeum* (21 Oct. 1865), observed of *The Blue Bower* that 'there is nothing to suggest subject, time, or place. Where we thus leave off, the intellectual and purely artistic splendour of the picture begins to develop itself. The music of the dulcimer passes out of the spectator's cognizance when the chromatic harmony takes its places in appealing to the eye.' (TGC, pp. 545–6).

10 O. Doughty and J. Wahl, *The Letters of Dante Gabriel Rossetti* (4 vols., Oxford: Oxford University Press, 1965–7), quoted in TGC. For full details of the provenance of the paintings from this period, see the TGC. Some prices include *The Blue Bower* (1865), 210 guineas (sold a year later for 500 guineas); *Regina Cordium* (1866), 170 guineas; *Mariana* (1865–70), £500; and *The Bower Meadow* (1871–2), £735.

11 The cost of *The Beloved* is cited in TGC, p. 211.

12 For comparative pricings see the exhibition catalogue, *The Pre-Raphaelites: Painters and Patrons of the North East* (Newcastle: Tyne and Wear Museum Services, 1989).

13 For full details of Margaret (Eustacia) Smith, see the exhibition catalogue cited in n. 12 above, pp. 129-30.

14 See Germaine Greer, *The Obstacle Race* (London: Picador, 1981) and Deborah Cherry, *Painting Women: Victorian Women Artists* (London and New York: Routledge, 1993) for a discussion of the women artists associated with the Pre-Raphaelite movement.

15 Pearce, *Woman/Image/Text* (n. 22, Ch. 1), pp. 31–45.

16 See TGC, p. 210, for details of the frame upon which the verses are inscribed.

17 In his famous statement on *Beata Beatrix* Rossetti wrote, 'The picture must of course be viewed not as a representation of the incident of the death of Beatrice, but as an ideal of the subject, symbolising a trance or sudden spiritual transfiguration. Beatrice is rapt visibly into heaven, seeing as it were through her shut lids.' (TGC, p. 209).

18 Several of the essays collected in Rosemary Betterton (ed.), *Looking On: Images of Femininity in the Visual Arts and Media* (London: Pandora, 1987) address the politics of body language. See especially Kathy Myers, 'Towards a Feminist Erotica', pp. 189–202.

19 Jordanova, *Sexual Visions: Images of Gender in Science and Medicine between the Eighteenth and Twentieth Centuries* (Hemel Hempstead: Harvester-Wheatsheaf, 1990), p. 89. Further page references to this volume are given after quotations in the text.

20 Virginia Surtees, *The Paintings and Drawings of Daute Gabriel Rossetti (1828–1832): A Catalogue Raissoné* (2 vols., Oxford: Oxford University Press, 1971), p. 42.

21 Judith Williamson, *Decoding Advertisements: Ideology and Meaning in Advertising* (London: Marion Boyars, 1978). According to Williamson, the majority of advertisements work by juxtaposing an image of the product (e.g. a car) with a supplementary signifier (e.g. a cheetah) in order to reveal the concept/signified being sold (e.g. speed).

22 Pearce, *Woman/Image/Text* (n. 22, Ch. 1), pp. 130–41.

23 See TGC, p. 211, for a representation of this painting.

24 See Pearce, *Woman/Image/Text* (n. 22, Ch. 1), pp. 46–58. Griselda Pollock discusses the two-dimensionality of Pre-Raphaelite paintings and the sexual threat they pose in her chapter, 'Woman as Sign: Psychoanalytic Readings', in *Vision and Difference: Femininity, Feminism and the Histories of Art* (London and New York: Routledge, 1988), pp. 120–54.

25 Thanks to Deborah McVea, and others, for pointing out to me the ambiguity of terms like 'black' and 'fair' in the Bible.

26 See TGC, p. 210.

27 See e.g. Helen (charles)'s essay '"Whiteness": The relevance of politically colouring the "non"', in *Working Out: New Directions for Women's Studies*, ed. Hilary Hinds, Ann Phoenix and Jackie Stacey (London: Falmer, 1992), pp. 29–35.

28 'Cultural capital' is a concept invented by the theorist Pierre Bourdieu to explain the way in which power is relayed in capitalist societies through the individual's access to/exclusion from the practices of 'High Culture' (e.g. a familiarity with opera, a knowledge of expensive wines).

29 See the Introduction to Pearce, *Woman/Image/Text* (n. 22, Ch. 1), a full discussion of the problems and possibilities of 'interventionist' readings.

30 For an explanation of the terms 'alternative' and 'oppositional', see the account of Raymond Williams's types of ideology in *Woman/Image/Text* (n. 22, Ch. 1), p. 8.

31 See Zoe Wicomb, 'Motherhood and the Surrogate Reader: Race, Gender and Interpretation', in *Gendering the Reader* (n. 3). A recent exhibition catalogue of Cindy Sherman's work reproduces a wide selection of her work, and also offers insightful commentary on the rationale behind it: T. Kellein, *Cindy Sherman* (Basle: Edition Cantz, 1991).

| 4 |

Dialogic Theory and Women's Writing

Their strength is the way they know each other, the wordless sensitivity that has grown between them; a private language constructed to express their connection with each other and their separation from the authorities: puns, quotations, riddles, Cockney. They laugh when no-one else does, because of the exquisite meanings they can give to events which seem banal to everyone else. Every act, and every movement, they translate and share, looking at one another secretly, waving private flags.[1]

The 'private language' enjoyed by Julie and Jenny in Michèle Roberts's *A Piece of the Night* signals the focus of my concerns in this chapter: namely, the way in which much contemporary women's writing is involved in the waving of 'private flags'. I shall be suggesting how some of the key concepts of Mikhail Bakhtin's dialogic theory can be used as a springboard to understand the gendered exclusivity of address that exists in literature by and for women and the dialogic intimacy represented both by female locutors and interlocutors within the text, as well as between the text and the ('female') reader (or, more precisely, the reader 'positioned as female').[2] I shall propose that this dynamic might help us to re-specify what we mean by 'women's writing' and/or 'feminist writing': texts written not only *by women,* and about women, but more especially written *for them.* Such discussion will lead me, hopefully open-eyed, into a quagmire of essentialist definitions: treacherous ground in these poststructuralist times, but inescapable for those of us who continue to teach courses on 'women authors', or, indeed, to make the sex of the author a criterion of choice in our private reading.

Bakhtin and the Dialogic

As Michael Holquist points out in his introductory book on Bakhtin, 'dialogism' was a term 'never used by Bakhtin himself'.[3] Instead it must be seen as a convenient epistemological 'catch-all', coined by his Anglo-American followers in an attempt to conceptualize the notion of *reciprocity* central to all his writings about language, literature, and what Holquist has called 'the modern history of thinking about thinking' (p. 15). Allowing, then, for the fact that all we now include under the umbrella of dialogic theory is, in effect, a broad inference of Bakhtin's own writings, I shall attempt through some selected quotations to convey a sense of the basic principles.

The following extract from the 1929 text *Marxism and the Philosophy of Language* (sometimes attributed to Bakhtin's co-author, V. N. Voloshinov) offers one of the most suggestive starting points:

> A word is a bridge thrown between myself and another. If one end of the bridge belongs to me, then the other depends on my addressee. A word is a territory shared by both addresser and addressee, by the speaker and his [*sic*] interlocutor.[4]

We see from this that Bakhtin's notion of dialogue is, at one level, extremely literal: it is predicated upon the everyday occurrence of two people conversing. What interests Bakhtin in such exchange, however, is the power of the addressee in determining the words of the speaker: each word, as he notes elsewhere, is 'directly, blatantly, oriented towards a future answer word'.[5]

For some literary theorists, the fact that Bakhtinian dialogue has its roots in a model of spoken language has been seen as a problem: they have doubted that a model so firmly grounded in the concrete analysis of 'speech-acts' can bear much relevance to the conditions of dialogue in literary texts.[6] It is true, indeed, that Bakhtin's own theorizing of dialogic activity frequently fails to register a difference between the written and the spoken word; but much of his analysis is concerned specifically with the written word.

His account of 'doubly voiced discourse' in *Problems of Dostoevsky's Poetics,* for example, proposes that 'dialogic relationships are possible not only among whole utterances' but 'toward an individual word, if that word is perceived not as the impersonal word of speech but as a sign of someone else's semantic position'.[7] From this perspective he shows how the individual words of literary works will frequently betray the controlling presence of another text. This will sometimes take the form of a stylization or parody of the other text or, in certain circumstances, give rise to the *active* category of exchange which Bakhtin called 'hidden polemic'.[8] In *Problems of Dostoevsky's Poetics* Bakhtin cites Dostoevsky's own *Notes from the Underground* as an example of a text in which the narrator's words are frequently in 'hidden polemic', with 'answer words' not present in the text itself, but personified into a censorious extratextual interlocutor. It is, indeed, the recasting of words and discourses, both textual and non-textual, as dynamic sites of reciprocal exchange, rather than fixed semantic positions, that makes Bakhtin's model so exciting for the literary critic – a sentiment summed up in Bakhtin's own observation:

Within the arena of . . . every utterance an intense conflict between
one's own and another's word is being fought out. . . . The utterance so
conceived is a considerably more complex and dynamic organism than
it appears when consumed simply as a thing that articulates the intention of the person uttering it.[9]

One final point needs to be made here concerning the ambiguous nature
of the 'addressee' in Bakhtin's writings: namely, the way in which the
interlocutor *inside* the text is frequently conflated with the reader *outside*
it. While the reader may, on occasion, inhabit or adopt the positioning of
an interdiegetic character (perhaps through an overt rhetorical strategy:
see below), this is not by any means the norm – although it is, perhaps,
fair to say that dialogic intimacy within a text *can* prompt and facilitate a
parallel text/reader interaction.[10] What the Bakhtinian model does not
make clear is the *multiplicity* of agents that can be represented by
'addresser' and 'addressee' of the text, including the whole army of
'implied' authors and narrators, and 'implied' or 'ideal' readers, proposed
by subsequent reader-theorists.[11] What the model lacks in its complexity
of vision, however, it certainly compensates for in its intensity (the
absolute insistence that every utterance is inscribed and directed by an
awareness of its potential audience); and this very confusion of speakers
and interlocutors inside and outside the text *does* appear to be a significant feature of much contemporary feminist writing, as I shall now go on
to show.

'I' as a Function of 'We': The Relationship between Speaker and Addressee in Contemporary Women's Writing[12]

One of a number of books specifically to address itself to the relationship
between feminism and dialogic theory is Anne Herrmann's *The Dialogic
and Difference: 'An/Other Woman' in Virginia Woolf and Christa Wolf*.[13]
In a fascinating comparison of the two writers, Herrmann shows that where
Woolf's texts always have one ear pointed towards an adversarial male
reader (a graphic instance of Bakhtin's 'hidden polemic'), Wolf casts hers as
a sympathetic female 'ally'. She writes:

> The rhetorical difference [i.e., the difference between Woolf and Wolf]
> lies in the difference of the addressee; Woolf constructs her addressee
> as antagonist, whose otherness is attributed to difference in gender
> and class. Wolf constructs her interlocutor as ally, as someone who
> mirrors her own point of view . . . for [Christa Wolf] any construction
> of the subject implies the inclusion of another subjectivity as a way of
> guarding against objectification. (p. 43)

Although, according to Bakhtin/Voloshinov, writing in *Discourse in Life and Discourse in Poetry*, the latter is only one of the relationships that may be held by the two parties, it is, he concedes, the most familiar one: 'Speaking figuratively, the listener [that is, the reader] is normally found *next* to the author as his [sic] ally'.[14] Similarly, although all writing by women certainly does not position the reader as a (female) ally, I would suggest that this is a distinguishing feature of much of the writing we think of as *feminist*.[15] In contemporary women's fiction, moreover, that comradeship, that sense of community, has frequently been brought to metafictional consciousness. Marge Piercy's novel *Small Changes*, for example, opens with the dedication 'For me. For you. For us. Even for them', a statement which deftly registers the bond between the gendered self and her female 'other', and positions them against the (implicitly) masculine third person plural.[16] As a dedication it thus acknowledges that, while men are free to read the text (they cannot, indeed, be prevented from reading it), they are positioned outside the boundaries of the inclusive address (me/you/us) which represents a specifically female continuum.

While a dedication is perhaps the most overtly political way in which a writer can identify her readership, many other fictional works postulate a special relationship between a speaker within the text and an extratextual addressee. The narrator of Margaret Atwood's *The Handmaid's Tale*, for example, tells her story to a nameless 'ally' who can be seen both as a fictional character in the text and also as the reader.[17] This ambiguity is brought to metafictional self-consciousness when, in one of several asides, Offred observes:

> A story is like a letter. *Dear You*, I'll say. Just You, without a name. Attaching a name attaches you to the world of fact, which is riskier, more hazardous: who knows what the chances are out there, of survival, yours? I will say *you*, *you*, like an old love song. *You* can mean more than one.
> *You* can mean thousands. (p. 50)

What is fascinating about this particular address is that it forces the reader to enter the text almost against her own better judgement. Offred's intimacy carries with it the risk of danger ('who knows what the chances are out there?'). Brought within the action of the text, into the dangerous future Offred inhabits, we as readers are cautioned about our own slim chances of survival. By joining with Offred and reciprocating her interlocutory need of us, we too risk punishment and death: a risk, indeed, which may also be read as an ironic metaphor for what it always means to accept our positioning as feminist (that is, politically conscious and committed) as opposed to merely 'female' reader. Atwood's novel is thus an excellent example of a text which *does* observe Bakhtin's own conflation of a fictional addressee inside the text (possibilities include her own 'lost' daughter) with the addressee, or reader, on the outside; though this deployment of an ambiguous second-person pronoun must be seen to be a very artful, and generally *untypical*, instance of literary rhetoric, and a different order of reader-participation entirely from those acts of 'identification' which are not linguistically signalled or cued by the text, and/or which do not register the coexistence of an interdiegetic addressee.[18]

A similar rhetorical strategy may, however, be attributed to Christa Wolf, in her famous post-war novel *The Quest for Christa T.* (1968), which makes devastating use of 'us' and 'we' in telling her heroine's story.[19] Once again we have a situation in which pronouns which might *technically* refer to the narrator and her friends in the novel – the people who shared the life of Christa T. – also look outwards to us, the reader. By means of the inclusive term we are brought into the experience of Christa T.'s loss; and, most importantly, forced to share in the responsibility for her death:

> She really might have died, almost. But she mustn't leave us. This is the time at which to think more of her, to think her further, to let her live and grow older as other people do . . . At the last moment, one has the thought of working on her . . . Useless to pretend it's for her sake. Once and for all, she doesn't need us. So we should be certain of one thing: that it's for our sake. Because it seems that we need her. (p. 5)

The intimacy and involvement that authors like Atwood and Christa Wolf make into a strategy of their text–reader address is seen elsewhere in contemporary women's writing in the relationship *between* the fictional characters. I want to move on now to look at some examples of texts which are more purely *descriptive* of dialogic relationships: relationships between female characters in which intimacy has given rise to what Michèle Roberts, in the extract from *A Piece of the Night*, referred to as 'a private language constructed to express their connection with each other and their separation from the authorities' (p. 49).

'A Territory Shared': The Private Languages of Women

The mode of writing which brings this exclusivity of address most prominently to light is the letter, and letters between women have obtained a special significance in contemporary feminist criticism precisely on account of their marginality to literary genres intended for a public audience. The letters of friends and lovers are invariably exclusive in their intimacy, their codes and shorthands sometimes proving an impenetrable barrier to any outsider trying to make sense of them. It is therefore no coincidence, I think, that research on letters written between women has become a major preoccupation of feminist critics, who have discovered in their cryptic surfaces an intimacy that is highly political in its exclusivity. This has been especially true of women researching lesbian writing: a good half of Lillian Faderman's

Surpassing the Love of Men (1979), for example, involves the re-reading and reconstruction of letters between women whose implications had previously gone unseen.[20]

It is significant, too, that many contemporary women writers have chosen the epistolary form to represent intimate relationships between women. The success of Alice Walker's *The Color Purple* (1983) is acknowledged as largely the consequence of her inventive reworking of the oldest of novelistic forms.[21] Celie's letters – addressed first to God, then to her sister Nettie – give a new immediacy to the oppressions of black women. I would suggest, moreover, that the hostility with which this text was received by reviewers critical of its treatment of black men can be explained by the gynocentrism of its address. As one of my students recently pointed out in an essay on the book, the *story* actually moves towards a reconciliation with the men: more threatening is their total exclusion from the circle of address.

Another text which does something extraordinary in terms of address is Jane Rule's novel *This Is Not For You* (1982).[22] It is a rare example of a fictional work – outside the conventional epistolary genre – written entirely in the second person. The first chapter opens like this:

> This is not a letter. I wrote you for the last time over a year ago to offer the little understanding I had, to say goodbye. I could have written again, but somehow your forsaking the world for the sake of the world left me nothing to say. Your vow of silence must also stop my tongue, or so it seemed. What a way to win an argument! (p. 1)

The dynamic established between the narrator (Kate) and her addressee (Esther) in this arresting 'first and last' paragraph returns us to the mechanics of Bakhtinian dialogue. Kate establishes the conditions of address by taking us to the point at which address is no longer possible: the point at which her words have lost their 'future answer words' in the voice of the woman to whom the text is addressed. Esther's 'vow of silence' (she has literally become a nun) stops Kate's tongue. Without an interlocutor to realize themselves against, words are not possible, and Kate can only go on to tell the story she does by addressing Esther in the past, according to the terms of their 'old argument'. Yet despite the fact that this dialogue between Kate and Esther is created retrospectively, its dynamic demonstrates as well as anything I've yet found the peculiar exclusivity of address that may occur between women. The image of two minds locked together in cryptic sympathy is symbolized by Kate's ability to decipher Esther's postcards:

> When I got back to Washington, the first of your cathedral cards had arrived. The message read, 'Mother likes Italy', which meant obviously that you didn't. Or you were recovering your sense of security enough to find your mother's company increasingly difficult. (p. 209)

Such 'writing in code' – which I've referred to several times in passing already – may be taken as a distinguishing feature of dialogic activity in feminist texts: a form of address that suggests a private conspiracy between one woman and another, a dialogue whose interests remain hidden, unseen by the outside world. This brings me to the final aspect of Bakhtinian theory I want to raise in this chapter: the importance of *intonation* and *extra-literary context* in the gendered positioning of the addressee.

Intonation and Extra-Literary Context

According to the Bakhtinian school, the intonation of an utterance is the element which registers most accurately the relationship between the speaker and the addressee in any verbal exchange. Clark and Holquist describe it like this:

> The purest expression of the values assumed in any utterance is found at the level of intonation, for the reason that intonation always lies at the border of the verbal and the non-verbal, the I and the other. Intonation clearly registers the other's presence, creating a kind of picture in sound of the addressee to whom the speaker imagines she is speaking. . . . Intonation serves as the material means for stitching together the sound, in the speech of the speaker, and the unsaid, in the context of the situation.
>
> (*Mikhail Bakhtin*, p. 12)

It will be seen from this description that what Bakhtin means by intonation translates roughly into what we refer to in everyday speech as 'tone of voice'; the premiss that the voice in which something is spoken – whether it is comforting, angry, pleading or ironic – often matters more than the words themselves. It is the reason, as Clark and Holquist explain, that when we overhear someone's telephone conversation we can quickly establish their relationship to the person at the other end even if we do not know who they are or what they are talking about.[23] In the essay 'Discourse in Life and Discourse in Art', Bakhtin/Voloshinov makes the same point by means of a short story. It goes like this:

> Two people are sitting in a room. They are both silent. Then one of them says 'Well!'. The other does not respond. [End of story]
>
> (*Bakhtin School Papers*, p. 99)

In the subsequent analysis, Bakhtin proves that the listener/reader can only make sense of the word 'Well!' if he or she knows more about the extra-verbal context in which the statement is made, and the particular intonation with which it is spoken. On the latter, he speculates:

> Let us suppose that the intonation with which this word was pronounced is known to us: indignation and reproach moderated by a certain amount of humour. This intonation somehow fills in the

semantic void of the adverb 'well', but still does not reveal the meaning of the whole. (p. 99)

At which point he invokes the additional necessity of being familiar with the 'extra-verbal context' of the situation, in this case the fact that:

> At the time the colloquy took place, both interlocutors *looked up* at the window and *saw* that it had begun to snow; both *knew* that it was already May and that it was high time for spring to come; finally *both* were *sick* and *tired* of the protracted winter – they were *both looking forward* to spring and 'both were *bitterly disappointed* by the late snow fall'. [Author's emphasis] (p. 99)

Returning to the Atwood passage featured earlier, I would suggest that both intonation and extra-verbal context are central to establishing a conspiratorial intimacy between this text and its reader. Through her repeated use of the word 'you', together with its defamilarizing italicization, Atwood induces the reader to savour the different ways in which the word may be spoken: to consider the many different things it might be made to mean according to different intonations.[24] While in the context of the *story*, therefore, 'you' might well be another, unspecified fictional character, the ambiguity of the address invites the reader to share in its (possible) warmth, intimacy and exclusiveness. Moreover, the inferred extratextual context of the action – the danger in which Offred stands as a woman in Gilead society – is instrumental in gendering the address and converting the 'I–thou' intimacy into an explicitly feminist bonding. Once again it is the conflation of the textual with the extratextual – in this case the woman reader's knowledge of the workings of patriarchy, both inside and outside this particular fictional narrative – that enable her to grasp the full connotations of the speaker's 'you' with the same expertise that Bakhtin's protagonist reads the word 'well'. Although women readers come to texts with a wide and differing range of cultural experience, we can nevertheless expect their inclusion in texts such as Atwood's and Walker's to be predicated upon a spark of 'recognition' which will enable them to respond to their own 'hailing' or 'interpellation' by that text.[25] The specialized cultural knowledge that makes the female reader privy to the text's intonation and extratextual context in this instance is also, therefore, the key to her entry and participation. The textual and the extratextual become, indeed, 'a territory shared'.

What I am proposing here, then, is that it is precisely these two elements, 'intonation' and 'extra-verbal context', that make possible the existence of Roberts's 'private languages'. Jordan, the male narrator of Jeanette Winterson's *Sexing the Cherry,* at one point registers this exclusion when he says:

> I noticed that women have a private language. A language not dependent on the constructions of men but structured by signs and expressions, and that uses ordinary words as code words meaning something other.[26]

Following on from feminist theorists like Elaine Showalter, who have attempted to explain this linguistic/communication difference in terms of cultural *marginality* (where women constitute the 'muted' but not 'silent' group), Bakhtin's model allows us to positively re-imagine that space in terms of the challenging and resilient dialogic principles upon which the *communality* is predicated.[27] An important (and not unproblematic) inference here, of course, is that the 'conspiratorial' dialogue we find in women's writing is predicated upon women's own exclusion from the circle of the (masculine) dominant: what the Roberts quotation refers to as 'their separation from the authorities' (p. 49). The reason why Jordan cannot understand the language of women is because they have developed a model of communication that functions according to different codes: a new linguistic 'territory', in which words, disguised and ironized by the gender-specific subtleties of intonation and extra-verbal context do indeed mean 'something other'. Meaning, according to this system, depends upon a highly developed sense of *relationship* between speaker and addressee; it exists, indeed, in the space(s) between them.

Conclusion

Whether or not the instances of conspiratorial dialogic address that feature in contemporary women's fiction constitute no more than a reactionary strategy, a bonding and a discursive exclusivity, brought about by the women's own marginalization as a group, remains a moot point. The pervasiveness with which the feature occurs is, however, sufficient for me to propose it as a defining characteristic of much of the contemporary women's writing that we would wish to call 'feminist'. Feminist fictional writing, according to this rationale, is thus writing which enacts or describes a dialogue between women *as allies*: a dialogue in which the meaning of any utterance depends upon, and is defined by, reciprocity of address within the consciousness of a gendered context.

I am aware, of course, that once such generalizations have been made they exist only to be knocked down. I feel nonetheless that for theory and politics to advance, the 'grand' and 'totalizing' narratives have still sometimes to be risked. In true dialogic fashion I will, however, attempt to anticipate some of the most obvious protests.

In the first instance there are those who will probably say, why bother with definitions of women's writing anyway? As Toril Moi observed in *Sexual/Textual Politics* (1985), 'to define Woman [and her texts] is necessarily to essentialize her'.[28] My reply to this is the justification that I offered at the beginning of this chapter: that as long as we persist in arranging our reading and teaching around such categories as 'women's writing' or 'feminist writing', we need at least to *attempt* to know what it is. Teresa de Lauretis recently reviewed her own political commitment as a feminist film critic in *Alice Doesn't: Feminism, Semiotics, Cinema* (1984: see n. 20 to Chapter 1) via an interrogation of the terms 'women's cinema' and 'feminist cinema', concluding:

> In sum, what I would call alternative films in women's cinema are those which engage the current problems, the real issues, the things actually at stake in feminist communities on a local scale, and which, although informed by a global perspective, do not assume or aim at a universal, multinational audience, but address a particular one in its specific history of struggles and emergency. (p. 17)

While it could be argued that de Lauretis's position causes her to be unnecessarily dismissive of feminist readings of 'non-feminist' texts, her statement does, once again, help us focus on the specificity of address that makes a text of itself 'feminist'. Although, elsewhere, my own work has been based on the assumption that if a reader is able to intervene in the production of a text's meaning it may be rendered feminist, I now believe, like de Lauretis, that we need to distinguish between those texts which have to be 'appropriated' and those which speak to us directly.[29] Like her, I also see the reason for this as one of political urgency: after spending ten years of my own life reading male-produced texts 'against the grain', I now want to engage with those which posit me as an 'ally'.

The de Lauretis quotation, with its focus on particular audiences, brings me to the second of the objections that may be raised against my hypothesis as it stands: that is, its universalized conception of the female addressee. As colleagues have pointed out, it is surely reductive to assume that one female addressee is the same as another? In my attempt to theorize what seemed to me a pervasive feature within contemporary women's writing, I overlooked the many other factors – race, class, sexual orientation – which position female addressees both inside and outside texts. In many ways, for example, it could be more productive to look at the *differences* between the addressees of *The Color Purple* and *The Handmaid's Tale*.[30] Both construct female addressees, but there is a fascinating tension in Walker's text between the black addressee in the text and the appropriation of that subject-position by a white readership. In such instances, the gender of the addressee is clearly a starting-point rather than an end in itself: as de Lauretis has proposed, we must envisage 'a female social subject engendered, constructed, and defined by multiple social relations' (p. 32).

There is the ultimate advantage, however, that a theory of feminism based upon a structural theory of 'relationship' can, with some artistry, sidestep these more blatant essentialisms. Although the subtext of this chapter has been to add yet another voice to the old question of whether women write differently, it has avoided the supposition that this 'difference' has anything to do with the biological sex of the author or, indeed, the reader, asserting simply that the texts concerned construct *gendered positions* for their speakers and addressees who will, of course, 'differ' from one another in other respects. Although I personally feel that much of the anxiety about essentialism in theory is misplaced, the notion of 'positionality' has been seized upon by critics like Julia Kristeva in order to show the importance of gender in 'women's lived experience' 'without naturalizing it' (Moi, p. 166). As Linda Alcoff has neatly summarized, 'Woman is a position from which a feminist politics can emerge rather than a set of attributes that are objectively identifiable'.[31] With this criterion in mind, it is possible for me to propose a redefinition of 'women's writing', or, more specifically, 'feminist writing', which makes gender at once central *and* provisional. A dialogic theory of feminist writing is not concerned with the relationship between 'women' *per se* (or, by extension, with a concept of 'relationship' based upon common experience), but with a set of self-consciously gendered textual positionings ('speaker'/'addressee', 'text/reader') which are not fixed, but historically specific and politically strategic. Furthermore, the 'feminism' of the texts I have considered rests finally in none of the positions (of how the speaker or the addressee is 'identified') *per se* but, more radically, in the dialogic engagement of the one with the other.

Notes

1 Michèle Roberts, *A Piece of the Night* (London: Women's Press, 1978), p. 49. Further page references to this volume will be given after quotations in the text.

2 Teresa de Lauretis identifies these two terms – 'by' and 'for' – as the criteria by which we may identify women's cinema ('Guerilla in the Midst': see n. 26, Ch. 1). Further page references to this article will be given after quotations in the text.

3 Michael Holquist, *Dialogism: Bakhtin and His World* (London and New York: Routledge, 1990), p. 15. Further page references to this volume will be given after quotations in the text.

4 Mikhail Bakhtin/V. N. Voloshinov, *Marxism and the Philosophy of Language*, trans. Ladislaw Matejka and I. R. Titunik (1929; Cambridge, MA: Harvard University Press, 1986), pp. 85–6.

5 Mikhail Bakhtin, *The Dialogic Imagination*, ed. Michael Holquist, trans. Caryl Emerson and Michael Holquist (1941; Austin, TX: Austin University Press, 1981), p. 280.

6 See Ken Hirschkop's criticism of Voloshinov/Bakhtin in his essay on 'Bakhtin and Cultural Theory', in *Bakhtin and Cultural Theory*, ed. Ken Hirschkop and David Shepherd (Manchester and New York: Manchester University Press, 1989), p. 14.

7 Mikhail Bakhtin, *Problems of Dostoevsky's Poetics*, trans. Caryl Emerson (1929; Manchester: Manchester University Press, 1984), pp. 184–5.

8 David Lodge offers a clear summary of these different types of 'doubly-voiced discourse' in his essay 'Lawrence, Dostoevsky, Bakhtin' (1985), now reproduced in his collected essays, *After Bakhtin: Essays in Fiction and Criticism* (London and New York: Routledge, 1990).

9 Katarina Clark and Michael Holquist, *Mikhail Bakhtin* (Cambridge, MA: Harvard University Press, 1984), p. 220. Further page references to this volume are given after quotations in the text.

10 For discussion of reader/viewing positioning based on a more general principle of character-identification, see discussion in Ch. 1 pp. 17–20.

11 Ever since Wayne Booth's celebrated separation of the 'real' from the 'implied' author in *The Rhetoric of Fiction* (Chicago: University of Chicago Press, 1961), quickly supplemented by Seymour Chatman's identification of 'narrator', 'narratee', 'implied reader' and 'real reader', in *Story and Discourse* (Ithaca, NY: Cornell University Press, 1978), reader-theory has assumed a complex hierarchy and interaction of multiple speakers and addressees to be present in every text, in such a way as to massively complicate how, and in what way, the reader (as 'addressee') is present in the text (see discussion in Ch. 1).

12 This subheading derives from Clark and Holquist's formulation: 'For Bakhtin, individual intention is a relative matter, in as much as the "I" is a function of "we".' *Mikhail Bakhtin* (n. 9), p. 224.

13 Anne Herrmann, *The Dialogic and Difference* (see n. 16, Ch. 2). Further page references to this volume will be given after quotations in the text. See also Dale Bauer, *Feminist Dialogics: A Theory of Failed Community* (New York: State University of New York Press, 1989), Dale Bauer (ed.), *Feminism, Bakhtin and the Dialogic* (Albany, NY: State University of New York Press, 1991) and my own *Reading Dialogics* (see n. 4, Ch. 1)

14 *The Bakhtin School Papers,* ed. Ann Shukman (Oxford: RPT Publications, 1983), p. 24. (This book includes the essay 'Discourse in Life and Discourse in Art', attributed to V. N. Voloshinov.) Page references to this volume will be given after quotations in the text.

15 It should be noted that although the ostensible addressee of Woolf's text is a male adversary, it is also possible to construct a covert female ally – thus ensuring the 'feminist' identity of this text. For more discussion of the gendered positioning of the reader in Woolf's texts, see Jane Marcus's excellent essay, 'Sapphistory: The Woolf and the Well', in *Lesbian Texts and Contexts*, ed. Karla Jay and Joanne Glasgow (New York and London: New York University Press, 1990).

16 Marge Piercy, *Small Changes* (Garden City, NY: Doubleday, 1973).

17 Margaret Atwood, *The Handmaid's Tale* (London: Jonathan Cape, 1986), p. 50. Further page references to this volume will be given after quotations in the text.

18 While the explicit inclusion of the reader in the text has long been a feature of the novel ('Reader, I married him . . .') the confusion of an inter- and extra-addressee is certainly less common, although Ann-Marie MacDonald's *Fall on Your Knees* (Toronto: Alfred A. Knopf, 1996) is another interesting example, similar to Atwood's text in its ambiguous (and intimate) address.

19 Christa Wolf, *The Quest for Christa T.*, trans. Christopher Middleton (1968; London: Virago, 1982), p. 5.

20 Lilian Faderman, *Surpassing the Love of Men* (London: Women's Press, 1981; repr. 1985).

21 Alice Walker, *The Color Purple* (London: Women's Press, 1983).

22 Jane Rule, *This is Not for You* (London: Pandora Press, 1982; repr. 1987), p. 61. Further page references to this volume are given after quotations in the text.

23 See *Reading Dialogics* (n. 4, Ch. 1), pp. 1–5 and 72–9, for further discussion of this.

24 There is, of course, also an issue of exactly how intonation can be expressed (and read) in written as opposed to spoken texts. My past research has, however, revealed that through careful attention to the power dynamic between speaker, listener and 'object of utterance' a textual intonation can be deduced. See ch. 3 of *Reading Dialogics* (n. 4, Ch. 1), pp. 121–48, for an application of this.

25 'Interpellation': Louis Althusser's term for the way in which we, as subjects, are

'hailed' and positioned by ideology. See Louis Althusser, 'Ideology and Ideological State Apparatuses', in *Lenin and Philosophy and Other Essays*, trans. Ben Brewster (London: New Left Books, 1971). See ch. 6 (pp. 212–13) of *Feminist Readings/Feminists Reading* (n. 35, Ch. 1) for further discussion of how this term may be also be used to describe the way in which texts 'hail' readers.

26 Jeanette Winterson, *Sexing the Cherry* (London: Bloomsbury, 1989), p. 29.

27 Showalter's two key essays which define 'woman' in terms of cultural marginality are 'Towards a Feminist Poetics' and 'Feminist Criticism in the Wilderness', both in her *New Feminist Criticism* (London: Virago, 1987).

28 Moi, *Sexual/Textual Politics* (London: Methuen, 1985), p. 139. Further page references to this volume will be given after quotations in the text.

29 See Chs. 1, 2 and 3 for discussion of my earlier reading practices.

30 These 'differences' of address subsequently become the basis for the reader-jealousy I describe in Ch. 2.

31 Linda Alcott, 'Cultural Feminism *vs*. Postructuralism: The Identity Crisis', *Signs* 13 (3) (Spring, 1988), p. 433.

PART

II

THE EMOTIONAL POLITICS OF GENDERED READING

Preface to Part II

The two chapters which comprise the central section of this book, 'The Emotional Politics of Gendered Reading', employ Roland Barthes's typology of the romance trajectory as a journey from '*ravissement*' to 'sequel' to explore a selection of the emotions associated with the processes of reading, and to investigate how the resultant *implicated readings* can be squared (or not) with our commitments as feminist readers.[1]

As I have already detailed in Chapter 1, my means of gaining access to this largely uncharted area of reception theory was to use my own readings, re-readings and re-memories of four texts (two novels, a film and a photographic exhibition) as the basis for a meta-commentary on how we might begin to make sense of our emotional involvement in texts: indeed, to determine what constitutes an 'affective' as opposed to a 'cognitive' response to a text, and what conditions make such an engagement possible.[2] Chapter 1 has also provided the short answer to this question. What seem to us to be emotional responses to texts can best be explained, using the theory I develop here, as readings based on the *structural* relationship of text and reader that I have named 'implicated'. These readings may be distinguished from 'hermeneutic readings' in as much as they are predicated upon the reader's dialogic engagement of a 'textual other', and *not* upon an external framework of *interpretation* (such as feminism itself) which is brought to bear upon the text.

While this is the bare outline of my thesis, however, it is hoped that the chapters themselves will do justice to the *complexity* (both pleasurable and traumatic) of what it means for readers to commit themselves to an implicated reading of a text. Both chapters in Part II will be concerned with questions of who or what constitutes a 'textual other', how that 'other' is identified and engaged, and how the subsequent relationship is sustained and managed in the face of the wide range of textual and extratextual pressures (including the pressures of 'feminist interpretation') that might threaten it. The analysis returns us also to the questions of 'reader-power' first introduced in Part I, this time exploring how the reader's changing perception of her agency *vis-à-vis* the text (and 'textual other') is a crucial factor in explaining her positioning within a model of reading as an implicated *process* as opposed to professional *practice*. There are many interesting twists and feints of logic to be contended with here, however, since my own readings demonstrate very clearly that readerly enamoration is a complex (and often self-deceiving) process, with the reader seeking to be both active (and/or empowered) and passive (and/or disempowered) simultaneously. Chapter 6, which focuses on the less happy 'sequel' of the reader-romance, also calls into question the *chronology* of readerly emotion, revealing how, for the reader at the centre of the experience, certain emotions that Barthes associates with the sequel (such as 'frustration' and 'anxiety') might seem to *precede* the *ravissement*, at the same time that the joys of that first enchantment may erupt (or be recovered) at any point. My general hypothesis here, indeed, is that *ravissement* is best characterized as the configuration of all those (readerly) emotions that are experienced as being *outside time*, whilst those associated with 'the sequel' all result from the subject's reawakening to a 'world in which various temporal agents . . . threaten separation and the end of love'.

While the rationale for my choice of the romance narrative, and in particular my engagement of Barthes's emotional 'dictionary', was dealt with in Chapter 1, I feel I should also take this opportunity to foreground – rather than evade – the obvious solipsism of my 'romance method'. As one reader of the book has pointed out to me, what is striking about these chapters is how 'romantic' my own readings are, implying that the discourse and narrative of romance are part of my *primary* engagement of the texts, as well as of the meta-commentary through which those readings are analysed. This, I feel, is totally correct. The reason Barthes's schema can be applied to these readings as easily and productively as it has been is due, in large part, to the fact that I went to those texts with that schema in mind: that my identity as a reader was already romanticized. As a point of method, however, I should perhaps point out that the actual selection of emotions I come to focus on was not worked out in advance of the readings/re-readings, nor did I work consciously to make my readings follow the trajectory of a classic romance narrative. The implosion of romantic discourse at the level of reading and analysis must, however, be seen to mark the self-conscious idiosyncrasy of the project I have undertaken here, as I attempted to make clear at the end of Chapter 1. It can also be pointed out, of course, that an overwhelming proportion of narrative texts are themselves 'about' romantic relations (whether this be part of their generic configuration or merely a 'subtext') and this further solipsistic twist (three of my own chosen texts may themselves be considered 'romances') will further explain why the text–reader relationship is well served by using the same discourse. The interaction of the text–reader romance with the interdiegetic romance, is, indeed, very much a feature of my readings of both *Written on the Body* and *The Story of an African Farm*, with the story of my own fluctuating relations with my 'textual other(s)' dialogizing with – if never actually *joining with* – the romance of the text's protagonists.[3]

The fact that it is the two novels in which my inscription by romantic discourse is at its most solipsistic also serves to draw attention once again to the cross-disciplinary nature of this project and the implications of this in theoretical and methodological terms. As I have already observed in Chapter 1, my rationale for the book in this respect has been one of courting the productive interactions across media rather than focusing on the non-translatable differences which would, I feel, have led me into another area of study (that of a comparison of reading processes and practices in visual and verbal texts). Since the primary aim of this project was to first identify and *name* some of the as-yet-unspoken processes of reading, in both literature *and* the visual arts, I preferred to make the cross-disciplinary differences of reading/spectatorship the means of reconceptualizing our practices in both areas of reception. In the readings and discussions which follow, it will be seen how it is often the negotiation of my readerly subject position in relation to visual texts that has enabled me to reconceive (and re-execute) my relationship to literary texts, whilst the narrativizing tendencies of all fictional engagements are very obviously transposed to my involvement in the visual texts. Rather than attending to how we (already) read differently across disciplines, then, I suppose I would like these chapters to illustrate how we might *learn* new ways of reading, by self-consciously transporting the readerly conventions from one discipline to another. This last point also relates to the way in which, in these chapters, 'reading' has also, very obviously, become 'writing'. The texts which my meta-commentary analyses, and which I refer to as 'readings', are also 'writings': texts which often (and sometimes very self-consciously) bear very little relation to the texts they are notionally 'readings of'. This, as I have already observed in Chapter 1, is an idea that has long been commonplace in poststructuralist *theories* of reading, but whose practice is more visible in implicated than hermeneutic reading, and here, especially, in our engagement of the visual arts (see the Preface to Part I). As a point of method, my position here would be that there is surely still much for us to learn from bringing this conceit of all *reading-as-writing* to still greater consciousness. This does not mean that I am advocating a new form of self-consciously writerly criticism (where every 'reading' becomes a 'rewrite' of someone else's story), but that we might understand more about the *politics* of the critical process if we recognize that this is what we are often *wanting* to do.[4]

This last point brings me, finally, to a few words on my use of the personal pronoun in the texts which follow. As I have already indicated in Chapter 1, I regard my first-person exploration of these texts as primarily *strategic*. What the 'I' offered me was a way of enunciating my dialogic relation to the texts from a position *within* them, and a means of making visible the dialogic 'I–thou' relation on which my theory of implicated reading has subsequently been based. Whilst this use of the 'I' might first appear to be a form of 'personalist criticism', therefore, I would prefer to distinguish it from a good deal of the (academic) writing that goes under that name.[5] It is important to recognize that an 'autobiography *of* reading' is *not* the same as the use of autobiography *within* reading or criticism, and that the purpose of this project was never simply to counter the alienation of contemporary academic discourse, or to join the movement of redefining 'the political' through a recommitment to 'the personal'. Whilst I think that such projects, properly handled, do have a place in current academia, I would prefer to see my use of the 'I' as very much a response to the specificity of a project which focuses on an exploration of the *dialogic conditions* of reading, rather than an autobiography of either 'myself' or 'myself as a reader' (although this was, of course, the focus of my interest in Chapter 2).

In terms of presentation, it should be noted that I have signalled the different layers of reading and commentary which comprise these chapters by the use of different typefaces. My 'original' readings, rereadings and 're-memories' of the text are reproduced in sans serif; my subsequent analyses of those texts by standard roman type.

Notes

1 Roland Barthes, *A Lover's Discourse* (see n. 41, Ch. 1). Page references to this volume will be given after quotations in the text.
2 'Re-memory': see n. 42, Ch. 1.
3 Jeanette Winterson, *Written on the Body* (see n. 41, Ch. 1); Olive Schreiner, *The Story of an African Farm* (see n. 1, Ch. 1).
4 'Criticism as re-writing': the practice of 're-telling' a story as a means of making a particular interpretation of it is, of course, a long-established (if little-acknowledged) critical method. Within current feminist criticism Judith Butler is an exemplary practitioner, as may be seen in the textual readings which comprise the latter part of *Bodies that Matter* (n. 50, Ch. 1).
5 'Personalist Criticism': see n. 51, Ch. 1.

5

The Emotional Politics of Gendered Reading I: Ravissement

Ravissement/ravishment

The supposedly initial episode (though it may be reconstructed after the fact) during which the amorous subject is 'ravished' (captured and enchanted) by the image of the loved object (popular name: *love at first sight*; scholarly name: *enamoration*).

(Barthes, *A Lover's Discourse*, p. 188)[1]

Imagining a corollary between the mechanisms of romantic love and our (gendered) experience of text–reader relations, this chapter sets out to explore the sexual/textual pleasures of Roland Barthes's *ravissement*: the emotional field associated with that euphoric first connection between 'self' and 'other' in which the amorous subject (reader) is swept away on a tide of abandonment, joy and devotion to the loved object (text). As I indicated in Chapter 1, my method of composition has been to interweave extracts from my readings, re-readings and re-memories of four texts – Olive Schreiner's novel, *The Story of an African Farm* (1899); Angela Grauerholz's photographic exhibition (1995); Jeanette Winterson's novel, *Written on the Body* (1992); and Jane Campion's film, *The Piano* (1993) – with a commentary which, while it does not purport to 'explain' the former, provides a theoretical frame through which to make connections across the different readings.[2] Since *ravissement*, in Barthes's own analysis, refers to a structural/historical moment in the lover's trajectory rather than an 'emotion' *per se*, I have sought to tease out a number of different emotions associated with this 'first phase' of sexual/textual dialogue, and to explore the reading event through this finely nuanced lens. The first of the emotional states I consider is *enchantment*.

Enchantment

In terms of interpersonal relations, most of us are at a loss to find words adequate to describe the first surge of emotion that marks our attraction to the 'other'. Barthes's approach is to make the amorous subject passive: the victim of a sudden ravishment or (more problematically in sexual-political terms) 'rape'.[3] He/she (regardless of actual gender) becomes the feminine subject who is *done to* through a sequence of emotions that serve first to 'activate', and then to 'immobilize':

> Love at first sight is a hypnosis: I am fascinated by an image: at first shaken, electrified, stunned, 'paralyzed' as Menon was by Socrates . . . subsequently ensnared, held fast, immobilised, nose stuck to the image (the mirror). (p. 189)

To consider the act of reading in terms quite as sensational as these is not something recent academic criticism has encouraged us to do, though adjectives such as 'gripped' and 'enthralled' are part of our common vocabulary for describing a 'good read'/viewing experience. This would suggest, as I outlined in Chapter 1, that reading is indeed a process predicated upon a self–other dynamic metaphorically similar to romance: whenever we 'open a text' (prepare to view it), we are liable to enchantment – though 'who' or 'what' the source of the enchantment might be remains a complex matter, as analysis of my own readings will subsequently show.

In Barthes's analysis, enchantment – the emotion which first marks our ravishment – is always 'prepared for' through the *induction* of a third party, who points out the desirability of the other (p. 137). This is part of his thesis, commensurate with the concept of the 'twilight state' (p. 190), that no *ravissement* is as spontaneous as it first appears. Despite our protests to the contrary, we 'fall in love' because we want to/have been waiting to – and because someone points us in the right direction. If we are not ready/willing for such an enamoration to take place, then presumably it will not happen; which could certainly explain (analogously) why certain reading experiences are rapturous and others not. In my own readings, indeed, the (preparatory) conditions of reception have evidently played a crucial role in determining my likely relationship with the text – although an initial 'resistance' does not necessarily mean that enchantment may not subsequently occur.

To return to the question of who or what the reading subject is likely to be enchanted *by*, Barthes's focus on the importance of the 'scene' as a crucial factor in *ravissement* is equally suggestive. 'The first thing we love is a scene,' he writes, because:

> Love at first sight requires the very sign of its suddenness (what makes me irresponsible, subject to fatality, swept away, ravished): and of all the arrangements of objects, it is the scene which seems to be seen best

for the first time: a curtain parts: what had not yet ever been seen is discovered in its entirety and then devoured by the eyes: what is immediate stands for what is fulfilled: I am initiated: the scene *consecrates* the object I am going to love. (p. 192)

As far as the amorous *reading* subject is concerned, the 'scene' can, of course, be thought of as both intra- and extradiegetic: the stage-setting within the text which, as in interpersonal romance, serves to introduce or frame the object of desire (a character, a discourse, a dialogic subject position), *or* the socio-cultural context in which the text is first received. The latter, like the whole question of 'induction', must be seen as crucially important in certain circumstances. As my own readings will reveal, the social and psychological context in which a text is consumed (re-produced) may strongly influence our disposition towards enchantment: for example, when our 'being in love' (or not) in the material world becomes part of the 'scene' which embodies the *intratextual* love object. Despite its highly visual connotations, however (and the fact that Barthes himself illustrates the 'scene' of enchantment with Werther's first vision of Charlotte as a silent spectacle), *A Lover's Discourse* also observes that the 'scene' may be *aural*:

The frame can be linguistic: I can fall in love with *a sentence spoken to me*: and not only because it says something which manages to touch my desire, but because of its syntactical turn (framing), which will inhabit me *like a memory*. (p. 192)

In terms of literary ravishment, this coda is obviously of vital significance, since our object of desire is always already linguistically inscribed. In certain of my own readings Barthes's observation is of special significance, however, since it is indeed certain syntactical turns which have caused me to become 'enchanted' by a particular 'textual other'.[4]

According to Barthes, another factor of vital importance in bringing about the state of enchantment is the unknown or mysterious quality of the 'other'. While I will discuss this aspect of *ravissement* in more detail under the heading of 'devotion', it is also important to register it here as a feature of the *coup de foudre*. Barthes writes: 'I am then seized with the exaltation of loving *someone unknown*, someone who will remain so forever: a mystic impulse: I do not know what I know' (p. 135). This mystery of 'otherness', which is experienced as an overwhelming condition of the initial attraction, is linked with another powerful emotion that marks *ravissement*: abandonment of self. Although, at times, such abandonment can be associated with the equally powerful impulse towards identification and merger, it is also experienced as an exaltation of difference – an emotion that correlates, in terms of text–reader relations, to the (risky) thrill of giving oneself up to both an alien discourse and/or a hermeneutic indeterminacy: the text is a narrative riddle that cannot (easily) be solved.

One final aspect of enchantment as figured by Barthes which is worth considering is the apparent paradox that the moment of first rapture is also the moment of greatest fulfilment. This has been something of a problematic issue as far as my own readings are concerned, since, as a conceit, it *can* be seen to oppose other (narrative) trajectories of 'classic romance', in which 'fulfilment' marks the end of a story in which various obstacles have had to be overcome to realize the promise (and *promise only*) offered by the initial *ravissement*.[5] There is a tension here, unquestionably, between Barthes's psychoanalytically predicated model of desire (which makes all desires inherently regressive and repetitive) and a socio-cultural model of romance determined by a well-defined structural sequence *ending* in fulfilment. My own readings, not surprisingly, can be seen to contain both expressions: fulfilment is both a gratuity of our intial attraction, *and* something to be subsequently sought after/regained.

With some of the mechanisms of sexual/textual enchantment thus set forth, I turn now to the readings in which I sought to record my emotional involvement in the reading process. I began the preceding discussion with a consideration of the contextual factors which prepared my relationship with the text in each case: the existence (or not) of an anticipatory 'twilight state' (p. 190)[1] and the role played by various third parties in inducing the 'romance'.

Of the four texts I finally decided to focus on in this. chapter, only one (the Grauerholz exhibition) was unknown to me when I began this project. In every other instance, therefore, the contextual factors affecting my first reception of the text are part of my 're-memory' of it, and separate from the powerful set of professional and personal interests that (in every instance) have affected my re-reading of it.[6] It is interesting to observe, moroever, that in both re-memories and re-readings I appear to have been somewhat reluctant to lay bare my sources: as though an admission of the route through which we first came upon the 'other' is indeed to undermine its special status. Thus of Schreiner's *African Farm* I note only that:

> It haunts me because its shadowy heroine, Lyndall, appeared to me at a crucial point in my own feminist development: the juncture at which a 'feminist identity' became both an object of desire and of identification.

This personification/beatification of the text (my use of the word 'appeared' gives it the agency and authority of an annunciation) can certainly be seen as an attempt to obscure or conceal its induction. The specialness of its impact in my life is diminished, perhaps, by the acknowledgement that it did not simply 'appear': although the 'third party' in this instance – Vera Brittain's War Diaries – situates it in a chain of texts that initiated my feminist education (in my early twenties) and is therefore not without its own romance.[7] In retrospect, I recall that Schreiner's text was a key item of emotional and intellectual exchange in the letters between Vera and Roland Leighton, and would therefore have come to me highly charged, especially as I received my first copy as a birthday gift from the person who was then, and for many more years would remain, the 'significant other' in my own life. Notwithstanding the romance of this particular induction, however, in my re-memory all adjuncts are lost; the specialness of Schreiner's text resides in its (exclusive) relationship with me: a relationship *so special* that (retrospectively) I can only think of it as a 'gift from God'. I would also observe that this is but the first of many instances in which we will see the discourse of feminism (the discourse which brought me to Schreiner via Brittain) displaced by that of a transcendent humanism: this, as we shall see, is a particularly dramatic instance of a text's political inscription (both textual and contextual) splitting from its emotional dialogue with myself, as reader.[8]

The induction processes that attended my first reading of Winterson's *Written on the Body* constitute a less romantic story and, although they are not repressed in either my re-memory or my re-reading of the text, it is clear that they would have to have been so, were this to be a successful enchantment. In fact, what the following extracts from my re-memory reveal is the major *obstacles* that were put in the way of my emotional engagment with this novel, and the desperate struggles I had to put up (as a former Winterson 'fan') to overcome them. I begin by situating my reading of *Written on the Body* in the context of my reader's 'romance' with the earlier texts, in particular *The Passion* (1989):[9]

What I remember especially about this first read [of *The Passion*] was that I started somewhere in the middle (probably with Villanelle's narration), kept going, and then started again at the beginning. It was one of those texts that moved me according to what I have recently discovered Raymond Williams referred to as 'the shock of recognition': despite the historical-fantasy location, the discourse on love and passion made profound humanist contact with me.[10] It was that special sense of having your own thoughts and feelings written out for you. Not only did I 'know' the truth of many of Winterson's aphorisms, I would also have chosen the same images and metaphors myself. Indeed, in my own writings I had already done so . . . So, 'death of the author' notwithstanding (and my own literary criticism by now in a rigorously *anti*-humanist mode), I took time out from my professional critical persona and allowed myself to play projection/introjection with the reconstructed author of this text. After quickly consuming *Oranges* (1985) and *Boating for Beginners* (1985) and catching up on some of the hype already surrounding Gore Vidal's 'most interesting young writer of her generation', I succumbed to a literary-specific form of fandom.[11] As with our involvement with any cultural icon, I was, of course, inscribed by a complex mixture of 'desire for' and 'identification with'. Winterson was to become the public embodiment of my own literary aspirations as a writer/scholar (at very least, my desire to be a 'published writer') but as the (uncanny) mouthpiece of my own thoughts and speech-acts she was also to become my intellectual 'other': the 'one who understands'.

What I describe in this extract of reader-autobiography, then, is the circuit of induction represented by the move from text-to-*oeuvre*-to-author-to-text: an embarrassingly 'retro' feature of our reading habits, unspoken of in today's literary theory. Yet what prepared me for my 'romance' with *Written on the Body* was my existing investment in the other texts and my relationship to them: 'Winterson' had become a principle to which I was committed.

As a subsequent section of my re-memory reveals, however, reception of this particular text was also inscribed by a powerful set of contra-indicators:

> *Written on the Body*, though, as I'm now remembering it . . . was launched onto the market amidst a barrage of negative publicity and criticism. Some of this was to do with the book, most of it was to do with what was seen as Winterson's own personal slide towards complacency, arrogance and hubris. Maybe it was that the press were getting tired with interviewing one so young and manifestly successful; maybe it was that Winterson did begin upping the ante at this time. What I remember, however, was the quality newspapers stamping their reservations all over the book: its politics (the issue of the 'genderless narrator'); its form (the slide from narrative towards 'panegyric' with a few recognizing that it was more like a (courtly love) poem, than prose); and inevitably – its ending.[12]

And so, how did this turn in Winterson's own critical fortune affect my own reception of the book? Although at the time I probably would have denied it, now I am inclined to say *profoundly*. As a Winterson surrogate, I was immediately put on the spot by friends and colleagues who wanted my opinion and direction. Had she 'sold out'? Did the book 'fail'? Was it the best (for a few were already claiming this) or the worst thing she had ever written?[13]

> As soon as I had read it (which I'm now remembering was, indeed, the first weekend it arrived in Lancaster) I did the honourable thing and defended it – and her. When people asked me how I thought it compared with the earlier texts I fudged the situation by saying that 'I no longer thought of Winterson's texts as separate entities': they were part of a larger discursive continuum. Well, *yes* . . . but no. Such loyalty is the requisite of all 'fans', something I know from my other life as a football supporter. Whatever you might secretly think or suspect, you never let on to 'others'. And so my memory of my reception of this text is of the public defence I was obliged to give on Winterson's behalf, and this responsibility is the first obstacle to a more honest emotional re-engagement. Indeed, it must be said that in my re-read-

ing of the text I will be confronting a spectrum of responses that I never addressed at the time because I was still 'half in love' with the text's author.

This acknowledgement of emotional fraudulence in our relationship to texts, the possibility that we might be faking our enthusiasm, is an indication of the complexities surrounding the emotional politics of reading. A sense of former dishonesty was, indeed, very marked in my re-reading of the text, where – questioning my involvement in its narrative trajectory – I write:

> Is my own (romantic) involvement with the text in line with that of the protagonists, following the same route? Not at all. The first fifty pages or so have seen me struggling desperately to make emotional contact – mostly through a (re)construction of the Winterson narrative persona [i.e. a persona I recognize from the previous texts]. But I see that in my original reading of the text I probably was faking it: the scenes of passion between Lothario and Louise alienate more than they fascinate. This is possibly because I am unable to find any satisfactory viewing position for myself; unable to achieve any meaningful intra-diegetic relationality. Only those fragments of texts which lose the body, which appear as white words on a black screen, offer my own heart a suitable jumping-off point. For example:
>
>> I didn't only want Louise's flesh, I wanted her bones, her blood, her tissues, the sinews that bound her together. I would have held her to me though time had stripped away the tones and textures of her skin. I could have held her for a thousand years until the skeleton itself rubbed away to dust. What are you that makes me feel thus? Who are you for whom time has no meaning? (p. 51)
>
> In line with the text's own struggle, then, my own point of contact with the erotic body is bones not flesh: it is the scaffolding of desire that works for me in this text, not the homage to its surfaces and minute particulars.

What I seem to be acknowledging here, albeit reluctantly, is the extent to which the advance publicity surrounding *Written on the Body* combined with my own feminist conscience to thwart my enchantment by the text. Although I wanted desperately to be 'shaken', 'stunned' and 'electrified' as before, I could snatch *ravissement* only in the exceptional passage, the odd linguistic turn, which escaped the problematic politics of Lothario's desire. Needless to say, I will return to a more particular analysis of the obstacles in the way of my emotional engagement with this text in the next chapter: here it is important to register only why the initial enchantment never occured.

In the case of Jane Campion's film, *The Piano*, the induction performed by friends and the media was more positive and, in my case at least, more successful. By the time I eventually got to see this film, it had already become a cult success on the feminist film circuit – although, as with Winterson's novel, political question marks (this time concerning the text's racism and its controversial presentation of female sexuality) were part of the gossip. Amongst *most* of my friends, however, there was approval and enthusiasm. 'You must see it', they said. 'You'll love it'. It is significant that in the re-memory of my first viewing, however, I present my enchantment as being circumscribed by a number of obstacles and anxieties that I'll consider in detail in the next chapter. The problem, as I perceive it in my re-memory, is that my inductors had done their job so well that I had already *anticipated* my likely pleasure in the film *before* I eventually got to see it – and that, like the pleasure of any daydream, it was bound to be disappointed.

> There is much about this film that I remember *not* enjoying. Ada's voice, while effectively wraith-like, was not the one I wanted to hear at the beginning of the film, and her whole person – the small, fragile, doll-like body – was not the one I wanted to see. My immediate route into the emotional economy of the film – via identification with/desire for the principal female character – was therefore blocked from the outset, though it is clear that I have subsequently been able to adopt/respond to her subject position in spite of this. Unlike *Story of an African Farm* and the Angela Grauerholz exhibition, then, my relationship to this text does not take the form of the typical romance trajectory *(ravissement + sequel)*. As with Winterson's *Written on the Body*, the *ravissement* may better be seen as the set of expectations with which I approached the text and which were initially displaced/disappointed when viewing began. Unlike my experience with Winterson's novel, however, this initial disaffection was subsequently overcome and my friends' promises of seduction fulfilled – though not, perhaps, in the way I had originally expected (e.g., through direct identification with the 'Brontëesque' characters).[14]

Important here is the clarification that not only can our pre-textual experiences constitute a Barthesian induction, but in certain instances *they are the ravissement*. In these readerly scenarios, indeed, the *sequel* begins with the first meeting.

It is also significant, however, that in my *re-reading* (as opposed to re-memory) of Campion's film I register that the induction associated with my original viewing has now been substantially revised:

> My experience of watching this film for a third time, for the purpose of this exercise, was not at all in line with the re-memory of it reconstructed the day before. The nature of my emotional involvement, which I thought I had sewn up, was sweetly and surprisingly different

from what I anticipated: for all my rationalizing of the text to a few key 'structures of feeling', my supposed alienation from the characters, my disengagement of the narrative – I found myself effectively transported into a text which worked on me *more* like a romance, less like a Freudian case-study, than on my previous viewings.[15] From the moment the music started, I felt myself cued in to the sort of pleasure that – at a theoretical level – I would not associate with this film. By some manner of means, it is clear that my relationship to this text had changed – been reconceptualized – between the times I saw it first, and now; and that this change is itself at odds with the rationalization I offered in my re-memory.

What I need to accept, therefore, is that *at the same time* as I have been working towards a theoretical explanation for my investment in this text, I must also have been internalizing it in quite a different way. My reference to the film-still postcard in the 're-memory' (Ada and Bains caught in the moment of rapture and reconciliation) is a clue to this 'other reading': between its first cinematic release and now, *The Piano* has mutated from a 'cult' into a 'classic' movie, and it seems that I, too, have been willing to participate in the change. Such re-packaging of a complex psychic (melo)drama as a simple romance is, however, possible only when we *know* the text's outcome and have rendered it 'safe': which is why, presumably, the potential for this sort of pleasure – the love-story of Ada and Baines – increases the more times you see the film. *The Piano* is a text which comes together and 'makes sense' only in its closing sequence, and the more familiar we become with that ending the more possible it is to 're-script' what comes before.

What this extract seems to point to is the fact that textual induction is manifestly cultural and historical, and that our relationship to a text will be significantly over-determined by changes in that context. My anticipatory pleasure in *The Piano* was keener and more straightforward the third time because my knowledge of the text, combined with the change in its commodity-status, permitted me to indulge a new relationship to it: one in which, once again, my political (feminist) anxieties could be suspended and/or rationalized.

As I acknowledged at the beginning of the chapter, the Angela Grauerholz exhibition was the only text I had not encountered previous to this project – although my reading was equally prepared in terms of the advance publicity with which I approached it.[16] As I record:

My first viewing of the photographs was on the first 'free' Wednesday night when Grauerholz was herself present, giving a gallery talk. The exhibition rooms were packed with people, to the extent that I could only snatch glimpses of most of the images as the crowd followed her around. Her talk was also in French, so I could only understand that, too, in part. However, by this time I'd already read the reviews and looked at the catalogue, so I had a good idea of the central themes and concepts of her work. It was the co-incidence between her theory of text–viewer relations and the one that I'd been developing in previous weeks that struck me most forcibly: the conceit of the reader/spectator as a ghostly participant in the text and the emotional configurations such participation gives rise to.

In contrast with the major emotional expectations which accompanied my first encounter with *Written on the Body* and *The Piano*, I would probably describe this induction as one of curiosity rather than instantaneous *ravissement*. In this respect, indeed, it was a prequel more in line with Barthes's own amorous trajectory: I was not enchanted with Grauerholz's works in advance of seeing them, nor was I 'stunned' and 'electrified' at the exhibition preview. Like glimpsing an attractive stranger in a crowd (which was, indeed, precisely the conditions of viewing that first night), I was, however, interested enough to return: in Barthes's terms, I sensed that there was something in those rooms which would 'match my desire' (p. 193), even if I did not yet know what it was.

When the time came for my return visit, however, the day I chose to perform the actual reading of the exhibition, there were a number of serious contextual obstacles blocking my prospective engagement with the text(s). What I record in my reading is both the 'advice' the viewer is given on how to respond to the works, and the inhibitions associated (for me) with museum space. About the former I write:

> The most significant feature about Grauerholz's own work in this respect – and the one that has put me off, kept me hovering on the threshold all these weeks – is the fact that this notion of participation is present in her work as an *injunction*. As with much contemporary art and literature, such theoretically self-conscious control of spectatorship threatens to steal the reader/critic's thunder: leave her (me) with little or nothing to say. The information board, situated at the threshold of the exhibition rooms and inscribed with curator Paulette Gagnon's 'explanatory' text, tells the viewer what Grauerholz expects her to do even if this is negatively phrased: 'a reading of the work allows the observation that the artist leaves the viewers free to find their own dimension'.[17] So there is no opportunity for me, as reader/critic, to make the exciting observation that we – as viewers – move in and out of these images like ghosts. We have already been told that this is what we're going to do; that this is the act of reading that we must perform.

'Induction', in this instance, has been taken to such an extreme that the amorous (reading) subject is denied the sense of 'surprise' that, for Barthes, is another condition of *ravissement* (see Barthes, p. 193).

Equally inhibiting for me, however, was the cultural anxiety and alienation which often afflicts me when I visit galleries and museums (see illustration 1.2). In the following extract I record my feelings immediately prior to making my reading:

> I am writing this on a bench placed near the exit of the exhibition. It is the only seat provided, so my reading (note-pad in hand) is going to be an awkward and tiring one. Before I make my way back to the first rooms I survey my context: white walls, dim lighting, pale wooden floors. From this distance the photographs look simply like large, black rectangles on the white walls. Despite the fact that I am the only visitor, a number of security guards pace restlessly about. Even with the absence of the crowd it doesn't feel like the ideal space to do what Grauerholz requires of me: least of all to open up myself up to the *emotional* experience of it all. But I also accept that for me – as a female, erstwhile working-class subject with a deficiency of the cultural capital that makes this sort of activity second-nature – there can be no comfortable space from which to view art.[18] However, I am here now as a professional – a critic, trained in textual analysis – and, gathering up paper and pen, I make a beginning.

In retrospect I am prepared to recognize, however, that this anticpatory discomfort is likely to be double-edged as far as a prospective *ravissement* is concerned. In terms of the romance metaphor, the analogy is clearly one of the amorous subject falling in love with someone beyond her own class and status. And since this is *the* convention of popular romance, perhaps my 'discomfort' on this occasion was really commensurate with my attraction towards what does, indeed, prove to be an extremely bourgeois reader-romance.

In conclusion, then, it may be observed that although the presence of a 'third party' *may* work as a powerful inductor in drawing the reader/viewer to a text, such informants (human or discursive) can also represent 'detractors', and create obstacles to a successful – or, at least, immediate – text–reader engagement. The Barthesian emphasis on such a conduit does nevertheless lead us very emphatically to the general importance of contextual factors in priming the site of *reader-ravissement*, and to the way in which many of the conditions of an implicated reading are established in advance of the actual textual engagement.[19]

I want to move on now to review the importance of 'the scene' in the process of text–reader enchantment. As I observed at the beginning of this chapter, in reader-terms the scene can be thought of as either *contextual* (hence relating to many of my preceding observations *vis-à-vis* induction) or part of the amorous staging performed by the text itself. As far as the emotional involvement with all my chosen texts is concerned, the scene has been an absolutely vital factor in determining the extent and nature of my enchantment. In the case of my two visual texts, indeed, it could be argued that the scene *is* the *ravissement*. As a ghostly participant in the text, my relationship is with the scenes that embody the text's own 'structures of feeling' (see note 15 above) rather than with the protagonists themselves. Put simply, it is not the characters with whom I 'fall in love', but the spaces/places they occupy.

In the case of *The Story of an African Farm*, scene is clearly of paramount importance in this respect, although – perhaps paradoxically – this is also the text in which I come closest to a desire for a humanistically conceived textual character. It is striking, none the less, that in my re-memory of Schreiner's novel (and in this case it was at least seven years since I had last read it) it is through the scene that I re-enter its emotional field:

> What I see when I first think myself back into this text is the exterior of the bush settlement where Lyndall and her sister come to live, although I can't recall exactly if the farm is isolated or if there are other buildings close by. In my mind, there are at least outhouses, sheds: a scattering of wooden structures. And beyond the dwellings is the bush: the distant hills, the kopje. If I concentrate some more I know that the earth is dry and red, the vegetation sparse. It is as hot, arid and alien as any place I know and not at all the sort of landscape I favour. I would never have chosen to read this novel on the basis of its location; indeed, the knowledge that it was about Boer farmers in South Africa would have assuredly put me off.[20] Quite another route brought me here, however, and now that I am back I am regarding the setting with a mixture of familiarity and confusion. It is, in every way, like co-ordinating yourself in a dream and – in my bodiless incarnation – I am in every way the dreamer.

Recognizable in this account is something of the same discomfort that marked my *contextual* experience of scene at the Grauerholz exhibition. Here, however, it is quite obvious that the alien landscape associated with this text has since become intrinsic to its romance: the heat, the red earth, the distasteful political system in which the protagonists live, constitute a highly charged 'difference' which, even in my re-memory, clearly raises a *frisson* of mixed fear and excitement. The ghost-metaphor, too, is a successful trope for enabling readers to 'explain' their ability to enter texts from which they are notionally excluded. My ghost, as will be seen, relishes her ability to wander amidst the scene of her past *ravissement*, while all the while feeling the discomfort *and* excitement of the trespasser:

> As I flit around the outskirts of these buildings, eyeing them from different vantage points, I succumb to a complicated sequence of emotions that represent my relationship to the text and its characters. Longing, loss, pride and regret crowd in upon one another in rapid succession, as all my past readings and revisitings collapse together. It is not simply that this is a text that, upon one reading, will produce a roller-coaster of emotional affect (though, of course, it is), but the

fact that different emotions are associated with different hauntings. And this, now, is part of the pain and the confusion as well as the fascination of my return. To return to this text is to return to the ghosts of all my former intra-textual selves: the reader-positionings I have occupied at different stages of my own personal growth and development: selves that I can never inhabit again although, as I wander around these buildings, I find myself drifting in and out of their fields of vision: now seeing as I once was, now as I am.

What this further passage reveals, moreover, is the way in which each new 'haunting' of the scene is loaded with the connotations of past visits. Therefore, to take Barthes's *Werther* analogy, every time the hero sees the heroine in a context similar to the one in which he first beheld her – 'framed by the door of her house (cutting bread and butter for the children)', p. 192 – his first enamoration is going to be overlaid and revised in the light of subsequent emotional experiences. Therefore, as is demonstrated in my own example, the scene becomes an effectual palimpsest of our changing relationship to our textual others.

The prominent significance of the scene in my relationship to Schreiner's text also goes some way to explaining my enchantment with Campion's film, in which the female protagonist never becomes the subject of my 'devotion' (see below) in the way that Lyndall does. Yet the fact that my re-memory of Lyndall is so radically decentred (de-humanized) in this focus on the scene, offers a clue to what it is that constitutes my object of desire in *The Piano*. In this instance, the significance of the 'scene' does not strike me immediately, but towards the end of the re-memory the connection is made:

Even as I write, however, something is coming back to me. When I focus on what it meant to participate in this film, all I think is forest . . . the primal space into which, I, too, plunged. It could be, perhaps, that this is because the forest (and the sea) represent the psychic backcloth of the film: the empty screen – devoid of characters – onto which we, as viewers, can project *our own* bodies and voices. There is a very real sense, indeed, that when I re-memory this film I am wanting to erase the characters and empty the woods. It is as though I want access to the 'structures of feeling' (see note 15) – the film's emotional infrastucture – without its own participatory cast. In the same way that I craved the glimpse of some person(s) known to me in Grauerholz's photographs, so am I re-peopling Jane Campion's script with them here. Which is why, presumably, Michael Nyman's film score has proven so successful: a parallel text which evokes the structures of feeling associated with the film *without* the specificities of the accompanying narrative. Because my involvement with this text is not directly mediated through the characters (like *Written on the Body* and unlike *The Story of an African Farm*), because I do not constitute them as dialogic 'others' whom I desire or with whom I identify – my participatory

mode is less one of merger than of *substitution*. I want to explore
Ada's dreamscape on my own without Ada in it. And in my re-memory I do. The central pleasure of this text for me is the (emotional) landscape it supplies me with: the dark forest of my own subjugated fears,
desires and redemption.

This 'clearancing' of a text in order to substitute one's own emotional or,
perhaps, erotic fantasies is an interesting idea, and the image of the novel or
film stripped of human participants could be useful in helping us further
conceptualize how Williams's 'structures of feelings' exist as an embodiment rather than an expression of certain emotional configurations.[21]
Imagine, for example, watching two hours of *The Piano* – following all the
same camera-shots – without the characters in them: a bizarre conceit, but
one that helps suggest something of the experience I am describing.[22] The
musical score, as I indicate in the re-memory, would seem to perform a similar function, providing us with the (remembered) connotations of the
romance (an abstract scaffolding of loss and desire) which we, as decontex-
tualized reader-participants, can then 're-settle' with our own fantasies.

Angela Grauerholz's photographs, on the other hand, do the clearancing
for us. What are her images, after all, if not the scene stripped of narrative
and protagonists? Although the curator's commentary stopped short of saying this directly (we are merely advised that 'the artist leaves the viewers free
to find their own dimension, forming their own interpretations of the photographs through their own thoughts in the face of the creative process'), the
invitation is clearly one to ghostly *participation*. Realization of this fact
comes fairly early in my own experience of the exhibition, although, as will
be seen from the following extract, at first I was clearly floundering in
Barthes's 'twilight state', anxiously searching for a 'textual other' which
would not appear:

Room 1

There are four images in this annex: three landscapes and one interior. They are large photographs: 122 x 183cms, and all are in
cibachrome – except the interior has been developed in sepia rather
than black-and-white.[23]
    I begin with *Landvermesser* (1992) [see Illustration 5.1]. This is a
woodland scene, photographed from a point of view within the trees:
slightly elevated, looking down. There is little that is distinctive about it
on first observation: no obvious tricks of composition, perspective or
production technique. Everything is square, everything in focus – until
you realize that the empty foreground space, bisecting path, and off-
centre sapling which feel, at first, like poor composition, are purposely
unsettling. We are so conditioned against the aesthetic impropriety of
the empty foreground space (a feature that occurs repeatedly in
Grauerholz's landscapes) that we overlook the emotional disturbance

Illustration 5.1   'And so I retreat from this text . . . feeling like I've somehow come the wrong way' (Chapter 5)

that helps explain *why* we don't like it. In this particular instance, I soon realize that my disquiet is associated with my sense of being lost. If I enter this landscape through the route that Grauerholz lays out for me I find myself floundering in this foreground space, heading for the path, not knowing which way to go. Woods, as most of us know, are the worst place to lose your way in: every direction looks the same. And even in this text, where the woodland is clearly part of a city park rather than the wilderness, I feel the same incipient anxiety overtake me. It is the middle of the afternoon: a place I've never been to before. I don't know what I'm doing here, and I feel like I'm wasting time. My problem is how to get away . . .

Now *File d'Attente* (1994) (see Illustration 5.2). Here is another location/destination that is unfamiliar to me and which confronts me with a similar feeling of confusion and disorientation. As I approach this queue of unfamiliar people waiting for a bus I, as an uninformed spectator, have no idea which city I'm in, which year it is, what time of day. Because the image is dark and grainy, it feels like it is about to rain and that it is a long time ago. But this is the illusion created by many of Grauerholz's photographs: a heavy, overcast summer afternoon which is the scene of waiting and weariness. These people, however, are in modern summer clothes, so I know this is recent history, and the light dresses and shirt-sleeves indicates that the weather is fair. As I haver towards them, across the pale wood gallery floor, I feel consumed by their anonymity. The blurred focus of the image means that even when I get closer I can't make out the faces: though I find myself thinking, curiously, what if I *did* happen to recognize one of these sub-

Illustration 5.2 'What if I *did* happen to recognize one of these subjects?'
(Chapter 5)

jects? The woman in the print dress who looks most directly towards
us, for example? How different, then, would this viewing experience
become. As it is, my eyes are arrested by her partly *because* I can't
see her well. There is the familiar cinematic lure towards identification:
by assuming her positionality I can escape my own awkward exclusion as a spectator. But there aren't enough suturing devices in the text
for me to sustain this fantasy for long. And so I retreat from this text,
like the first one, feeling I've somehow come the wrong way.

What is interesting about my intervention in these first two images is the
way in which the conceit of the scene, and my participation in it, gradually
takes hold. With the first photograph, *Landvermesser*, I'm clearly at a loss
as how to situate myself. All I can think, when I enter the text, is: what am
I doing here? And the disquiet at what I am *being asked to do* quickly translates into a (political) 'interpretation' of the text, based on the projected
unease of being a woman alone in the woods. As far as this first image is
concerned, then, I am quite unaware of the romantic potential of the scene
I have entered, and am not thinking that it and the subsequent texts may
somehow conceal/reveal my own textual other.

The inclusion of figures in the next photograph, *File d'Attente*, gives me
my first opportunity to focus my disorientated emotions. By acknowledging
that part of my alienation derives from the fact that I do not 'recognize' any
of the people waiting in the queue, I go on to speculate on what it would feel
if I *did* happen to identify one of them. More to the point, what would I feel
if s/he were suddenly to become *the one*? With this second image, therefore,
a discourse of fascination has been established, and from this point on all

my *unheimlich* feelings start to explain themselves through the notion of *something missing*.[24] What this would seem to indicate, if nothing else, is just how eager we are, as readers, to convert our unspecified emotional response to a text into some sort of *narrative*, even if the reflex is in most instances unconscious. Because this reading of Grauerholz's exhibition was undertaken as part of a project in which I had already begun figuring the text–reader relationship as a kind of romance it is, of course, unsurprising that this was the narrative that occured to me here. It is my speculation, however, that similar 'management' strategies help rationalize our emotional response to all texts, though the discourses providing the focus will, of course, vary.[25] I thus complete my tour of the first exhibition room with my readerly identity already firmly established. I might not yet know who or what I am *looking for*, but I know that I am looking – and my emotional anxiety, whilst not resolved, has at least been brought under control. Here is my analysis *in situ*:

> The images in this first room, then, have not seduced me as much as ambushed me. These are all spaces/places that I, as a single woman, have entered by accident and from which I have soon retreated. Although these are very much the landscapes of our dreams, therefore, they are not yet the landscapes of desire. The best way to understand them is probably as the metaphorical as well as physical *anterooms of desire*: the streets and rooms through which we stumble in our quest for something else. And so I pass on to the second room of the exhibition, hoping to find the 'something else'.

Room 2 does, indeed, yield a true 'scene of romance', and from this point on my interpellation as the amorous subject of these texts is confirmed. Although the public, male-defined spaces of *Le Bureau (1993)* and *La Bibliothèque* (1992) (see Illustrations 6.1 and 6.2) represent something of an obstacle in my quest, *Mozart Room* (1993) (see Illustration 5.3) may be considered the scene of my first full 'enchantment':[26]

> *Mozart Room* turns out to be my first fully pleasurable viewing experience in the exhibition. I don't recognize this immediately, because the image is apprehended in the context of the other interiors I have just described and categorized as excluding of me as a female, culturally disadvantaged subject. Despite its title, however, this image – the corner of a room with twelve-pane window photographed on a slightly skewed angle – is open to me precisely because it is free of the semiotics of high culture that have marked the other texts. The lack of a narrative subject enables the viewer to focus on many of the atmospheric features present in all the photographs with a new intensity. The blurring of focus caused by the over-exposure, the grainy surfaces, and the extreme light/dark contrast are connotative of age and dust. When I enter this text, for example, I am imagining the windows to be

Illustration 5.3 'A space in which to desire?' (Chapter 5)

grimy, the net curtains thick with brown dust, despite the fact that there is no *evidence* for this set of associations. I also imagine it to be another historical moment: World War II, probably. Like the photographs in the first room, this image creates the illusion of my having come upon this place by accident: but unlike the other images, in which that space was experienced as mistaken and hostile, I am led towards the corner of this room as if it were a refuge . . . And thus I stand in front of the image of *this* window: dreaming. I may not yet have found what it is I'm looking for in these rooms, these images, but I have found a space in which to desire.

Another emerging subtext here, and one that has already erupted elsewhere in this chapter, is the way in which my feminist consciousness (reading the images through an awareness of gendered space) is seemingly at odds with my 'romantic' suture into the text. Whilst it is clear that my implication in the image is in its own right gendered and sexualized, a more overtly political engagement constitutes an obstacle to a more personalized and emotional one. Thus, while my theoretical consciousness frowns and tells me that this is *surely* a false dichotomy (politics is emotional; emotions are political), my reading *practice* is still to separate the one from the other.

I want to move on now to consider the role of the *linguistic scene* in facilitating my enchantment by the other three texts. Returning to Schreiner's *Story of an African Farm*, it is obvious that my enchantment by the character, Lyndall, is predicated almost entirely on the instances of direct speech through which she is presented to the reader. What Barthes refers to as a 'syntactical turn' (see the discussion at beginning of this chapter) becomes, for me, the defining quality (the 'essence') of the loved object. Hence I write:

My first encounter (re-encounter) with Lyndall as a child is marked by two verbal statements: 'I try' (in connection with her sewing) and 'he has been crying'. As soon as I began re-reading this text I quickly understood that what had caused me, once, to fall in love with this character was not the representation of her 'personality' and 'inner thoughts' by the narrator, but the *direct speech* she is granted.[27] Her entry is marked, in other words, by an exhibition of resolve and perspicacity. *Vis-à-vis* her observation on Waldo's crying, we are also assisted by the narrator: 'She never made a mistake'. This is a child, then, who is immediately singled out for possessing a 'knowingness' beyond her years, and who is already on the offensive against 'life', in particular its trickery and deceptions.

In our culture such 'knowingness' is gendered, and it is not gendered female. From her first entrance, then, the female character who is to become the object of my fascination is *not* destined to become the conventional heroine of the text. While some of the structural markers are in place – she is, after all, an orphan – her lack of innocence and trust signals her transgression. Although the fate of the adult Lyndall is to be thwarted by the material reality of her position 'as a woman', and although Schreiner is to guarantee her femininity through repeated references to her physical appearance (in particular, her smallness and delicacy), the linguistic/discursive field she occupies from page seven onwards is unambiguously masculine. It is Waldo who weeps the 'girl's' tears; Lyndall who stands by 'curious'. As a female reader, then, I would not *have* to identify as a lesbian to establish this transgressive relationship with the central protagonists. In structural terms, Lyndall and Waldo are introduced to us already role-reversed. In her brain and in her speech it is Lyndall who is the boy.

It will be seen that, in the reading itself, I have already gone some way to trying to explain *why* certain syntactical turns should have such a charismatic effect, and my reasoning is that Lyndall's repeated recourse to declamatory statement is strikingly transgressive in gendered terms. What I am 'shaken' and 'stunned' by, then, is a sexually coded incongruity that instantly renders Lyndall an object of fascination and 'devotion' (see below). Her linguistic 'cross-dressing' throws into instant confusion both her role in the text and my relationship to her, but I know also that somewhere in this destabilizing of conventional gender roles she exists as my textual other. (I will return to this linguistic 'inscription' of Lyndall's character in the section on 'Devotion' below.)

Despite the fact that I have hitherto presented my enchantment by *The Piano* in largely scopophilic terms (my conceit of 'clearancing' the 'scene' was emphatically visual), my (re)reading of the text reveals that, as with Schreiner's novel, my emotions are also engaged by the 'syntactical turns' (Barthes), first, of Ada's voice-over and second, of Baines's declaration of love. As the following extract suggests, the former continues to 'electrify' me even though I am watching the film for the third time:

> It is very obvious, moreover, that the multiple sensory pleasures one derives from a film produce an emotional effect very different to the written text. *The Piano* exploits its multi-media facility to the full, overwhelming the viewer with a combination of visual and aural effects. Once the hermeneutic code is relaxed ('what is this a film about?'), the opening sequence of the film becomes a sensory feast: the breathtaking beauty of the photography (exploiting all manner of 'defamiliarizing' devices: multiple points of view; the world seen through Ada's fingers; the beach and coastline made huge and wet and wild by the bizarre imposition of a grand piano in its midst; the emotional and historical connotations of the musical score (we are cued in to 'historical romance'); the voice-over).
>
> The effect of the latter, juxtaposed as it is to a set of strikingly unfamiliar visual images and a seductive, though reassuringly familiar musical score (Nyman's soundtrack is widely regarded as a brilliant pastiche of nineteenth-century piano music), is startling. Although in the 're-memory' of my previous viewings I expressed a discontent with Ada's voice – its high and eerie pitch – this time I was much more struck with the nature of its rhetoric. Extended dialogue is sparse in *The Piano* – it is a text that depends upon visual rather than verbal language to move and explicate the narrative – but the 'speeches' that do occur (Ada's voice-overs, Baines's declaration of love, Stewart's ventriloquizing of Ada's voice 'in his head') are marked by the strangely authentic 'artificiality' of nineteeth-century literary language:[28]

> The voice you hear is not my speaking voice, but my mind's voice.
>
> I have not spoken since I was six years old. No one knows why, not even me. My father says it is a dark talent and the day I take it into my head to stop breathing will be my last.
>
> Today he married me to a man I've not yet met. Soon my daughter and I shall join him in his own country. My husband said my muteness does not bother him. He writes and hark this: God loves dumb creatures, so why not he!
>
> Were good he had God's patience because silence affects everyone in the end. The strange thing is I don't think myself silent, that is, because of my piano. I shall miss it on the journey.
>
> (*The Piano*, p. 3)[29]

As someone familiar with this sort of language, another cultural code has clearly been sparked into action for me, intensifying my emotional involvement and helping to explain something of the anticipatory pleasure I experience at the beginning of the film. Several of the reviews mentioned Emily

Brontë's writing as one of Campion's acknowledged nineteeth-century 'intertexts' (see note 14), and, as a former devotee of both this author and this literary period, the rhythms and inflexions of the language are wonderfully evocative for me. Although, like Nyman's music, Ada's speaking voice is no more than a pastiche of such diction, it serves its purpose.

Baines's declaration of love, meanwhile, would seem to operate as another crucial linguistic frame (Barthes) for my emotional reception of this text. Although, as I will discuss in the next section of this chapter, my *ravissement* cannot, in this instance, be reduced to desire for/identification with any of the principal characters, Baines's expression of his own helpless enchantment (he is, to quote Barthes, 'ensnared, held fast, immobilised', p. 189) becomes one of the key 'structures of feeling' (see note 15) to which I (the enchanted reader) relate:

> While the depiction of the sex itself can be given a pro-feminist reading (Ada is shown to be very much the active and desiring sexual subject, as she pulls Baines's body into her), Stewart's voyeurism renders the scene a bizarre viewing experience, with our own potential intradiegetic involvement thwarted by comedy. It is one of those odd cinematic moments in which scopophilia is turned upon itself. Viewing sex – through a window, on the screen – is, for the most part, a silent and alienating experience; the sight of *them* merely confirms *our* exclusion (cf. Freud's 'primal scene'). The more we see, the less we feel – or the more we feel our distance from their emotional engagement. Thus, while this consummation scene satisfies the desire for narrative closure in my relationship with the text, it does not engage my emotions. What does – and this goes back to my earlier point about the inter-textual points of reference that bind me to this text – is Baines's 'confession' in a stilted stylization of nineteeth-century literary language:
>
> > 'Ada, I am unhappy . . . because I want you. Because my mind is seized on you and I can think of nothing else. This is how I suffer . . . I am sick with longing, I don't eat, I don't sleep . . . So if you've come with no feeling for me, then go'. (p. 150)
>
> Like Ada's voice-overs, this statement clearly draws on a cultural code full of erotic resonance for me, and serves to reconnect me with the text's author-function (in whose script-writing I participate).[30] Such privileged super-textual positioning also protects me from the alienation I might otherwise feel from being aligned with Stewart in what follows. This is a text, after all, that speaks the power of the word through its absence: although we experience Ada and Baines's relationship as a primarily silent spectacle, much of its emotional impact hangs on its (rare) use of spoken language – a significance echoed in Stewart's own desperation to know whether Baines had ever heard Ada speak.

While I will discuss the implications of my identification with the author/narrator more fully in the next section ('Devotion'), my reasoning, as far as the linguistic scene is concerned, is that the resonance of Baines's declaration for me depends not only on its intertextual connotations, but also on the fact that I feel involved in its scripting. Thus, while this is not a (cinematic) scene in which I identify with the character, I *do* identify with the author/narrator of the 'linguistic scene', and am hence interpellated into its romance.

The linguistic scene, meanwhile, is possibly *the only means* by which I am successfully sutured into Winterson's text. I have already indicated some of the major obstacles to my enchantment by this text in terms of (negative) induction processes, together with the fact that it is 'only those fragments of text which lose the body, which appear as white words on a black screen, that offer my own heart a suitable jumping-off point' (see above). The section of text I quote to demonstrate this provides, however, another illustration of how the reader/viewer can, on occasion, extract 'scenes' from their (narrative) contexts, and insert herself in their clearanced emotional spaces (see extract and discussion, pp. 97–8 above). The scene I refer to here is linguistic rather than visual, but it is the same conceit that I used to describe my colonization of Campion's film.

What has emerged in this survey of reader-enchantment, then, is recognition that the reader is certainly more active in creating, sustaining and negotiating her *ravissement* that it might at first appear. Although the vocabulary associated with this phase of the romance trajectory traditionally casts the lover as victim of a barrage of chemical, ideological or even supernatural forces outside his or her control, the fact that the *coup defoudre* (for amorous readers as well as for lovers in the material world) is prepared for by a 'twilight phase' (Barthes), in which a host of inductors are set to work, suggests – at the very least – an active collusion with the gods. As far as my own readings are concerned, it is clear that my emotional response to the texts – my ability, or not, to be seduced by them – has been substantially influenced by the contextual factors which have determined my receptivity towards them. This is not to claim that we can engineer a positive reception of any text (Winterson's *Written on the Body* is a clear instance of how *ravissement* cannot be called to order, or powerful contra-inductors overruled), but that our predisposition – as in 'real-life' romance – is of crucial importance.

Barthes's assertion that 'the first thing we love is a *scene*' (p. 192) has also been useful in revealing the reader's active collusion in his/her enamoration. The different means by which the reader-lover can exploit the potential split of scene from narrative content is, as we shall see, but the first of many ways in which s/he can displace dissonant textual details and re-people the text with his/her own emotions (embodied or disembodied). While the Grauerholz exhibition could be seen to be inviting this degree of reader-power very (inter)actively, my reading of Campion's film is a good example of how our enchantment by a text can be sublimely dissociated from its own narrative articulation and/or reader-positioning. All that we require, it seems, is the bare bones of a structure – a discourse, a 'syntactical turn' (Barthes) – which we recognize, and we're off: which is not to imply that the text becomes inconsequential in determining our emotional response, but that a good deal of our reader-pleasure comes from the creative management of those emotions through active intervention in the textual process. As with any good romance, desire is whetted by challenge, and what my readings seem to reveal about reader-enchantment is ingenious ways in which the reader is able to manoeuvre herself into a position in which to be ravished.

Devotion

In this section I move on to consider another of the emotions central to the sexual/textual *ravissement*: the aspect of romantic love that we know as 'devotion'. Our devotion *to* a loved object can, indeed, be understood as the obverse of the raging (unsatisfiable) need *for* him or her. Although both emotions belong to the provenance of the *ravissement* (when we fall in love we both 'want' and 'want to give' simultaneously), I will deal with those emotions associated with a sense of 'lack' in the next chapter since, although they are initiated at the moment of enamoration, their refinement belongs more properly to the 'sequel'.

One of the reasons that lovers are overwhelmed with a sense of gratuitous devotion to the loved object is clearly because the *ravissement* by the other seems, itself, such an unasked-for miracle and blessing. As Barthes writes:

> It has taken many accidents, many surprising coincidences . . . for me to find the Image which, out of a thousand, suits my desire. Herein a great enigma to which I shall never possess the key: why is it that I desire So-and-so? Why is it that I desire So-and-so lastingly, longingly? Is it the whole of So-and-so I desire (a silhouette, a shape, a mood)? And, in that case, what is it in the loved body that has the vocation of a fetish for me? What perhaps incredibly tenuous portion – what accident? (p. 20)

To this extent, our devotion to the object of desire seems no more than a reciprocating gesture: an expression of the overwhelming gratitude we feel towards him or her for having appeared in our life ('at last'). While all of us are now probably scrambling through our personal histories to test the 'truth' of this, I would suggest that a similar reflex embraces our relationship to chosen literary and other texts. Leaving aside, once again, what it is exactly that we love or desire in a work of art, most of us will recognize a feeling of devotion towards those 'special texts' (perhaps very few in number) that have made it onto our 'life list'. This aspect of text–reader relations is, of course, emphatically overlaid with the discourse of religion, and 'sacred' is (interestingly) a word that we would probably use more comfortably of texts than of people.[31] We speak of books that have become our 'bible' (Vera Brittain and Roland Leighton thought of *The Story of an African Farm* as their bible, for example), and the Bible is itself the quintessential symbol of the consecrated text: something that is not only an 'aid' to worship, but to be worshipped for itself. My own readings, as will be seen, offer plenty of evidence of this sort of 'devotion', attended in each instance by another quasi-spiritual emotion that I would probably describe as 'grace': the sense of miracle at having our needs met and our desires fulfilled:

> In the encounter, I marvel that I have found someone who, by successive touches, each one successful, unfailing, completes the painting of my hallucination; I am like a gambler whose luck cannot fail, so his hand unfailingly lands on that little piece which immediately completes the puzzle of his desire. . . .The Encounter casts upon the (already ravished) amorous subject the dazzlement of a supernatural stroke of luck: love belongs to the (Dionysiac) order of the Cast of the dice. (p. 198)

Returning to the earlier Barthes quotation, it will also be seen that the impulse towards devotion is tied up powerfully not only with the miraculous appearance of the other, but with his or her unique and enigmatic specificity. As Barthes writes elsewhere:

> The other whom I love and who fascinates me is *atopos*. I cannot classify the other, for the other is, precisely, Unique, the singular image which has miraculously come to correspond to the speciality of my desire. (p. 34)

In terms of the text–reader relationship, this enigma will take many forms, and may describe our 'special' relationship with character, narrator, discourse or some formal idiosyncrasy of the text. In addition, the fact that the act of reading is, in some instances, overdetermined by the 'will to interpretation' means that the hermeneutic impulse attending this aspect of 'devotion' is intrinsic to the relationship. The 'insoluble riddle' that Barthes invokes to describe the mystery of romantic desire *per se* is part and parcel of the reading process:

> To expend oneself, to bestir oneself for an impenetrable object is pure religion. To make the other into an insoluble riddle on which my life depends is to consecrate the other as a god. (p. 135)

Once again, my own readings will furnish many instances of this mystification of the textual other, a readerly impulse that is frequently in interesting conflict with my critical/theoretical responsibility to explain and analyse. In literary criticism, after all, we are trained to believe that hermeneutic (and other) codes exist to be broken; and this distinction, as will be seen (and as has already been previewed in Chapter 1) lies behind my naming of these two models of reading as hermeneutic and *implicated*.

Apart from this uncomprehending prostration before the loved object, there are other ways in which the amorous subject can express his or her devotion. The first of these is through the use of the 'dedication'. This romantic impulse is described by Barthes as follows:

dedicace/dedication

An episode of language which accompanies any amorous gift, whether real or projected; and, more generally, every gesture, whether actual or interior, by which the subject dedicates something to the loved being. (p. 75)

In this entry Barthes goes on to describe the different forms the dedication might take, focusing, not surprisingly, on the *writer's* ability to dedicate his/her work to a loved one. His conclusion, however, is that such dedications are effectively tautological, in as much as the writer can give the dedicatee back only a version of the self that s/he has already inscribed on the text. While I consider this reasoning somewhat tautological in itself, the tension is an interesting one. But if the writer is liable to such frustrations in his or her inability to demonstrate devotion through dedication, what of the *reader*? What constitutes an act of dedication for us, 'passive' as we are? The answer must be through making the act of reading into an act of writing: through paying tribute to the text, as I do here, through the practice of criticism, or through merely 'retelling' it (with approval) to friends. In addition, the reader may express dedication to the (special) text by gifting it to a (special) other, in such a way that the dedication to the one 'stands in' for the dedication to the other, and personal and textual devotion are romantically interfused. (I read somewhere once that the inscriptions on the flyleaves of books are possibly *the* most revealing indicators of our romantic pasts.)

A similar way in which the amorous reader subject might show devotion towards the special text is through his or her 'fetishization' of it.[32] This impulse, which we might see expressed in the way that certain books become prized personal possessions, for example, compares with the emphasis placed on 'objects' connected with the beloved in the lover's discourse, and is defined by Barthes as follows:

objets/objects

Every object touched by the loved being's body becomes part of that body, and the subject eagerly attaches himself to it. (p. 173)

What is interesting, here, in terms of the politics of reading in general, is the difference to which it points between the 'private' and the 'public' consumption of art. Texts which are consumed in the public domain are not so easily fetishized in this way, although the culture-industries associated with both film and 'high art' pander to the desire for a conspicuous identification with the product, through reproductions and associated merchandise which can become the surrogate 'possession' of the reader/viewer. In this respect the catalogue I acquired at the Grauerholz exhibition, and the postcard (see p. 93 above) and musical score I have of *The Piano,* may be considered fetishistic items which 'privatize' my relationship to the texts themselves. Making a text (or its substitute) a treasured item in this way is clearly a means of demonstrating our 'devotion' to it, and there is no question that, in my own readings, Schreiner's novel and Campion's film have acquired something of that status for me.

Another way in which devotion to the loved object reveals itself is through the associated emotion of *compassion.* This is an aspect of romantic relationships that is rarely discussed; probably, once again, because the psychoanalytic analysis of desire has been predicated upon an economy of supply and demand (in which desire = demands waiting to be met). Compassion, however, can be considered another important feature of the *ravissement*: that first (gratuitous) outpouring of care and sympathy for the other, in which the amorous subject 'loses herself'. Barthes documents the emotion thus:

compassion/compassion

> The subject experiences a sentiment of violent compassion with regard to the loved object each time he sees, feels, or knows the loved object is unhappy or in danger, for whatever reason external to the amorous relation itself. (p. 56)

In terms of my own readings, as will be seen, this is an emotional reflex associated principally with my relationship to textual characters, although my early defence of 'Winterson' (the author) could probably also be thought of in the same light. It is in my readings of *The Story of an African Farm* and *The Piano* that devotion and compassion are of central importance, however, revealing much about the dynamics of the reader's relationship to a textual realm she both can and cannot participate in; and for this reason my discussion in this section will be limited to these two texts. I begin my commentary with a consideration of how my readerly expression of devotion is predicated upon my attraction to a 'unique' and 'unclassifiable' (Barthes) 'textual other'.

As I have already indicated, Lyndall is the textual character that I come closest to desiring/identifying with, in an 'authentic realist' sense, in the course of these readings.[33] I have already noted also how my initial enchantment by her is marked by the 'linguistic scene' she occupies (that is, the gender-subversive syntactical turns of her direct speech). It is clear, too, when I return to these same extracts, that it is the verbal statements which are the agent of my (instant) *devotion*, functioning as they do in an overtly evangelical way:

In the midst of the burlesque parable of Bonaparte Blenkins, then – the surreal context for the first part of the novel – Lyndall and Waldo are revealed to us through a series of highly staged actions and state-ments. It is these semiotic positionings that I am myself positioned by, nevertheless: 'recruited' with a vengeance.[34] As she holds forth to Em and Waldo in Chapter Two, for example, Lyndall's statements of aspi-ration and intent become detached from the context in which they are made. When I go back over these pages, it is the declarations them-selves that echo, reverberate: send a chill down my spine:

> 'There's nothing helps in this world . . .but to be very wise, to know everything – to be clever.' (p. 16)

> 'When he (Napoleon) said a thing to himself he never forgot it. He waited, and waited, and waited, and it came at last.' (p. 19)

> 'Has it never seemed so to you, Lyndall?' [Waldo]
> 'No, it never seems so to me.' (p. 22)

What this reading acknowledges, moreover, is that these are themselves statements 'out of context'. Even as they appear to refer only tangentially to the plot (what the children are suffering under the tyranny of Blenkins), so neither are they the pronouncements of the average child. Thus I continue:

> Children (especially female children) are not usually granted this much seriousness, this much authority in their speech. Lyndall, on the other hand, speaks with the assurance and dignity of the prophet: a Christ-like girl-child who knows the world, sees the future, and tells us how we should meet it. My involvement with this character, then, has clearly been marked by the discourse of religious faith: 'Lyndall' is not simply someone to desire, but someone to *believe in*. (Though there are those for whom the two are, of course, inseparable.) Positioned alongside the respectful, if uncomprehending, Em and Waldo, I listen to Lyndall's naïve and arrogant proposals and am prepared to follow. I can see from my adult perspective, from my former reading of the text, that her judgement is faulty, her confidence misplaced, but I am prepared to follow all the same. Such *conviction* in another is per-haps, for me, the prerequisite of desire.

Even in the process of reading, then, I was sharply aware that my enchant-ment by Lyndall was bound up in the discourse of religion. 'Devotion' in this instance is therefore not a casual adjunct of textual attraction, but its central expression. I devote myself to Lyndall because of *her* devotion, which is unspecified as yet, but signalled by the firmness of her opinions (see her statements above). The Christ-analogy is far from spurious.

The issue of *who* the Lyndall is to whom I instantly commit myself is, however, more complicated. As my reading of the 'lock-in' scene reveals (when Lyndall and Em are punished for misbehaving, following Otto's dismissal), my attraction to one so young is something that has to be explained and (consciously) negotiated:

> Re-reading it [the scene], I recognize this as the moment when I lay myself down at Lyndall's feet: although what interests me now is that my emotional expression as a reader cannot be understood in quite these metaphorical terms. Indeed, as I stand (at the window/in the doorway) my heart aches with the *intransitivity* of my position. This is one of the moments when I, as a reader, literally do not know what to do with my feelings. I am strung out somewhere between an overwhelming respect and admiration for Lyndall's strength and resolve, and an equally overwhelming desire to comfort her. Both these are emotions conceived as verbs of action: Lyndall exists for me as an other that I want either to prostrate myself before (signifier of devotion), or else take in my arms and comfort (signifier of care). Both such expressions are, of course, denied me. As a reader of the text I can never express the dialogic relation I feel, but must remain strictly intransitive: I can only watch and listen, listen and watch:

>> Lyndall lay on the bed with her arm drawn across her eyes, very white and still. . . .

>> 'I wish you would be quiet', said Lyndall, without moving. . . .

>> 'Do you think you will be able to?' [Em]
>> 'No, but I am trying.'

>> 'Oh, Lyndall, what are we to do?' [Em]
>> Lyndall wiped a drop of blood off the lip she had bitten.
>> 'I am going to sleep', she said. 'If you like to sit there and howl till morning, do. Perhaps you will find that it helps; I never heard that howling helped anyone . . .'

>> Long, long after, when Em was really asleep, she lay still awake, and folded her hands on her little breast, and muttered:
>> 'When the day comes, and I am strong, I will hate everything that has power, and help everything that is weak'. (pp. 72–5)

My relationship with Lyndall, here, is not one predicated upon identification. As I look through the text's window, the emotional struggle takes the form of a dialectic between self and other. If I could simply merge with Lyndall the whole experience would be much easier – but I cannot. Instead, the scene has set up a whole host of immensely uncomfortable subject positions which I try out and reject. Part of me has wanted to be Em, for example: to experience that trust in Lyndall's ability to get us out of this situation; to have her offer me her solicitude . . . But Em is also unreconstructed femininity: the sister whose innocence, simplicity and servitude set her up as the quintessential 'victim':

Lyndall's opposite. So there is no way that I would want to be Em permanently. To be the object of care and pity is not commensurate with my need to be, myself, a desiring subject and in another, even more improbable scenario, the interlocutory object of desire.[35]

So, this mediation rejected, what pose do I strike as I hover in great emotional tumult outside of Lyndall's window? In subsequent episodes my position will be much easier in as much as there will be Waldo to align myself with. But Waldo is not here just now, and the textual other that I am wanting/worshipping is (I must remember) a young child.

It is the realization of the extent to which I have been transgressing the *narration* of this text by refusing to relate to Lyndall *as a child* that intensifies the complexity of my position. The 'I' that has been loitering outside this room is manifestly not a child herself, and neither is the consciousness that uses a penknife to try to prise open the shutter and burn down the window. Such acts of defiance are, at the very least, adolescent, and it is certain that in my reception of this text I have interpreted this as an 'adult' crisis.

This degree of licence accepted, the range of options for my position as a viewing subject increases. Liberated from the chronotopic present I can, perhaps, relate to Lyndall's spirit in another form: the adult narrator who (via the narrator) is scripting this scene retrospectively.[36] As the child, Lyndall, lies on the bed, 'arm drawn across her eyes, very white and still' (p. 72), so do I reach out and take the hand of her future self. By recasting the scene as a *past*, I am able to communicate my desire and become (notionally) transitive. I can (hypothetically at least) tell Lyndall's extradiegetic projection what I could never tell her interdiegetic self because it has become an emotion once removed . . . Somewhere in this out-of-time, then, one adult feminist consciousness enters into dialogue with another and finds a way of transcending the exclusions of 'time past'.

This is certainly a complicated – some might even say desperate! – reader-manœuvre. It is, however, brought about by an aspect of the reading/viewing experience that has not (to my knowledge) been given any serious attention: namely, how we deal with the obstacles in the way of our 'participation' in those texts in which we become most involved, and in which merger/identification with one of the characters *is not* an immediate solution. This is also the moment when the reader-as-ghost metaphor comes into its own, describing as it does the *partial* inclusion of the reader in the text. What is striking about the above extract, for example, is the way in which I situate myself both *inside* and *outside* the textual action. As I indicate repeatedly, *I can see but not be seen*.

In terms of an expression of devotion, this sense of my own 'intransitivity' is at first experienced as an overwhelming obstacle. To show devotion, we need 'access' to the loved one, and this is emphatically denied me. My solution – which is also a means of circumventing the issue of Lyndall's age/status – is, indeed, ingenious, but on this occasion it satisfied me. By extracting both Lyndall and myself from the text – the time/space in which we could never meet – and proposing an extradiegetic 'meeting', I was able to 'communicate' with 'her' as with an equal consciousness; to *show* devotion and to *give* compassion.

Devotion is not, however, an emotion associated only with the first throes of sexual/textual passion; indeed, it is to an extent defined by 'the test' to which it is subsequently put, and thus becomes part of the 'sequel' of romance. This is certainly the case in my reading of *The Story of an African Farm,* and for this reason I have decided to disobey the chronological logic of these two chapters and deal, here, with how the emotion is negotiated 'after the fall'.

Without wishing to anticipate too much of the discussion in the next chapter by going into details of how Lyndall's failed ambitions present the (feminist) reader with feelings of anxiety, betrayal, frustration and disappointment, it is enough to register that all these emotions *do* ensue, putting our initial faith and belief in her under considerable strain. I record my own crisis thus:

> Such disappointment in one's textual heroes is extremely hard to bear. And yet having made my own commitment several pages back – having effectively yielded my heart and soul to Lyndall – it is too late to suspend my involvement. Indeed, it is too late even to feel something as simple as 'disappointment'. My heart aches for Lyndall even as she deviates from what she promised to be. Rather than condemning her for her 'weakness', I am compelled to share in her suffering. This, in turn, makes me even more uneasy. So easy to slide towards her own sense of irony and defeat: the 'bitter silvery laugh' (p. 197). But in this, too, it is already too late. Now, when Lyndall falls, she will take me with her.

What is interesting here is the way in which Lyndall's fall from grace marks a shift in my relation to her, from 'desire for' (one who is above me), to 'identification with', as admiration slides into sympathy. While this new relationship can also be constructed positively, however, the power-balance has been shifted dramatically, and Lyndall is in serious danger of slipping from her throne. It is important to recognize that, if this slide were to continue, *The Story of an African Farm* would become a very different reading event for me, and would probably be dislodged from my library of 'special texts'. Because of what was offered 'before the fall', however, I am like a lover desperate to keep faith with one in whom I have invested much; and the following extract is another example of the ingenious lengths to which the reader will go in order to preserve the feelings associated with the first *ravissement*:

The reader's commitment to the fallen Lyndall is reinforced by Waldo's commitment to her. Though it is clear that he only partly comprehends what Lyndall says in Chapter 4 (Part II), his role as 'interlocutor' of her passion (and she has no other) puts him in the privileged position that I, too, seek to inhabit. When, moreover, Lyndall transfers her own thwarted ambition onto him, a new contract is enjoined. Her outburst at the wedding:

> 'We must not, Waldo; I want your life to be beautiful, to end in something. You are nobler and stronger than I . . . and as much better as one of God's great angels is better than a sinning man. Your life must go for something.' (p. 232)

throws down a gauntlet that I feel I, too, must seize. From this point on, Lyndall is no longer my saviour and protector, but my mentor: she challenges me to do what she couldn't do herself, but on her behalf. No matter that in the text this gauntlet is thrown to a man. For myself, as a feminist, her clarion call reverberates with the politics of her earlier speeches in Chapter 4, and I feel myself called to duty. This is a complex re-negotiation of a relationship, but one which keeps the former power dynamic intact. Lyndall might have given up on her own account (a potentially devastating default for myself, as an adoring follower), but by *commanding me* (via Waldo) to realize her unfulfilled ambitions, she retains the authority and integrity that I am so heavily invested in. Although she 'fails', Lyndall never becomes a victim. And although it is I that am now expected to perform her work, she continues to direct it. The crucial thing (for *my* continued belief in her) is that she remains strong. And up until this point in the narrative, indeed she does.

It is through her extensive 'soundings' of Waldo, then, in Chapters 4 and 6 of Part II, that I re-negotiate my own relationship with Lyndall. The terms of the relationship have changed, but although I can no longer expect to live my life *through her* (in the same way that the heroines of classic romance submerge their own identities in the lives of the heroes), she is still my guiding light. The faith she has invested in me makes me responsible to her in a new way, and I feel myself, like Waldo, to be setting out on a quest on her behalf.

Through this artful manipulation of my relationship to Lyndall via Waldo, then, she remains an object of unconditional devotion. To extend the biblical metaphor, he and I are now her 'disciples', and our 'belief' is no longer in what she will 'do', but in what she represents. This new (textual) positioning, in which she is sublimated into the interlocutor of our greatest hopes and fears, is certainly the mechanism by which her initial 'enchantment' is preserved, overriding the *narrative* sequel which serves to bring her down. My reading of the text thus closes in a stubborn alignment with

Waldo's vision (in which Lyndall is still the bright angel) and a rejection of Gregory Rose's story of her defeat:

> If Gregory Rose's story offers the reader the material inscription of Lyndall's tragedy (death-as-the-consequence-of-complications-due-to-childbirth), Waldo offers us the mythic version in which Lyndall sheds her mortality and becomes an heroic model of desire and aspiration. She becomes this, moreover, not through any story that Waldo tells of her, but through the *interlocutory role* in which she is cast. It is as Waldo's guiding light that Lyndall achieves her mythic stature and endures as my all-time heroine. Thus the one I worship becomes, in the end, not a 'text' in herself but the one to whom *my text* is addressed: not so much a projection, as a projected space: the *ideal reader* of my own ambitious script.

The Piano is another text for which I feel devotion, though who or what the subject of devotion is in this instance is even more difficult to determine. While my earlier comments suggest, rightly, that my positive feelings towards the text have been influenced in part by the marketing and publicity that has enabled me to respond to it *as* a romance, I feel that I must also attempt to understand how these responses are mediated by the text itself (even if it is not the source of them).

As I note repeatedly in my reading (and my re-memory), there are no characters in this text which I desire as I desire Lyndall. Although, as we have already seen, it can be argued that I was enchanted by the film through devices associated with the major characters (the 'syntactical turns' of both Ada and Baines, for example), it was not the 'uniqueness', the 'great enigma' (Barthes) of either one of them that was, in itself, the cause of my *ravissement*. Indeed, my challenge as a reader/viewer was (as I began to explain in the previous section) to find a means of participating in the text's 'structures of feeling' (see note 15) *without* identifying explicitly with the narrative trajectories of the interdiegetic characters. This said, the characters are still the means (the 'language'/sign system) by which those 'structures of feeling' are revealed in the first place, and it is therefore reasonable to expect that my devotion to the text will, in some convoluted manner or means, express itself *through* an enchantment by the characters and their relationships.

My solution to this problem, which became a conscious part of my third reading/viewing, was inspired by some of the ways in which I had already come to explain my relationship to Lyndall in *The Story of an African Farm*. As we have already seen, my attraction and subsequent 'devotion' to her slipped repeatedly from the inter- to the extradiegetic: from an 'authentic realist' image of her as a material presence, to one in which she became a decentred 'collection of semes', or a dialogic reader-positioning (see especially my analysis of the 'lock-in' scene, pp. 112–14 above).[37] This move from the inter- to the extradiegetic is certainly one way, also, of beginning to understand my devotion to both Ada and Baines despite the fact that I do not desire/identify with their interdiegetic selves. What I formulate, as will be seen in the following extract, is a readerly scenario in which my involvement is with the author/narrator of the text rather than with her (textual) representatives:

> But if I'm now fair set to re-read this as a romance, how am I to dialogize with characters that I previously regarded as mere semes and functions? What is to be my new point of emotional entry? The answer would seem to be 'from above'. In my re-memory I made a big point of my personal involvement in this text depending upon my 'evacuation' of its own characters and narrative(s), and of inserting myself (and my own textual others) in the resulting 'clearances' (see note 21). With this viewing, however, I quickly discovered a means by which I could relate to Ada's story without either fully occupying her subject position or fully displacing it with my own. The solution – partly recognized in my re-memory – is to align myself with the Ada of the 'voice-over': the ghostly persona who narrates *not* what happens to her, but how she remembers it, from a point of view that is both 'above' and (in temporal terms) 'beyond'. It is precisely because this Ada is disembodied – and not the presence that we see on the screen – that I can merge my own story-telling self with hers most successfully.
>
> From my seat in the clouds (the perspective favoured by much of the film's photography) I enter into this text with new sympathy for what is going on below.[38] I care for the characters because they are my own fictional representatives on earth. The first occasion on which this relationship is able to express itself is through the view of Ada standing on the cliff-edge, looking down on the abandoned piano. It is an absurd image – a grand piano dumped in the middle of a vast beach – but its surrealism makes the symbolism more potent. What Ada gazes down upon (accompanied by strains of music) is, of course, the 'coffin' of her own lost past, which has been made newly visible by its radical de-contextualization. As a viewer/participant the image causes me a rush of identification at one remove. Because this 'Ada' is not me, but my representative, I both empathize and sympathize. I have stood where Ada stands, experienced this particular reflex of desire and loss (the loss of past desire), but I also have (externalized) care for her suffering.

The readerly reflex which this extract demonstrates is one of undisguised narcissism. My 'object of devotion', the thing that I treasure as 'rare', 'enigmatic', *'atopos'* (Barthes), is none other than the script with which I *over-write* Campion's. It is not so much that I 'identify' with the implied author of the text, so much as that I *supplant* her. Through this (highly active) intervention, I have commandeered *The Piano* as *my* text (as with Ada, repeatedly, of the piano: 'It's mine!'), and what I subsequently 'feel' for Ada and Baines (including, it will be noted, considerable 'compassion') is what I feel for my own projections/creations. And this is a very different relationship to one of simple 'identification' with either 'author' or 'character'.

It is clearly my violent appropriation of this film's 'structures of feeling', then, that has caused it to become an object of devotion for me: a text which doesn't 'tell' my story as much as enable me to (re)write it by providing me with a set, plot and characters: a rich source of props with which to rationalize its trauma. To this extent, indeed, *The Piano* works for me as the classic 'dream text' – providing the fictive 'displacements' and 'condensations' that enable us to process emotional distress obliquely.[39]

In this section I have focused on the different forms our textual devotions can take and, in particular, on the *obstacles* to that devotion: namely, the problems we have in, first, *identifying* the textual others who are to become the focus of that devotion, and then in finding a reader-position from which we can demonstrate and sustain our emotional commitment. The convolutions of my own readings, indeed, may be seen as a testament to the considerable lengths to which the reader can go once her passions have been engaged – although I must also allow for the probable idiosyncrasy of my own strategies and devices.[40] The prevalence of religious discourse in my text reminds us how strongly we are in need of persons/ideals in which to 'believe', and how this discourse is readily incorporated into that of romantic love. The political colouring of this particular reader-emotion will depend, meanwhile, on how the textual other is itself identified/ defined. Whilst the devotion I express towards Lyndall and her 'cause' in Schreiner's novel may be seen as explicitly pro-feminist, for example, the narcissistic devotion to my own romantic script which dominates my reading of *The Piano* could be viewed as the means of avoiding the serious feminist complaints that have been levelled at the film (see discussion following, and Chapter 7). Such apparent differences can, however, be shown to be superficial and misleading. As I shall go on to argue at the end of this chapter (and as I have already anticipated in Chapter 1), it is now my belief that *all* implicated readings, like the ones I describe here, are structurally incommensurate with politically determined readings *per se*, and that the feminist inscription of one's textual other is not, in the last analysis, equivalent to a feminist engagement of the text itself. The cruder implications of this are, indeed, seen in my relationship to the character of Lyndall, which very clearly depends upon her dialogic structuring *vis-à-vis* myself rather than on what she embodies or represents in terms of feminist politics. It is, indeed, because of this that my investment in her is able to survive her own ideological compromise. For textual devotion, like its worldly counterpart, is predicated upon faith, not judgement, and will become wilfully blind in order to protect the 'unique' and 'enigmatic' being who was the source of the first enchantment.

Fulfilment

As I indicated at the beginning of this chapter, there is some dispute about where – in the romance trajectory – we should expect 'fulfilment' to occur. According to the classic *narratives* of romance, it is the resolution we look forward to once all the obstacles have been removed (the 'marriage' which ends the story); but for Barthes (whose *ravissement*/sequel dyad is *without* a happy ending), it is more properly thought of as an expression of *ravissement*: the first appearance of the 'other' (following the empty twilight phase) is received as such a miracle and blessing that the amorous subject feels (temporarily) that s/he wants for nothing. To quote Goethe (Werther): 'I am living through days as happy as those God keeps for his chosen people; and whatever becomes of me, I can never say that I have not tasted the purest joys of life.'[41]

The feeling of fulfilment associated with *ravissement* depends very much on the illusion that time has been suspended: the (improbable) sense that this moment can last forever and consume all others. Thus, going back to his analysis of the importance of 'scene' at the moment of enamoration, we find Barthes writing: 'What is immediate stands for what is fulfilled' (p. 192). This sense of gratification is also a feature of the amorous embrace: one feature, which is admittedly in tension with the erotic 'will-to-possess', but which we might think of as dominating the period of *ravissement* and first encounter:[42]

> Besides intercourse . . . there is that other embrace, which is a motionless cradling: we are enchanted, bewitched: we are in the realm of sleep without sleeping. . . . In this companionable incest, everything is suspended: time, law, prohibition: nothing is exhausted, nothing is wanted, all desires are abolished, for they seem definitively fulfilled . . . A moment of affirmation; for a certain time, though a finite one, a *deranged* interval, something has been successful: I have been fulfilled (all desires abolished by the plenitude of their satisfaction): fulfilment does exist, and I shall keep making it return: through all the meanderings of my amorous history, I shall persist in wanting to rediscover, to renew the contradiction – the contraction – of the two embraces. (pp. 104–5)[43]

This sense of being fulfilled because time has been arrested is not, upon first consideration, one that we would associate with the reading process in which there is such a drive towards 'closure', frustrating any premature satisfaction. If, however, we see the *whole* textual experience as one that involves the suspension of worldly time (the proverbial sensation of being lost in a good book), then maybe the analogy holds – especially with those texts in which the joys of *ravissement* are never (completely) displaced by the pains of sequel (as in my reading of *The Story of an African Farm,* for instance). There is, moreover, an important difference between media in this

respect: whilst (diachronic) 'narrative' is a feature of most artistic production, the visual arts (painting, photography and, to some extent, film) tend
to offer viewing experiences in which the discrete 'scenes' or images which
make up the (narrative) whole possess a notional autonomy.[44] As we wander around an exhibition, for example, we can pause in front of a certain
image, resisting the pressure to move on and through. Films, too, often col-
lude in this particular mode of reader-pleasure, through a range of narrato-
logical devices and special effects (the use of slow motion, for example)
which play up the moment 'out of time'. Whilst different texts and media
may vary in the extent to which they facilitate this freeze-frame reading
practice, however, it could be argued that it is always *possible* to read syn-
chronically and enjoy the (temporary) fulfilment of what Barthes refers to as
the 'deranged interval' (p. 105). This is certainly borne out by all my readings here, with the exception of Winterson's text, which, unlike her earlier
novels (see discussion above), fails to provide any real satisfaction, even of
a temporary kind.

I begin my discussion with an extract from my reading of the Grauerholz
exhibition. The texts which provide the key to my readerly fulfilment in this
case belong to the installation 'Filling the Landscape' (1994), which was the
centrepiece of the exhibition, and which is described in the catalogue thus:

> *Eclogue* or *Filling the Landscape* occupies a square room in which a
> transparent, six-drawer cabinet has been placed, containing more than
> 200 landscape photographs enclosed in 27 cases. A list of related
> words categorizing these photographs is displayed on each case, form-
> ing a kind of poem. The various images suggest parks and gardens –
> both public and private, with and without people – natural and
> groomed landscapes, and representations of water in different forms
> (lake, river, pond, reservoir and canal) . . . As if the lens granted admit-
> tance to forbidden places, Angela Grauerholz considers photography
> in terms of the setting which receives it and which she transforms by
> determining its qualities. In the manner of Jean-Jacques Rousseau, she
> practises the art of collection as inventory. The collection mounted
> according to archival principles is an itinerary. However, collecting is,
> above all, to select – the root meaning of the word eclogue (from the
> Greek *ekloge*, selection). Angela Grauerholz divides landscapes by
> classifying them, placing them into memory so that they remain a per-
> manent reminiscence, a self-reflection. Through a kind of sublimation,
> the artist begins to favour idea over image by concealing something,
> and thus agitating the consciousness. Will the visitor sense the differ-
> ence in the outward appearance of things, in the hidden shimmer of
> photographs, somewhere under the surface appearances? (Catalogue,
> pp. 54 and 53)

How I experienced the 'agitation of consciousness' which Gagnon here presents as part of Grauerholz's conscious design will be dealt with in some

detail in the next chapter. As far as the discussion here is concerned, it is necessary to indicate simply that it was only when we got to Box 3 of the exhibit (the boxes are opened and their contents displayed to visitors by an attendant at certain times every day), did I realize what it was that I had been looking for:[45]

> The third box (No.1), ENTERING THE LANDSCAPE, contains a series of larger photographs, all of which feature figures in the landscape. Even after the first photograph – a group of people (shot from above) file through a narrow trail in a wood – I am excited: this glimpsing of figures in natural landscapes is very evocative to me, though evocative of *what* it is hard to say. The tantalizing nature of the fleeting figure is, of course, enhanced enormously by these special viewing conditions: we never get a chance to lean forward and inspect the text minutely which, paradoxically, seems to increase the sensation of partial 'recognition'. If my experience of this exhibition is conceived in terms of a narrative (romance), then it is clear that, here, I am drawing near to my object(s) of desire and/or moment of *ravissement*. In this respect, moreover, it is important to recognize that this sensation is the product of the conditions of viewing themselves rather than a response to the figures represented. The blurred figure of the older woman who passes through an overgrown garden (gooseberry bushes?) is not, herself, my object of desire, but the manner in which I behold her produces a charged response[46] *(see Illustration 1.3)*. As the images flash by me one after another I think that at any moment I may see her, recognize her – and the fact that I don't makes me think only that the presentation itself was so fast that I missed it. As with reading a literary text, it is the activity of reading itself and the mental spaces/places that it opens up that is more important than what is being read. As we move to the next box I have, in Grauerholz's terms, already 'filled the landscape' with the reflex of my own desire.
>
> Box 4 is entitled WOOD/WALK/NARROWING/SINGULAR/PATH/CURVING/ ENDLESS and the photographs are, once again, much smaller, signifying an increased privacy. The tension here appears to be between the wild and the cultivated landscape: a path through woodland on the one hand, formal gardens on the other (the latter in sharp focus/contrast). Once again, however, I'm most attracted by the images which blur this distinction: the overgrown formal gardens symbolic of a secret past gone astray. This narrative is continued in the fifth box (No. 2) – LANDSCAPE/PERFECT/PICTURESQUE/PRETTY/SEDUCTIVE/BEAUTIFUL/ IDEALIZED/PRIVILEGED/CENTRED – which would seem to be a sequence shot in the grounds of a large house. For myself, connotations of the nineteenth-century novel make this the ideal romance landscape, and having had my expectations whetted by the contents of Box 1 ('ENTERING THE LANDSCAPE'), I am now waiting hungrily for a glimpse of my own

textual other. There are no figures in these photographs, however, just the traces of their past presence in the stone balustrade overgrown with ivy, the stagnant pond, the path through trees. The only living creatures we see are some pigeons in the formal gardens and a cow in tangled undergrowth. There is no question, however, that this is the most provocative box as far as I'm concerned. Now that the conditions of viewing have been established and I know what I'm looking for, these images provide me with the perfect landscape for my own imagination to fill. Indeed, in my imagination the landscape is filled by myself in the process of searching.

Re-reading this commentary in the light of the catalogue entry (which I had not read at the time of the visit), I am amused at how well I have performed in Grauerholz's exercise: the 'ideal' reader/viewer caught in the nets of my own will-to-seduction. What the artist has (unwittingly?) achieved, indeed, is a kind of joke at the expense of both herself and the bourgeois intellectual visitor, in which the latter is unable to resist replicating the former's privileging of 'individual experience' and 'the private life'. No matter how engineered my response might be, however, the 'fulfilment' I experienced upon 'filling the landscape' with my own imaginings *was* powerful (as the reading itself testifies), and meant that I left the exhibition in a heady state of *ravissement*. In terms of the amorous trajectory, this is clearly an instance in which 'fulfilment' is simultaneous with the first rapture and – as I shall explore in the next chapter – the mild anxieties, frustrations and disappointments I experienced in the earlier rooms, may thus be thought of as belonging to the 'twilight state' (preceding *ravissement*) rather than to the 'sequel'. Once I had discovered *how* to gratify my own fantasies *vis-à-vis* Grauerholz's images, moreover, I was able to bring my 'reading' of the exhibition to a satisfying *hermeneutic* closure (the closure of the 'professional' as opposed to the 'implicated' reader) by producing an after-the-event 'interpretation' of the enigmatic *Draped Foot* (1993) (see Illustration 5.4) which was used to publicize the exhibition and provided a descriptive focus for the press:[47]

I would like to say that the key to how these landscapes might be filled with images from Grauerholz's own repertoire was part of the actual viewing experience, but this is not the case. It is subsequently, intellectually, that I have finally been able to make the connection between the fetishized images of the draped foot and the ghostly other I've been stalking . . . From footsteps (literally) to feet . . . But when you look at this image again, which is semiotically overlaid with a multiplicity of images from the history of Western art (not least all those pietàs) you realize that it is narrative as well as *icon*. This foot is the 'missing part', certainly – the truly Freudian fetish – but it is also an embodiment of our own restless search: hence the 'view down' – what we are seeing is our own foot as it strides out before us. Here, then, as throughout the exhibition, the

Illustration 5.4   'How "the search" *becomes* the fulfillment' (Chapter 5)

relationship between the viewing subject and subject in the text is blurred; in Grauerholz's romance trajectory the textual other is, in fact, a fusion (collapse) of self and other as we comply with her instruction and 'fill' the landscape.

On the issue of amorous fulfilment, what I would now add to the above postscript is the equally clear realization that, as far as this reading/viewing event is concerned, the foot is an obvious symbol of how 'the search' *becomes* the fulfilment. *Ravissement*, in this instance, does not depend upon the appearance of an/other, but simply the acknowledgement of who/what one is searching for.

In my discussion of the readerly reflex by which I become the 'author' of *The Piano,* meanwhile, I have already given some indication of where the 'fulfilment' of that textual experience is to be located. By making Campion's characters the 'actors' of my own narrative, I feel the film to function as a romanticized fictionalization of my own emotional history: a representation which is at once cathartic (it helps me 'process' the pain of my own experience) and 'fulfilling'. Like Grauerholz's exhibition, this text confounds the classic romance trajectory in as much as (in *my* reading) it *combines* the '*ravissement*–sequel' narrative (the sub-textual story of Ada's past affair with Delwar Haussler) with that of 'twilight-enchantment' (her relationship with Baines).[48] Meanwhile, because it is the function of this second narrative to dominate and subsume the first (the negative emotions associated with the sequel of the old romance are displaced by the positive ones associated with the new *ravissement*), my *own* textual fulfilment is to be located in those scenes/episodes in which Ada's new life triumphs over the old whilst not denying its (continuing) significance. This thesis is given its clearest, most triumphant expression in the closing sequence, of course, and it was therefore inevitable that, in this viewing of the film (my third), it was the scenes which anticipated this cathartic denouement that afforded me the most emotional gratification.

While the fulfilment offered me by this text therefore originates with my own, highly autobiographical (re)scripting of its ending, it is the connections which the text itself makes between the final sequence and the preceding action that help me identify (and 'fill in') the other moments of affirmation. In other words, it is by the scenes which prefigure Ada's climactic death/resurrection that I am most ravished, most fulfilled.

One of the most visible ways in which the film effects this prefiguration is in its use of acceleration/deceleration devices: the variation in camera speed which would seem to symbolize the tension between Ada's old life (the 'slow-motion' pain and suffering of the 'sequel') and the *coup de foudre* of the new. This tension, and the set of emotions associated with it, is noted in the following extract from my reading:

> The next section of the film, featuring the consummation of Ada and Baines's relationship, is dominated (in my reading) by a polarization

of images: the (accelerated) *escape towards* is countered by the (decelerated) *pull back*. This pattern begins with the shot of Ada plunging through the forest towards Baines's hut (she has made up her mind, and casts off even her daughter in pursuit of her desire). The forest echoes the urgency of her mission through the sound of the wind that sweeps through it. This 'flight towards' seems to me to be the central theme of the musical score also, making this (rather than the consummation scene itself) the climax of the action. It is paralleled and inverted, very obviously, by Stewart's interception and attempted rape of Ada on her way to Baines the next day. In my reading, then, the slow-motion filming symbolizes all the forces that now stand to drag Ada back and down – and although the ostensible agent of this action is Stewart, he can be regarded as an externalization of Ada's own doubts and 'lack of faith'. Will she act upon her newly realized desire and choose Baines, or will she allow her previous failure in love to accept the punishment Stewart (*in loco parentis*) is about to serve on her? To this extent she is still a victim of her past: not because she is still in love with Haussler (her affection has been transferred to Baines), but because she is afraid to trust the chance of the new life that has been offered her.

Something of this forward-upward/backward-downward dynamic is also inscribed in the consummation scene itself. During the crisis moment, after Baines has told Ada to 'go' and she has responded by hitting him furiously, she sinks to the floor – and their love-making begins with him raising her up again (in a movement which anticipates the re-surfacing of her body at the end of the film). This 'resurrection' is accompanied by the return of the music. A notable technical feature of this scene is the illusion of variable camera speed: Baines's attempt to propel Ada out of his house and her angry response to this is achieved by a rapid sequence of edits, but the filming appears to slow down again (i.e. the camera maintains a single point of view) once Ada submits to her own passion and rises up to meet Baines's arms. This 'acceleration' is deployed at a number of other key moments in the film, to which this one – the central transfiguration – of course refers. Other instances include: Stewart's axe striking the ground when he closes his deal with Baines; Baines's first sexual 'assault' of Ada (when he rushes up to her from behind, puts his hand around her neck, and then kisses it); Ada's fourth visit to Baines in which he rips her camisole in a pseudo-rape; Ada's first sight of Baines naked (he suddenly appears from behind the curtain); Stewart's interception of Ada on the way to Baines (though *his* attempted rape is filmed, significantly, in slow-motion); the sequence in which Stewart chops off Ada's finger; the piano rope uncoiling, catching Ada's foot, and pulling her overboard . . . and, finally, her re-surfacing into Baines's arms.

What I now see all these episodes representing – episodes in which time is apparently accelerated – is an 'abandonment of self': an emotional surge which is itself integral to the (sudden and miraculous) 'fulfilment' experienced at the moment of *ravissement*.[49] Although this (self-) 'abandonment' is associated with all the principal characters, not just with Ada, I have chosen to read it as symbolizing the (violent, frightening, but *necessary*) suspension of 'the will' that facilitates her own rebirth. And because, as I have already indicated, my own readerly fulfilment by the text is bound up in this autobiographically driven 'interpretation', all these scenes (culminating in the drowning) become profoundly satisfying and cathartic. I end with my attempt to articulate something of the gratification I find in the film's ending:

> For me, now, all the emotion of this film is concentrated in the final sequence. This ending could not have its impact without what goes before, but its moment of blinding catharsis dominates the whole text. And once you have seen the film before, this is all you are (I am) waiting for: the moment when she dies and is reborn simultaneously; the moment Baines pulls her out of the water and holds her in his arms – probably the most affecting image of the film, with its connotations of birth and pietà. I watch and re-watch this sequence, my throat aching with grief, wondering whether I, too, have really chosen the new life over the old?

If the dislocation of time (Barthes's 'deranged interval') characteristic of amorous fulfilment is anticipated in *The Piano* by a speeding-up of the action, in Schreiner's novel it is characterized by temporal suspension. The episode that I am thinking of here, in particular, is Waldo's leavetaking: the romantic non-climax of the narrative which nevertheless manages to perform that sexual/textual function, despite the fact that the emotional crisis is ambiguously defined. In the following extract I describe my feelings concerning the success/failure of the Lyndall–Waldo relationship, and consider how, sutured into the text as Waldo's surrogate, I achieve vicarious fulfilment in this (romantic) farewell:

> It is true, however, that when I read the book first I craved a simpler romance. I went back to this section – Lyndall and Waldo sitting together in the waggon at the wedding – repeatedly, searching for the alternative script. The episode has all the makings of the classic love-scene: the darkness, the intimacy, the space away from the crowd, Waldo's imminent departure – so why doesn't it happen? In a sense, of course, it *does*. Lyndall tells Waldo that she loves him:
>
> > 'Waldo', she said gently, with a sudden and complete change of manner, 'I like you so much, I love you . . . When I am with you I never know that I am a woman and you are a man; I only know that we are both things that think'. (p. 223)

Unfortunately, such intellectual androgyny is at the expense of passion. It is not love that is lacking in the Lyndall–Waldo relationship, but sex. The collapse of difference signals the end of romance within the heterosexual economy in which Schreiner's text participates. For a feminist and/or non-heterosexual reader, this conservative perception is, of course, especially frustrating; but it does facilitate an easy alignment with Waldo. It is because the sex/gender roles have been so confused in this relationship that romance is impossible. Throughout the text, as we have already seen, it is Lyndall who plays the boy's role; who (literally) *takes the lead.* And she, regrettably (as we will shortly see), can only realize her own sexuality through subservience to a 'masculine' authority. Indeed, she spends her own short life searching for one stronger than herself; one who she might 'submit to' in just the way that we (myself, Waldo) have submitted to her. So our tragedy is this: Lyndall's love – the love that has taken responsibility for Em and Waldo and 'the position of women' – is incommensurate with her own (sexual) desire. This is a hard fact to confront three-quarters of the way through a text, at the point where your own commitment has become unconditional – but it is the fact, nevertheless. This is a love that will never convert to passion.

As with all thwarted romances, however, the 'truth' takes a while to sink in. Indeed, the implications of all this are still far from clear the next morning, when Waldo takes his leave and sets off on his 'quest'. Despite the limits that have now been set upon their relationship, the parting is decidedly ambiguous in romantic terms. Waldo is not, and is never going to be, Lyndall's lover, but at some level she knows (and *we know*) that he *ought to be.* There is a strong resistance to sexual/textual destiny in this scene: it is the crossroads moment at which life might have taken another turn:

> 'So you are ready', she said.
> Waldo looked at her with sudden heaviness; the exhilaration died out of his heart. Her grey dressing-gown hung close about her, and below its edge the little grey feet were resting on the threshold.
> 'I wonder when we shall meet again, Waldo? What you will be, and what I?'
> 'Will you write to me?' he asked of her.
> 'Yes; and if I should not, you can still remember, wherever you are, that you are not alone . . .'
> They stood quiet.
> 'Good-bye!' she said, putting her little hand in his, and he turned away; but when he reached the door she called to him: 'Come back, I want to kiss you'. She drew his face down to hers, and held it with both hands, and kissed it on the forehead and on the mouth. 'Good-bye, dear!'

> When he looked back the little figure with its beautiful eyes
> was standing in the doorway still. (p. 239)

And I, of course, as Waldo's alter-ego, find myself poised with him on
the same threshold, wondering, hoping – even at this late stage –
whether the scales might not suddenly tip otherwise. . . . The possibility hangs in the air, but nothing is resolved: she kisses Waldo on the
mouth, but she also calls him 'dear' – a mark of affection, not desire.
Thus when the chapter ends I (the implicated reader) am dazed, bewildered, yet paradoxically fulfilled. Too many emotions have been
raised and then denied for any of it to make sense. I know that I (like
Waldo) have cemented my contract with Lyndall, but I don't know
what the exact terms of that contract are.

This scene, then, would seem to conform perfectly to Barthes's hypothesis
that the fulfilment of romantic love is best understood as an expression of
the *ravissement* itself: 'when what is immediate stands for what is fulfilled' (p. 192). Although we are told little of Waldo's feelings throughout
the text, my own reading reveals very clearly that we are fulfilled through
the simple expression of our own enamoration: an emotion so overwhelming that it swallows us up, suspending the laws of time and space.
This 'arrest' of the temporal is figured in the text by the references to
'stillness' and 'quiet', characterizing this as Barthes's 'other embrace' (see
quotation earlier, p. 119). This 'blessing', or moment of grace, occurs,
moreover, *despite* the ambiguity and uncertainty in which it swims, thus
re-emphasizing the fact that the pleasures of romance/reading occur gratuitously and are often isolated from the (diachronic) thrust of the narrative
per se. To this extent, indeed, it is probably better to think of *ravissement*
not as the first phase of romance (as implied in its pairing with the sequel)
but as the achronological accumulation of all those moments out of time
when 'the story' (the sequel) is suspended.

The ease with which I appear to occupy Waldo's subject-position in this
farewell scene makes it an exceptionally straightforward fulfilment in reader
terms, with the crisis in interdiegetic action coinciding with my own maximum implication in the text via a shared textual other. Elsewhere in the
reading, my access to this sort of emotional fulfilment is more complicated,
involving me in interlocutory manœuvrings of the kind I have already
described in the section on 'Devotion'. One of the episodes which best illustrates this type of readerly renegotiation is Lyndall's *attempt* to care for
Waldo after his father, Otto's, death:

Lyndall's care of Waldo following Otto's death is, for me, the text's
centre of grace. In a novel weighed down with grief and longing we
are granted this brief spell of beatitude in which Lyndall walks
amongst us, offering up solace and care mixed with the promise of
revenge:

'Come', she said, bending over him, 'I have been looking for you all day. . . .'

'You have had nothing to eat. . . .You must come home with me, Waldo. . . .'

She made him take her arm, and twisted her small fingers among his. . . .

'You must forget. . . . Since it happened, I walk, I talk, I never sit still. . . .'

'There is a candle and supper on the table. You must eat', she said authoritatively. (pp. 85–6)

Lyndall's care, like her relation to the world generally, is marked by her authority. Hers is not a characteristically feminine sympathy made manifest in gestures of consolation and protection (the soothing voice, the mother's arms), but rather the leader's command: 'You must eat' (p. 85). Why this species of care – doubtless unrecognizable as such to some – has so much appeal (to myself) is that it is inscribed with *responsibility*. In the midst of the present crisis has come someone who understands the measure of our affliction: someone who has confronted its extremity, looked it in the eye. And someone who will now tell us what to do next. The blessing of such authority in crisis situations is that it enables us to stop thinking: we can consign ourselves to another to, literally, pull us through. With such a faith in someone's ability to 'know best', there is no limit to what might be borne. And this 'forgetfulness', based on the pragmatic insistence that he return to the present, is precisely what Lyndall offers Waldo on this occasion.

It is significant, however, that it is an offer that Waldo himself rejects. In response to Lyndall's advice that 'forgetting is the best thing' (p. 85), Waldo hisses the apocalyptic 'There is no God!' (p. 86). This, of course, is hardly a 'reply' to what Lyndall has been saying; rather, its *non sequitur* marks the emotional and intellectual distance between them. On this occasion, as in the future, Lyndall protects herself by avoiding the big questions Waldo torments himself with. Where Waldo asks 'why', Lyndall asks what is to be done: 'we must not think so far, it is madness' (p. 231).

Having already invoked Waldo as my alter ego in the text, the next question is: where does his rejection of Lyndall's comfort leave me? Does his refusal to be consoled render void my earlier comments which identified this as the text's moment of grace? Not at all.

Although I might, indeed, feel myself positioned alongside Waldo on account of what I perceive to be similarities in our world views, the most important aspect of the positioning as far as I am concerned is his relation to Lyndall. And it seems that I am able to occupy this relation without necessarily (always/on all occasions) occupying his own emotional field. This is to say that, in the scene I have just discussed, I can accept the care that Waldo rejects. Where he shrugs off Lyndall's offer to take responsibility, screaming 'There is no God', I take her hand and go quietly. And so we see my readerly spirit separate itself from its host and walk away, leaving Waldo and his grief seated on the ground.

The transgressive possibility of *partly* inhabiting a subject position, or of moving in and out of a vicarious 'identity' whilst sustaining the positionality, helps to counterbalance the painful intransitivity of reading that I have alluded to elsewhere. It also, on this occasion, allows myself – as reader – to resist the text's narratorial authority. In response to Waldo's rejection of Lyndall's comfort the narrator opines:

> In truth, is it not life's way? We fight our little battles alone; you yours, I mine. We must not help or find help. When your life is most real, to me you are mad; when your agony is blackest, I look at you and wonder. Friendship is a good, strong stick; but when the hour comes to lean hard, it gives. In the day of their bitterest need all souls are alone. (p. 87)

As part of a broad, humanistic discourse there is 'truth' here that we will all recognize. In other circumstances – indeed, in former readings – I have responded to this unflinching verdict with recognition. But not now, not in this reading, in which I am marking, in particular, the trajectory of my romantic involvement with Lyndall as my textual other. While for the characters in the text (Waldo included) her special qualities are part of their shared history, for me they are the key to my recent *ravissement*. Thus I reject the pessimism of the narrator even as I reject Waldo's failure to be consoled, and should Lyndall offer me her arm I would accept it gratefully.

As in the extract dealing with my readerly positioning in relation to the 'lock-in' scene (see the previous section), this text demonstrates my ability not only to move between interdiegetic subject positions which will provide me with access to the text, but also to inhabit the positioning without the identity which goes with it. Thus, on this occasion, I suture myself into Waldo's role but replace his rejection of Lyndall's care with my own acceptance, hence realizing the fulfilment of my own desires. Although this degree of negotiation might suggest that there are no limits to what the reader might/might not do to achieve her own textual fulfilment, however, I should also anticipate some of the discussion in Chapter 6 by pointing out that the movement in and out of subject-positions is neither always 'voluntary' *nor* in the reader's interest. At the end of Schreiner's novel, for example, I find myself ripped away from Waldo's positioning – the position which enables us (that is, he and I) to sustain our 'devotion' to Lyndall despite her own 'failure' – and cast out into my own (extra-textual) sea of grief in which there is no hope of (textual) consolation. But all this is to anticipate Chapter 6: what this reading has shown is an instance of the creative power the reader has to participate in the more gratifying 'structures of feeling' represented by a text.

As in the case of 'devotion', my readings here reveal that the reader's ability to find emotional satisfaction in a text depends largely on her ability to discover/create a subject position through which she can *enter* it. Perhaps more obvious than in the previous section, however, is the extent to which this participation may involve displacing the interdiegetic action with one's own extratextual projections. In the case of the Grauerholz exhibition and *The Piano,* especially, my sense of emotional fulfilment depends largely upon my becoming 'author' of the text, and using its structures to creatively explore my own self–other relations. This is not a surprising conclusion (any commonsense investigation of our emotional involvement with texts would assume – as does Raymond Williams's naming of the 'structures of feeling' – that there will be a necessary connection between the text and 'personal experience'); but it *does* emphasize the fact that the extent to which the text mediates that experience will vary, and that sometimes the textual component in the dialogue will be very minimal indeed. Grauerholz's photographs are, of course, a superb metaphor for this, illustrating as they do the reader's ability to project enchantment, devotion and fulfilment (for an extratextual 'other') onto an empty landscape.

Conclusion

This chapter has sought to explore some of the ways in which we, as readers, might first 'fall in love' with texts ('enchantment'), and then considers two of the principal emotional configurations associated with the textual *ravissement* ('devotion', 'fulfilment'). The exploration reveals that, as in any romance, it is a relationship which depends upon us first *identifying* an 'other' to whom we are attracted. In terms of the text–reader relationship, this other can be a character in the text (like Lyndall in my reading of *The Story of an African Farm*), a 'textual positioning' (that is, not 'Lyndall' *per se,* but her interlocutory positioning of me as dialogic addressee), an 'author-function' (as in my relationship with the Winterson persona and my usurpation of Campion's directorship) or simply the ('empty') 'scene' of romance (as in the Grauerholz photographs and the Campion film) which we can 'fill' with our own scripts and fantasy projections. Identification with/desire for a humanistically conceived subject is thus only one of the many forms the reader's *textual other* might take; and this is something that has not been given any significant acknowledgement in existing reception theory (see the discussion in Chapter 1).

In most instances there are at least *some* obstacles to our establishing a relationship with this textual other once we have identified who/what it is. A successful *ravissement* thus depends upon our 'entering' or *participating in* the text in some way, and this is achieved through a number of (highly creative) reader-strategies, including character-identification (such as my identification with Waldo in *Story of an African Farm*); subject-positioning which does not involve identification (like my inhabiting Waldo's 'role' in the narrative whilst rejecting his feelings/behaviour); extradiegetic projection (my 'dialogues' with an adult Lyndall in a space 'outside' the text); becoming the surrogate *author* of the text (my rescripting of *The Piano*); and supplying the *subject* of the text (such as my clearancing/re-peopling of both Grauerholz's photographs and Campion's film).

What this (partial) list of strategies suggests, of course, is that the reader has considerable power/freedom in determining her relationship to a text. Once she has identified the prospective 'other' she has a number of means of engaging him or her in 'dialogue', even if this involves some very complex and ingenious manœuvres. In terms of the feminist politics of reading, meanwhile, what my own readings also indicate is the reader's apparent ability to transgress fixed sex/gender roles and inhabit any number of (shifting) 'positionings' in terms of gender and/or sexuality. This discovery sits comfortably alongside the arguments – and textual analyses – of Queer theorists like Judith Butler, though it raises the same questions about identity, choice and commitment that have become the critical focus of much of their work – are we really as 'free' to adopt different (reader) identities as such models seem to allow, and to what extent does such mutability risk slipping back into a non-gendered, transcendent humanism?[50] All this is besides what I feel to be the bigger political question, which I introduce in the chapter itself (and which has been outlined in Chapter 1): namely, the extent to which *implicated readings* of the kind I practise here can ever be thought of as properly feminist (or politically invested in some other way) on account of their particular structural articulation. As I have already suggested, emotion and politics appear to tear apart from one another in most reading events, for the good reason that we (as readers) *cannot read or see both the 'other' and the context in which the other appears simultaneously.*

With respect to the perennial question-mark over the respective roles of text and reader in the production of meaning, meanwhile, this exploration of textual enamoration would seem to place the ball firmly in the reader's court. Once the reader's heart (like Baines's) has 'seized' on its object of desire/devotion, there appear to be few obstacles (to a successful *ravissement*) that cannot be overcome or out-manœuvred.

Such easy thrill and gratification is not, however, the whole story of the reader-romance, even if it is its (notional) beginning. Indeed, as we progress towards the darkening skies of 'the sequel', it could be argued that for amorous readers – as for lovers everywhere – the period of *ravissement* is, by definition, the period of empowerment. For although, as Barthes himself indicates, the lover experiences the initial *coup de foudre* as something that is *done to him* or her, it is s/he who is really the active 'discoverer', 'surprising' the self through the 'surprise' of the 'other' (p. 193). What has characterized all the (positive) emotions associated with sexual/textual enamoration in this chapter, indeed, is that they have their source in the reader/subject's projection onto the other of her desires and fantasies: desires that are identified, processed and fulfilled through the other's simple act of 'being', and which require nothing of the other in return. Not so, of course, 'the sequel', which may be thought of as a new (and newly temporalized) self-other relation, in which the object of desire/devotion (the textual other) is supposed to respond to all that has been invested in him/her. In terms of text–reader relations, this marks a shift from the (comparatively easy) procedure of 'gaining access' to a text (in order that one might show 'devotion' to the other), to waiting to see if the devotion will be reciprocated. The sequel, then, is characterized by the reader/lover's effective *disempowerment* and, as we shall see, all the negative emotions associated with the reading process are really a symptom and an expression of this sense of impotence. It is, indeed (as it is for Barthes's lover), a frankly desperate scenario, in which the reader must wait to discover not only if his or her love/desire is reciprocated, but also if her huge emotional investment in the other (based on such sudden, first impressions!) is to be proved worthy. As many texts fail in this expectation as do lovers; but I take us into the next chapter refusing the assumption that this disillusion will win out, if only because – as we have already seen in my own readings – the heart does not always attend to the narrative trajectories (including Barthes's) that have been written for it, and will sometimes manage to sustain the 'hypnosis' (Barthes) of the first enchantment against all the assaults subsequently levelled at it.

Notes

1 Roland Barthes, *A Lover's Discourse* (see n. 41, Ch. 1). Further page references to this volume will be given after quotations in the text. All Barthes's quotes are from this particular volume unless otherwise stated.

2 See n. 41, Ch. 1 for full references to all these texts. Page references to the Schreiner and Winterson texts will be given after quotations in the text. See n. 17 below for details of the Angela Grauerholz exhibition catalogue.

3 Female/feminist readers may well have problems with Barthes's metaphorical characterization of the *ravissement* as a 'rape'. Many of us feel that because of the very specific suffering it causes to women in the material world, rape should not be used as a trope in this way. The conceit also draws attention to his gendering of love relationships generally, since he observes the classic stereotyped association of passivity (the lover as s/he is swept off her feet) with femininity, meaning that the lover is always typified as female whatever his/her biological sex. Barthes nevertheless mixes the sex of his pronouns throughout *A Lover's Discourse* in a way that certainly does not preclude the possibility of homosexual relations, especially if we assume his 'I' persona is autobiographical (at least in the particular of its gender).

4 'Textual other': see n. 8, Ch. 1 and discussion following.

5 'Classic romance': for a detailed discussion of the formulas of classic romance and the ways in which its scripts have been rewritten, see the Introduction to *Romance Revisited* (see n. 44, Ch. 1), pp. 15–24.

6 'Re-memory': see n. 2, Ch. 1.

7 See Vera Brittain, *Chronicle of Youth: The War Diary 1913–1917* (New York: Morrow, 1982). The diaries offer a moving portrait of Brittain's relationship with Roland Leighton during World War I.

8 Humanism: as I also observed in Ch. 1, the irreconcilable tension between feminist and humanist discourse (with what we think of as 'emotions' situated firmly in the latter) was the first hypothesis I used to explain the apparent impossibility of incorporating affective and political reading practices. I subsequently realized that the problem was one also one of *structure*, as this chapter goes on to show.

9 Jeanette Winterson, *The Passion* (Harmondsworth: Penguin, 1987).

10 'Shock of recognition': see Raymond Williams, n. 33, Ch. 1. Although this is another complex concept, meaning differently in different contexts, it helps to explain the way in which 'structures of feeling' are recognized by individuals as part of their 'lived experience'. See Elspeth Probyn, n. 6, Ch. 1 , pp. 22–3.

11 Jeanette Winterson, *Oranges are not the Only Fruit* (London: Pandora Press, 1985) and *Boating for Beginners* (London: Methuen, 1985). Gore Vidal's pronouncement was reproduced on the back cover of the Penguin edition of *The Passion*.

12 This impression of the media reception of *Written on the Body* was confirmed by the LEXUS-NEXUS computer search I made of all the newspaper reviews written in the year following the novel's publication.

13 See e.g. Pamela Petro (*The Atlantic*, February 1993), who writes, 'Winterson has always been a sorceress with language; her slim books are packed with the stuff of speech and reflection in pure, concentrated form . . . *Written on the Body* is the best evidence yet to support Vidal's claim' (see n. 11 above).

14 'Brontëesque characters': Campion herself cited Emily Brontë's *Wuthering Heights* as a source for *The Piano* in an interview with Jay Carr in *The Boston Globe*, 14 Nov. 1993, and many of the film's reviewers refer to this fact in their analyses (see Ch. 7).

15 'Structures of feeling': see n. 33, Ch. 1.

16 The Angela Grauerholz exhibition was held at the Musée d'Art Contemporain in Montréal from 27 January to 23 April 1995. Full details of the photographs are supplied with the List of Illustrations.

17 Paulette Gagnon, *Angela Grauerholz*, exhibition catalogue: see n. 16 (Musée d'Art Contemporain et Les Publications du Quebec, 1995). Gagnon's catalogue essay is entitled 'Creating Ambiguities of Time and Experience'. Page references to this essay will be given after quotations in the text.

18 'Cultural capital': see n. 28, Ch. 3. When giving talks on this aspect of my research several members of the audience have expressed scepticism at my claim to a lack of 'cultural capital' and have implied that, at very least, I should by now have got over my feelings of insecurity, inauthenticity and a lack of entitlement within the art institution. The whole strength of Bourdieu's formulation, however, is that cultural capital is effectively a 'birthright', which cannot be 'bought' through education and acculturation: indeed, it is precisely that which *cannot* be 'acquired' (to the extent that it seems 'natural').

19 'Implicated reading': for a full discussion of this term see Ch. 1 pp. 28–8.

20 My blindness, complicity and 'turning aside' from the central issues of race and ethnicity in this text may be compared to the responses of some of the readers who participated in my reader-survey in Ch. 8.

21 'Clearancing': my concept is predicated on the practices of the nineteenth-century lairds (many of them absentee English landlords) who evicted tens of thousands of Scots crofters from their homes in order to turn the Highlands over to sheep. During the mid- to late nineteenth century between 50,000 and 60,000 Scots emigrated to Nova Scotia (Canada) alone, and evidence of their sudden and violent departure is to be found in the ruined villages and townships that are spread throughout the Scottish Highlands. I should also add that my choice of this concept is far from gratuitous, since part of my purpose is to *emphasize* the imperiousness of this particular readerly strategy.

22 Another significantly more kitsch, but extremely graphic, way of conceptualizing my reading practice here is a form of 'readerly karaoke', in which I, as author-narrator, assume the leading role in someone else's textual production.

23 Grauerholz's blurred and grainy images are the product of some complex technical procedures aimed at making the fixed (ostensibly atemporal) image 'fluid' and temporal. See Paulette Gagnon's discussion in the catalogue essay (n. 17 above).

24 *Unheimlich*: Freud's term for the 'the uncanny', which encapsulates the particular unease created by the 'homely' and 'familiar' (the 'recognizable') being simultaneously 'alien' and 'unfamiliar'. See entry on the uncanny in Elizabeth Wright's *Feminism and Psychoanalysis: A Critical Dictionary* (Oxford: Basil Blackwell, 1992), pp. 436–40.

25 'Management strategies': although coming from a rather different perspective, this notion of readers controlling and managing their emotional responses to (and investments in) texts echoes some of the conclusions of Norman Holland in *The Dynamics of Literary Response* (see n. 9, Ch. 1). See especially ch. 4 of this volume.

26 *La Bibliothèque* and *La Bureau* will be considered in more detail in Ch. 6.

27 See my discussion of the significance of direct speech and intonation in my reading of *Wuthering Heights*, in *Reading Dialogics* (n. 4, Ch. 1), pp. 121–48.

28 This 'artificiality' is commensurate with Bakhtin's category of 'stylization', one of his four types of doubly voiced speech (see n. 8, Ch. 4).

29 The text here is from Jane Campion and Kate Pullinger's 'book of the film', *The Piano* (New York: Hyperion, 1994). Page references to this volume will be given after quotations in the text.

30 'Author-function': see Michel Foucault's 'What is an author?' in Donald F. Bouchard (ed.), *Language, Counter-Memory, Practice*, trans. Donald F. Bouchard and Sherry Simon (Ithaca, NY: Cornell University Press, 1977).

31 The interpolation of religious and romantic discourse is also manifest in the texts of many of Jackie Stacey's respondents in *Star Gazing* (see n. 19, Ch. 1). See especially pp. 142–5 on 'worship'.

32 'Fetishization': my use of this term is intended to *evoke* the full Freudian connotations (the overdetermination of an object as a phallic substitute, hence mitigating the fear of castration), whilst starting from the more everyday usage of a more simple over-valuation, objectification and 'othering'. Whilst the Freudian connotation will have different implications for male and readers in terms of gender, meanwhile, it is impossible to generalize what those might be, since (as the variable positioning in this chapter so aptly demonstrates) the text–reader relationship is not fixed in terms of either gender or power.

33 'Authentic realism': see n. 35, Ch. 1.

34 'Recruited': the concept employed by Louis Althusser to describe the way in which individuals are *interpellated* by ideology. See n. 25, Ch. 4.

35 Although on first consideration it might seem fantastic and improbable that we, as readers/viewers, can *ever* become the subjects/objects of a *text's* 'desire', certain positionings might well give us that illusion: see the discussion of my interlocutory positioning 'by Lyndall' (via Waldo) below, pp. 128–31.

36 'Chronotopic': the chronotope is Mikhail Bakhtin's concept for the 'intrinsic connectedness of temporal and spatial relations'. See my *Reading Dialogics* (n. 4, Ch. 1), p. 67.

37 'Collection of semes': see Roland Barthes, *S/Z*, trans. Richard Miller (New York: Hill and Wang, 1974): 'The person is no more than a collection of semes (inversely, however, semes can migrate from one figure in the text to another, if we descend to a certain symbolic depth, where there is no longer any respect of persons: Sarrasine and the narrator have semes in common)' (p. 191).

38 My own 'bird's-eye' relationship to this text was, of course, prompted in part by Stuart Dryburgh's camera-work, which repeatedly shows characters and landscape from 'a seat in the clouds'.

39 'Dream text': see Freud's *The Interpretation of Dreams, Standard Edition of the Complete Psychological Works of Sigmund Freud*, trans. and ed. by James Strachey (London: Hogarth Press, 1953–73), vol. 4. According to Freud's theory, dreams are 'the guardians of sleep', and the unconscious invokes strategies like condensation and displacement to protect the dreamer from things *too* potentially disturbing.

40 As I observed in the Preface to Part II, the idiosyncrasy of my own readings – directed towards a particular intellectual exercise, and working within a very specific trope/discourse – has to be acknowledged. However, it is also my belief, as already stated, that readers of all kinds, in all circumstances, engage in processes of similar ingenuity and 'management' (see n. 25 above) even though these may not be brought to full consciousness.

41 'Werther': the romantic hero of Goethe's *The Sorrows of Werther*, a classic romance text which is a repeated point of reference for Barthes's own meditations in *A Lover's Discourse* (see n. 41, Ch. 1). See especially p. 119.

42 'Will-to-possess': see *A Lover's Discourse* (n. 1), pp. 232–4. Here the strength of this conceit is explained through the (rhetorical and psychological) impossibility of its inversion: the 'non-will-to-possess'.

43 Barthes's model here is, of course, thoroughly conservative and (hetero)sexist, assuming as it does that intercourse is at the centre of all sexual relations and that all non-penetrative (and non-arousing?) erotic or sensual encounters are implicitly incestuous.

44 Diachronic/synchronic: linguistic concepts originating in the work of Ferdinand de Saussure, which contrast ongoing, 'chronological' ('diachronic') time with the ('synchronic') 'moment in time'.

45 The viewing arrangements for the contents of the 'Eclogue' cabinet were very specific. At a fixed time on certain days a curator was available to open the boxes and display the photographs, but under clear instruction to control the speed of the presentation (viewers were not allowed to study individual photographs for longer than a few seconds). The presentation was also random: boxes were not opened in any particular order, hence the 'double-numbering' in my readings (the order in which I saw the boxes/their own numbering).

46 Although it is obviously impossible to reproduce any of these 'hidden' images, certain photographs in the cabinet were either reproductions or variations on those mounted in the main exhibition. This particular image (of the ghostly woman in the bushes) was very similar (if not identical) to *Disparation* (see Illustration 1.3).

47 See Ann Duncan, review of Angela Grauerholz exhibition, *The Gazette* (Montréal: 28 January 1995), p. J2.

48 According to the story as it is told in 'the book of the film' (see n. 28 above), Ada's former relationship was with her former music teacher, Delwar Hausser, who was also Flora's father. After finally seducing Ada (through protracted sessions at the piano, of course!) Hausser disappeared.

49 'Abandonment of self': according to Barthes (see n. 41, Ch. 1) this sensation
   (otherwise conceived as 'engulfment') is intrinsic to the *ravissement*: 'This is how
   it happens sometimes, misery or joy engulfs me, without any particular tumult
   ensuing: nor any pathos: I am dissolved, not dismembered; I fall, I flow, I melt'
   (p. 10).

50 See Judith Butler's *Bodies that Matter* (London and New York: Routledge,
   1993) and my discussion of some of the problems associated with the consequences of Queer theory in Ch. 7 of *Feminist Readings/Feminists Reading* (n. 35,
   Ch. 1).

6

The Emotional Politics of
Gendered Reading II:
The 'Sequel'

The 'sequel' is the long train of sufferings, wounds, anxieties, distresses, resentments, despairs, embarrassments, and deceptions to
which I fall prey, ceaselessly living under the threat of a downfall
which would envelop at once the other, myself, and the glamorous
encounter that first revealed us to each other.

(Barthes, *A Lover's Discourse*, pp. 197–8)[1]

Cassie looked over at Rona. Rona was staring into the middle distance, the butt-end of a smile left on her face. A book flopped open on
her skirt, pages riffling. Cassie shifted from one buttock to another,
full of redundant energy. It was no good. Cranking up conversation
about the book was a non-starter. Rona hadn't read the bloody thing,
and anyway, ordinary conversation wouldn't do. Cassie didn't feel
ordinary. She felt fired up, needing to know what was true. Own fault
though. You made the choice to read, you lived with the consequences. Alone. You were on your own whatever happened to you
and as a result it was your own fault.

(Janice Galloway, *Foreign Parts*, p. 134)[2]

However various the tumult of feelings associated with the first throes of
love, the nuances of emotion associated with the 'sequel' are well known to
be infinite. All romantic involvement – whether requited or unrequited –
brings with it a vast sea of anxiety which is manifested in a variety of emotional reflexes. The high cost of *ravissement* is also a feature of the readerly
romance; and here, too, it sometimes seems unfair that we are obliged to
'pay' for something which *appeared* to happen to us involuntarily (see discussion at the end of Chapter 5). Yet these are terms and conditions that
most readers are familiar with, covertly at least. Like Cassie, the character
in Janice Galloway's novel quoted above, we learn to accept that our commitment to books, as to people, brings with it a chain of emotional consequences that we must be prepared to face up to on our own. Despite her

efforts to get Rona to share her readerly experiences with her, Cassie knows that discussion will only partly help to alleviate the tension between herself and her chosen texts. The struggle, ultimately, is between her and them; and, as in any emotional involvement, she has first to overcome the resentment towards the thing that made her so vulnerable: the (textual) other to which she has opened her heart.

Infinitely subtle and various as the emotions associated with the sexual/textual sequel are, however, the constraints of *this* textual space mean that I am able to consider only a few of them. The four that I have finally selected – anxiety, frustration, jealousy and disappointment – do, nevertheless, embody associated others. Anxiety, for example, incorporates some significant variants such as 'suspense', 'panic' and 'fear of abandonment' by the other. 'Disappointment', meanwhile, is another important emotional hub, existing in dynamic relation to 'despair' on the one hand and 'disillusion' on the other. How such precise distinctions manifest themselves in terms of the text–reader relationship is the focus of the discussion which follows.

Anxiety

Anxiety is intrinsic to the amorous condition. As soon as the subject realizes that the 'other' who has so miraculously 'revealed' him- or herself might, at any time, and for any reason, once again disappear, *angoisse* sets in. And whilst this anxiety might mutate into different forms at different stages of the relationship, the psychic fear upon which it is predicated – the thing that we want most will be taken away – is never erased, even (especially?) in situations where love is requited and promises made.

The first textual expression of such anxiety that I wish to deal with here is that associated with *waiting*. Although in Barthes's own 'scenography' this particular torture is firmly located in the latter stages of a relationship (when the beloved's behaviour is only too well-known!), it is also interesting to mark its presence in the 'twilight phase' (before *ravissement* occurs) and to recognize how the feelings of fear and (expected) loss are prepared for even *before* the other is identified, in the sense, 'I know that as soon as I find you I must live in danger of losing you again'.[3] In the scenography associated with the already-committed lover, meanwhile, Barthes offers a graphic description of how the anxiety associated with waiting can become so all-consuming that the subject loses all sense of him- or herself and his/her ability to 'act':

> Waiting is an enchantment: I have received *orders not to move*.
> Waiting for a telephone call is therefore woven out of tiny unavowable interdictions *to infinity*: I forbid myself to leave the room, to go to the toilet, even to telephone (to keep the line from being busy); I suffer tor-

ments if someone else telephones me (for the same reason); I madden
myself by the thought that at a certain (imminent) hour I shall have to
leave, thereby running the risk of missing the healing call, the return of
the Mother. All these diversions which solicit me are so many wasted
moments for waiting, so many impurities of anxiety. For the anxiety
of waiting, in its pure state, requires that I be sitting on a chair within
reach of the telephone, without doing anything. (pp. 38–9)

Barthes's 'explanation' of the psychosis of waiting is self-consciously psychoanalytic (our immobilization replicates our infant dependency, when so
much of our time is spent waiting for the mother to 'return'); but it could
also be argued that waiting is a culturally encoded (in)activity, in which the
sufferings of the lover replicate the suffering of all those rendered *passive*, if
only temporarily, such as job applicants or people awaiting medical attention or legal jurisdiction. The agony of waiting, in these instances, is predicated upon a power-imbalance that is social and economic rather than
psychic; and I would argue that the waiting endured by the romantic lover
(especially in terms of its gendered and historical specificity) is thus
informed by cultural as well as psychoanalytic discourse. The fact that
Barthes's own illustration associates the agony with powerful 'interdictions'
(not to move, not to give our attention to anything else) can be directly associated with the 'conditions' of waiting in the public realm, for example. He
registers something of this, of course, when he genders his 'waiting' lovers
feminine, regardless of their actual sex ('a woman waits for her lover, at
night, in a forest', p. 37); but – as we shall see – it is important to register
just how many of the 'negative' emotions associated with the sequel have
their discursive origins in the cultural inequalities of gender difference, as
well as in the psychoanalytic models of 'desire' and 'loss'.

The *degree* of suffering that attends waiting would seem to depend,
moroever, on just how powerless the subject feels before the loved object.
As her confidence in herself (and her powers to win/keep the beloved)
diminishes, so, too, will the agony increase. According to this scale, the anxiety of waiting can thus range from a vague restlessness, through an (active)
search that, becoming desperate, culminates in the immobilizing fear of
total abandonment (usually figured as the 'death' of the other: see Barthes,
A Lover's Discourse, p. 38). This cline of anxiety is, moreover, readily
transferrable to the text–reader relationship, where the distresses of the
sequel are closely bound up in fluctuations of power, as the following analysis will show.

In some respects my reader-experience of Winterson's *Written on the
Body* could be said to be wholly consumed by the anxiety of waiting for the
missing (textual) other of my memory/expectations to (re)appear.[4] Although
I do not bring this point forward to full consciousness in my re-memory of
the novel, my approach to this new Winterson text was clearly attended by
considerable nervousness. Amidst all the negative publicity, it is obvious

that I had my own gnawing doubts about whether my 'Winterson' would come back to me, though what the following extract reveals is my determination to overcome this loss of faith:

> Having been 'prepared' by the press reviews for the so-called 'genderless narrator', this aspect of the reading process was not the obstacle for me it might have been.[5] My briefing, as I remember, even included the information that women tended to read the narrator as female, while men assumed 'him' to be male. For those wishing to make a lesbian reading of the text, moreover, the choice was obvious. And so did I, too, begin with this pre-determination – brushing aside the problems of Lothario's blatant inscription by heterosexual codes of behaviour (whatever his or her sex) in the early pages of the book. How I made the text work for me, as I remember it now, was by meeting its tendency towards humanist abstraction head-on. I willingly embraced all the aphoristic statements on love, desire, the fear of loss, and downgraded the specificities of history, culture, gender. For many critics, this was exactly what Winterson intended us to do (was the whole point of refusing to fix the narrator's sex), and was what a good deal of them (notably the feminists) criticized her for.[6] One side of my brain clearly entertained the same doubts and anxieties (I quickly realized it would be difficult to make a positive materialist-feminist reading of the text, for example!), but my commitment to Winterson was such that I was prepared to play the game of 'willing suspension'. Thus as soon as the narrative came to focus on Louise as an idealized love-object and to lose all pretensions to contextual specificity I became more comfortable. There was much here that could be read as a continuation/re-inscription of the discourses of the earlier novels: the absolute, essential, intransigent nature of 'true love' set against the freaks of bodily mortality and time.

As some of my discussions in Chapter 5 will already have demonstrated, the effort I put into quelling the anxieties which surrounded my first reading of the text was distinctly lacking when I came to re-read it for the purposes of this project. The 'I' who approached the text in 1992 clearly had enough faith in her power as a reader (and in her commitment to 'Winterson') to believe that the text could be *made* to satisfy her expectations, and my re-memory suggests that this defence is precisely what I *did* achieve, via my humanist realignments and my theory (see Chapter 5) that the 'Winterson' novels are best regarded as a textual continuum. By the time of my re-reading, however, all such conviction has disappeared, and anxiety predicated upon hope is replaced by the fear (certainty?) of disappointment. Despite this new scepticism, however, it is interesting to see that part of me is still waiting for the old 'Winterson' to return – with my text scrambling desperately to explain her disappearance, and think of (textual) places where she might yet be found:

Coming back to the novel after a short break, I suddenly realize my point of emotional contact with the Winterson *oeuvre* and understand why this text partly succeeds, partly fails, in its interpellation of me.[7] Unlike my experience of the Schreiner novel where my involvement was very much mediated through characters to whom I related, my dialogue here is with the author-narrator herself: the mouthpiece identity that – for all my poststructuralist training – I trace back to an originatory 'Jeanette Winterson'. Although what I'm talking about technically is probably some version of the 'implied author', I need also to acknowledge the fact that the Winterson text is very much bound up with the Winterson *intertext*: the interviews, the reviews, the gossip – the preaching.[8]

In this first section of *Written on the Body* my sense of the Winterson narrative-persona is patchy. Despite the fact that Lothario speaks almost continually in the aphorisms that are the mark of his narration, only sporadically is their sentiment spiked with the irony and quirkiness that I have come to associate with the Winterson persona. In Bakhtinian terms, it is a classic instance of hearing two types of speech struggle for control.[9] Mostly what I'm hearing here is Lothario aping Winterson (Bakhtin's category of *stylization*); occasionally it is 'Winterson' herself, for example: 'Nevertheless, it wasn't the terrorism that flung us apart, it was the pigeons . . .' (p. 22). And why is this 'Winterson' and not the other? Because it catches my own humour in a conspiratorial 'hidden dialogue': a positioning that is cultural, historical – and not, it must be said, contaminated by Lothario's (hetero)sexualized innuendo.[10] What it comes down to, then, is this: the narratorial voice that provides me with access to the text's 'structures of feeling' is the one that is somehow in dialogic conspiracy with me: this, if anything, is what 'Winterson' has meant for me.[11]

Through this hastily conceived account of who/what I have related to in previous Winterson texts, I temporarily revive the hope that the missing textual other of *Written on the Body* might yet be found. This other, I speculate (loosely identified, here, as the text's 'implied author'), could be lurking *behind* the principal narrator (Lothario), waiting to (re)emerge, or be (re)discovered?, at a crucial moment. As it is, this dim hope is never realized, and the thesis upon which it is predicated disappears from my text: at some point in the reading I – the 'abandoned' reader/lover – will have given up and stopped waiting for 'my' Winterson to return. Although this moment of final reader-renunciation does not declare itself in my reading, the associated grief and pain find their expression obliquely in my account of the text's ending:

I read the final section of the novel in a single sitting, without making notes or attempting to carve it up into sections for closer analysis. This was facilitated by the fact that it has a unity that the first section lacks, both temporal (it follows the chronological passage from March–October when Lothario begins his/her search for Louise) and in terms of its 'structure of feeling'. At last Lothario's guilty bragging abates, and the focus settles – gets serious. At this point the rhetorical angst about love and sex – how to distinguish one from the other, how to *prove* the latter, how to know the real thing from its shadow – give way to the simpler rhythms of possession and loss, presence and absence. Despite the text's hysterical insistence on the materiality of the lover's body, we see it evaporate – amid rising doubt and panic – into thin air. Thus the text wheels dizzyingly, via Lothario's deranged consciousness, around all the spaces/places Louise might be, *but is not*. The nature of the loss is also defined by the provisionality which surrounds it and which is made part of the plot: the assumption is that Louise is still alive *somewhere*, and that (with effort) she may be found. At the point Lothario begins his active search of her, however, the latter becomes less certain, and the growing panic he suffers as a consequence is an effective dramatization of a key ingredient in all mourning. None of us, it seems, is able to register the permanence of physical loss very easily; it is difficult to adjust to the fact that someone isn't there any more when they remain alive and kicking in your unconscious. As Lothario observes *vis-à-vis* the death of another friend:

> When I recovered from her death in the crudest sense I started to see her in the streets, always fleetingly, ahead of me, her back to me, disappearing into the crowd. I am told this is common. I see her still, though less often, and still for a second I believe it is her. (p. 155)

What the final section of this novel enacts, then, is two contradictory emotional pulls. On the one hand there is an accelerating search for the missing object, which may be thought of as the horizontal axis. On the other hand, there is the downward pull of certainty that she is gone (the vertical axis). ('The more I know it to be true, the more desperately I search').

Unable, it seems, to articulate my own loss (of 'Winterson'), I let the text do it for me. In the same way that Lothario waits for Louise, so do I wait for 'Winterson'. Both of us have kept up the search long after we know it to be 'hopeless', and both of us share the mourner's inability to accept that 'it' (this life, this romance) is finally over.

The Story of an African Farm is another text in which the anxiety of the reader's 'waiting' is given dramatic expression by the action of the text itself.[12] Waldo's separation from Lyndall, which climaxes in his return to the farm and the unfinished letter, is the conduit for my own anxiety that 'she' might be lost to both of us:

> So I grew miserable; a kind of fever seemed to eat me; I could not rest, or read, or think; so I came back here. I knew you were not here, but it seemed as though I should be nearer to you; and it is you I want – you that the other people suggest to me, but cannot give. (p. 285)

The intensity of Waldo's suffering here, as his anxiety moves from 'restlessness' to 'immobilization', replicates my own reader-panic that the character in which I have invested so much is not only missing but irreplaceable. As I speculate earlier in the reading:

> Having entrusted herself to a textual character to the extent that I now trust in Lyndall, the reader is in a position of unprecedented vulnerability. I am less than half way through the text and the woman I have committed myself to has not yet reached adolescence. If she changes, if she turns out to be 'less' than I hoped, I am doomed to pain and disappointment. If she is destined to suffer, it follows that I must suffer too. Worst, if she forms attachments that usurp my own relation to her I will feel betrayed.
>
> And how should I avoid any of these things? In the text, as in the material world, time marches on. Identities are provisional. Relationships change. The particular configuration of semes with which I fell in love cannot be set in stone. As Lyndall grows, so will she become something other . . . Thus I am betrayed not by her but by the impossible conditions of my own desire.

The feelings of 'betrayal' and 'disappointment' which are also part of this reading experience I will deal with later. What is important, here, is simply the realization of the acute anxiety the sequel brings with it: the fact that we (as amorous readers) are destined to wait helplessly/hopelessly for the moment of *ravissement* (and the 'first embrace') to return.

It is at this point that I, the reader, need to come clean and explain that Waldo's letter was the moment when, in terms of my *implicated* reading of the text, Schreiner's novel exploded before my eyes. Despite the fact that I had, by this point, already prepared the rationalization for how my 'devotion' to Lyndall could be preserved intact and the period of readerly *ravissement* extended (see Chapter 5), Waldo's expression of 'anxiety in its pure state' (Barthes, p. 38) blasted me through the textual frame to an existential world in which I, too, was waiting for the irreplaceable one who will never return:

> But all this is to run ahead, and in its explanation – its rationalization – to seriously cheat on the matter of this text's emotional impact on me. For my re-reading of Schreiner's novel on this occasion – notwithstanding my preparatory re-memorying, and despite the academic purposes towards which this exercise is directed – has proved a tortured undertaking. The quotation cited above, for example [Waldo's], made me literally cry out when I first re-encountered it: the emotional ambush

of a phrase I had long forgotten: *'you that the other people suggest to me but cannot give . . .'*

How to write about the experience now is, of course, another problem. Having already prepared the rational explanation for my recuperation of Lyndall at the end of the text, how do I now present the pain that tears apart from this romantic closure? Alignment with Waldo's subject-position (the position that preserves Lyndall as a feminist heroine) comes at a cost. His success at producing her as the 'ideal reader' of his own text is simultaneously undercut by the realization of her loss as it is announced by Em:

> 'I am very helpless, I shall never do anything; but you will work, and I will take your work for mine. Sometimes such a sudden gladness seizes me when I remember that somewhere in the world you are living and working. You are my very own; nothing else is my own so. When I have finished I am going to look at your room door –'.

> 'Waldo, dear,' she [Em] said, putting her hands on his, 'leave off writing.'

> He threw back the dark hair from his forehead and looked at her.
> 'It is no use writing any more,' she said.
> 'Why not?' he asked.
> She put her hand over the papers he had written.
> 'Waldo,' she said, 'Lyndall is dead'. (pp. 286–7)

What this scene, of course, represents on a psychic level is the realization of our greatest fears: the moment when we recognize that all our sexual/texual waiting really has been in vain and all our anxiety justified. As Barthes writes: 'I have just shifted in a second from absence to death' (Barthes, p. 38). In terms of my own reading experience, moreover, this was the moment not only when anxiety converted to despair, but when I said goodbye to the text and its characters to confront my own private grief and loss:

> But to explain all this is to slide away, once again, from the express nature of my own positioning at this crisis moment. In my original notes I wrote this:

> > Impossible. What a text to have chosen. I was doing fine until p. 285, thinking what an excellent text this was in its analysis of the alienation of labour (Waldo's letter) . . . But then the bombshell. The devastating moment of 'truth' that I had forgotten lurked here. Waldo's truth. My truth. The truth of the heart that mocks all our future stabs at life: *'it is you I want —you that the other people suggest to me but cannot give.'*

This entry continues with another page or so of more personal confession that it is not necessary to disclose. It is enough, here, simply to register that the source of the bombshell is an explosive configuration of the textual with the extratextual. Thus I conclude my notes with the observation:

> At this stage in the reading process I am very outside the text. In the split second I become Waldo (i.e. adopt his subject position), I also escape and fly away. I am in my own deep corner now, he in his – just as the text has warned me (Schreiner, p. 86).

What is interesting here is the way in which the splitting of myself from Waldo replicates what happened earlier in the text, though with very different consequences (see Chapter 5, pp. 114–16). Where before I was able to voluntarily separate myself from Waldo's grief in order to accept Lyndall's comfort, here I am torn away from him by what *feels* like an involuntary reflex. Although I am still inhabiting Waldo's 'structure of feeling' (it is this, after all, that has brought about the crisis) I am no longer suffering it through him. Indeed, both he *and* Lyndall have disappeared from view, and I am left wailing in an empty space somewhere between the text and the world. And the pain is such that it stops my reading, puts an end to all textual engagement. This is the moment the book falls from your hands and you crawl away to your bed or some other primitive space to finish the thing off on your own: not the story, but its catharsis.

And it was because this moment, the end of Waldo's unfinished letter, was so much the end of my own personal trajectory through this text that I had problems – on this reading at least – with the subsequent chapters. Despite the fact that Lyndall is the vicarious object of desire upon which all this emotion has been levied, her part in *my* reading stops at this point, first, because I have (through Waldo's positioning of her as the 'ideal reader') brought my own romantic investment in her to a successful closure, and second, because through the conduit of Waldo's own simultaneous loss of that ideal I have been catapulted out of the text into a private grief that the text can never solve (despite the narrator's efforts to offer just this sort of philosophical comfort in Chapters 13 and 14).

I want to move on now to consider some of the forms reader-anxiety can take other than that associated with waiting for the textual other to (re)appear. The most significant of these, in terms of the readings I have performed here, is the anxiety associated with the pressure for a professional – and 'political' – interpretation of the text. Whilst such a perspective cannot be easily integrated into my implicated readings (for the reasons outlined at the end of Chapter 5), this classic demonstration of 'reader-guilt' nevertheless lurks in the margins of my texts.[13] The anxiety here, that the text you have implicated yourself in will turn out to be incompatible with the moral and political values you elsewhere subscribe to, may thus put serious pressure on the 'I–thou'/text–reader relationship, by questioning their worthiness. The obvious analogy within the romance narrative is with the anxiety caused by parental disapproval: a pressure which may jeopardize the romance by undermining the status of the textual other *and* by destroying the rarefied 'scene of romance' (see Chapter 5). As the prospective *author* of a text advertising itself as 'feminist' (that is, espousing a particular political ideology), it is true to say that *all* the readings I undertook for the purposes of this project were overlaid with this anxiety – and with a degree of self-consciousness that would not necessarily attend my non-professional textual engagements.

As some of the extracts from my reading in Chapter 5 will have already revealed, my emotional relationship with both Winterson's *Written on the Body* and Campion's *The Piano* had to be forged amidst very public debates on the feminist 'legitimacy' of both texts.[14] The fact that I subsequently yielded to *ravissement* by one and not the other thus raises some interesting questions about how political reader-anxieties can or cannot be overcome: why was I consistently able to repress a critical feminist reading of *The Piano*, for example, when my complaints against Winterson's text surface on every other page? Was it because Winterson's text really *is* more politically 'suspect' (something I doubt), or simply because, as in all romance, a successful enamoration will cause us to suspend such judgement (temporarily at least)?

The ease with which I lose and displace my anxieties over *The Piano* is certainly a striking feature of the reading, with most of my doubts consigned to parentheses. Despite the fact that, in the following extract, I admit to a certain anxiety with regards to Baines's behaviour ('a state of tense suspension'), I am clearly happy on this, my third reading, to accept my own rationalization of why his abuse of Ada 'becomes' acceptable:

> The other major obstacle that I have had to contend with – and which has been *the* issue for most feminists dealing with the film – has been the sexual conquest at its heart: the dilemma that, in the mid-1990s, we are back with a text so pro-Freudian that 'no' does indeed mean 'yes'.[15]
>
> My memory of dealing with this uncomfortable fact on first viewing was a desperate scramble of my theoretical resources to frame Baines's 'purchase' of Ada's body/heart in such a way that it would be politically acceptable. Although I do not remember sharing the problematic erotic pleasure that some of my friends have talked about in their viewing of the protracted strip-tease of Ada's body, I clearly felt enough investment (implication) in the film – even at this point – to want *not* to disengage with it because of political principles. What I remember is being in a state of tense suspension regarding Baines: ready to judge him/dismiss him, but reluctant to do so. Once Ada reciprocates, moreover, the political tension is resolved: I, along with thousands of others, seem to have been quite prepared to accept that 'no' did indeed mean 'yes', and that

because it did, Baines's very *unacceptable* behaviour is somehow made magically acceptable.

This is, in many ways, another devious reader-manoeuvre. By rationalizing my reading in terms of my own 're-writing' of the script I quickly close the doors on other, less palatable readings, implying that because quasi-objective 'interpretation' is not my objective I somehow have the 'right' to make the reading I do. This is, however, a spurious liberalism, because – as I am well aware – the (poststructuralist) 'belief' that we can make *many readings* of a text does not alter the fact that feminists should be commited to making feminist readings, or, at very least, to presenting them alongside the other possibilities. Something of this 'conscience' *does* find its way into the following extract (inspired by Baines's predatory encirclement of Ada as she plays the piano on the beach); but its lack of serious commitment is, once again, denoted by the parentheses in which it is confined:

> (In the midst of this reverie, I am brought up short: suddenly realising to *what extent* I am writing the script of what I see/want to see. With a pang of conscience I am aware of the fine Marxist-feminist reading I would once have made of this text, seeing in it quite other 'structures' to the affective ones I now indulge. This, after all, is a text which offers its heroine some very narrow choices: she exists, materially, as an object of exchange between her father and three men (her former lover, Stewart and Baines), and her piano is most literally interpreted as a symbol of sublimated (hetero)sexual desire. The reading I have thus been performing up to this point works only if this political critique is wilfully suspended or, at least, if caveats are imposed. My suggestion that Ada's desire is somehow 'in excess' of sexual desire is a classic example of the latter, and a for-mula that I have invoked in my earlier writings.[16] All in all, however, it would seem that my emotional engagement with this text depends upon the same sort of 'de-contextualization' that I felt most uneasy about in the readings of Pre-Raphaelite paintings).

All that this transitory anxiety reveals in this instance, however, is how easily it is overcome. This is not to say that in a different writerly context, amongst a different set of interlocutors, I would not feel obliged to make a more serious feminist engagement with the text, but that on *this* occasion my interpellation by the ideology of romance *has* been at the expense of a more material politics. In terms of the structural incompatibility of impli-cated and hermeneutic reading discussed at the end of Chapter 5, mean-while, it is very striking how this has worked to my advantage. The parentheses illustrate perfectly my inabilility to perform the two types of reading simultaneously (cf. my analyses of other readers in Chapter 8), even if my meta-conscious explanation of that 'failure' still focuses on discourse rather than structure.

When I look back over my re-reading and re-memory of the Winterson text, meanwhile, it is clear that the 'disappointment' I blame on its problematic politics was not preceded by much anxiety *per se*. This is because, at the time of my first reading, I was (as I confess) still 'too much in love' with 'Winterson' to admit the possibility of impediments, while by the time of the re-reading (for this project) serious disillusion had set in: a form of readerly *disenchantment*, which I looked to my feminist politics to explain. The fact is, however, that an increased political consciousness (conscience?) alone cannot be blamed for the end of this particular reader-relationship; nor do I regard this particular *text* as the significant turning point in Winterson's career. What had changed, between 1992 and 1995, was rather my own frame of emotional reference, with the consequence that my dialogue with 'Winterson' finally ceased. As I record in my re-memory:

> Without question, this text was the beginning of the end of my special relationship with 'Jeanette', though it would take a while (perhaps until now) for me to fully acknowledge it. At this point, at least, she ceased to be my prophet and mediator – but maybe that's because I no longer needed her to be? There have been profound changes in my own personal life between *Sexing the Cherry* (1989) and this publication, and a new set of interlocutory relations have opened up for me . . .[17]
>
> I feel considerable sadness and loss to acknowledge this, even now, but it does make my emotional response to *Written on the Body* all the more interesting. What does it feel like to *fake* emotion as a reader? What does it mean to face up to the fact you're faking? And how do you rationalize the loss of feeling? What criteria of discrimination and criticism might I, or might I not, reach for? What I am attempting to acknowledge – to be honest about before I start – is that the 'failure' of this novel for me never was, and never will be, purely textual. Whatever the criticisms of the reviewers might have been based on, I am recognizing that the shift in my own allegiance is not the responsibility of text and author alone.

While I will return to the issue of 'fake emotion' later in the chapter, what this attempt at readerly candour would seem to confirm (in my own instance at least) is that our relationships to texts are so profoundly tied up with changes in our own dialogic identity (who/what constitutes our present interlocutory 'other') that its success or failure (emotional and/or political) will *never* be the responsibility of the text alone. To this extent, it is perhaps fair to say that our textual others are *always* in competition with extratextual others (whether 'intimates' or members of various interpretive communities: see Chapter 8), even though the conditions necessary for a successful readerly *ravissement* requires us to pretend otherwise. To return to Barthes, the crucial factor in our first enchantment is 'matching' or 'correspondence': 'Something accommodates itself exactly to my desire' (Barthes, p. 191). When I read 'Winterson' now (and I include all the works, not only *Written*

on the Body) it no longer 'matches', and since the 'something' her texts once
represented to me has been lost I read them *without* anxiety: *disappointment* has enabled me to swallow all my fear.

Like *The Piano*, meanwhile, *The Story of an African Farm* is a text which
ought to inspire more political anxiety than it does in my readerly relation
to it. What my re-memory reveals in this instance is the rather shocking
admission that the feminist discourse at the heart of this text is not the
explicit focus of my engagement with it (I had completely forgotten
Lyndall's long speech in Chapter 4, Part II, for example), although my
'devotion' (see Chapter 5) to Lyndall is, of course, associated with the feminist values she represents. While, in the re-memory, I interpret this strange
dislocation partly in terms of a prioritization of 'embodied' rather than 'dis-
embodied' discourse (I remember what Lyndall *represents*, in terms of feminism, rather than what she and/or Schreiner say about it), in the re-reading
I am forced to be more accountable for my relationship to the text's politics.
This accountability brings with it a degree of anxiety, as is illustrated by the
following extract, which deals with Lyndall's return to the farm after she
has been away at school:

> When Lyndall returns from school, my expectations and anxieties are
> mediated through the figure of Waldo. *Wuthering Heights* is to the
> fore once again here – although Lyndall [unlike Cathy] has brought
> back feminism as well as femininity with her.[18]

> I recorded in my re-memory of this text that it was my forgetting of
> Lyndall's great feminist speeches in Chapter 4 that puzzled me the
> most. This still appertains, although I have since found a way of
> explaining why this has become a gap in my own reading. The prob-
> lem is the fact that the feminism is so mixed in with the femininity.
> Lyndall's bold manifestos (totally in keeping with her childhood vision)
> are circumscribed by her own defeat at the hands of patriarchal ide-
> ology:

>> 'I'm sorry you don't care for the position of women; I should
>> have liked us to be friends: and it is the only thing about which
>> I think much or feel much – if, indeed, I have any feeling about
>> anything . . . My head swings sometimes. But this one thought
>> stands, never goes – if I might but be one of those born in the
>> future; then, perhaps, to be born a woman will not be to be
>> born branded.' (p. 194)

>> 'Let me take your arm, Waldo. How full you are of mealie dust.
>> – No, never mind. It will brush off. – And sometimes what is
>> more amusing still than tracing the likeness between man and
>> man is to trace the analogy there always is between the progress
>> and development of one individual and of a whole nation . . . It
>> is the most amusing thing I know of; but of course, being a
>> woman, I have not often time for such amusements. Professional

duties always first, you know. It takes a great deal of time and thought always to look perfectly exquisite, even for a pretty woman.' (pp. 207–8)

And so we see Lyndall focused on 'what really matters' with a conviction that we should have expected from her . . . but at the same time shaking mealie dust from her white dress. Although her feminism is fully conscious of this contradiction – indeed, the absurd conventions of femininity are at the centre of her critique – she has nevertheless submitted to them. Lyndall's great feminist pronouncements are undercut with irony and bitterness: and satire, as we have repeatedly been told, is the last weapon of those who no longer believe in the possibility of change:

> 'But what does it help? A little bitterness, a little longing when we are young, a little futile searching for work, a little passionate striving for room for the exercise of our powers, – and then we go with the drove. A woman must march with her regiment. In the end she must be trodden down or go with it; and if she is wise she goes.(p. 196)

Even now, reading these words for the umpteenth time, I cannot say whether Lyndall's statement of defeat – jarring as it does with her commitment to a better world – makes me love her less or more. The desire and determination are still there, but she has given up on the means of achieving her goal (even as a child she eventually gave up on getting Em and herself out of their room and lay down to sleep). To have so much conviction running alongside such bitter resignation is very difficult for me as a feminist reader. It also threatens the foundations of my relationship with Lyndall, which was based on my belief that she would stay true to her word, that she would keep fighting (on my behalf). Both Em and the narrator have previously promised me, seduced me, with the information that Lyndall 'always does what she says' (p. 55). Now Lyndall has gone away to school to get a serious education, realized that this is impossible for a woman, and effectively given up. She has manifestly *not done* what she said she would do. And this is the woman to whom I have entrusted my own 'life'!

While I will deal with the wider implications of this extract under the heading of 'disappointment', it also betrays the uneasiness I experienced at this point in my re-reading of the novel: an emotional tensing of muscles, as I realized exactly how much work I would have to do to sustain and justify my devotion to Lyndall. Although this political anxiety is qualitatively different to that associated with *The Piano* and *Written on the Body*, in as much as it is a character in the text rather than the text itself that is under scrutiny, since Lyndall is – in this instance – my textual other the threat is equally serious. Indeed, in some respects the desperate lengths I go to in

order to discover subject-positions which will enable me to preserve a positive relationship with my heroine (see Chapter 5) are an index of the
extreme *anxiety* I felt when I realized just how much she had it her power to
'disappoint' me.

The final category of reader-anxiety I wish to deal with *vis-à-vis* these
readings is the one peculiar to the Grauerholz exhibition.[19] This is an anxiety which is contextual rather than textual, in as much as it concerns what I
have described as an 'anxiety of entitlement': the lack of 'cultural capital'
which makes my own reader-relationship with 'high art' extremely angst-
ridden (see extract reproduced on pp. 93–5 above).[20] Although my description displaces my own tension onto the figures of the security guards that
'pace restlessly', the extract gives a fair impression of how, even now – after
many years of 'viewing art' – I have considerable problems in legitimating
my presence in these spaces/places of 'distinction'.[21] In terms of romantic
conventions, the experience can best be likened to the anxiety (female)
lovers suffer in relation to their wealthy, upper-class (male) suitors: an
inequality which it is, of course, within love's power to redress.

In terms of this particular set of text–reader relations, however, I have
never yet been so enraptured by a visual image in a gallery-situation that I
have completely forgotten the hostile environment in which our supposed
interaction is taking place. No matter how much the artist/curator has critically and ironically commented on the white/bourgeois/patriarchal conditions of viewing (and this, after all, has been a feature of a good deal of
feminist art), the institutional context still inhibits my relationship with the
text concerned: a constraint which is graphically illustrated in my viewing of
Grauerholz's 'Filling the Landscape':[22]

> On this particular afternoon I am not expecting to have access to the
> installation, since a presentation isn't scheduled for this time. When
> the curator/gallery assistant (?) appears with two women who have
> evidently requested a special showing, however, I take the opportunity
> to join them. They are speaking in French, with an accent I find diffi-
> cult, so I'm not going to understand much of what is being explained:
> this could be an advantage in as much as what I am exploring here is
> my own response to the texts, but it will also have an inescapably
> alienating effect. Fortunately, because I have already been at work in
> my professional mode for a couple of hours, my latent cultural anxiety
> is blunted.

Although the account emphasizes my determination not to be intimidated
by the highly alienating circumstances in which I'm viewing these texts, and
despite the fact that the account goes on to describe a generally positive
viewing experience (see Chapter 5), there is no doubt that Grauerholz's
intention to make viewers feel 'uncomfortable' when confronted with this
exhibit more than succeeds with me.[23] Whilst the catalogue guides us
towards the awkward feelings associated with voyeurism, however (the

'public' viewing of 'private' images), my own anxiety combines this with a profound cultural illegitimacy, symbolized by the curator addressing all her 'explanations' to two very expensively dressed women in French. If they are being made to feel uncomfortable about snooping through the drawers of someone's private desk (and they don't look it!), I am still expecting to be thrown out for 'trespassing' in the driveway.

Another important feature of this reading experience, moreover, was the way in which the alienating high-cultural context in which I was obliged to view Grauerholz's photographs was also the 'subject' of many of the images. Here is my discussion of two of the photographs in Room 2, for example:

> A quick glance around this second annex suggests that I am likely to be disappointed [in discovering my 'textual other']. Here are more interior public spaces that I know are unlikely to be welcoming to me as a woman. I head immediately for what appears to be the strongest image, probably on account of its compositional substance and solemnity. This is *Le Bureau* (1993) (see Illustration 6.1): an office featuring several tables stacked with papers and a large central reading lamp. Elegant wood-framed upholstered chairs are scattered loosely around, though the disorder is minimal, and the general impression of *gravitas* is enhanced by the bases of four massive stone columns. There are semes here that, as an academic, I recognize, and although the text is labelled *Le Bureau* it connects in my mind with numerous university libraries. As a (female) student and lecturer I have myself spent a fair amount of time in such places, but now – with its occupants absent –

Illustration 6.1   'This rock-face of learning' (Chapter 6)

this room makes me feel, once again, that I am trespassing in another masculine territory. Another woman might feel that she would like to sit down on one of those chairs, undo the ribbons on the stacks of papers, but not I. This time I don't retreat so quickly, however, and my feelings are more mixed: part of me is seduced and would *like* to stay. I linger a moment or two, relishing the same curious blend of alienation and envy that marks all my visits to Oxford, Cambridge and the British Library. I know there is pleasure here, but I know also that it is forbidden to me.

Much of what I have just written in relation to *Le Bureau* also applies to the photograph, *La Bibliothèque* (1992) (see Illustration 6.2). The gendered semiotics of this interior are almost identical with the last: the same civilized calm, the same patriarchal grandeur. In this text two male figures in the foreground, their outlines stretched and softened by over-exposure, consider serried rows of books. The massiveness of the library, its apparent infinity, is accentuated by the low camera-angle which emphasizes both the vertical and horizontal axes. The figures themselves are rendered small and transient in relation to this rock-face of learning. As a female scholar I feel my marginality is even greater, though both the room and the feeling are something that I am at least familiar with. I could linger here for some time without too much discomfort, but once again cannot expect much pleasure. The thousands of copies of leather-bound volumes, while offering a certain fetishistic attraction, are unlikely to contain much that is of interest or relevance to me. Time to move on again.

Illustration 6.2   Trespassing?

Considering that my relationship to the exhibition has, by this time, been 'framed' by a romance narrative (see also my experience with 'Mozart Room': see Chapter 5, pp. 101–2), these bourgeois public interiors (the Office, the Library, the Opera) take on the surreal and nightmarish quality of the rooms and houses we rush through in our dreams, as we flee away from something we fear *towards* something we desire. Since it is an anxiety brought to intellectual consciousness, however, I am also keenly aware that this 'fright and flight' mechanism is very explicitly gendered. My lack of entitlement in relation to these images focuses on the fact that no amount of education and other cultural privileges will ever make me feel comfortable in these spaces/places historically defined as male territory.

Looking back over my reading, I perceive that my sense of alienation at this point in the exhibition was acute; but I recognize also that this profound anxiety of entitlement (what am I doing here? How can I relate to these images?) was *mixed* with the (amorous) anxiety of waiting for the textual other to appear (as indeed it was made to: see the discussion in Chapter 5, pp. 101). It is this complication – the fact that anxiety is an expression of both hope *and* fear – that accounts for its over-determination of the reader's whole emotional repetoire. What all my readings indicate, indeed, is that this is a readerly emotion that looks in both directions: back towards what has (possibly) been lost, and forwards to what might (possibly) be (re)discovered. To this extent, it is an emotion that, as with the Grauerholz exhibition, can be seen to belong to the prequel as well as the sequel of the reader–romance trajectory – to circumscribe, indeed, the whole relationship, with the glorious exception of the *ravissement* itself (that extended moment apparently 'outside of time') where, as we have already seen, nothing is asked for, and everything is given.

In as much as it situates its anxiety at the intersection of the textual and the contextual, these readings of the Grauerholz exhibition, like most of the other readings considered in this section, bring the 'emotional' and the 'political', the 'implicated' and the 'hermeneutic' into more explicit tension with one another than with many other of the emotional headings I deal with. The inference here is clearly that a good deal of reader/spectator anxiety comes from a fear that the 'special' relationship with our textual others is under constant attack from 'external' forces, that either threaten to take the beloved subject/object away or else despoil it in some way. What the readings in this section therefore demonstrate is that reader-anxiety is most often located on the borderline between the implicated and the political reading of a text: a defensive guard, perhaps, that seeks to preserve and protect our relationship with our textual other(s) from the doubts, questionings and *knowledge* that will surely corrupt our state of rapturous innocence.

Frustration

Although, in terms of the romance trajectory, the various nuances of emotion we experience as 'frustration' might sometimes appear to be virtually simultaneous with *ravissement*, it is actually a concentration of feelings better understood within the context of the 'sequel': as an expression of the amorous subject's desire to *get back to* the plenitude of the first (gratuitous) enamoration. This is certainly the case with the two literary texts I deal with here, though with the case of *The Piano* and the Grauerholz exhibition it is more obviously a feature of the *prequel*: an expression of the many obstacles that hindered (though not permanently) my implication in these particular texts.

Frustration, like anxiety, is an expression of the subject's feelings of impotence towards the (textual) other; though where anxiety (as we have seen) is an emotional torture associated with the inability to act, frustration is rather an expression of not knowing how to do so. It is the state of feeling that *we must do something* to make the textual other (re)appear and/or reciprocate our love, but not knowing what that action might be.

Barthes's own text (under different headings) offers examples (see p. 59) of some of the ways the frustrated lover might attempt to overcome his/her feelings of impotence. These include, first, an obsession with finding an *explanation* for both one's own feelings (what is love? why am I feeling it?) and the other's behaviour (why is the other being 'silent' or evasive? why is my love not being returned?). This strategy helps to displace the pain of being in love by making it into a hermeneutic 'mystery' and, within the arena of text–reader relations, is familiar to us through the act of criticism itself. (Although we might ostensibly be offering an interpretation of the text, what we are also doing is attempting to rationalize and/or avenge the indifference the text shows to us as readers.)

Intimately bound up with the hermeneutic strategy is the reader-lover's recourse to *writing* (*A Lover's Discourse*, pp. 97–100). Writing is both one of the ways in which we can attempt to articulate our 'incomprehension', and a means of positioning a recalcitrant (that is, silent/unresponsive) textual other as an interlocutor whether s/he wants it or not. Although Barthes's entry on 'writing', which focuses on its inability to 'express' love ('To try and write love is to confront the *muck* of language', *A Lover's Discourse*, p. 99), regards it as further evidence of the lover's *powerlessness*, my own feeling is that, in text–reader relations especially, writing is the (only?) means through which the reader/lover can effectively deal with the frustration of his or her own silence/inactivity. What is the practice of criticism, after all, if not turning the tables on the one that has had us in its thrall? By making the textual other *our* interlocutor, moreover, we are able to relieve our frustration by declaring our love/devotion. While Barthes reflects scathingly on the ultimate futility of such an exercise (see p. 100), it seems to me that writing *does* confirm the status of the other (as lover) through its act of dialogic positioning, even if, paradoxically, their textual presence signals their existential absence. In my own criticism, at least – including the readings I have produced here – the act of writing has been crucial in expiating the various frustrations I have experienced in my role as passive consumer of the text.

The other way in which the implicated reader might be expected to handle their frustration, as I have already indicated, is through an *obsession with their own behaviour*. In as much as frustration is an expression of not knowing how to act, a self-reflexive absorption with tactic and strategy becomes in itself an effective way of gaining control over the emotion. What relieves the tension, in other words, is intense speculation on *what might be done*: an amorous reflex that might be directly compared to the reader/critic's obsession with *methodology* (because I don't understand what this text is doing to me, or because I can't make it 'respond' as I want, I therefore obsess myself with the problem of 'how to approach the problem'). This is another circumstance, indeed, in which the reader's relationship with an interdiegetic textual other might be seen to be displaced onto a metaphorical (and extratextual) substitute.[24]

In terms of my own readings, meanwhile, emotional frustration centres largely on the problem of my subject-positioning as reader. Once my textual other has been identified – be this a character in the text (Schreiner), 'implied author' (Winterson) or 'scene' of romance (Grauerholz and Campion) – my challenge is clearly to create/sustain the dialogic relationship that precipitated my first *ravissement*. In terms of the strategies for alleviating this frustation, moreover, this theoretical and methodological focus on 'positioning' can be seen as a classic example of the (amorous) reader converting the text's apparent silence and indifference into an obsession with her own behaviour: I attempt to 'cover up' for the other's evident 'lack of interest' by trying to work out what *I have got to do* to win that interest back. In other words, the emphasis on reader-positioning can be regarded as both an expression of frustration *and* an attempt to contain it.

How I, the desiring reader (of Schreiner's novel), managed to discover inter- and extratexual locations in which to *rendezvous* with Lyndall was discussed in some detail in Chapter 5 (see especially the section, 'Devotion'). As I have already indicated, however, the ingenuity of these manœuvres (in particular my strategic alliances and dis-alliances with Waldo) are really a measure of the extreme frustration and panic I experienced on the numerous occasions I felt my textual heroine slipping away from me. Even in my re-memory I was acutely aware, for example, not only of *her* insubstantiality (as a 'collection of semes') but also of *my own*.[25] My frustrations, indeed, are well illustrated by the metaphor of the ghost who can never make her presence felt (as in the text reproduced in Chapter 1, pp. 1–2). This 'ghost' metaphor also helps us clarify a little more the nature of the reader's sense of disempowerment, which, with respect to my reading of this text, is focused almost entirely on my inability to *actively* dialogize with the characters. This frustration exists *despite* my ability to intervene in the text in other ways, such as bringing the narrative to a satisfying closure, unravelling its numerous hermeneutic and cultural codes, and aligning its various intellectual and political discourses with my own interests.[26] The problem is that all these interventions, although undeniably a part of my total reader-pleasure, still fail to satisfy my need for an *interactive* dialogue with my textual other, in this case the character of Lyndall. What I am looking for as a reader, and which I sometimes get but more often fail to get, is intertextual *attention*: the interlocutory sense (illusion) that – despite my ghostly status – I have been 'recognized'.[27] Without such recognition the reader becomes self-consciously aware of herself as a voyeur of the text rather than an interactive participant, and this becomes a source not only of frustration (what can I do to make the other see me?) but also of alienation, as I record in the following extract:

> As I mark these textual inscriptions and their affect upon me I ponder the extent to which the sufferings of the voyeur have been taken seriously, either in theories of spectatorship or in with respect to inter-diegetic characters. Schreiner's primary intertext here, for example [*Wuthering Heights*] positions Heathcliff in much the same way as I have just been positioned when he is forced to watch Cathy through the illuminated window of Thrushcross Grange. The painful confusion of his feelings, as I remember them, is one of pride (in Cathy's shining superiority) mixed with the frustration of his own exclusion. Such is his intimacy/identification with Cathy at this time, indeed, that the 'view-in' is tantamount to a schizophrenic splitting of himself: he is looking at a part of himself which has become forbidden to him.

As I go on to explain, however, my readerly voyeurism in relation to this text is not mitigated by any *identificatory* reflex (see the extract reproduced in Chapter 5, pp. 111–13). Whilst in Chapter 5 I used this extract (and what follows) to illustrate how such feelings of exclusion can be rationalized and strategically overcome, here I want simply to draw attention to the intensity of the frustration that precedes the resolution. By this point in the reading experience, desire for the other has expanded to include a host of attendant emotions, such as care and compassion, and my impotence is realized not only in Lyndall's apparent indifference to me (she does not know that I am there) but also, more painfully, in my inability to offer comfort to her. At another level of readerly intervention I can, of course, alleviate this suffering (hers and mine) by rewriting the script, which is effectively what I do with the end of the novel; but this does not satisfy the immediate need for dialogic contact. The fact that I achieve this only through the most devious means (see Chapter 5, pp. 130–1) remains, as I have already indicated, the clearest testimony to the profundity of my frustration *and* my devotion.

If my strategy for dealing with the difficulty of my reader-positioning in Schreiner's text is expressed as an obsession with my own behaviour (see above), in the case of Winterson's *Written on the Body* I prefer to turn my frustration against the text itself:

> What to do with this opening? Here we are *in medias res*: the blind confusion that swamps the discourse of love; the mixing up of 'I' and 'you' and 'she' a testament to the fact that none of us is able to make sense of it, though we are compelled to try. We are desirous of precision, as the text says. We loathe the clichés, and yet we also need them. Love is decidedly *not* something to be looked straight in the eye, nor is it something we can ever get sufficient distance on to control. In Elspeth Probyn's terms, love above all things thwarts the passage from ontology to epistemology.[28]
>
> Two pages, then, that challenge the reader to test the truth-value of every assertion against their own experience. I frown at the prospect of yet more readerly authentication. Yet how else engage with this text? As a literary critic I could doubtless find ways to avoid the obvious (analysis of genre, structure, discourse etc.), but every reader will also be obliged to plumb their own hearts, to savour the meaningfulness of each and every cliché. None of us is beyond this, although we might like to be . . .
>
> In terms of the *morality* of love, the sentiment here echoes that of the earlier Winterson novels: it's not adultery *per se* that's wrong, but the lack of courage in making 'the right choice' and seeing it through. This is a sentiment that I can relate to, though it must also be said that gender and sexuality weigh heavily in such cases. If Lothario is a woman, for instance, one might be inclined to have more sympathy for the qualms of her lovers, though none of Winterson's novels can be said to have much patience for those who remain closeted. However, it must also be said that on this reading Lothario isn't a very convincing woman to me: his/her role in the heterosexual economy of marriage/adultery is too prototypically masculine, and Louise too stereotypically feminine. While nothing in his self-presentation genders him especially . . . , his positioning of the other as 'an other' is indicative. The other option is to separate sex from gender and read this as a lesbian butch–femme masquerade which may be perceived as either reactionary or chic depending upon one's mood and/or politics. Whichever way the reader chooses to set it up, however, I only know that this time round the unresolved gender and indeterminate sexuality made me feel uncomfortable, alienated. It's not that I'm resistant to this sort of gender dynamic in lesbian relationships – simply that without confirmation that Lothario *is* a 'she', the text's re-working of heterosexual romance conventions lose their potential transgression: the clichés are reproduced without necessarily being defamiliarized.
>
> It will be seen, then, that my emotional response to the opening pages of Winterson's text is very much circumscribed by political and

theoretical considerations. It's as though I can't get to what I feel because I know too well what I ought *not* to feel, and now – unlike the period surrounding my first reading – I seem incapable of engaging sufficiently even to fake a more positive connection. At this point, even the humanist reading of the text – pleasure in the recognition of certain universal truths – is proving difficult to access. Lothario is implicated in a world just material enough to thwart full participation on this 'higher' plane; and the fetishization of Louise's body doesn't help either – this is a version of femininity which I neither aspire to nor desire. In general, then, it would seem that these characters – unlike Lyndall and Waldo in *The Story of an African Farm* – block rather than mediate my access to the text's 'structures of feeling'.

Although the word 'frustration' is not actually used in these opening pages of my reading, what strikes me in retrospect is how immensely *irritated* I appear to be with the text, how obviously loath to engage with it. Frustration, here, has quickly turned to exasperation as I resist the humanist authentication of romantic experience provoked by the aphorisms. Despite the fact that this is a mode of expression typical of the Winterson *œuvre* – and one by which I have previously been seduced – I am notably reluctant to play the game. If the imperative to sexual/textual frustration is a desire to reunite with the 'original' object of desire (at the moment of *ravissement*), then these trite expressions should return me to Winterson's earlier texts. The fact that they do not is clearly an indication that I am seriously 'out of love' with this author-function even *before* I begin reading, and all that the opening page does is remind me of what I no longer feel.[29] My 'frustration', indeed, is very typically that of the ex-lover who looks back on the source of his/her late obsession and thinks 'what did I ever see in him/her'? As the text moves me from the aphorisms to a revelation of Lothario's character, I can barely conceal my disgust; although, in the manner of all those most threatened, I conceal my negative emotions with a veneer of objectivity by raising my criticisms to a supposedly political level. But the fact of the matter is that, now that I have consciously marked my estrangement from 'Winterson', *everything* her pen touches appears strangely alien to me in my attempt to distinguish myself from my former implication. My frustration is thus, ultimately, a frustration with my readerly self.

An interesting aspect to the obstacles blocking my participation in this text is the role played by its narrative structure and transgression of generic conventions:

Any thoughts I might first have had about the possibility of re-positioning myself within the text as the consequence of Lothario's need to purify himself are, however, frustrated by its narrative structure. Even though it is clear, after the initial consummation, that this is his destiny, the record of his purgatorial quest is delayed until the final (much shorter) section of the novel. The first continues with the pattern of alternating panegyrics to his love for Louise with cynical narratives of his past affairs. The repetition of the phrase, 'I had a girlfriend/boyfriend once . . .' becomes a disruptive incantation, reminding the reader just how much work Lothario will have to do to prove that his love for Louise is 'different'.

What I am suggesting here is that my opportunity for relating to Lothario's chastened self – the self that is bound to Louise and no other – is frustrated by these continual reminders of his promiscuous past which are sutured into the main narrative. This is because I approached *Written on the Body* with the desire/expectation that it was a 'romance', in the manner of Winterson's previous novels – which is to say, that it would subscribe to highly conventional values (such as monogamy, destiny, the existence of eternal love) at the same time as challenging traditional sexuality/gender roles – only to be presented with a 'Don Juan' whose past exploits undermine all his supposed devotion to Louise.[30] Once again, however, what this 'complaint' against the text actually reveals is the overwhelming prejudice with which I *approached* it. It was a text doomed to fail in its ravishment of me (at least, this second time around) because it does not abide by the same romantic conventions as its predecessors; and it is amusing to see how, in this and other extracts, I effectively blame all my own ('fake') emotional response (which I now regard as a symptom of my first reading of the text) on Lothario's 'inauthentic' desire. The failure of my own reader-romance is thus bound up, ironically and somewhat peevishly, with the 'failure' of the interdiegetic romance: its destabilization of essentialist values ('somewhere love is written in tablets of stone') frustrates my own enchantment and confirms just how conventional a good deal of reader-pleasure indeed is.[31] Thus, although I *know* romantic love to be an ideology determined by a complex web of narrative and cultural conventions, I also know that I have been very effectively interpellated by them, and that a good deal of my reader-activity depends upon my actively colluding in their (re)production. My frustration with this text therefore rests with the fact not that it deals in 'fake emotion' (Lothario's), but that it has stopped me from continuing to fake my own.

As with the case of *Written on the Body*, my initial frustrations with *The Piano* can be seen to derive from the expectations with which I approached it: expectations which had advanced so far by the time I *did* see it that I was was already imagining the script and peopling it with my own characters (see the extract reproduced on pp. 92 of Chapter 5). The way in which this initial frustration was overcome, through my strategy of making the characters pawns in my own highly personalized (re)scripting of the film, nevertheless confirms the source of such readerly angst to be linked to our sense of impotence and lack of dialogic interaction. As with Winterson's text, my re-memory of Campion's film shows my initial frustration and disappointment as deriving from my inability to sustain/restore the period of *ravisse-*

ment (which, as I have already observed, *preceded* my encounter with the actual text). Once I discovered that I could achieve this by 'clearancing' the text of Campion's own characters, however, and by using its 'structures of feeling' simply as a springboard for my own (covert) rescripting of the narrative, all the frustration vanishes.

My frustration with the Grauerholz exhibition, meanwhile, combines a further instance of the problems of reader-positioning which have dominated the three previous readings, with the context-specific problem of obtrusive curatorial 'instruction' on how to read the text (see extract reproduced on pp. 94 of Chapter 5). By being giving such clear (and already theorized) advice on how to view the photographs, I the academic reader/critic was, not surprisingly, frustrated at having my role usurped and the *ravissement* to which I looked forward made a common property (see also 'Jealousy', following).

In terms of reader-positioning, meanwhile, the biggest obstacle I faced with this 'text' (that is, the exhibition) was the photographs in Room 3, in which the (nude) female figures seriously intruded on the search for my own textual other.[32] As I fled through the empty rooms, woods, alleys and overgrown gardens in search of ghostly traces, these fleshly embodiments (of someone else's fantasy) were *not* what I wanted to see:

> Taking the room as a whole, however – which juxtaposes the female nudes, the torso of a male figure, *Lessing* (1992), and two large 'landscapes', *Druid I* (see Illustration 1.1) and *Druid II* (1990–1) – I achieved a more positive, if intellectual, appreciation of these texts.[33] By regarding the tangled weave of thick and knotted branches of *Druid I* and the close-up representation of tree bark in *Druid II* as the aspects of the landscape *beheld* by the male and female subjects of the other photographs we are able to read the series as a challenging comment on the dynamic interaction between figure and landscape: literally what it means to be a figure (seeing) *in* the landscape. Such intellectual 'explanation' undoubtedly sidelines the viewer's emotional involvement in the texts, however, and for this reason this room ultimately offered fewer reader-challenges than the previous ones.
>
> The exception to this is *Druid I*, whose tunnel through trees and undergrowth was recognizable to me as another dream-landscape, reproduced in a number of classic intertexts such as 'the road to Manderley' in du Maurier's *Rebecca* or the forest through which Ada plunges in Jane Campion's film *The Piano*.[34] Responding to the sensations of fear and excitement evoked by my experience/memory of such scenarios, I found myself turning again, with increasing frustration, to the nude figures. This dialogue between figure and landscape, self and other, was so theoretically satisfying that the nude *ought* to function as the object of desire/identification at the centre of this

exhibition. I look again, but still the self-conscious artistry associated with these images works as an obstacle and interdiction.

What the extract points to in total, however, is the rather more complex realization that a text can offer us reading-positions that are enabling (seductive) and frustrating simultaneously. Whilst some theorizing thus allows me to make a useful intellectual connection between the figures and what they 'see', their presences nevertheless intrude on the 'fiction' I am beginning to make out of my own dynamic interaction with the text(s). As with the case of *The Piano*, frustration occurs when the text's own story (and protagonists) threaten to drown out my own.

In conclusion, what all these readings reveal is that readerly frustration – when understood as a reflex of our first textual enchantment – is predicated upon the reader's desire to achieve (resume) a fully dialogic interaction with the text. For this reason, such frustration is voiced most clearly *vis-à-vis* the problems of reader-positioning: how to achieve (and sustain) a location from which to engage the texual other. In Schreiner's novel, in which that other is a textual character, the frustration derives from the reader's sense of her own intertextual insubstantiality: the fact that, although she can participate in the text *to an extent*, she is nevertheless 'unseen' (and hence unvalidated) by the object of her devotion. In *Written on the Body*, meanwhile, what the readings covertly reveal is a frustration with myself (as reader) for no longer being able to fake a satisfying emotional response, which is then displaced onto the text and rationalized (into, say, 'obsession with one's own behaviour': see above) as a (methodological) problem of positioning. Because my textual other must, in this case, be construed as my former relationship with the Winterson *œuvre*, I construct a scapegoat (Lothario's promiscuous sexual mores) which is seen to stand in the way of my (conventionally) romantic relation to the text and its characters. Finally, with respect to *The Piano* and the Grauerholz exhibition, where the textual other has its source in my own narrative scripts that are very clearly projected *onto/into* the texts' own 'scenes' and 'structures of feelings', 'frustration' occurs whenever a didactic discourse obtrudes itself upon my *ravissement* (or movement towards it) and interrupts my ghostly dreaming.

Jealousy

As readers of Chapter 2 will be aware, it was jealousy that precipitated my original interest in the emotional politics of reading. So shocked was I to discover that the reading process could give rise to emotions as base and unscholarly as this one, that I was provoked into exploring what other unspoken relations might be at work.

Like anxiety, jealousy is intrinsic to the discourse of romantic love (or, at

least, to how love is conceptualized in the Western world). Thus Barthes
writes: 'To be jealous is to conform. To reject jealousy ("to be perfect") is
therefore to transgress a law' (*A Lover's Discourse*, p. 145). What produces
this conformity is, of course, the exclusivity upon which such love is predicated. Although there are other models of relationship which avoid the logic
of the nuclear couple, it remains one of the defining aspects of most romantic discourse, and accounts for a good deal of the obsessional behaviour of
the amorous subject.[35] Jealousy is quickly aroused, for example, when one
suspects another of claiming to 'know' the beloved. As Barthes writes:

> The other is my good and my knowledge: only I know him, only I
> make him exist in his truth. Whoever is not me is ignorant of the other:
> 'Sometimes I cannot understand how another *can*, how he *dare* love
> her, since I alone love her completely and devotedly, knowing only
> her, and having nothing in the world but her!' (p. 229)

This quotation also raises the complicated question of who, or what, is the
focus of jealousy in the amorous relationship: although we might, at first,
assume it to be an emotion directed at the one who is in competition for the
love of the beloved, the fact that this other becomes a threat only if the
beloved submits to their attentions means that it is directed (guiltily, shame-
fully) at the beloved too. Indeed, it could be argued that many of the negative feelings associated with the other wo/man are, in fact, the product of
one's lack of trust in the beloved, and are associated with oneself for one's
lack of trust.

When we turn to the manifestation of jealousy in text–reader relations, it
is quickly obvious that the same confusion of 'who/what is to blame'
applies. Whilst this is fairly straightforward in the case of Schreiner's *The
Story of an African Farm,* where the focus is on a textual character
(Lyndall), in the case of the other texts significant *contextual* forces are also
at work. With respect to Winterson's *Written on the Body,* for example, my
re-memory (as we have already seen) makes it quite clear that I was, at different times, both jealous of the author, 'Winterson', for having written the
books I would have liked to have written, and of other members of the feminist reading community who also claimed a special relationship with her
work. With respect to the Grauerholz exhibition and *The Piano,* too, this
jealousy of the 'special text' applies: a jealousy whose emotion is once again
directed primarily at those other readers and viewers with whom I have had
to share the discourse that has such a personal (secret?) bearing on my own
life.

Because it was Winterson, indeed, who was one of the first authors to
make me aware of the existence of 'reader jealousy', I begin my discussion
by returning to the re-memory of my early infatuation with her work (see
the extract quoted on pp. 89–90 of Chapter 5). It will be seen that this 'narrative of implication' is also an excellent illustration of the way in which
'jealousy *for* the subject' can be mixed with 'jealousy *of* the subject'.

Although I am quick to turn my first engagement with Winterson's texts into a positive experience, the confusion of 'desire for'/'identification with' which characterizes this particular relationship also bends the feelings of envy and jealousy in two directions: I both wish to be the exclusive inter-locutor of Winterson's texts (which I will share only with my own signifi-cant others) and to be (to displace) 'Winterson' herself.

By projecting the dynamics of this early relationship onto my reading/re-reading of *Written on the Body,* moreover, it is possible to see the latter in the guise of the other 'wo/man' that stole Winterson from me. My jealousy, in this respect, is directed specifically at the way in which the treacherous text interpellates an 'ideal reader' who is not me. Despite this negative press, plenty of my friends and colleagues enjoyed this text a good deal – and because, ultimately, I have conceded that *I did not,* my own special rela-tionship with the Winterson *œuvre* was clearly at an end.

The Angela Grauerholz exhibition, meanwhile, provides another interest-ing example of how reader-jealousy which begins outside the text is dis-placed onto scenes and subjects within it. Since, as I established in the previous section, the 'other' of this text is, in effect, the 'empty space' which I people with my own inscriptions, the primary source of both frustration and jealousy must be those things that stand in the way of my projections. In the same way, therefore, as I am 'frustrated' at having the exhibition curator, Paulette Gagnon, tell me how to approach the exhibition (see p. 162 above), so I am also jealous of her for suggesting things about the text–viewer relationship that I wanted, first, to discover for myself, and sec-ond, to claim as a unique and personal engagement with the text(s). This unwelcome intrusion of another onto my private space is then replicated in my reading of the texts themselves in the form of the female nudes who peo-ple the fantasy landscapes of Room 3 (see the discussion in the previous sec-tion, pp. 162–3). Once again, moreover, the extract I used to illustrate my frustration can also be used to illustrate my jealousy: not only are these fig-ures an obstacle to the fulfilment of my desire, they are also a 'threat' to its sustenance, in as much as they have stolen the 'scene' on which my own fan-tasy projections depend.

The jealousy predicated upon usurpation of the reader's own imagination is not, however, the only one to discolour my relationship with the Grauerholz texts. In the course of my wanderings through these interior and exterior landscapes, in pursuit of my own elusive textual others, I am peri-odically arrested by spaces/places where I would like to stay – places, indeed, that might 'hold the key' – were it not for my anxiety of entitlement (see above) about being there. Consider again the account of my response to *Le Bureau* and *La Bibliothèque* (reproduced above on pp. 153–4). Although I originally considered this extract as a statement of the profound 'anxiety' that marks the prequel/sequel of my Grauerholz romance, it is interesting to foreground the jealousy embedded in my readerly neurosis. In this instance, the subject at which the jealousy is directed is, I would like to suggest, myself – or rather, the 'other self' I might have been in a different life. What I describe when considering the first image is the strange sensation of slipping into another ghostly body/persona, only to be wrenched out of it again, as my 'lack of entitlement' forbids me to linger. Therefore, although most of my negative emotions with respect to this public space are focused on what I perceive to be the obstacles to my pleasure (the men and their symbols of patriarchy), another obstacle, and one of whom I am profoundly jealous, is the self that dares to walk amongst them – and in whose embodiment I might have laid claim to my textual others more quickly.

As the previous sections of this chapter will have revealed, *The Piano* is a text of which I have become extremely possessive. The rescripting in which I have engaged in order to people it, like the Grauerholz photographs, with my own fictional representatives has served to make me jealous of all who appear to be laying claim to it in a similar way. When I heard that the journal *Screen* was producing a special 'debates section' on the film and its reception, for example, I felt instantly resentful – not so much from a professional point of view (because it was a text I wanted to write on myself), but because of the other, personal, investment which made me resent its public status.[36] Very little of this is recorded in the re-memory or readings themselves, however, so we must assume that this is another text in which jealousy *per se* has been repressed and/or displaced.

Apart from the viewers and critics who threaten my privileged relation to this text, the other obvious target for my jealousy is the film's director, Jane Campion. The only place, however, that Campion surfaces in the reading is on the few occasions in which the heavy hand of the director interferes with my own reverie (see the discussion above, p. 117–18). Looking back over my reading now, I see the principal competition to my own special relationship to this text to lie not with its scriptor or re-scriptors, but with the *discourse of heterosexuality* which allows the romance to strain all the conventions to breaking point, but still offer the reader the satisfaction of a traditional closure. My own reading contains many gaps and silences in this respect, particularly with regard to the sex scene, the discussion of which is endlessly (and symbolically) deferred. By making my own highly sublimated reading of Ada's desire (see the discussion in Chapter 5) I avoid the issue of how this section of the film positions the non-heterosexual reader, not least because of the erotics of gendered power which makes Ada into transferrable 'property' between Stewart and Baines. Although an orthodox feminist reading is obliged to see this as her 'tragedy' (she is a woman denied autonomy, sexual or otherwise), it is also possible to feel residual desire for a 'self-abandonment' so all-consuming. Whatever the power dynamics of individual lesbian relationships, for example, the yielding of oneself to a protector/saviour (as Ada yields herself to Baines) is never going to be affirmed and supported in the public realm. Therefore, although no note of jealousy appears to touch my response to the two great romantic climaxes of the film (when Baines first raises Ada up into his arms prior to the consummation; and again, when he pulls her out of the water at the end of the film), I feel that some small twinge of envy must be mixed with my vicarious satisfaction. What such a feeling amounts to, of course, is a jealousy for a very ideologically incorrect subject position, and it is consequently no surprise at all that in my own reading I should attempt to deflect and disguise it by focusing on what Baines's 'strong arms' represent in terms of Ada's psychic drama (see the extract quoted in Chapter 5, pp. 124–6). Apart from representing the (symbolic) triumph of the new life over the old, however, what Baines's embrace also represents is the social and political legitimation of such a surrender: the 'coming home' that many of us cannot even dream of, because the 'loving arms' (Barthes, *A Lover's Discourse*, p. 104) belong to a person of the 'wrong' sex.

This jealousy of heterosexual privilege is much more to the fore in my reading of Schreiner's *Story of an African Farm*. In this text–reader relationship, indeed, it is Lyndall's perverse but apparently involuntary and irrevocable sexual passion for 'the Stranger' that presents the most serious challenge to my devotion to her as an embodied subject. While Chapter 5 analyses the way in which I managed to overcome this impediment, it is worth looking at the section of text where I acknowledge just how potentially alienating this episode of the novel is:

> Unfortunately this 'still centre' [the emotions associated with Waldo's departure: see Chapter 5] cannot hold. The carefully negotiated, carefully preserved ambiguity in my relationship with Lyndall – the fine line that keeps it a positive (reading) experience – is sullied with the appearance of 'the Stranger'. While I am never jealous of Waldo's heterosexual claim on Lyndall's affections, I am jealous of this relationship. Jealous, of course, because it engages Lyndall sexually in a way that the other doesn't; and jealous because it renders her something 'other' – something which I can no longer admire, no longer approve. This is the moment of crisis as far as my readerly romance is concerned: the test of my loyalty. It is also, however, the test of Lyndall, and while I might have preferred a more idealized script, I am partially appeased by the irony and disdain with which she regards her own 'weakness':
>
> > 'I love you when I see you but when you are away from me I hate you. . . . But all this is madness. You call into activity one part of my nature; there is another higher part that you know nothing of, that you never touch. If I married you, afterwards it would arise and assert itself, and I should hate you always, as I do now sometimes'. (pp. 254–5)
>
> This is a very fine emotional/political line for myself as a feminist reader, and I know that I will react to it differently upon different readings and in different moods. The fact remains that the passive fate that Lyndall chooses for herself – to reject marriage, but to travel the world

as 'the Stranger's' mistress – *isn't* the only one available to her, although her lack of an independent income is correctly and crucially central to her dilemma. The big issue for the feminist reader at this point is whether we see her refusal to marry as heroic enough in itself. Sometimes I do, sometimes I don't. And on this point hangs the issue of whether we will regard *Story of an African Farm* as a 'noble' tragedy or not.

It is here that the distinction between textual and 'real-life' romance becomes crucial, however. If Lyndall were an existential other, my discovery of this relationship – the fact that she loved the Stranger ('Because you are strong. You are the first man I was ever afraid of', p. 257) – would almost certainly have closed the doors on my lesbian/feminist investment. In a textual romance, however, there is the possibility of shutting the doors on the part of the narrative that threatens our desired trajectory. Not totally, perhaps. And not always. (Hence the significance of the contexts in which we read.) But sometimes. In my re-memorying of the text, for example, there was no mention of Lyndall's 'Stranger' or the heterosexual imperative that is the source of her doom. In the same way that I chose to look in on the scene that showed the child, Lyndall, plotting to escape from her bedroom, so can I choose not to look through the window revealing her sitting on the Stranger's knee. I can reject, that is to say, the omnipotent viewing position of the narrator and situate myself elsewhere. What I do on this occasion, indeed, is realign myself with Waldo. Although Waldo is to learn of Lyndall's elopement in due course, he is spared meeting the Stranger himself, and he is spared hearing what passes between them on this particular night. Indeed, he is spared the details of all Lyndall's subsequent tragedy. Her story ends for him with their conversation in the waggon shed, and in terms of the emotional coherence I am seeking for myself as a reader, perhaps it ends there for me also.

Although, taken as a whole, what this extract demonstrates are the strategies available to the actively 'devoted' reader to defend her relationship with the textual other (see Chapter 5), it is clearly a close call. Whilst the re-scripted nature of my relationship with *The Piano* means that my jealousy of Ada and Baines remains largely discursive (even in my more candid reading, the focus of my envy is what Baines's arms *represent* rather than the arms themselves), the textual other of this reading has been an interdiegetic character who now presents herself as the victim of her own (hetero)sexual desires. When I consider where the jealousy the scene provokes is directed, moreover, I realize – in some confusion – that it is not *ultimately* jealousy that I feel. Although 'the Stranger' certainly ought to be the target of my resentment (for stealing Lyndall's attention from Waldo and myself), the ambiguity of Lyndall's feelings for him (see the speech quoted above) quickly turns my feelings back towards her – and that feeling is now less one of jealousy than of *disappointment*. Despite all the valiant attempts to preserve my heroine intact, her choice of another who is necessarily less worthy than myself has the inevitable effect of 'diminishing' both of us. Barthes defines this subtle mixture of jealousy and disappointment as *irksome*: '[A] sentiment of slight jealousy which overcomes the amorous subject when he sees the loved being's interest attracted or distracted by persons, objects, or occupations which in his eyes function as so many (unworthy) secondary rivals' (p. 110). Lyndall's distraction – by a persona and by an ideology – does indeed bring her, and my sexual/textual relationship to her, to what we might consider the crisis point of the sequel: the moment the 'Image-repertoire' (Barthes) slips, and a lacuna opens between the 'other' and the (idealized) object of desire. It is this deadly trajectory, beginning in 'disappointment' and ending in (total) 'disillusion', that spells the real end of romance. Whilst anxiety, frustration and jealousy are part of the pain that keeps love alive (and, paradoxically, help sustain the feeling of *ravissement*), the smallest prick of irritation can signal its doom.

Before moving on to an analysis of what factors contribute to the tragic demise of the readerly romance, it is worth noting in conclusion just how chameleon an emotion reader-jealousy is. What my own readings suggest, indeed, is that this is an emotional reflex that can be directed at any number of textual and extratextual subjects (some personified, some not) which threaten the reader-viewer's special relationship with the textual other. Whilst in the case of my readings of the Grauerholz exhibition this is focused mostly on my desire to protect my own (surrogate) authorial control over the text, in the case of *Written on the Body* my jealousy and resentment move between the author-function *and* the 'other readers', whom I now suspect of being more implicated in the text than I am.[37] With respect both to *The Story of an African Farm* and *The Piano*, meanwhile, the jealousy settles most firmly on the text's discursive privileging of heterosexuality. The key readerly issue here is that whilst my own intervention in/rescripting of these texts enables me to establish my own alternatively sexualized relationship with my textual others, this is necessarily at the expense of a number of the romantic conventions (such as 'self-abandonment') associated with a socially sanctioned heterosexual relationship. My 'fulfilment', in other words (see Chapter 5), can never be as complete or as simple as it is for the interdiegetic characters, and I am uncomfortably reminded, once again, of the liminal/invisible nature of my own (ghostly) romance.

Disappointment

Horrible ebb of the Image. (The horror of spoiling is even stronger than the anxiety of losing.)

(Barthes, *A Lover's Discourse*, p. 28)

For lover and reader both, the loss of the other through one's disappointment in them is a different order of catastrophe entirely from the pain and anxiety suffered when their image still burns bright. As Barthes writes under the entry for 'Exile':

> Mourning for the image, in so far as I fail to perform it, makes me anxious; but in so far as I succeed in performing it, makes me sad. If exile from the Image-repertoire is the necessary road to 'cure', it must be admitted that such progress is a sad one . . . A double lack: I cannot even invest my misery, as I could when I suffered from being in love. In those days I desired, dreamed, struggled; the benefit lay before me, merely delayed, traversed by contretemps. Now, no more resonance. Everything is calm, and that is worse. Though justified by an economy – the image dies so I may live – amorous mourning always has something left over: one expression keeps recurring: 'What a shame!' (pp. 107–8)

It is this 'double lack' of disappointed love on which I wish to focus in the concluding section of this chapter: a lack which compounds the loss of the textual other as a presence in one's life with the loss of one's desire for them. The resultant emotional distress which, as I indicated at the end of the previous section, heralds the end of romance, distinguishes itself from the 'despair' brought about by 'fear of abandonment', because the amorous subject/reader knows s/he has brought about the loss herself, through her own dis-illusion or cessation of 'belief'.

Although, upon first consideration, despair might seem a more extreme emotion than disappointment, since it matches desire ounce for ounce, the latter exacts a slow and steady torture in which the amorous subject actively colludes. To the extent, indeed, that s/he first notices (imposes) the stain on the face of the beloved (textual) object, the subject becomes a murderer: but a murderer that kills *herself* ('not by inches, but by fractions of hair-breadths')[38] along with the other:

> In real mourning, it is the test of reality which shows me that the loved object has ceased to exist. In amorous mourning, the object is neither dead nor remote. It is I who decides that its image must die (and I may go so far as to hide this death from it). As long as this strange mourning lasts, I will therefore have to undergo two contrary miseries: to suffer from the fact that the other is present (continuing, in spite of himself, to wound me) and to suffer from the fact that the other is dead (dead at least as I loved him).
>
> (Barthes, pp. 106–7)[39]

It is the fact that 'the end of love' is marked by this reinstatement of self-responsibility that makes its suffering all the worse. Although, as we will see, the 'corruption' of the other can be precipitated by a number of 'external' factors, it is the doubt of (that is, the loss of faith in) the amorous subject herself that sets the seal. After believing that she has been the passive victim of both *ravissement* and 'sequel' the reader/lover is thus finally forced to face up to her active collusion in the (textual) romance – including responsibility for its failure. As will be seen in my own readings, this is a painful acknowledgement, and the subject will often attempt to evade his or her shame and guilt by displacing it back on the (textual) other, or by attempting to contain and conceal his or her doubts.

How, then, does the rot first set in? Who or what is responsible for disfiguring one previously considered so perfect (to the extent that s/he 'matched' so exactly my own desire)? Barthes describes the 'spoiling' as an 'alteration' brought about by the 'abrupt production', within the amorous field, of a 'counter-image' of the loved object:

> In the other's perfect and embalmed figure (for that is the degree to which it fascinates me) I perceive suddenly a speck of corruption. This speck is a tiny one: a gesture, a word, an object, a garment, something unexpected which appears (which dawns) from a region I had never suspected, and suddenly attaches the loved object to a *commonplace world*.
>
> (*A Lover's Discourse*, p. 25)

For Barthes, this re-inscription of the 'other' into a 'commonplace' or mundane existence is the key to the disenchantment. The moment we perceive the other as 'ordinary', they fall from the charmed circle of our desire, and the special person/text is special no longer. Whilst the 'agents' of this disillusion may be as various as they are trivial, it is worth noting the role played by (textual) 'third parties', either in the role of rivals for the beloved's affections/attention, or as 'informers' who are responsible for casting the first seeds of doubt/dismay in the amorous subject's mind. Something of the harmful effect of the first group was dealt with under the heading of 'jealousy' above: by showing interest in someone/something that the subject will inevitably deem 'unworthy' (because less important than him/herself), the beloved may cheapen himself/herself in his/her lover's eyes. Similarly, a trivial piece of gossip – something which allows the amorous subject a vision of the beloved leading an ordinary life without them – can serve as a serious disenchantment. As Barthes writes (on the damaging role of the 'Informer'):

> What I want is a little cosmos (with its own time, its own logic) inhabited only by the two of us. Everything from outside is a threat; either in the form of boredom (if I must live in a world from which the other is absent), or in the form of injury (if that world supplies me with an indiscreet discourse concerning the other). By furnishing me insignificant information about the one I love, the Informer discovers a secret for me. The curtain rises the wrong way round – not on an intimate stage, but on the crowded theatre. (p. 139)

The third party's role of rival and informer is, as we shall shortly see, a key factor in text–reader disappointment. Barthes's description of the lover's world as a chronotope disassociated from the common world is also, as we have seen, characteristic of the special conditions which give rise to (and sustain) the textual *ravissement*.[40] It is also true, however, that this distraction will occur only *if the amorous subject permits it*, and what is interesting as we move on to my analysis of the four readings is the variable extent to which I am able to block out the corrupting voices of these detractors. As we saw in the section on frustration, such challenges are present in all textual relationships from the beginning, and it is often difficult to know why or when we begin to listen to them.

Of all the readings performed here, it is, of course, my engagement with Winterson's *Written on the Body* that is most bitterly circumscribed by disappointment. As the other sections of this chapter have already revealed, this text heralded the end of my special relationship with the Winterson *œuvre*: a readerly act of murder which I could claim was provoked by others (the insidious voices of the informers), but which I must really take responsibility for myself. This, indeed, is a classic instance of the amorous subject refusing to hear the criticisms of others until she is ready to: what my re-memory confirms is my cool indifference to (and imperfect memory of) such 'slander'. And my defence, as I remember it, was amusement: the media discovered Winterson to be 'arrogant' only because they insisted on taking her so seriously.

Even now, I am unsure of the role of these informing voices in my own disenchantment with 'Winterson', though it could certainly be said that the massive public exposure to which she has been submitted has had the effect of making her and her writings disenchantingly 'commonplace'. A connection can probably be made, however, between the effect of the adverse publicity and my changing relation to the texts themselves as they relate to the discourse of the body. I remember, for example, the hard ('redemptive') work I had to do to explain and justify the nude photograph of Jeanette Winterson which appeared in *The Guardian*.[41] This making public of the author's sexual body (even if it was without the author's consent) may be seen to correspond with my growing discomfort with the commodification of her work. The fact that this 'exposure' also anticipated a newly explicit emphasis on the sexual body in her writing therefore becomes metaphorically contiguous. As has already been implied in the previous sections of this chapter, the discourses of romance and of sex are, for me, largely incompatible, and the unveiling of the perfect sexual body in this novel (as in the newspaper photograph) set a paradoxical 'stain' upon the body of Winterson's works as a whole. Although sex should, admittedly, function as the secret shrine at the heart of romantic love, its (literal) 'publication' converts the sacred (and secret?) body into a 'paltry image' (p. 26) and hence kills romance. Something of my own confusion and disappointment at this 'alteration' may be seen in the following extract:

> It occurs to me that this is the first book in which Winterson has attempted to describe sex in a major way. In the previous novels,

the encounters are dealt with obliquely: the discourse of passion juxtaposed with fleeting images of the sexual body. In this text, however – whose mission, after all, is to 'embody' desire and loss – the sex between Lothario and Louise is moved to centre stage. Most interesting, in this respect, is the way in which both the text and Lothario are engaged in a struggle to justify this celebration of the carnal: to prove that this 'super-sex' bears little relation to shadowy imitations, and therefore warrants its central reference point in life and art.

The sexual body is not, however, the only body to appear in this novel. Winterson's representation of the *cancerous* body has also caused me many problems, though here the 'stain' of disappointment derives (paradoxically) from its idealization:

> There is, therefore, a necessarily huge gap between my first reading of this text and my present reception of it *vis-à-vis* the cancer narrative – and what I find myself resisting now is its elision of the sexual body and the diseased (and dying) body in an aesthetics which is instrumental in Lothario's purge:

> > Cancer treatment is brutal and toxic. Louise would normally be treated with steroids, massive doses to induce remission. When her spleen started to enlarge she might have splenic irridation or even a splenectomy. By then she would be badly anaemic, suffering from deep bruising and bleeding, tired and in pain most of the time. She would be constipated. She would be vomiting and nauseous. Eventually chemotherapy would contribute to the failure of her bone marrow. She would be very thin, my beautiful girl, thin and weary and lost. There is no cure for chronic lymphocytic leukaemia. (p. 102)

> What is most unacceptable to me here is the sentence 'She would be very thin . . .' Indeed, I am unable to read it without having images of Dante Gabriel Rossetti's *Beata Beatrix* (see Illustration 2.1) flash before my eyes, together with the infamous Holman Hunt quote that Elizabeth Siddal (the model for the painting) had been seen 'looking more ragged and more beautiful than ever'.[42] Whichever way this and related descriptions in Winterson's text were intended, I am unable to read the juxtaposition of beauty and serious illness as anything other than a glamorization of the fact. It is something I feel passionately not only because I have witnessed and been on the receiving end of pain so extreme that there is no way that it can be aesthetically 'framed', but because as a teenager I was very much inclined to the idea of illnesses (especially of the pale and wasting kind!) as an ideal. Thus I am sensitive to the text's own investment in this discourse on the grounds of my own past collusion with it.

Apart from my objection to the integration of the sexual and dis-
eased body at an aesthetic level, I am also resistant to discourses
which – like that in *Written on the Body* – look to serious illness and/or
death as the 'realization' of love and the apotheosis of desire. In my
experience, illness silences love and kills desire because it arrests the
dialogue and intersubjectivity on which those emotions are based: for
those who are sick, the only relationship which is meaningful is the
one with the illness and/or the pain. . . . For the lover/witness, too,
the experience is the same: the person whom we used to know so intimately we can relate to no longer because their primary relation is no
longer to us but to their body and their body's suffering. This implosion
of the self through suffering is, for me, the ultimate tragedy of illness,
and certainly the one that is most under-represented in the arts (where
death-beds continue to function as the site of all manner of affecting
reconciliations).

And so, what does this digest of personal experience cause me to
feel about Winterson's novel? That its measuring of love by illness and
death is hopelessly inauthentic and misguided? That, despite their cou-
pling in the history of Western art and literature, romance and illness
are really incompatible discourses? Yes, though my bigger objection
is the way in which this 'untruth' is used in the service of Lothario's
own purgation to the extent that cancer may be seen as merely a plot
device. The 'loss' that Lothario is compelled to measure his love
through is the loss of the (sexual) body of his desire. Cancer takes this
physical body away from him in order that he can prove a 'higher'
spiritual love. This is a reductive reading of all that the text can be seen
to be doing in the last section, I know, but I find myself making it nevertheless. The problem is (as I noted earlier) that it is a discourse with
which I am all too familiar not to see its imprint here:

> There is nothing distasteful about you to me: nor sweat, nor
> grime, nor disease and its dull markings. Put your foot in my lap
> and I will cut your nails and ease the tightness of a long day. It
> has been a long day for you to find me. You are bruised all over.
> Burst figs are the livid purple of your skin. . . . You were milk-
> white and fresh to drink. Will your skin discolour, its brightness
> blurring? Will your neck and spleen distend? Will the rigorous
> contours of your stomach swell under an infertile load? It may
> be so and the private drawing I keep of you will be a poor repro-
> duction then. It may be so, but if you are broken then so am I.
> (pp. 124–5)

Although Lothario expresses some self-awareness of the extent to
which his distance from Louise's illness enables him to idealize her
body through the act of memory, as a *romance* the text is absolutely
dependent upon the maintenance of the illusion. The function of her ill-

ness is to enable Lothario to cleanse and spiritualize his love through an act of renunciation, but this is only convincing if she remains an 'unmarked' object of desire. Had Lothario actually attended Louise during her treatment it is likely that he, along with other lovers in these circumstances, would have had to contend too with feelings of horror and repulsion with regards to the changes in Louise's body: his sexual renunciation of her would become involuntary. As it is, the love is supposedly transformed ('proven') while the desire (like Louise's body) remains intact: as the final image of the ghost-Louise confirms, she is etherialized but not changed:

> From the kitchen door Louise's face. Paler, thinner, but her hair still mane-wide [no obvious effects of chemotherapy here!] and the colour of blood. (p. 190)

While this reminds me of the stories about Lizzie Siddal in her coffin, it is not like any of the cancer stories I have ever heard or read and – because the latter have come too close to me – as a reader, I object.[43]

It is nevertheless important to recognize, in conclusion, that the 'spoiling' of my relationship with Winterson's work cannot be finally reduced to authentic realist dissatisfaction and/or moral indignation.[44] Indeed, it cannot be reduced to the (re)reading experience of this one novel. As the other sections of this chapter have made clear, both prejudice and disappointment were in place long before I began this reassessment, suggesting that the words of her detractors – the 'gossips' and 'informers' – might have had more influence than I have given them credit for. Looking back over my own text, indeed, it is clear that I was reading like a betrayed lover determined to discover when the 'stain' first appeared on the stainless body of the relationship. Reading backwards in this way, I can, of course, recognize Lothario's prototype in the earlier heroes and heroines, and berate myself for not spotting the 'signs' (of 'errancy': see below) sooner. The origin of my disappointment can thus be likened, if somewhat melodramatically, to the rogue cells of the cancer patient which fail to present themselves until too late. In this instance, the 'deadly secret' can be thought of as a subjugated discourse (the discourse of 'the sequel') which I, the erstwhile enchanted reader, blindly refused to see. For Lothario's Don Juanesque career, which casts a retrospective shadow over my relationship with the entire Winterson *œuvre*, is no more than an expression of what all lovers know, but most refuse to admit: that romantic love (no matter how apparently unique) is an emotion capable of reproducing itself over and over again. This is a tendency that Barthes refers to as *errancy*:

> Though each love is experienced as unique and though the subject rejects the notion of repeating it elsewhere later on, he sometimes discovers in himself a kind of diffusion of amorous desire; he then realises he is doomed to wander until he dies, from love to love.
>
> (*A Lover's Discourse*, p. 101)

Whilst Winterson's text may thus be seen to face up to this amorous 'fact of life', my own reading shows me stubbornly rejecting it. In an ironic disjunction of the intertextual discourse and my own reactionary stance as an 'unreformed' romantic reader, Lothario's errancy thus becomes the spoiling 'stain' that finally brings my disappointment with 'Winterson' to consciousness (which is not to say that it is the *cause*), and which therefore signals the 'end of love'.

It is clearly no coincidence that my (passing) disappointment with the Grauerholz exhibition is also focused on the representation of the sexual body: namely, the female nudes featured in Room 3. As this section of my reading indicates (see the extract quoted above, pp. 162–3), the (public) exposure of the body is, for me, at odds with the private ('secret') discourse of romance, and my romantic engagement with the text depends here – as with Winterson's texts – upon keeping the paths hidden, the body clothed. Although my reading explains my discomfort with these figures on the ostensibly political grounds that, as I remark, 'the female nude in Western art is so circumscribed by patriarchal and (hetero)sexual discourse', it is evident that my discomfort is overdetermined by the same reactionary idealism that caused me such problems with Winterson's text. In both instances I constitute the discourses of romance and the erotic as fundamentally incompatible, and this 'materialization' of the body fills the gap that needs to be left in my own imagination.

How the Grauerholz bodies differ from the Winterson ones in this respect is, however, in their provisionality. In terms of my viewing experience of the exhibition as a whole they are as transitory and impermanent as the fleeting movements they are engaged in (both figures are pictured running and leaping), and if they *do* constitute a 'stain' on the face of my textual other (in this case, the 'scene' of romance), it is by no means indelible, thus indicating that a small wavering of the Image-repertoire need not necessarily signal the end of romance.

In terms of indelibility, Lyndall's 'staining' in *The Story of an African Farm* presents me – the 'adoring reader' – with a challenge somewhere between the Grauerholz exhibition and *Written on the Body*. My heroine's fall from grace, as already indicated in this and the previous chapter, is a severe test of my loyalty, commitment and readerly ingenuity. As we have seen, I have to work extremely hard to find a new position from which to dialogize with Lyndall after the collapse of her own ambitions, and the 'solution' I come up with in Chapter 5, although intellectually persuasive (to myself at least), cannot quite remove all traces of my dis-illusion: an emotion that I am reluctant to admit, even to myself.

Looking back over my reading, in particular the extract relating to Lyndall's return from school (see pp. 150–1 above), it is interesting to see how anxiously this textual disappointment was prepared for. Although my *re-memory* is hazy on my relationship to this section of the narrative (I quite 'forget' Lyndall's feminist speeches), in my re-reading I am intensely aware of what is to come, as is signalled by the desperation of my lines: 'If she changes, if she turns out to be "less" than I hoped, I am doomed to pain and disappointment. . . . Worse, if she forms attachments that usurp my own relation to her I will feel betrayed. And how should I avoid any of these things?' What this implies, of course, is that our experience of sexual/textual *ravissement* is not quite as blind as it first appears. Even whilst the reader/lover is gripped by the full 'uniqueness' and 'originality' of her experience, a darkly repressed knowledge of the sequel constantly threatens her sense of euphoria and plenitude; as we saw in the first section of this chapter, love is not a minute old before it is circumscribed by the anxiety of loss.

The disappointment that threatens my relationship with Lyndall, then, differs from that which afflicts my relationships with either the Winterson or the Grauerholz texts through a matter of timing. Whereas, with Winterson, I *began* my reading with the expectation of disappointment, here the anxiety emerges as part of the process. Because the Grauerholz photographs were *new* texts, moreover, and because the nature of my readerly desire was still unspecified during that reading process, the momentary disappointment I felt about the female nudes was but one feeling amidst a kaleidoscope of unclassified emotions. With respect to Schreiner's novel, however, I begin the second section fully conscious of what I currently possess (my commitment to Lyndall) and what I therefore stand to lose.

The two 'flaws' that appear on the body of Lyndall's character are her femininity and her (hetero)sexuality. Reviewing the extract where I describe how my 'faith' is challenged when she returns from school (see pp. 150–1 above), it seems important to separate out what is problematic about her politics *per se* (some of which I have already dealt with under the heading of 'anxiety') and her 'body politics' (the white dress; the descriptions of her coquetry), which I clearly find more disturbing. Although, in the reading itself, I merely use the latter to question the former (what value should we ascribe to her feminist speeches against, in my phrase, 'the absurd conventions of femininity' if she has nevertheless submitted to them?), my disquiet at the way in which she shakes mealie dust from her dress is clearly in excess of this. As with the episode in *Wuthering Heights* where Cathy returns from Thrushcross Grange, I am disturbed by a disruption of the Image-repertoire. The gender transgression that marked Lyndall's childhood (see Chapter 5) is jeopardized by this small gesture of feminine propriety (brushing dust off a white dress); and I – like Waldo, like Heathcliff – am confused and embarrassed about how to relate to one whose identity, both intellectual and sexual, was formerly characterized by its androgyny. This is not to say that my reading had fixed/fantasized Lyndall in a masculinized role, but that my conception of her person/behaviour did not allow (despite the *narrator's* repeated and immensely irritating references to such matters as her 'smallness') for *this degree* of femininity. With respect to the 'Image-repertoire' I had created, indeed, this incongruity (which I receive as a shock, an 'aberration') 'stains' my relationship with Lyndall by linking her to a commonplace world (see Barthes, above, p. 171): a world which I believe belittles her *despite* the irony and contempt with which she treats it.

Whilst, in my reading, I manage to contain the damage done by this 'alteration' (Barthes, p. 25) to the beloved's self-presentation by convincing myself that it is a 'masquerade', the complex re-positioning this involves me in (in terms of both gender and emotions) clearly puts my devotion on the defensive (see Chapter 5).[45] An even more damaging 'stain', potentially, and one that I do not contain so much as evade, arises out of Lyndall's insistent heterosexuality. Although, once again, the cynicism with which she approaches her relationship with 'the Stranger' in some ways makes her 'betrayal' (of myself and Waldo) easier to bear, the existence of a sexual imperative at odds with her emotional and intellectual affiliation (she desires this man, but she does not love him) remains, for the lesbian/feminist reader, provokingly perverse. My strategy for dealing with this disappointment is, as we have already seen in Chapter 5, to pretend it never happened: to lop off the text at the point Lyndall passes from Waldo's field of vision, and so edit out both the night she spends with the Stranger and the tragic coda to her story. The fact that the sustenance of my relationship with Lyndall requires such a major repression of the plot is evidence, however, of just how big this 'spoiling' potentially is, and when I go back to the novel itself I see many 'counter-images' (Barthes, *A Lover's Discourse*, p. 25) of Lyndall that could become the focus of a major dis-illusion. Apparently trivial alterations in appearance, clothing and behaviour produce a severe disruption within the idealized/idolized Image-repertoire, for example:

> From under their half-closed lids the keen eyes looked down at her. Her shoulders were bent; for a moment the little figure had forgotten its queenly bearing, and drooped wearily; the wide dark eyes watched the fire very softly. . . .'Poor little thing!' he said, 'you are only a child'.
> (p. 258)

The irony here, of course, is that *yes,* Lyndall is now more of a child than she ever was in the book's early chapters. And what has infantilized her, paradoxically, is the feminizing and sexualizing process of 'becoming a woman'. In terms of the politics of gendered *reading,* however, the mystery remains of how I am able to body-swerve this degradation of my textual other, whereas in other textual relationships the first hint of alteration will signal the 'end of love'. Looking back over all these readings, the answer would seem to lie, not surprisingly, both with the text's reader-positioning and with the reader's own 'will-to-possess' (Barthes, p. 232). What Schreiner's text clearly allows me to do, which Winterson's does not, is adopt reader-positionings which will enable me to protect my relationship with my textual other. *Written on the Body,* meanwhile, offers no such footholds, and because I am unable to escape the domination of the narrator (Lothario) for long enough to form alternative relationships with other characters/discourses/'scenes' within the text, I am trapped in my disillusionment. Thus, although Schreiner's narrator is at times every bit as didactic as Winterson's, and is, after all, the one responsible for demeaning Lyndall before my eyes, I am nevertheless able to overrule her authority.

Whatever textual indeterminacy facilitates the maintenance of my textual romance, however, it is clearly strongly supported by my own 'will-to-possess' (and preserve) this particular textual other. Because Lyndall is such a powerful icon for me, I am resolutely determined (in this reading, at least) not to give her up. Admitting disappointment here, indeed, would represent not only the loss of the 'other' but, even more seriously, of the 'desire to desire'. The prospect of a life/textual event *not* structured by such emotion is clearly why we fight disillusion (and its consequences) at all costs. As Barthes writes, of the panic of the lover's 'self-exile' from the Image-repertoire (that is his/her attempt to give up the other):

> I try to wrest myself away from the amorous Image-repertoire, but the Image-repertoire burns underneath, like an incompletely extinguished peat fire; it catches fire again; what was renounced reappears; out of the hasty grave suddenly breaks a long cry.
>
> (Jealousies, anxieties, possessions, discourses, appetites, signs, once again amorous desire was burning everywhere. It was as if I were trying to embrace one last time, hysterically, someone for whom I was about to die: I was performing a denial of separation.)
>
> (*A Lover's Discourse*, pp. 108–9)

In terms of my ongoing relationship with Schreiner's text, then, it is clear that I am not yet ready to yield my 'will-to-possess'. As Barthes's psychoanalytic explanation of the reflex makes clear, and my own reading in Chapter 5 supports, I am still prepared to go to enormous lengths to avoid separation. At what point a reader/lover *will* stop making efforts to protect his/her desire in this way is unpredictable, however, and clearly depends, as in the case of my relationship with 'Winterson', on a congruence of contextual as well as textual factors. I have also the sense that this is where a reader's 'involvement' with a textual character constitutes a different order of relationship to that with the 'disembodied' textual others with which I have been dealing. However illusory, it is the reader–character relationship that comes closest to mimicking/replicating our relationships in the material world. For me to admit the blemishes in Lyndall's character/behaviour is more immediately threatening to *my identity* as a desiring reader/subject than to find similar 'alterations' in Grauerholz's 'scenes', or even, it seems, the 'body' of a ('beloved') author's works.

It should be clear by now that my reader-relationship with both the Grauerholz exhibition and *The Piano* are far less threatened by the shadow of the sequel than are the two novels. This is partly for the good reason that they are both newcomers to my library, and have not yet been subjected to the same (con)textual sea-changes as the others. In both instances, indeed, the readings I have analysed here were written when my *ravissement* was still fresh, and such disappointments as do threaten are ephemeralized amid the swirl of other first impressions. This fact obviously has some bearing on how we choose to think of the chronology of *ravissement* and sequel, to which I will return in the conclusion to this chapter but it also points to how central is the changing context in which a text is received – of personal, intellectual, social and historical circumstances – in determining our relationship to it. As far as *The Piano* is concerned, indeed, it could be said that no significant signs of disappointment stain the reading I deal with here; potential disruptions to the Image-repertoire (such as Ada looking different to the way I imagined her) are overcome through the radical and pre-emptive re-scripting of my relationship to the text and its characters, as described in Chapter 5.

If this text of Campion's fails to engender disappointment, however, it does dramatize it. Looking back to my earlier discussion of Winterson's novel, we can see that Ada's story is another inscription of Barthesian 'errancy', inasmuch as the plot hinges on the transference of her love from one suitor to another. In this respect, and as I indicated in Chapter 5) we can see her seduction by Baines parallelling the degenerative sequel of her relationship with Haussler. Every key she wins back from Baines takes her further down both routes, until the climactic dis-illusion with the one coincides with the *ravissement* of the other. Once again, the chronology of this raises questions with respect to the articulation of prequel/*ravissement*/sequel, but it is also an interesting instance of how the 'spoiling' of an old relationship can be most simply caused by the arrival of a new (textual) other.

Although I have already explained my ability to avoid disappointment by this text in terms of my active intervention in its production, it is nevertheless interesting that the 'structure of feeling' I appropriate so readily here (the cathartic displacement of one romance by another) is nevertheless an expression of the same 'errancy' I made the source of my disappointment with Winterson's text. What this would seem to indicate is just how wilfully blind our ideological inscriptions are: whilst I seize the hypothetical possibility of the *coup de foudre* striking twice, I am still resolutely opposed to the discourse of romance as serial monogamy. It is clearly but a hair's breadth in our moral and emotional reasoning that separates enchantment by one text (or aspect of a text) from disappointment by another: the configuration of discourse and personal experience that determines when and why we will fall 'out of love' (with a text/with a person) is clearly as finely nuanced as that which generates our *ravissement*.

Conclusion

Whilst this chapter has dealt with 'the long chain of sufferings' characteristic of the romantic sequel under four headings, a further subdivision can clearly be made between the distress predicated upon *unrequited desire* (anxiety, frustration) and that which accompanies the *end of desire* (disappointment). Jealousy, as we have seen, occupies a treacherous middle ground somewhere between these two positions, since, while it arises out of a desire for the other, its unpleasant discoveries (a glimpse of the beloved in rapt dialogue with an unworthy rival, for example) can themselves become the 'spoiling' that precipitates disappointment, disillusion and the other's 'death'. For readers and lovers alike, moreover, I would argue that whilst the agony of unrequited love might seem so unbearable at the time that we constitute it as despair (see Barthes, p. 48), its unhappiness is nothing compared to the 'horror' (Barthes, p. 28) associated with the death ('murder') of that love: the moment of unbounded panic and emptiness when we see the other (text/person) deform/dwindle/combust before our erstwhile adoring eyes, and we look into the yawning abyss of a world that is no longer held together by our desire for (an)other.

What my readings here have, of course, shown is that, in terms of text–reader relations at least, this last scenario is so terrifying that the reader will do everything she can to avoid or forestall it (as with the case of Schreiner's novel), or else face up to it *only* when another has arrived to 'fill the gap' (as illustrated by my belated renunciation of 'Winterson'). Readerly disappointment, like its counterpart in our interpersonal relations, has to be strongly managed in this way precisely because it constitutes the moment when we take responsibility for our emotions: for most of the preceding *ravissement* and sequel we have felt ourselves to be the passive recipients of our suffering, but to acknowledge an imperfection in the other is also to acknowledge our part in their former (ideal) construction.

This recognition returns us to the question of power in text–reader relations. As the preceding discussion suggests, and as my conclusion to Chapter 5 also indicated, there are some complicated issues at work here, precisely because the reader/lover's *perception* of their empowerment/disempowerment does not necessarily match the 'true' (that is theoretically explicable) state of affairs. We have already observed, for example, that during the period of *ravissement* the amorous subject feels herself to be the passive (if blessed) recipient of some magical and gratuitous gift, while the plotting and scheming that accompanies this phase (as the subject strives to achieve the 'positioning' that will give him/her maximum access to the beloved) shows her to be supremely active and in control of her (readerly) actions. In this respect, while our ability to find 'satisfaction' in a text would seem to depend hugely on our ability to achieve dialogic interaction with the textual other (see the discussions in Chapter 5), this 'other' might provide us with no more than the generating 'spark' for our own projection/production.

When we turn to the emotions associated with the sequel, meanwhile, the power-play is superficially reversed. Now the reader/lover feels herself *more active* (it is up to her to remove the obstacles that are causing her so much emotional frustration); yet, at the same time, because her actions are unsuccessful she also feels herself significantly *less empowered*. Because of this somewhat contradictory relationship between activity/passivity and empowerment/disempowerment, it becomes extremely difficult to construct a hypothesis of our emotional involvement in texts that maps onto existing reader-theories concerning the relationship between 'pleasure' and 'participation' (see the discussion in Chapter 1). Whilst the analysis of the readings I perform here certainly does indicate that a good deal of the unhappiness we experience in text–reader relationships depends, as in our interpersonal relationships, on the feeling of disempowerment, this does not necessarily coincide with our sense of the text being the 'dominant partner' in meaning-production, merely that – as in the case of my reading of *Written on the Body* – we are unable to *utilize* (for whatever reason) our potential reader-agency.

When dealing with emotions, whether textual or otherwise, this project has, however, caused me to feel strongly that such attempts to *explain* the complex psychological proceedings that will cause us to experience 'pleasure' here or 'distress' there are something of a red herring: the fact that our feelings of 'enchantment', 'devotion', 'frustration' and 'jealousy' are the products of certain ideologically inscribed reflexes that all relate (somewhere) to an 'imaginary' (that is 'false') understanding of the relationship between the self and the other. Starting from this premiss (which is the one I employed in my analysis here), the reason why I experience my reader-positioning as sometimes passive and empowered, and at other times active and disempowered, is ultimately less important than the emotions to which these configurations give rise. It is only by recognizing that the text–reader romance functions according to the same ideological 'illogicality' as all romance that we can analyse what 'really' happens in the reading process, rather than what 'ought' to happen.

This brings me on to the question of the *chronology* of the text–reader romance. Although, as I discussed in Chapter 5, romance is a discourse that we construct and experience as a narrative, most of use would also agree with Barthes's assertion (*A Lover's Discourse*, pp. 6–8) that, *in medias res,* it is experienced as an overwhelming muddle of emotions in which the pleasures of *ravissement* are virtually simultaneous with the anxieties of the sequel. What this chapter has revealed, indeed, is the enormous battle which the reader fights to protect her first enchantment from the 'chain of sufferings' that threaten it from the moment of its birth, and how certain emotions which belong to the first wave of passion (such as 'devotion') are to a large extent defined by the 'stains' and 'corruptions' which threaten them (see, for example, the discussion of *The Story of an African Farm* in Chapter 5). In this respect, indeed, I feel it would be better to understand the different sets of emotion associated with *ravissement* and sequel, not in terms of their chronology, but in terms, first, of their (admittedly confused) relationship to power and agency as discussed above (that is, *ravissement* as 'passive' empowerment; sequel as 'active' disempowerment), and, second, of their *experiential temporal status*. By the latter I mean that whilst the emotions that characterize the *ravissement* are all marked by a sense of 'union' and 'fulfilment' that is somehow 'outside time' (as exemplified by the 'motionless cradling' of the 'amorous embrace', Barthes, p. 104), the anxieties, frustrations and jealousies of the sequel all result from the subject's reawakening to a temporal world in which various agents (such as rivals, daily life and human ageing) threaten separation and the end of love. It is through this differential subjective temporality, then, rather than through a narrative chronology as such, that we can see the amorous emotions separate out into *ravissement* and sequel: in the first set, the reader/lover is 'at one' with the textual other; in the second, she is desperately chasing it, all the while wanting to get back to the space/place where time stands still, and the need and the fulfilment are one.

It is the recognition that in the text–reader romance, as in our relationships in the material world, the joys and sufferings of our relationship do not follow a smooth trajectory from 'birth' to 'death' which makes the experience both more thrilling and more alarming than we would otherwise expect. What the analysis of my readings here will hopefully have confirmed is that, for the feminist reader especially, the emotional rollercoaster on which we travel each and every time we engage in a new textual encounter is thus a challenge as well as a thrill: that reading is not only about 'pleasure'. And although *all* readers are liable to the same dynamics of 'inclusion/exclusion' and 'acceptance/rejection' that I have described here, for the politically motivated reader (such as the feminist) the undertaking will be loaded with a heavy and exacting burden of responsibilities and desires that will make our relationships with our textual others more difficult both to define and defend.

Translating this last point into my thesis concerning the structural and ideological incompatibility of implicated and hermeneutic reading, then, what these readings from the sequel seem to confirm is that political frameworks such as feminism are most often invoked to *explain* our disappointment with a text in which we are no longer (emotionally) implicated. Although it is, of course, possible to cite instances in which feminist discourse (as embodied by a textual character, perhaps) is itself our textual other, this construction is separate from the notion of feminism as a *reading practice,* whose dialogic relationship is not with an other *in the text* but with an extratextual point of reference (for example, the reader's own audience or 'interpretive community'). Indeed, in this respect my readings here of Winterson in particular anticipate perfectly some of the discussions that follow in Chapters 7 and 8. Like the professional critics and journalists writing on *The Piano*, and like the members of the feminist reading groups, my own text slips frequently into a highly professionalized rhetoric of feminist critique as a response to my failure to sustain a more implicated reading. Feminism (or some other political value-system) becomes, then, the means through which we can scapegoat the text and textual other who has

disappointed us, whilst recognizing (as we must) that the failure of the relationship was due to more than an ideological disagreement.

As I indicated earlier, however, the mechanics of how and why we
become emotionally involved in texts to the extent that we do probably
matters less than the fact that this dimension of the reading process is at
least recognized. Whether our involvement stems from a passionate interaction with some aspect of the text (as in my relationship with Lyndall),
or an (equally passionate) projection onto it (as in the case of my reading
of *The Piano*), the 'politics' I have been struggling to bring to consciousness here is as follows: that it is precisely because the (implicated)
text–reader relationship is *structured like a romance* that we will continue
to fall out of love with texts, as with people, in ways that 'reason' (and
much existing theory) tells us we ought not to.

Notes

1 Roland Barthes, *A Lover's Discourse* (see n. 41, Ch. 1). Page references to this
   volume will be given after quotations in the text. All Barthes's quotes are from
   this particular text unless otherwise stated.
2 Janice Galloway, *Foreign Parts* (London: Jonathan Cape, 1994).
3 Scenography: Barthes writes 'There is a scenography of waiting: I organize it,
   manipulate it, cut out a portion of time in which I shall mime the loss of the loved
   object and provoke all the effects of a minor mourning' (p. 37). See also p. 190
   of *A Lover's Discourse* for a description of 'the twilight state'.
4 Jeanette Winterson, *Written on the Body* (see n. 41, Ch. 1). Page references to
   this volume will be given after quotations in the text.
5 See e.g. Nicolette Jones (*The Sunday Times*, 13 September 1992): 'The gender of
   the book's narrator is unspecified, eliminating any distinction between homosexual and heterosexual love . . . Some of the narrator's attitudes smack of a gener-
   alizing hostility towards men; others are self-serving in a way you feel the old
   Winterson would have satirized'. Elizabeth Pincus, writing in the *San Francisco
   Chronicle* (7 February 1993) is more indulgent: 'Call it a political tactic (to
   demonstrate that lesbian love is no less potent, no less real than hetero love), or
   call it a philosophical dissection of our gendered society. In any case, the central
   conceit of "Written on the Body" elevates the novel to a new plane of inquiry
   about the nature of the human heart'.
6 See e.g. Natasha Walter's review in *The Independent* (19 September 1992) which
   makes the point that it is *not only* the narrator's gender which is unspecified.
   Walter writes: 'Yet she leaves out not only the specification of gender, but blurs
   all the other contours of her narrator's personality. The narrator has no childhood, no colour, no class, and no past – except for a succession of lovers'.
7 'Interpellation': see n. 25, Ch. 4.
8 'Implied author': see n. 11, Ch. 4.
9 'Speech types': see my discussion of Bakhtin's different types of 'doubly voiced'
   discourse in *Reading Dialogics* (n. 4, Ch. 1), pp. 51–4.
10 'Hidden dialogue': see *Reading Dialogics* (n. 9), pp. 53–4.
11 'Structure of feeling': see n. 33, Ch. 1.

12 Olive Schreiner, *Story of an African Farm* (see n. 1, Ch. 1). Page references to this volume will be given after quotations in the text.

13 'Reader-guilt': I am indebted for this concept to a member of the audience at the University of Rochester, New York, where I gave a paper based on this material, although I am still uncertain whether or not to name 'guilt' an emotion. In other circumstances I have argued that guilt is itself a 'fake emotion', or at least one that conceals/evades more honest desires.

14 Jane Campion, *The Piano* (see n. 41, Ch. 1).

15 '"No" means "yes"': a reference to Freud's theory of how repression causes individuals to say the opposite of what they really desire, and for which he has been taken to task by (some) feminists, especially with reference to his deployment of this paradox in the case history of 'Dora'. See vol. 7 of *The Standard Edition of the Complete Psychological Works of Sigmund Freud* (n. 39, Ch. 5).

16 For further discussion of this theory of alternative/sublimated desire see my essay, 'Another Time/Another Place: the Chronotope of Romantic Love in Contemporary Feminist Fiction', in *Fatal Attractions* and *Cultural Subversions*, ed. Lynne Pearce and Gina Wisker (London: Pluto Press, forthcoming).

17 Jeanette Winterson, *Sexing the Cherry* (London: Bloomsbury, 1989).

18 See ch. 1 of *Feminist Readings/Feminists Reading* (see n. 35, Ch. 1), pp. 38–39, for further discussion of Cathy's feminization and its effect on Heathcliff.

19 Angela Grauerholz exhibition: see n. 41, Ch. 1.

20 'Cultural capital': see n. 28, Ch. 3.

21 'Distinction' (Bourdieu): see n. 20 above.

22 'Filling the landscape': see discussion in Ch. 5, pp. 120–41.

23 That it was Grauerholz's intention to make viewers uncomfortable in the process of their 'filling the landscape' is certainly the opinion of Paulette Gagnon in the exhibition catalogue (see n. 17, Ch. 5). Gagnon writes: 'The confrontation with situations which combine effects of surprise and anonymity is a stunning one. In the isolation of the instant, the subjects' triviality cannot transport us elsewhere or account for our experience. In the ensuing disappointment, the key to the disconcerting elements of the image can be found through a recourse to imagination and personal interpretation' (p. 51).

24 Textual others: this notion that the reader/viewer's primary dialogic relationship may be transferred from an 'other' in the text to one who forms part of the *context* of reading (e.g. a member of the reader's own interpretive community) will become a focus of attention in Chs. 7 and 8.

25 'Collection of semes': see n. 37, Ch. 5.

26 'Hermeneutic/cultural codes': see n. 18, Ch. 1.

27 'Recognition': but see the section on 'devotion' in Ch. 5 for an instance of how such recognition of the reader's presence *may* be suggested.

28 'Ontology/epistemology': see Elspeth Probyn (n. 6, Ch. 1) and discussion of how these terms relate to the reading process in Ch. 1 pp. 25–6.

29 'Author function': see n. 30, Ch. 5.

30 I admit that these values are *highly* conventional, and they have certainly been modified in many more recent encodings of romantic love. See the Introduction to *Romance Revisited* (n. 5, Ch. 1).

31 Jeanette Winterson, *Oranges are not the Only Fruit* (see n. 11, Ch. 5), p. 170. See also my essay '"Written on Tablets of Stone"? Roland Barthes, Jeanette Winterson and the Discourse of Romantic Love', in *Volcanoes and Pearl Divers: Essays in Lesbian Feminist Studies*, ed. Suzanne Raitt (London: Onlywomen Press, 1995), pp. 147–68.

32 Angela Grauerholz, *Nude* (1992), 161.5 × 50.8cm and *The Leap* (1992), 161 × 50.8cm. Reproduced in Exhibition Catalogue (see n. 17, Ch. 5), p. 24.

33 See the exhibition catalogue, pp. 30–1 (n. 17, Ch. 5) for reproductions of *Lessing* (1992), 161.5 × 244cm, and *Druid II* (1990–1), 244 × 161.5cm.

34 Daphne de Maurier, *Rebecca* (London: Victor Gollancz, 1938).

35 See again the Introduction to *Romance Revisited* (n. 30 above) for discussion of alternatives to this monogamous version of romance.

36 See *Screen*, Reports and Debates (ed. Jackie Stacey), vol. 36(3) (Autumn, 1995) pp. 257–87. The three articles included in this section, and to which I refer in Chapter 7, are as follows: Stella Bruzzi, 'Tempestuous Petticoats: Costume and Desire in *The Piano*', pp. 257–66; Lynda Dyson, 'The Return of the Repressed? Whiteness, Femininity and Colonialism in *The Piano*', pp. 267–76; and Sue Gillett, 'Lips and Fingers: Jane Campion's *The Piano*', pp. 277–87.

37 This resentment echoes the ones I discuss in Ch. 4 with regard to contemporary feminist fiction.

38 See Emily Brontë, *Wuthering Heights* (Harmondsworth: Penguin, 1965), p. 321.

39 See Freud on 'Mourning and Melancholia', in vol. 14 of *The Standard Edition of the Complete Psychological Works* (n. 39, Ch. 5), for discussion of the subject's need to 'introject' the lost object, this being the 'logic' that clearly subtends the Barthes quotation. (Thanks to Jackie Stacey for pointing this out.)

40 'Chronotope': see n. 36, Ch. 5.

41 Kate Campbell, 'Whatever turns you on', *The Guardian* (6 November 1990), p. 36.

42 See Dante Gabriel Rossetti, *Beata Beatrix* (Tate Gallery, London, *c*. 1864–70): see Chapter 2 of my *Woman/Image/Text: Readings in Pre-Raphaelite Art and Literature* (Hemel Hempstead: Harvester-Wheatsheaf, 1991), for a full discussion of this image.

43 See e.g. Barbara Rosenblum, 'Cancer in Two Voices: Living in an Unstable Body', in *An Intimate Wilderness: Lesbian Writers on Sexuality*, ed. Judith Barrington (Portland, OR: Eighth Mountain, 1991), pp. 133–8, and Jackie Stacey's *Teratologies: A Cultural Study of Cancer* (London and New York: Routledge, 1997).

44 'Authentic realism' (see n. 35, Ch. 1).

45 'Masquerade': a concept that has been appropriated by many contemporary feminist theorists in connection with the 'performance' of femininity. See especially Judith Butler in *Bodies that Matter* (n. 50, Ch. 1).

PART

III

THE POLITICS OF
FEMINIST/S READING

Preface to Part III

Although many of us subscribe to ways of thinking and value-systems that are supposed to embrace difference (feminism being one of them), it is important to recognize how much anxiety and distress even small differences of opinion can cause, especially amongst groups of friends, colleagues and variously defined communities who believe they are operating within a common context and with a common goal. This is nowhere more true than within communities of feminists as readers and viewers, where disagreements over what a text means, or what it represents in political terms, have often been enough to shatter both personal and professional partnerships. While such disagreements within a politically defined group are most easily explained in ideological terms (feminism is such a broad church that it is inevitable that investments will vary), my research into the reading process has revealed that other factors are also at work. As emerged with respect to my own readings in Part II, our differential structural relation to a text – whether we are operating within a hermeneutic or a implicated model of text–reader relations, for instance – will also affect the total reading event, and will have a bearing on whether we experience it as positive and fulfilling or negative and disappointing. In the following two chapters the implications of this thesis are taken further, as I explore the reading processes of readers other than myself. In Chapter 7 these are the professional readers and critics of Jane Campion's film, *The Piano*; in Chapter 8, the participants of my own small ethnographic survey of groups of feminist readers based in Britain and Canada.[1]

Both these chapters, then, were conceived with the object of learning more about what causes readers – especially those constructed as having common interests and investments – to have such different reading/viewing experiences. In both instances I begin by assessing the ostensible (that is, 'declared') reasons for the readers' like or dislike of the text in question (because readers nearly always begin to make sense of their reading experience through the process of *evaluation*), before moving on to a consideration of other, often unspoken factors, such as the role of audience and the interpretive community. The latter may be seen to have a major bearing not only in providing readers with their evaluative frames, but also in determining their structural relationship with/within the text and whether or not they are 'permitted' to engage in a more implicated reading. The evidence, taking into account both the groups of readers considered here, together with my own readings in Part II, is that these extratextual 'others' will often obstruct and inhibit the reader's (actual or potential) relationship with an other within the text, thus frustrating a more interactive exchange. Disagreements between readers, and between groups of readers, may thus be explained in terms of different models of reading as well as differences in ideology.

I realize that there is a danger that this hypothesizing of two different models of reading could all too easily be misinterpreted as my advocating the one (the 'implicated') over the other (the 'hermeneutic'). This is not at all my objective. Indeed, it is my hope that these chapters, like those in Part II, will alert feminist readers to the *dangers* of implicated reading from a political standpoint: an issue to which I will return again in the Conclusion to the book as a whole. My interest, both with respect to my own readings and those considered here, has merely been to discern and conceptualize the different forms the text–reader relationship *may* take – and we can be sure that, whatever else may emerge, there will be more models, and more ways of conceptualizing them, than the dyad I have presented here.

These two chapters have also presented me with my most difficult challenge in methodological terms, and in such a way that gives the lie to any idealized dialogic model of either reading or ethnographic research. Despite my own self-reflexive practices in the writing of Chapters 5 and 6, the early drafts of Chapters 7 and 8 revealed me all too eager to resume my former textual practices. This included the almost total disappearance of my own readerly 'I', and the reinstatement of the text (and, in this case, *the texts of other* readers) as my own hermeneutic 'object' of investigation. While my resumption of this professional practice of 'othering' the text/textual practice was very easy to pass over in my analysis of the journalists and critics whom I discuss in Chapter 7, the implications raised by the rather less anonymous texts/readers who constituted my reading groups in Chapter 8 was not. As one of the readers of an early draft of this chapter pointed out to me: 'You are doing to their texts exactly what you accuse your readers of doing to Atwood's story'.[2] Whilst it was never my intention to 'accuse' (implying as it does that there are 'right' and 'wrong' ways of reading), it is certainly true that I was using my privileged position as researcher and commentator in such a way that it 'othered' my participants. In the light of the all the excellent work that has now been done in alerting researchers to the problematic power-structures which attend any sort of ethnographic research, I have subsequently attempted to make my commentaries in these chapters much more self-reflexive and, indeed, more 'implicated', drawing parallels, wherever possible, with my own reading practices elsewhere, and therefore hopefully signalling that I do not exempt myself from the practices and processes I describe.

Notes

1 Jane Campion, *The Piano*: see n. 41, Ch. 1.
2 Margaret Atwood, 'Death by Landscape', in *Wilderness Tips* (London: Bloomsbury Press, 1991). This is the text that my reading groups worked with (see Ch. 8).

7

Readers in Disagreement

Love, as we know, is blind. But what is it that makes readers similarly willing to indulge weaknesses, inconsistencies and flaws in some texts and not others? In this chapter I will be following up the discussion from the end of the last section by investigating the ways in which *readers as critics*, some of them identified as feminists, some not, seek to explain and legitimate their like or dislike of a particular text. These 'professional' readers/viewers have been drawn from the ranks of the journalists and academics who, like myself, have produced readings and reviews of Jane Campion's *The Piano*, thus providing thematic as well as theoretical continuity with the preceding chapters.[1] Although my account will deal with only a few of these readings in any detail, they are representative of a much bigger sample based on a computer search of all the newspaper and magazine reviews published in the year immediately following the film's release (1993), together with a selection of more academic pieces.[2]

(Re)constituting critics as readers of the texts they analyse is not, of course, the same as reviewing what they say. In this respect, this chapter should not be considered a survey of feminist responses to *The Piano*, any more than the last chapters were a straightforward reading of the same. As previously, the subject of my investigation is 'reading' itself: reading as it engages the affective as well as the cognitive faculties – focusing on the process of text–reader engagement as well as on the act of interpretation and meaning-production.

In as much as it considers the readings of others, this chapter also functions as a bridge between the analysis of my own textual engagements in the previous section and my work with groups of other feminist readers in Chapter 8. Whilst producing a reading of a text for publication, sometimes to an audience of thousands, is necessarily a very different process to 'reading for oneself' or, indeed, reading for the purpose of an academic exercise (as both I and my respondents have done), many of the same processes of engagement, evaluation and rationalization would seem to obtain. The issues of 'pleasure' *vs.* 'politics', or affective *vs.* cognitive analysis – how we deal with our composite intellectual and emotional response to a text – are still pertinent, though admittedly more hidden or disguised within the discourse of professional textual analysis. One of the purposes of this bridging chapter is, then, to explore the extent to which professional readers – both journalists and academics – appear to base their judgement of a text on values (whether aesthetic, intellectual or political) which are set apart from a more personal and/or emotive engagement with it, even though (in the journalism especially) the processes of 'involvement' and 'identification' are a recognized condition of reader/viewer pleasure and the text's chances of 'success'. We find a situation, then, in which the critics will evaluate a text's affective qualities in relation to its potential audience, whilst remaining silent about their own positioning in this regard. This, as we shall see, is also true of the academically trained respondents to my questionnaire (see Chapter 8), who could only comment on their personal and/or affective inscription by the selected texts with great awkwardness and difficulty. None of this is a surprise, of course: as I indicated in Chapter 1, this whole project, especially the focus on the emotional dimension of the reading process, was undertaken on the premiss that it is our increasingly sophisticated training as readers within various (and variously related) intellectual communities that has served both to define and disguise what happens in the reading process: we *do* read as we have been taught and according to certain marked codes and expectations, but we also mix these 'official' practices with cruder, less directed readerly behaviour in which, as evidenced by my readings in Chapters 5 and 6, the reader's 'I' is clamouring for involvement in, or recognition by, their 'textual other'.

Reading, within interpretive communities sharing a basic training in literary analysis, may thus be said to be circumscribed by the restraining hand of connoisseurship. As Lynda Nead has observed in her recent work on art and obscenity, 'disinterestedness' with regard to a potential emotional or libidinal engagement by a text is integral to the whole history of criticism and connoisseurship, marking as it does a clear distinction between the educated and the non-educated, the refined and the unrefined: between 'good' and 'bad' taste.[3] As we have seen throughout this book, those of us interested in understanding the more messy, unauthorized processes of reading have to contend with several centuries' worth of anxiety and discrimination when it comes to *any* aspect of reader-involvement. As Nead has shown, the mark of one's sophistication is precisely one's ability to keep a proper distance from one's object of study: to remain disinterested and unmoved.

Such 'connoisseurship' is evident both in the readings of the critics discussed in this chapter and in those of my respondents in the next. It has also erupted persistently in my own textual analysis, even where, as in Chapters 5 and 6, I was consciously trying to lay the conventions of my professional training aside. As will emerge, one way of understanding this constraint, and the means by which it creates such tensions for the way in which we negotiate our affective and cognitive responses to texts, is the more simple fact that no reading experience is ever an exclusive, private, bilateral exchange between text and reader. As I have speculated elsewhere, any dialogic relationship (and this includes the text–reader one) always involves some sort of third party – who, in Bakhtinian fashion, may be seen to direct (or, more menacingly 'to police') our reading.[4] Reading, as I have observed, is thus always a 'reading to': an act of engagement and/or interpretation somehow, and somewhere, determined by another (silent) witness who sits in active judgement, whether critical or benign, on our response. In the readings of *The Piano* which follow there are a number of instances in which the critic's analysis appears to have been very obviously determined by an interlocutor *other than* the ostensible audience of the piece, and this divided response may be seen as the readerly corollory to the multiple *textual* address and reader-positioning discussed in Chapter 3. Even as texts may be seen to address different readers simultaneously, so will readers (in their own readerly re-writing of a text) direct their response to a number of addressees.

Speculating on what theoretical mechanisms make the reading process as complex as it is, however, still does not necessarily help us in describing the sheer chaos of what it means to *be* a reader caught in the cross-fire of so many positionings and interpretive frameworks. This is registered by the fact that many of my respondents in the next chapter expressed considerable anxiety in commenting on their reading practices. Whilst most of them had a clear idea of how they were *meant* to read, in an academic context at least, all knew that this professional analysis of a text (from a feminist or other standpoint) was *not* the sum total of their reading experience. All were aware that other factors, including the issue of their 'involvement' with the text, and the questions this raised about personal connections and affective responses, were at work – but many said they had no vocabulary, no legitimated framework, with which to deal with them. This readerly confusion over 'how we read' as against 'how we ought to read' seems crucially important to keep in mind as we move on to consider the question of disagreement and dissent within feminist reading communities. What the following analyses of critics and respondents seem to confirm (following on from the conclusions drawn from my own readings in Part II) is that 'differences' which are presented and authenticated as political and/or aesthetic can often be seen to conceal a differential structural relation to the text that casts them as either 'hermeneutic' or 'implicated' readers. This is not so simple as saying that readers and critics consciously reach for ideological and aesthetic criteria to disguise or justify their own personal engagement with/alienation from a text (though sometimes it can *appear* as simple as this), but that the confusion and discomfort resulting from our 'implication' might cause us unconsciously to cling to the security of apparently depersonalized interpretive frameworks. It is, above all, our *relationship with the text* that we seek to deny and silence as we hastily brush aside the messy nature of our involvement, the feints and refinements of which were exemplified by my own readings in Part II.

While it is not, of course, possible to 'prove' this panic at the heart of the reading process – in as much as we can never gain access to readers'/authors' undirected thoughts – the symptomatic reading of the texts which follows reveals a number of ways in which aesthetic and political dissent would seem to mask a more complicated relationship to the text, the reading community and, indeed, to reading itself.

In this chapter I explore the way in which supposedly 'aesthetic' and 'political' differences manifest themselves in published readings/reviews of *The Piano*, a text which has provoked a divided response within feminist circles. Like Jeanette Winterson's *Written on the Body*, it has come under heavy criticism for its representation of certain politically sensitive issues (sexuality, class, ethnicity, and rape), but has also proven overwhelmingly successful in terms of both 'arts' and 'mainstream' cinema audiences.[5] In the analysis which follows I compare the critics' ostensible reasons for either defending or rejecting the texts with speculation on the more covert mechanisms at work, including: the role of the reader's interpretive community; the controls imposed by the reader's own interlocutors – both the official (public) audience and the unofficial (private) one; and the reader's (often repressed) 'implication' in the reading event. Whilst the official readings made of the texts may thus be located within supposedly 'external' frameworks and value-systems (broadly separable into the 'aesthetic' and the 'political'), the *reading process* reveals itself at those points at which meaning is seen to be an intimate, and dialogic, relationship between text, reader and the reader's readers: when, in other words, the reader's own involvement in the text becomes visible. This is the difference between reading as performance (an act of interpretation) and reading as event (a relationship, however construed, between a readerly self and a textual other). Looking ahead to Chapter 8, I also pay particular attention to the way in which issues of ethnicity and national identity are set up as major sites of dissent and disagreement between readers, and how this politics is articulated alongside, or in opposition to, a feminist agenda.

Making Readings/Masking Feelings

One of the first things to be observed when considering the 'readings' produced by newspaper and magazine journalists is, of course, their supreme intertextuality. A survey of reviews over a twelve-month period reveals a global bush telegraph in which opinions, judgements and their concomitant rhetoric and vocabulary get endlessly reiterated and embellished. Besides an emerging set of 'differences' amongst readers there is also an enormous common currency, which is then in turn passed on to the consumer to facilitate/structure his or her own reading.

I will demonstrate this readerly intertextuality by looking first at some of the common, and ostensible, reasons why critics have 'liked' and 'disliked' Campion's film, grouping them under the following *aesthetic* and *political* headings: visual pleasure; representation of characters; narrative form; feminism; and ethnicity/national identity.

Visual Pleasure

In the thousand or so entries I scanned for this exercise, I discovered near-universal applause for *The Piano's* cinematography, with reviewers obviously feeling compelled to match the film's own visual excesses and subtleties with their own rhetoric. Thus Jeff Simon (*Buffalo News*, 18 November 1993) declares:

> Sometimes you look up at the screen and it registers that you're seeing things you've never seen before and hearing things you've never heard before – plot turns you couldn't possibly have guessed or new sights or phrases so freshly minted that the shine on them makes you laugh out loud. And then, on the rarest of occasions, you look up at the screen and realize that it is filled with an entire world you've not only never seen before up there but never quite imagined was possible.

Similarly, Stuart Klawans (*The Nation*, 6 December 1993), whose overall evaluation of the film is, as we shall see, less than enthusiastic, praises its intense visual 'defamiliarization':[6]

> Nor could the most hardened skeptic doubt the beauty of *The Piano*. Campion has set the film in the wilds of New Zealand where silver waves pound the beach beneath a misty, purplish horizon and lush greenery sprouts from primordial muck. Yet Campion is such a formidable image-maker that the landscape, for her, is more of a surplus than a necessity. In an early scene, for example, Hunter and her movie daughter (Anna Paquin) must camp out for one night on the beach. Campion has them take shelter beneath a hoop skirt, which, lit from within, shines on the screen like an improbable Chinese lantern. That's how good Jane Campion is – she transforms everything she sees.

For many reviewers, this 'transformative' visual power is invoked to help explain the emotional impact of the film – how it 'involves' or, indeed, 'possesses' its viewers – and the word 'haunting' is used repeatedly in this context. Thus Marylynn Uricchio (*Pittsburgh Post-Gazette*, 19 November 1993) writes, 'In a movie filled with striking images and haunting scenes, the shot of Ada's piano, crated and forlorn on the beach, is the most unforgettable'; whilst Michael Wilmington (*Chicago Tribune*, 19 November 1993) declares:

Campion is a visual master. Her images haunt your mind. A little girl
with shimmering angel's wings frolics on a hillside, and answers vio-
lently, 'Hell!' when her stepfather asks where her mother's gone. . . .
Campion and cinemaphotographer Stuart Dryburgh make the New
Zealand bush unforgettable as well: a weird vegetal landscape – unde-
veloped, wild – resembling weedy underwater depths, drowning in a
blue, witheringly cold light.

While the film's 'magic' and 'mystery' are also explained in terms of plot,
as we shall see below, its visual distinctiveness has clearly proved the easi-
est way to explain its effect (and, indeed, *affect*) on cinema audiences, yet
within a discrete, 'aesthetic' rationale that enables reviewers like Klawans
(see above) to be critical of its other aspects. Klawans's implication that
the film's visual gorgeousness is somehow *in excess* ('more of a surplus
than a necessity') is picked up by other reviewers, however: from the
laudatory Steve Persall (*St. Petersburg Times*, 19 November 1993) who
insists that, despite being 'a visually exciting work, filled with indelible
imagery', this aesthetic revelry is less important than the 'authenticity' of
its characters ('Campion could have filmed her actors against a blank
backdrop and their expertly defined passions would still shine through'),
to the chary Joseph Cunneen (*National Catholic Register,* 10 December
1993) who is supposedly troubled by 'one of the most talented directors
working today . . . creating images for their own sake'.[7]

   This determination to separate the visual aesthetics of the film from the
other levels on which it functions is in significant contrast to most of the
academic articles which I surveyed. Both Stella Bruzzi ('Tempestuous
Petticoats', pp. 257–66) and Sue Gillett ('Lips and Fingers', pp. 277–87), for
example (*Screen*, Autumn 1995), see every element of the film's visual repertoire as inseparable from its feminist political statement.[8] The splendours
and idiosyncrasies of Campion and Dryburgh's camera-work are never gratuitous, indulgent or superfluous: each image is a part of the film's radical
narrative, its attempt to challenge and rewrite the specificities of female sexual desire and (hetero)sexual relations. Thus the bizarrely defamiliarizing
image of Ada's hooped skirt made into a tent at the beginning of the film,
alluded to by a number of reviewers (see Klawans above), becomes, for
Bruzzi, a symbol of the 'protective function' of nineteenth-century female
clothing in a thesis which explores the way in which such clothing is alter-
nately affirming and undermining of the dominant social order.

   Although Bruzzi's article makes a suggestive connection between the aesthetic and the political, however, undermining the view prevalent in the journalism that, for better or worse, the visual pleasures of *The Piano* belong to
a culture of 'art for art's sake', it can be seen that all the commentators (with
the exception of Gillett, to whom I shall refer again below) are using apparently autonomous discursive frames of reference in a way that short-circuits
themselves as readers, and makes invisible the reading process itself.

Characters

By and large, the 'success' or 'failure' of the film's characters are also dealt with within an aesthetic frame which is broadly liberal-humanist, and which requires them to be 'believable', 'authentic' and 'sympathetic'. The exceptions, once again, are the academic pieces, which also invoke political criteria (in terms of feminism and ethnic awareness) to evaluate the representations of the characters. Whilst drawing on the same interpretive frames, however, there are some profound disagreements amongst these 'professional readers' on whether the representations succeed. At the one extreme we have Steve Persall (*St. Petersburg Times*, 19 November 1993) who finds the characters so 'authentic' and 'expertly defined' that 'we always know what's going on inside Ada's mind and, even more impressively, we learn enough to expect her next reaction'; whilst others such as Christopher Tookey (*Daily Mail*, 29 October 1993) and Anne Billson (*The Sunday Telegraph*, 31 October 1993) find them unsympathetic and unbelievable in the extreme. The latter is particularly interesting, in as much as she explains her whole 'disappointment' with the film on the grounds of her failure to 'identify' with any of the central characters:

> Now all this is fascinating stuff, so I naturally assumed my indifference was due to having watched the film the wrong way. Perhaps it required more emotional commitment and less detached analysis. I tried letting the fabulous and memorable images wash over me – the baby grand on the beach, a crinoline converted into a makeshift tent, acres of mud and blood and the intricate braiding of Hunter's hair . . . I even tried fancying Harvey Keitel . . . What makes an art movie work? This year I have liked a whole bunch of them, and in every case it's because I've empathised with one of the characters and wanted to wear their jackets. Hunter casts aside restraint with her layers of corsetry, but despite her impressive performance, the film keeps us at a safe distance from her journey of self-discovery. *The Piano* is perfectly formed and hermetically sealed.

Despite the fact that Billson's analysis is more openly self-reflexive than most of the other reviews – she 'writes herself in' as a reader in order to account for the text's failure – the rationale for her 'disappointment' is highly conventional. It is a judgement predicated upon the assumption that characters are either 'believable' and 'sympathetic' or not, and – despite her use of the personal pronoun – it says nothing about the reading process itself. There is no attempt to understand why she, as an individual reader/viewer, has not been sutured into the action when millions of others, as she acknowledges, have been.

Stewart Klawans, meanwhile, whose resistance to the text's heroine is indicative of a more complex (if similarly occluded) reading process, explains his objection on the grounds that Campion's presentation of character is too didactic:

> The difference between admiring *The Piano* with reservations and believing in it wholeheartedly comes down to one's willingness to identify with the heroine. That's a tricky business. In current film criticism, especially the hard-core stuff, identification has become [the] key concept, as if it were general to narrative film-making. But with whom would you identify in *Citizen Kane*? . . . So, to address the crudest form of identification theory, the 'chick's movie' slur: Yes, I am willing to adopt the point of view of female protagonists. Because of certain oddities in my up-bringing, I'm even more willing to identify with piano players . . . So my failure to plunge into the being of the piano player in this new movie very likely reflects some shortcoming in the production – perhaps Jane Campion's insistence that I should, I must, I will identify with Holly Hunter.

Like Billson, this is manifestly another instance in which the professional reader shows himself adept at turning his discomfort with, and disappointment in, the text back on the text itself: there is obviously some 'shortcoming in the production' that has prevented his engagement. As I will argue in the second part of this chapter, however, there are clear signs – even in the short extract quoted above – that Klawans's stumbling rationalizations (many of them contradictory) are concealing a more complicated viewing experience. As a critic he has an interpretive framework with which to dispatch this type of irritation and discomfort very quickly (the characters 'fail': intransitive); as an 'implicated reader', however, he is, perhaps, troubled in a way he cannot easily explain, and this disturbance causes some visible stress within his wonderfully cavalier text.[9]

For the academic readers, the text's characters, like its imagery, are dislocated from their humanist and/or narrative function to become pawns in Campion's wider political project. For both Bruzzi and Gillett, all the characters – male and female – are seen as agents of a transformative feminist politics, whilst for Lynda Dyson (also *Screen,* Autumn, 1995, pp. 267–76) they are regarded, rather less enthusiastically, as agents of 'colonial reconciliation'.[10] Bruzzi and Dyson (Gillett is an interesting exception in this and most other respects), meanwhile, locate their approval/disapproval of these characters *wholly* in this political realm: it is not a question of 'who they are' in terms of their subjectivity (humanist or otherwise) but *what they represent.* Thus Bruzzi 'reads' Ada's character as an exploration of the possibility of *masquerade*:

> If the masquerade is to be a feminist strategy, then its use should in some way facilitate the implicit presentation of woman as not merely spectacle: the locus of the 'collective fantasy of phallocentricism'. It follows that the reappropriation of male-designated roles for women

is fundamental to the development of Ada's relationship with Baines. . . . Similarly *The Piano* suggests that Ada's progression from passivity to activity is related to her defiance of objectification and a sexual defiance reliant on the hierarchical exchange of looks. (p. 264)

For Dyson, meanwhile, 'the development of Ada's relationship with Baines' is a sign not of feminist resistance but of colonialist appeasement:

The fantasy of colonial reconciliation is played out through the developing sexual relationship between Ada and Baines. At the end of the film, Ada chooses 'life' after jumping overboard with her piano. She leaves the instrument (the symbol of European bourgeois culture) at the bottom of the ocean, thus severing her connection with the imperial centre and thus begins her life anew with her man who has already 'gone native'. They become born-again New Zealanders living in a gleaming white house where the mute Ada rediscovers her voice. (p. 268)

What strikes me about the juxtaposition of these two readings, a striking demonstration of 'readers in disagreement', is the conceptual *similarity* of their arguments. Whilst Bruzzi approves the text and Dyson disapproves it, the rationale for both evaluations lies in 'de-humanizing' the characters and reading them as a collection of politically inscribed 'semes'.[11] I am not suggesting that there is anything wrong with this: in fact, it is very much the way in which poststructuralist theory has 'trained' me and thousands of others to read (see Chapters 2 to 4). But it is important to register how, as a technique, it effectively removes the reader from the reading. Neither Bruzzi nor Dyson appear to engage with the characters in any way other than to extract them from the text and insert them in relevant theoretical/political frameworks which then do the reading for them.

Sue Gillett's article is an interesting counter to this mode of analysis, making visible as it does the tension between a hermeneutic and an implicated reading of text and character. Whilst she too depends on the former to justify her love-affair with the text (see the discussion concerning 'feminism' below, pp. 208), she also seeks to represent her readerly involvement with the characters in ways that exceed and/or displace her 'political' analysis of the text. Rather than attempting to integrate these two types of reading, moreover, her fragmented text – written in different voices/registers – is a testament to the split between 'making a reading' and reading-as-process. Thus while, within the bounds of academic discourse, she makes a rational defence of Ada's character-function (she is not a simple 'victim' of rape, and so forth), the alternative/alternate sections explore the heroine's character through Gillett's (identificatory) relationship to it: a method similar to the one I myself employ in Chapters 5 and 6:

If I open my lips will you take this as an invitation? If I open my lips will you step inside and take up residence? Must I keep opening my lips so that I can show you the way out?

If I tighten my lips, each upon the other, will you turn away, as if from a closed door? If I tighten my lips, this one upon this one, will you hammer at me as at a door which is barred to you?

What are you waiting for me to say? What do you want to hear? Listening is an art. It is an act of love, requiring patience and courage.

Perhaps you do not know how to open me. Perhaps I do not know how to speak myself open. But one thing I know. I cannot be forced open. And I cannot be tempted. You would lose what you are trying to find and we would both be damaged.

Do not make me a whore. I gag on the word. (pp. 277–8)

It will be seen that in Gillett's text it is never made explicit who is speaking, or to whom. Whilst the context may lead us to assume that it is Ada's repressed voice that is being represented, we know that it is also Gillett's, since the act of ventriloquizing makes the speaker and the host co-existent with one another. But it is clear that the 'you' of the text may/must *also* be Gillett (as well as being Baines, Stewart, or indeed, ourselves, the audience). What Gillett has shown is just how mutable all these illocutionary and interlocutory positions are: as readers we are simultaneously speakers, the spoken and the spoken to. 'Characters', that are defined in the readings discussed above as 'instruments' of the text (and this applies both to the broadly aesthetic and the broadly political readings) are, here, the sites of dialogic interaction.

Narrative and Form

As would be expected, narrative and form have provided *Piano* readers with another key structure through which to analyse the text *without* appreciable attention to the reading process. In terms of generic classification, many of the reviewers follow Campion's own cue (in an interview with Jay Carr for the *Boston Globe*, 14 November 1993) and draw attention to its 'fairy-tale' or 'mythic' status: a distinguishing characteristic that some use to explain their disapproval (for example, Stuart Klawans, *The Nation*, 6 December 1993: '*The Piano* is too bound up with the specifics of time and space to be a fairy tale, though not enough so to be an historical drama'), but to which the majority turn in order to explain its 'magic', 'mystery' and hold over millions of viewers. Indeed, generic/narrative form, more than any other interpretive frame of reference, is what is most commonly held responsible for *The Piano*'s success, with the notion of the 'primal' and 'archaic' (as modalities which 'explain' the enduring significance of the folk-tale in contemporary culture) neatly subsuming – and hence silencing – questions of the text's emotional politics: the specificities of its dialogic engagement. For example, this is how Edward Guthman (*San Francisco Chronicle*, 19 November 1993) sums up the relationship between 'structure' and 'feeling':

Magical and haunting, 'The Piano' has the power and delicate mystery of a gothic fairy tale. There's something timeless in the story that New Zealand film-maker Jane Campion creates here – the quality of a myth re-telling it with each generation, the harshness of a romantic fable, full of violent passion that one of the Brontë sisters might have told.

Similarly rationally enraptured is Joanna Connors (*Plain Dealer Publishing Co.*, 19 November 1993):

Jane Campion's is a strange and wonderful movie . . . watching it, I was thrilled by this limitless and mysterious quality – thrilled and moved by its mute, mysterious heroine, its primal fairy-tale setting, its poet's cache of allusions and its vision of eroticism.

Whilst Jay Carr goes a little further in suggesting exactly how form can 'structure' emotional responses:

Campion, who wrote and directed it, is an original. Even when she remakes a classic, as she has here remade Emily Brontë's 'Wuthering Heights', there's so much of her sensibility in it, it's so subliminal that it seems primal, pre-conscious, something floating up from the depths, dreamlike, not something reworked and refashioned.

The 'primality' implicit in the Gothic/fairy-tale genre is here linked, though not explicitly, to the structures of the unconscious, with the implication that Ada's 'piano' is a symbol for the repressions of some great 'collective unconscious'. Much criticism, of course, exists to support this view of the appeal of certain narrative forms, in particular the folk-tale, though it seems to me that the real key to Carr's own enchantment lies in his dialogic relationship to the text, which I will go on to analyse below.[12] Another, more purely structuralist aspect of Carr's analysis is, however, one shared by many other reviewers: namely, the text's hermeneutic complexity. Whilst this is presented by many as simply an aspect of its 'fairy-tale' genre, the film's *obstacles* to meaning/resolution are certainly perceived to go a long way to explaining its emotional hold. Thus Guthman (*San Francisco Chronicle*, 19 November 1993) writes: 'That's one of the mysteries of Campion's film: We never learn what her life was like in Scotland, or who fathered her daughter, or why she consented to marry a stranger. We're left to imagine these things: that's one of the gifts of Campion's film'; whilst Jonathan Romney (*New Statesman and Society*, 29 October 1993) draws attention to the text's Machereyan 'gaps and silences':[13]

No one can bear the fact that Ada might have a secret knowledge and a secret past. Hers is an erotic silence indeed. Her piano playing is explicitly seen as a sexual force. As Stewart's frosty Aunt Morag comments with a shudder, 'Her playing is like a mood that passes into you.'
The Piano pretty much passes into you with the same mysterious

charm: endlessly eloquent and suggestive, but in its silences as much as its exceptionally rich discourse of themes and images. There's so much going on that you can't help wondering how much of the melody is evading you. You just have to keep listening.

For others, meanwhile, the film's hermeneutic conundrums are a source of major irritation and disaffection: instead of the mysterious key to its compulsion, the narrative aporia are experienced as profoundly alienating. John Simon (*National Review*, 27 December 1993), for example, has this outburst:

> We never find out anything about Ada's background, her first husband, and how Stewart acquired her in marriage. Or why she gave up speaking . . . Jane Campion prides herself on leaving much unexplained. She has every right to be proud: at leaving things unexplained Miss Campion is a champion . . . The consequences [of when Ada sends the piano key to the illiterate Baines] are dire, of course, but in an utterly loony way. Miss Campion claims kinship with Emily Brontë, but *Wuthering Heights*, another overheated spinsterish fantasy, makes a lot more sense, and has a little thing called genius going for it.

Whilst Simon's grumble that 'we never find out anything about Ada's background' has now been rectified (if somewhat contentiously!) by the publication of 'the book of the film' where all these matters are carefully filled in, part of me remains surprised that more readers, professional and otherwise, have not *attempted* to 'join up the dots' themselves.[14] This is largely because my own pleasure in the text (see Chapters 5 and 6) depended so much on reading, explaining and *legitimating* the action in the narrative present of the film (including, it will be remembered, the nature of Ada's 'seduction') in terms of my own scripting of the characters' narrative past. For myself as a reader, *The Piano* is a film as much 'about' a love affair in the past as it is about the new one in the present. The text is hermeneutically compelling precisely because it causes us to reconstruct this past according to our own personal investments, or according to recognized 'structures of feeling' (see Chapters 5 and 6).[15] For the majority of the professional readers surveyed here, however, the text's hermeneutic mysteries seem to have been received as an end in themselves: regarded as an easy explanation – in accordance with the thriller/Gothic genre – for *why* the film has entranced so many. In terms of accounting for the difference between hermeneutic and implicated reading, this may thus be seen as a further example of how the former can silence or deflect the potential for a more dialogic analysis of text–reader interaction.

All the frameworks of analysis that I have surveyed so far in this readerly review may be thought of as broadly 'aesthetic': the readers concerned have reached for a number of tried and tested criteria, most of them derived from a broadly humanist or New Critical literary training, to deal with (by and large) the popular success of Campion's film, though a number (Klawans, Billson, Simon, Tookey) have used the same evaluatory principles – defamiliarization of the visual, authenticity of character, hermeneutic (over)complexity – to discredit it.[16] What is important, however, is that both camps, as I indicated earlier, have depended on the same 'objective' critical referents, making their 'disagreements' relatively superficial ones. They are differences of 'position' merely; not differences (with the notable exception of Sue Gillett) based on a different *reading method*.

I turn now to the other 'grid' that enables us, as professional readers and critics, to perform effective readings of texts: the political. As I indicated at the beginning of this chapter, the specific frameworks I have chosen to focus on in Campion's film are feminism and questions of ethnicity and, in particular, the articulation of the two.

Feminism

We have seen already that scholarly readers – in this case Bruzzi, Dyson and Gillett – are the most likely to reach for the political frame as a means of expounding or, perhaps, 'explaining' their like or dislike of the film. All these readers have, indeed – in different ways, and to different degrees – displaced aesthetic criteria with political ones. Ada's character is fought over not in terms of its 'authenticity' or 'integrity', but according to what it represents in terms of the film's political vision. For the journalists, however, aesthetics and politics would appear, for the most part, to exist as separate frames of reference, with a distinct tendency for the latter to exist as a subsidiary concern in the film's overall evaluation. The most common response to the film's 'feminist message', indeed, is to see it as present but 'unforced'. Thus Hugo Davenport (*Daily Telegraph*, 29 October 1993) describes *The Piano* as:

> A triangular love story, deeply imbued with the spirit of the nineteenth century, yet uncompromisingly modern in its treatment of sex. It is a harsh, poetic exploration of the effects of erotic obsession in a milieu lacking the means to articulate or accept them. In the broadest sense, this is a feminist film – though its feminism emerges in an unforced way. The writer-director displays a sure touch in her handling of the contrasts between the white settlers and the indigenous Maori, drawing astute parallels between the relations of the sexes and the commerce of cultures.

In similar vein is Brian Johnson (*Maclean's*, 22 November 1993), who uses *The Globe*'s interview with Campion to praise the film's 'unspoken feminism':

> An unspoken feminism seems to inform Campion's attitude, and her sense of humor. 'But at the time I was writing *The Piano*', she recalls,

'I thought I wouldn't like to be pigeon-holed as a feminist. Now I think that yes, I really am a strong feminist, in the sense that I like women a lot and I am curious about women. Also, men do seem to have the obvious, literal power and wealth.' Campion appears unimpressed by the obvious. But, after improvising a career out of the intangible, with *The Piano* she has found her voice and taken her place as a diva among directors.

Both these reviews by male journalists may be seen to write out, or at least marginalize, the film's feminism whilst giving it tacit approval. It is a good instance of how an ostensible post-feminism (registered as an approving nod at certain shared values and principles) quickly translates into no feminism at all. This text is inscribed by feminist politics; but this isn't what it is 'about'. Its value lies in its wider humanist, and emphatically non-gender-specific, vision. Even reviews like Steve Persall's (' "Piano" is grand entry into feminist film history': *St. Petersburg Times*, 19 November 1993), which declare the film 'a magnificent feminist fable', unwittingly neutralize the force of their sentiment by emphasizing the universal, supposedly trans-historical, cross-cultural nature of the message:

> With Ada McGrath, however, Campion has created a fascinating feminist hero for the ages. How many women throughout history have been silenced by male domination, whether unintentional or sadistic? How many have had to compromise themselves – sexually or submissively – to retrieve at least part of that voice? Ada's dilemma mirrors all female casualties of the battle of the sexes; a repressed spirit capable of happiness and blocked from it. That Campion can address these issues in such an artistically entertaining fashion is her gift to film lovers.

Once again, it will be seen, politics surrenders to aesthetics in the final analysis.

Whilst the last reviewer is fairly specific in defining what he understands by the film's feminism (namely, its representation of the struggle against patriarchy at a psychological and sexual level), others are less specific. In the more negative accounts of the film's politics, feminism is implicitly reduced to the fact that this is a 'woman's film', or, more especially, a film about 'women as victims'. Thus Christopher Tookey (*Daily Mail*, 29 October 1993), probably the most hostile of all the reviewers, makes the film's politics the *bête noire* of his disapproval:

> The appeal of the central character, I suppose – especially for women – is that she is a survivor: she's willing to buy back her piano from Baines, even if it means selling her body. Then, as in so many films recently, she finds herself attracted to the man who has bought her .... My main problem with Ada – and I don't think it's just because I'm a man – is that I found her not sensitive but hard, not spunky but

passive . . . Everything Ada does, she seems to do for herself, with no thought for her child's welfare.

But the actors have little chance to flesh out characters written in a kind of politically correct short-hand. Feminists will smile knowingly at the way Ada is punished: it fits neatly with modern preconceptions that men will countenance no threat to their phallic supremacy . . .

But, all in all, the film is a bore and depressingly conventional in treatment . . . Its attitudes have the stale whiff of seventies, women-as-victims, feminism: the underlying notion is that the world owes women a loving.

I shall return to the more covert processes at work in such readings in the next section of this chapter. For the moment, however, it is sufficient to observe that none of these male reviewers is reading the text *as a feminist*, though Davenport, Johnson and Persall are notionally sympathetic. In no instance is feminist politics something which readers themselves are seen to be *productive of* through an interactive engagement with text. There are, however, exceptions. Apart from the scholarly articles which I will deal with directly, Jay Carr (*The Boston Globe*, 19 November 1993) is the journalist who goes furthest towards expressing a dialogic encounter with the film's feminism and, by extension, to positioning himself as a feminist reader:

Ada's voicelessness, except at the keyboard, is a telling metaphor for her society's silencing of women's voicings of their deepest feelings. Then her harsh, closed world is challenged. The tension between the bush, exploding with fertility, and Ada's subversive silence grows unbearably. Each character broods . . . until you know something's got to give . . . The combination of long-deferred contact with her deepest essence and his [Baines's] inarticulate yearning is what gives their eroticism such extraordinary potency. In strictly epidermal terms, their few sex scenes don't differ vastly from those in a dozen other films of far lesser impact. What sets them apart from almost all other movie sex is a rare feeling of something behind the sex, a feeling of total and almost mystical immersion in it. Each makes us feel the growing fascination of each with the other's body.

We can see that, in this section of commentary, Carr's reading of the film's feminism slides into his account of its *emotional politics*. The sex scenes are important 'not in themselves' but (in a leap in his own argument that Carr fails to observe) through *our own* 'mystical immersion' in them and, by extension, the tortured sexual politics of repression out of which they arise. The force of the 'us' in the final sentence is, in this respect, especially strong: 'Each makes us feel the growing fascination with the other's body' (that is, we become surrogate participants in this process). Unlike other reviewers, like Michael Wilmington (*Chicago Tribune*, 19 November 1993), who conflate the film's emotional impact with its sexuality in a way that does not (self-consciously, at least) involve the reader/viewer, Carr's account describes well the movement between sexuality (within a discourse of feminism) and its reception through the viewer's suturing into the text.

A similar 'personalizing of the political' is attempted, this time self-reflexively, in Sue Gillett's academic article on the film, though as we have already noted, the tension between a hermeneutic and an implicated reading of the text becomes a key source of frustration here. While she makes many concerted attempts to 'contain' her pleasure in the text within a feminist rationale, her *experience* as a reader is clearly one of her dialogic involvement in the text *not* being entirely reducible to its laudable political project (though the latter is expounded in some detail, as we have already seen, in order to 'defend' her more complex pleasures). She speaks explicitly of the problems caused by this tension in the concluding section:

> *The Piano* affected me very deeply. I was entranced, moved, dazed. I held my breath. I was reluctant to re-enter the everyday word after the film had finished. *The Piano* shook, disturbed and inhabited me. I felt that my own dreams had taken form, been revealed. I dreamed of Ada the night after I saw the film. These were thick, heavy and exhilarated feelings. The problem of reading *The Piano* through the questions concerning rape or sexual harrassment is that it then becomes extremely difficult to articulate and appreciate this powerful affective dimension of the film. ('Lips and Fingers', pp. 286-7)

A little later she pushes this split between the affective and the cognitive even further:

> The legal definitions of what constitutes rape continue to be an important part of feminist work. However, *The Piano* offers other readings than those based on legalistic discourse . . . It is a story which envisions the 'logical' drama of external events, interactions and exchanges as interwoven with a counterface of inexpressible but nevertheless tangible passions. This is more than a two-tiered layering of conscious and unconscious realms within the subject. (p. 287)

It is interesting to see how, in this instance, even a trained academic reader, belonging to a clearly defined poststructuralist interpretive community (see discussion below), is forced back into a binary postulation of the conscious *vs.* the unconscious; the speakable *vs.* the unspeakable; the cognitive *vs.* the affective. I will return to this perverse and somewhat exasperating state of affairs in the final section of this chapter, but it is sufficient here to use Gillett's piece as final and consummate acknowledgement of the vagaries of the reading *process*: the way in which the complexity of the 'experience' manifestly resists the conscious will to *either* model of reading.

Ethnicity and National Identity

To recap, then, Carr and Gillett's relation to the film's feminism may be seen to differ from that of the other readers and reviewers on account of the fact that they register their participation and involvement in its political processes. Most of the latter were happy to use the text's 'strong feminist message' as a simple locus of approval/disapproval, though another interesting twist comes into this equation with Lynda Dyson's article, 'The Return of the Repressed', in *Screen* 36 (3) (Autumn 1995), which accuses the film's feminism of obscuring its colonialism and covert racism: the implication here is that the ostensible focus on one 'identity' detracts from its treatment of others.[17] The celebration of *The Piano* as a 'magnificent feminist tale' has excused and made invisible its problematic ethnic politics:

> My analysis of the film highlights the way in which it draws on and reproduces a repertoire of colonial tropes. The critical acclaim surrounding the film constructed *The Piano* as an exploration of nineteenth-century sexuality and tended to ignore the way in which 'race' is embedded in the text. Whilst the construction of gender and sexuality is obviously a central theme in *The Piano*, the film's representation of a colonial landscape must necessarily be considered within the context of the contemporary debates over national belonging in New Zealand – debates which have resonances within the wider field of postcolonial theory. (p. 267)

The three *Screen* articles (see note 36, Chapter 6) do indeed set up an interesting debate, or site of dissent, *vis-à-vis* these competing discourses. Although Dyson accuses the one of silencing the other, both Bruzzi and Gillett – presumably in dialogic 'hidden polemic' (Bakhtin: see note 3 above) with voices like Dyson's – make a special effort to show the text's feminism and its post-colonial 'awareness' to be closely implicated with one another. In a short section on 'whiteness' Bruzzi thus argues, 'In *The Piano* whiteness is a similarly inconsistent signifier which in turn represents aggression (the colonial invasion), the potential sensuality of the colonial male body (the close-up of Baines and Stewart) and unaestheticized pallor (Ada)' (p. 263). In direct contrast with Dyson, Bruzzi argues that Ada's skin is never 'fetishized' in the way Richard Dyer talks about in his account of Hollywood cinema:

> Ada's defiance extends to her skin, the whiteness of which is never fetishized or aestheticized, so jarring with, rather than complementing, her attractiveness and sensuality; in the scene in which Stewart pursues her in the woods, the distorting lens and flat blue light de-eroticize her face completely. (p. 263)[18]

Dyson's reading, as we see, could not be more opposite:

Ada's cultural and racial 'purity' – exemplified by her shimmering whiteness and her sublime relationship to her music – is reinforced by the class differences represented within the film. The two plump white female servants are accorded the status of characters but, like the Maori women, they are desexualized . . . Whiteness as purity is a recurring motif in the film. While the Maori are at one with the bush (to the extent that they are even visible) the film continually privileges whiteness through the play of white against dark, emphasizing the binary oppositions at work in the text. This whiteness is enhanced by the use of filters, which means that while the darker skin tones of the Maori are barely discernible in the brooding shadows of the bush, the faces of Ada and Flora, framed by their bonnets, take on a luminous quality . . . This 'glow of whiteness' and its association with light, purity and cleanliness recurs throughout the film, for example in an early scene in which the Maoris approach Ada and Flora on the beach exclaiming, 'They look like angels'.

But what are we to make of such disagreement? What does it tell us about how different readings are produced? My response is that, as with the dissent over the text's feminist status, the difference is less of a difference than it might at first appear. This is because, once again, the two readers are using similar frames of theoretical reference (in particular Richard Dyer's essay, 'White'), in tandem with a reading method that locates 'meaning' (and in this case 'political meaning') very firmly in the text and its 'author' (Jane Campion), *not* the reader. Both critics, in a word, are seeing the same thing (Ada's white, European face 'glowing' in the dark, 'primitive' bush) but attaching different authorial intentions (and responsibilities) to that representation. Their 'difference' thus hinges on their own respective desires to read the film as 'reproductive of' (Dyson), or 'interrogating of' (Bruzzi), European colonialism *without* acknowledging their own implication within this meaning-production. What I would suggest, therefore, and what I will attend to in the final section of this chapter, is that we need to look beyond the ostensible reasons for this sort of political difference: to go beyond the different, but effectively superficial, responses to the same frames of reference, and examine what it is in the reading process itself (with an emphasis on the reader's dialogic relation with the text and her interpretive community) that might cause him or her to proclaim it radical or reactionary, 'good' or 'bad'.

It should be noted in conclusion, however, that for the most part the journalistic reviews are silent on the text's post-colonial status, although Joseph Cunneen (*National Catholic Reporter*, 10 December 1993), who does not like it for various reasons, declares that 'ultimately, the movie's use of the Maori is unintentionally exploitative'. Others are undoubtedly guilty of *reproducing* the familiar colonialist eroticization of the untamed landscape in their accounts of the film's 'exploration of sexuality' (see Carr, Persall, Wilmington and Billson), so that – in terms of its reception and circulation, at least – Dyson's criticisms *are* justified. Indeed, it is in a text such as Carr's, rather than in the more academic, overtly feminist readings, that the film's colonialism and racism are most visible, precisely because (as I shall directly argue) the reader is overtly complicit in the meaning-production.

Unmasking the Reading Process

Interpretive Communities

In the final section of this chapter I thus move on to see how a number of dialogic aspects of the reading process – interpretive communities, audience and implicated readership – undermine the hermeneutic readings produced by the critics surveyed in the previous section, and point to more complex reasons for their 'disagreements' over Campion's text.

It is clear from this review of an international field of 'readings', focused on a particular text/textual event, that many of Stanley Fish's views on the significance of interpretive communities and how they function still hold true.[19] His assertion in the Introduction to *Is there a Text in This Class?* (1980), that it is the social and intellectual milieu in which a text is consumed rather than its author or reader *per se* that makes and guarantees its meaning ('In other words, there is no single way of reading that is correct or natural, only "ways of reading" that are extensions of community perspectives', p. 16) would seem to explain the vast consensus in the frames of reference employed by *The Piano*'s professional readers. According to this theoretical model, the text itself as an autonomous and authoritative source of meaning-production disappears, and is replaced by a set of discourses circulating within a given community at any one time. In the case of the community of film critics analysed here, these discourses must be seen to be disappointingly conservative: a set of antiquated aesthetic and political criteria aimed at the evaluation of a text in an attempt to understand and authorize its popular success.

But there are, I would suggest, other more radical and productively dislocating ways of looking at Fish's interpretive communities. As well as seeing them as the source of the fusty and beleaguered 'frameworks' through which a text like Campion's is classified, fixed and approved – in other words, as the 'makers of readings' (see the previous section) – they may also be understood as more troubling agents in the *reading process*. Whilst Fish's celebrated accounts of how interpretive communities function tend to emphasize the almost shocking ease with which interpretations are made and meaning conferred within certain academic reading communities, a closer look at some of the readings discussed in the previous section of this chapter reveals a more anxious and dynamic model. What Fish's argument seems to overlook is the fact that, in as much as the interpretive community 'replaces' the text as the site of meaning-production, so does it become, itself, a *text* (with its own constituent 'textual others') – and is thus subject to the same 'self–other' dynamics and power-relations that are associated with the reader and the 'original' text. In other words, an interpretive community does not represent a set of fixed, and shared, values with which the reader mindlessly agrees, or to whom s/he defers. Rather, it should be thought of as its own site of struggle: a group whose 'position' is constantly being renegotiated and re-legitimated by its constituent members even while its consensus is publicly upheld (see also the discussion in Chapter 8). If we turn to a reading like Lynda Dyson's (*Screen*, Autumn 1995) with all this in mind, we see quickly that, while a very particular interpretive community provides the critic with a ready-made grid of interpretation and evaluation (this is an article very clearly 'produced' out of current scholarship on issues of race, ethnicity and colonialism), it could also be said to set up an anxious relay of exchanges with that community whose 'policing' lends a certain paranoia to the reading process.[20] One could argue, indeed, that Dyson is so concerned with making the 'correct' reading of this text that *this* becomes her reading experience: her dialogue is with Bakhtin's extratextual 'other' rather than anything in the text itself. This '(self-)policing' is visible both in the extract on the film's representation of 'whiteness' quoted earlier, and in the following:

> This romantic melodrama is set in a landscape where 'natives' provide the backdrop for the emotional drama of the principal white characters. The Maori are located on the margins of the film as the repositories of an authentic, unchanging and simple way of life: they play 'nature' to the white characters' 'culture' . . . This opposition draws on the discourses of primitivism which have historically constructed the colonial Other as a 'noble savage' inverting (rather than subverting) the hierarchies which have legitimized the colonial project in white settler colonies. (p. 286)

This comment is followed, in Dyson's text, by a footnote referencing Nicholas Thomas's *Colonialism's Culture* (1994), thus making very visible the interpretive community out of which her own 'reading' has been produced and, more importantly, in which the 'reading process' has taken place.[21] What I am proposing, therefore, is that we *could* see Dyson's dislike and disapproval of Campion's film as the product not of its own political failure *per se* (both Bruzzi and Gillett have shown us how, through a shift of authorial intentions, its 'position' can be read quite otherwise), but as a more unconscious anxiety and discomfort with the restrictions placed upon her by her own interpretive community: restrictions which have clearly not allowed her to engage pleasurably with the text in its function *as* a 'romantic melodrama'. This is not to imply, of course, that Dyson's is a 'wrong' or 'inauthentic' reading: there are many instances, and this may well count as one of them, when our politics makes it imperative that we *do* adopt the perspective of our interpretive communities rather than surrender to a 'blind' implication in the text. It should, however, have drawn attention to the way in which disagreements over texts – whether or not we like them, whether or not we perceive them to be 'good' or 'bad' – will depend upon criteria which are interactively rather than objectively communicated to us. It is the process through which we engage our interpretive community, rather than what the community 'represents', that will ultimately determine our relationship with the text itself.

Audience

Interpretive communities, in as much as they become 'others' to which our readings are directed as well as locations from which those readings may be said to 'derive', are not easily separable from audiences. For the purposes of my discussion here it is, however, useful to keep the two separate: to see the way in which the reader's audience, as another set of interlocutory presences (perhaps very different to the reader/critic's dominant interpretive community) will also direct the reading by its intervention in the reading process.

While a number of the reviews and articles discussed in the first half of this chapter reveal the presence of the audience in the reading process, the one that came to intrigue me the most was Stuart Klawans's review for *The Nation* (6 December 1993). As we have seen, Klawans represents one of the small minority of newspaper journalists that signalled discontent and disapproval with Campion's film. Although using the same interpretive and evaluative critical frameworks as his peers (a liberal-humanist engagement of highly conventional aesthetic and political criteria), Klawans has come to very opposite conclusions to theirs. For him the film failed, ostensibly at least, in terms of its unspecified and hybrid genre (see above), its 'unsympathetic characters' and its lack of hermeneutic interest ('it intuits no secret cause'). Reading between the many lines, I have discerned some other possible causes for Klawans's disaffection with this movie relating to his gender identity, his audience and the processes of reading. Although in the review (as we have seen) Klawans declares that his failure to identify with the central character has nothing to do with fact that he is a man ('So, to address the crudest form of identification theory, the "chick's movie" slur: Yes, I am willing to adopt the viewpoint of female protagonists'), there seems to me a certain anxious maschismo in the address to what may be identified as his journalistic peer group, an audience that is implicitly separate from the 'general reader'. Whilst he assumes that, whatever he says, the latter group will continue to 'swallow the movie whole', his criticisms appear to be addressed to fellow 'skeptics' and 'connoisseurs'. This interlocution is marked in his reading by a swaggering irony that makes the plot seem sentimental, improbable, and – we must infer – a stereotypical 'chick's movie':

> Sexy stuff then happens between Baines and the strong-willed Ada, who doesn't like him at first but then does – just as her daughter abruptly starts despising Stewart and comes to adore him (as Darryl Zanuck used to decree in his celebrated script conferences, 'Her love turns to hate!') Eventually, Stewart gets wise and locks up his wife, who responds by playing finger exercises on his spine. Now remember, Stewart is a thoroughly rigid, shuttered man – the kind who would abandon a large piece of symbolic furniture on the beach . . . Yet he has the exquisite sensitivity to wait for a mail-order wife to come to his bed. When she does, he also has the spiritual refinement to hear her unvoiced words. Naturally, an experience of such depth and tenderness lead him to violence (his love turns to hate), in the course of which, though a clumsy man, he performs a feat requiring near-miraculous fine-motor control. After that, three more reversals occur without the benefit of motivation, whereupon the film reaches as satisfying a happy ending as Zanuck himself might have engineered, or even Louis B. Mayer.

Amidst all the eulogy to Campion's 'masterpiece', there is much about this review which I personally enjoy: the wit and irreverence is a welcome antidote to the earnest, if often flamboyant, rhetoric of the other reviewers. This is not to say that I am blind to its gendering, however, even when this is a critical discourse in which I (as an erstwhile reviewer) have participated. What Klawans seems to me to be doing is securing his position within a readerly 'out-group' which is as élite as it is marginal: he belongs to the group of boys in the back row of the cinema making fun of the film's bourgeois, and implicitly feminine, sensibility. Such a gendered reading experience is not, of course, sex-specific: as I have already indicated, part of me is there with them. But the larger part, as has been demonstrated in Chapters 5 and 6, is involved in a very different relationship with the text, based on a different interlocutor (of my own address) and a very different set of interpretive communities (part feminist, part liberal-humanist).

Another way of understanding Klawans's resistance to the text in terms of his audience/peer group is more simply as a 'will to difference'. Like Anne Billson (*Sunday Telegraph*, 31 October 1993), he seems determined to separate himself from the majority view in a move that might be construed as a more flagrant, less anxious form of connoisseurship. Instead of being fearful that his fellow journalists will consider him emotionally gullible for 'getting involved' in a bourgeois, art-house movie, his response *may* be construed as no more than 'playful': this is the 'professional reader' flexing his muscles, showing us what fun he can have with a text – any text – in order to produce good copy. In both cases, however, this is clearly another instance in which the 'reading process' has impacted on the 'reading': and in such a way that the reader's reasons for disliking the text, for disagreeing with others, depend upon much more than the 'objective' frameworks, the aesthetic and political codes, that are the ostensible source of the evaluation. This professional reader's peer group has, in other words, become his 'textual other'.

Text–Reader Interaction

The indisputable significance of audience and interpretive community on both the reading process and meaning-production inevitably calls into question the status of my next dialogic category: the interaction of text and reader within a model of implicated reading. If all reading is mediated by the presence of 'others' outside the text, is it still possible – or meaningful – to think about our relationship to the text in this one-to-one way? My opinion is that it is. Even if the separation of a textual other from an extratextual one is always necessarily false (in as much as the extratextual 'others' are always already there in some shadowy or not-so-shadowy form), dialogic intimacy – the sense that we, as readers, have connected with a textual other in an exclusive and excluding way – is, I feel, one of the most important readerly 'illusions'. My own readings of *The Piano* and the other texts in the previous section display this readily, even as they also show the extent to which the 'special relationship' is frequently disrupted by the intrusion of the extratextual others (the interpretive community, the public and private audience) of our readings. This question of the relative power of textual and extratextual others will be considered further in Chapter 8.

This intimate positioning of the self in relation to the text which, as I established at the end of Part II, is perhaps one of the best ways of explaining our emotional involvement in the reading process, remains largely unacknowledged by professional readers and critics. As we have already established, this is partly to do with residual critical anxiety about the way in which this sort of text–reader construction appears to slide into an unproblematized authentic-realist model, in which readers are relating to texts according to their own 'experience'.[22] Whilst the reader's own subjective history is also part of the relationship I am describing, this is within a very different, and profoundly interactive, context; one in which the reader does not simply 'project' her experience onto the text, but engages that experience in a *new relationship* with it.

Because of the taboo of presenting one's reading as an 'experience' of the authentic-realist kind, then, very few of today's academically trained readers are likely to be openly self-reflexive about their 'relationship' to the text. The one notable exception among the texts surveyed in this chapter is, again, Sue Gillett's *Screen* article, which, as we have seen, makes the tension between 'making a reading' and the reading event central to her discussion. Rather than reproduce this admirably self-reflexive example, however, I have chosen to focus instead on Jay Carr's review for *The Boston Globe* (19 November 1993), which seems to demonstrate a similarly implicated relation to the text, even though this is not brought to the level of conscious commentary.

Carr's, it will be remembered, is an enthusiastic review, which draws on the same interpretive frameworks as Klawans (see above) to come to very different conclusions. What interests me in this piece, however, is the way in which Carr positions himself in relation to the text, to the extent that, as in the following extract, the distinction between the characters', director's and reader's emotional characteristics become amusingly blurred:

> Campion does not flinch from feminist indictment of the way men bring trouble on themselves and the world by refusing – literally and figuratively – to listen to women. But she's just as interested in serving the intense feelings of her characters with fidelity. What she has to say is that there is salvation in heeding feelings and trying to get them expressed, and there's an intelligence rooted in sensation. And her compassion extends even to Neill's myopic and – in one shocking scene – brutal husband. If there's any justice, Campion and Hunter will be showered with awards for their inspired work here. For Hunter it's a wonderful breakthrough into new emotional territory and scale. It confirms Campion as one of today's most potent image-makers. And Keitel derseves high praise, too, for his less showy but just as deeply felt work. Lush, convulsive, impassioned, unforgettable, 'The Piano' is a one-of-a-kind film.

Particularly indicative, in this respect, is the final string of adjectives – 'Lush, convulsive, impassioned, unforgettable' – which, while notionally attached to 'the film' (as subject), could seem to apply to Campion, Carr or any of the characters and actors that he names. Whilst the argument of this concluding paragraph situates the film's emotion very firmly in Campion's characterization and the actors' outstanding performances, it seems to me that Carr has also entered this 'new emotional territory' – and without restraint! The zeal of the rhetoric reminds me, indeed, of Bakhtin's 'discovery' of Dostoevsky as the 'inventor' of the 'polyphonic novel' when, as I have argued elsewhere, the 'invention' can clearly be seen to be a 'reading method' of Bakhtin's own.[23] One could argue similarly that *The Piano* could never have been such a consummate success without the willingness of Carr, Gillett and millions of others to engage with its 'textual other' (whatever that might be: see Chapters 5 and 6) in this dialogical manner. In this respect the casual comment of another reviewer, Jeff Simon (*The Buffalo News,* 18 November 1993), rings sententiously but suggestively 'true': 'I feel a bit sorry for those who can't be captured by it – a little bit, at least. It may well mean that in some fundamental way, they're hooked up wrong. Something is missing.' Whilst I would never wish to suggest that not responding to *a* particular movie, or, indeed, to *this* particular movie, could declare an individual 'emotionally challenged', it would indeed be depressing to think that some readers/viewers *never* had access to this sort of participatory reading experience – never knew what it was to relate to a textual other in this way.

There is also, of course, a pressure to see this most romantic model of text–reader relations as 'gendered feminine' in the same way that Klawans's satirical distancing presented itself as 'masculine'. Such gender-stereotyping of the reading process would seem to me both useful and problematic: useful, to the extent that it alerts us to the fact that all models of reading must necessarily have their origins in social as well as textual discourses, and are thus only improbably 'gender-neutral', but problematic in that it could quickly be elided back into sex-based theories of men and women 'reading differently'. Carr's own text sets up a useful echo with Julia Kristeva's work in this respect, with its recourse to a typically 'semiotic' vocabulary reminding us that men, as well as women, have access to the psychological/cultural mind-sets that privilege more intimate models of being (and reading): 'Even when she remakes a classic . . . there's so much sensibility in it, it's so subliminal that it seems primal, pre-conscious, something floating up from the depths, dreamlike'.[24] The fact that I began this survey unclear whether the reviewer 'Jay Carr' was a man or a woman actually helps my point here: if this is a 'feminine reading', and if we do think it pertinent to gender readings in this way, then their relation to the biological sex of the reader must remain productively ambiguous.

With the second part of this chapter I have attempted to illustrate how the reading *process* informs the readings we 'make' of texts: how a whole range of selfother relations – both textual and extratextual – create the conditions in which the text is experienced and meanings produced even though the 'meanings', the act of interpretation, often conceals and represses all signs of the process. This recognition becomes especially important, I have argued, when attempting to explain 'differences' between readers with regard to a particular text: why we end up approving or disapproving of a work will often depend as much on the (*interactive*) processes at work in the reading as on the ostensible frames of reference, aesthetic and political, to which we refer. In the next chapter I use this theory to explore the differences between feminist readers, as they further problematize what it means to 'belong to' – to read as part of – a notional 'interpretive community'.

Notes

1 Jane Campion, *The Piano* (see n. 41, Ch. 1).
2 My source for this material was the computer search-organ LEXUS-NEXUS, which identifies newspaper headlines from around the world. My original plan was to conduct a similar analysis of media responses to Jeanette Winterson's *Written on the Body* (see n. 41, Ch. 1), but preliminary research showed that most of the criteria for readerly evaluation and participation merely repeated themselves. Since this is not a survey of the critics' responses *per se*, but rather an investigation of

their reading method, I therefore decided to focus on *The Piano* alone. It is, however, interesting to observe the comparative status of film and written text in terms of media coverage. Whilst entries for Winterson's text numbered between 400 and 500 in total, the coverage of *The Piano* was phenomenal, exceeding 1000 entries for 1993 alone (the year immediately following its release).

3 Lynda Nead: see n. 13, Ch. 1.

4 See *Reading Dialogics* (n. 4, Ch. 1), pp. 202–4. My reference here to the more 'menacing' interlocutor draws on Bakhtin's concept of 'hidden polemic': according to the Bakhtinian analysis of speech types, this is a form of double-voiced discourse in which the speaker in the text is in hostile or antagonistic dialogue with an (unidentified) 'other' (person or discourse) outside the text. Bakhtin illustrates this sort of antagonism, drawing particular attention to the paranoia that accompanies the speaker's sense of being 'policed' with reference to Dostoevsky's *Notes from the Underground* (1864; New York: Bantam, 1981). See my *Reading Dialogics*, pp. 52–4, for further details.

5 Jeanette Winterson, *Written on the Body* (see n. 41, Ch. 1).

6 'Defamiliarization': a concept invented by the Russian Formalists to describe the various devices employed by literature to 'make strange' (and hence newly significant) that which has become jaded and familiar. See Terence Hawkes, *Structuralism and Semiotics* (London: Methuen, New Accents, 1978), pp. 62–3.

7 It is, of course, interesting to contrast Persall's statement with my own determination to 'clear' the text of its characters in Chapters 5 and 6 whilst *preserving* the 'backdrop'.

8 Stella Bruzzi, 'Tempestuous Petticoats: Costume and Desire in *The Piano*', *Screen*, 36(3) (Autumn, 1995), pp. 257–26, and Sue Gillett, 'Lips and Fingers: Jane Campion's *The Piano*', *Screen*, 36(3) (Autumn), 1995. Page references to this volume will be given after quotations in the text.

9 I feel I should also acknowledge the cavalier tendencies of my own early writing: see discussion in Ch. 2!

10 Linda Dyson, 'The Return of the Repressed? Whiteness, Femininity and Colonialism in *The Piano*', *Screen*, 36(3) (Autumn, 1995), pp. 267–76. Page references to this volume will be given after quotations in the text.

11 'Characters as semes': See n. 37, Ch. 5.

12 Critics like Bruno Bettelheim, *The Uses of Enchantment: The Meaning and Importance of Fairy Tales* (1956; Harmondsworth: Penguin, 1985), have found the archaic structure of fairy-stories particularly conducive to psychoanalytic interpretations and psychoanalytically based speculation on the positioning of the reader.

13 'Gaps and silences': see n. 9, Ch. 1.

14 Jane Campion and Kate Pullinger, *The Piano* (see n. 29, Ch. 5).

15 'Structures of feeling': see n. 33, Ch. 1.

16 New Criticism: the literary criticism, focusing on the work of Americans like John Crowe Ransom (*The New Criticism*, 1941), which centres on the work of art as an object in itself, removed from both historical context and authorial intention.

17 The notion of one 'identity' necessarily marginalizing others has been well-rehearsed within the arena of Queer theory. See, for example, Judith Butler's 'Imitation and Gender Insubordination', in the *Gay and Lesbian Studies Reader*, ed. Henry Abelove *et al.* (London and New York: Routledge, 1992), pp. 307–20, and also *Gender Trouble* (London and New York: Routledge, 1990) and *Bodies That Matter* (London and New York: Routledge, 1993). In the latter she writes: 'As much as identity terms must be used, as much as "outness" is to be affirmed,

these same notions must be subject to a critique of the exclusionary operations of their own production' (p. 227).

18 See Richard Dyer, 'White', *Screen*, 29(4) (Winter, 1988), pp. 44–65.

19 See Stanley Fish, *Is There a Text in This Class?* (see n. 9, Ch. 1), and discussion of this text in Ch. 1. Page references to this volume will be given after quotations in the text.

20 'Paranoia' and 'policing': see n. 4 above on Bakhtin and 'hidden polemic'.

21 Nicholas Thomas, *Colonialism's Culture: Anthropology, Travel and Government* (Princeton, NJ: Princeton University Press, 1994).

22 'Authentic realism': see n. 35, Ch. 1.

23 See Mikhail Bakhtin, *Problems of Dostoevsky's Poetics* (n. 13, Ch. 2) and also my discussion in *Reading Dialogics* (see n. 4, Ch. 1), p. 44.

24 For an account of Julia Kristeva's theory of the semiotic and how it has been associated with 'feminine writing' (although not necessarily writing by women) see our discussions in *Feminist Readings/Feminists Reading* (n. 35, Ch. 1), pp. 155–6.

8

Emotion/Reading/Politics: A Case Study

In this chapter I continue my investigation into how we can begin to think about reading in new ways. In particular, I consider the difference between 'making a reading' and 'the reading process', which acknowledges a more dynamic, interactive and *implicated* relationship between text and reader. As with the last chapter, I shall analyse these processes at work in the written texts of readers other than myself, although here the focus will be on members of five groups of feminist readers convened especially for the purpose of answering my questionnaire on the subject of feminism, ethnicity and national identity.[1] My hope was that these groups, based in five regional locations in Canada (Montréal, Toronto, Halifax [Nova Scotia]) and the UK (Lancaster and Sheffield), could be used to interrogate the concept of Stanley Fish's 'interpretive community': to what extent are readers constrained/enabled by specific national, cultural, intellectual and political affiliations?[2] And to what extent can these differences of affiliation then be used to explain *disagreements* between feminist readers who notionally constitute an interpretive community in their own right? Do these disagreements merely remind us of the wide variety of positions and investments now gathered under feminism's large umbrella, or do they rather (in line with my own emerging thesis) point to the way in which *different models of reading* (such as 'implicated' or 'hermeneutic') impact upon both the textual experience *and* meaning-production?

It should be made clear from the outset that this is not an ethnographic project *per se*: not only are my five groups of readers too small a sample to furnish us with any serious quantitative conclusions about how feminists read or, more specifically, how questions of ethnicity and national identity are articulated within a feminist consciousness, but I do not wish to present their data as simple *qualitative* evidence of the different readings that can be produced by individuals, groups and international 'communities' either. My purpose, rather, has been to use my readers' responses to question how we, as feminist scholars, might begin to analyse the reading process *as a process*:

to use the differences and points of disagreement *symptomatically,* in an effort to understand what textual/contextual factors cause us to produce different readings, and to enjoy radically different reading experiences, in the first place. In other words, the object of this project is not to evaluate differences across the readings themselves (such as the fact that Canadian readers might be more aware of questions of national identity when reading Atwood than British ones), but to assess the *structural* impact of things like peer-group pressure, meted out through both interpretive community and 'audience', on how we engage (or not) with texts. To this end I have followed my practice in Chapter 7 of comparing the more ostensible reasons for readers' 'engagement with'/'rejection of' certain texts (their 'declared' readings) with what I perceive to be the more 'covert' processes at work: namely, the role of the interpretive community, audience(s) and our practices as 'implicated readers'. I should also signal immediately, however, that my naming of some of these processes as 'covert' does not imply blindness and ignorance on the part of the participants themselves. Since most of the women (and one man) who volunteered to take part in this project are themselves academics working in various fields of textual criticism, I have assumed that they, like myself, are only too aware of the maze of factors that impact upon a reading event, *including* the extent to which some are far less visible – or, at least, less 'spoken' – than others.

The fact that this study has been conducted in order to investigate the *processes* of reading rather than to evaluate differences *across* readings is also vital in excusing the cultural narrowness of my survey. All my reading groups are constituted from individuals connected, in some way, to academic institutions, and all have – or are in the process of acquiring – a university degree. This means that they constitute a very small proportion of women readers globally. There seems to me little question that readers with different educational and cultural backgrounds would respond to the texts used in this survey differently, and would 'make' significantly different readings. At the same time, I would expect the factors attending to the *processes of reading* which I look at here (interpretive community, audience and the dynamics of text–reader interaction) to remain relevant.

Since part of my rationale for undertaking this study was, however, to explore how differences in reading are made/experienced within a group sharing a supposedly *common* politics and cultural site, the narrowness of my target group can, perhaps, be justified. As I noted in the Preface to Part III, one of the most troubling aspects of 'reading as a feminist' is often the sharp, and swift, recognition that it will not necessarily guarantee consensus with other feminist readers. It is this recognition of inevitable dissent, and the fact that it cannot be explained purely in terms of differences of political and/or theoretical affiliation, that these two chapters set out to recognize and investigate.

Apart from their homogeneity in terms of a feminist identity and educational background, however, there were many significant differences between my readers and between the groups as groups. The participants were of different ages (ranging from 20 to 60), nationalities, ethnic backgrounds, social classes, sexualities and levels of educational attainment – though the questionnaire only invited them to specify the latter together with their ethnicity/nationality (see Appendix). In terms of education this means that some of the participants were students engaged in their first degree, some were postgraduates studying for a higher degree, while others were post-doctoral and/or working as lecturers/professors in institutions of higher education. Whilst a number of the participants were attached to departments of English Literature or Art History, moreover (disciplines whose 'training' will have a necessary bearing on readings of literary and visual texts), some were from other disciplines in the humanities and social sciences. Such differences in specialism have inevitably made themselves felt in the readings/reading-processes produced, and have been vital in interrogating the concept of interpretive communities. In this respect it is also important for me to comment on the composition of the different groups themselves and my role within them. Some of the groups, such as those in Montréal and Lancaster, for example, were comprised largely of individuals who knew each other, and had worked together, prior to the exercise; others were formed specifically for the purpose of the exercise (such as the one in Toronto). The two others (Halifax, Sheffield) combined individuals who had worked together before with those who had not. As far as my own relationship to the groups was concerned (a point of key importance in a research exercise which I wished to be as self-consciously 'dialogic' as possible), the situation varied from my never having met or worked with any of the participants before (Toronto and Montréal), to knowing one member well (Halifax and Sheffield) and, in the case of Lancaster, knowing all the members of the group extremely well and within a ready-formed research context. As we will see, the variable nature of these interactions has a significant impact both on the participants' returns and on my analysis of them.

The project in which all these readers were asked to participate required them to 'read' a selection of texts – two short stories and two paintings – and then record their responses on a questionnaire. Although the format of the questionnaire was very open (see Appendix) I was able to meet with all the groups before the exercise and explain the purpose of the project in some detail: most of the groups also heard me a give a paper based on the 'emotional politics' section of this book, and the 'guidelines' to answering the questionnaire specifically invited the readers to articulate their responses to the texts in these terms: 'To what extent did you feel included/excluded by each of the texts *vis-à-vis* ethnicity/national identity? What aspects of the texts involved you as a reader, what aspects alienated you? And did you feel these emotional responses to the text sometimes contradicted your intellectual and/or political response?' Such explicit reference to my own work and interests in the guidelines meant that, although the questionnaire lacked 'directed' questions, it nevertheless 'primed' the readings in a very explicit and self-conscious way. Indeed, it was very much my intention to make my own agendas, and the function of the exercise within this book as a whole, as upfront as possible in response to the methods used by earlier ethnographers.[3] In line with my own emerging thoughts on how we read, and on making meaning, I wished this to be a self-consciously *dialogic* exchange between myself and my readers, and among the readers themselves. Moreover, because all my respondents had the benefit of a higher education (even if it was not a specifically literary one), I was able to share this rationale with them in the background notes (see Appendix) which explained the context of the research, the composition of the groups, the nature of the participation and a discussion of the relationship between myself as researcher and themselves as participants. Despite the fact that the readers were presented only with a blank sheet on which to record their responses to each text, therefore (after a few brief notes on each of the texts), my interests – if not my requirements – were very explicit, and far more detailed than in most existing surveys of this kind.

Apart from being asked to comment on their emotional involvement with each of the texts (which necessarily invited them to reflect upon the 'processes' of reading), I also specifically requested that my participants *avoid* making literary-critical style readings of the texts (see Appendix). The fact that so many of my readers found this an impossible instruction is, of course, another matter (if a somewhat predictable one!).

As well as steering the participants towards responses which would themselves focus on the processes of reading rather than simply offer interpretations, I also requested them to think about the texts in relation to *feminism* and issues of *ethnic* and *national identity*; and the background notes (see Appendix) made it very clear how these factors appertained to the project as a whole. The fact that, once again, *all* my readers had problems keeping these objectives in mind whilst 'responding' to the texts in the 'non-professional', emotional and self-reflexive way I had also invited is, of course, further testimony to the difficulties of reading with different purposes, and within different frames, which are also reflected in my own readings in Chapters 5 and 6. In no way should it be taken as an indictment of these particular participants or their textual competency.

In terms of the nature of the exercise, and its reader participation, I should finally mention that it was suggested to all the groups that they might like to meet up after they had completed their readings and questionnaires, and share their experiences. An extra sheet at the end of the document then invited them to reflect upon what struck them as most interesting about the follow-up discussion: 'What do you see to be the most significant points of difference between yourself and the other participants, for example?' Whilst I was able to be present at some (but not all) of these follow-up meetings, I have not used verbal comment of any kind as the basis of the analysis which follows. As I made clear to the participants themselves in the background notes, this is an exercise which – following the work of several other reader/spectator theorists – 'acknowledges the impossibility of gaining access to the "authentic" (i.e., 'spontaneous', 'original') responses of readers in so much as all reading is "always already" mediated by previous textual and theoretical experiences' [quoted from the Appendix].[4] My own attention is therefore focused on these texts as (written) texts, and not as expressions of the individual readers who produced them. At the risk of tautology, what follows is therefore a reading of readers' writings about reading: the reading and the writing, the response and the address are, as we will see, very profoundly entwined.[5]

Although my original intention in inviting the participants to meet together in this way was both to make the exercise more interesting and meaningful, and to give them an opportunity to define and comment on their differences and disagreements *themselves,* before I submitted their texts to my own analysis, I nevertheless underestimated the extent to which anticipation of this 'feedback' session would impact on the readings/writings they felt able to produce. Whilst this has provided me with even greater insight into how (both public and internalized) audiences direct and control the nature of our textual engagments (see discussions in Chapter 7 and below), it was evidently at the expense of the more implicated, less 'professional' readings which the participants might otherwise have made. Although the various groups were constrained/enabled by the prospect of the feedback to variable degrees (and it would be wrong to think of it as an entirely 'negative' pressure), the implications have nevertheless caused me, retrospectively, to redefine the status of the research, and to observe that this was an exercise designed to tell us more about the impact of *contextual* factors on the processes and practices of reading than about the reader's relationship with the text *per se.* This last concern is, however, somewhat mitigated by my attendant hypothesis that *all* readings are in dialogue or polemic with a third party of some kind (see the discussion in Chapter 7, pp. 195), as will emerge in the discussion which follows.

The final point of methodology that needs to be discussed is the choice of the texts themselves. My rationale here was to present my participants with a combination of texts, visual and verbal, which were, first, relatively accessible in stylistic terms; second, of reasonable length; and third, which included subject matter which would invite readers to reflect upon issues of feminism, ethnicity and national identity as part of the reading process. Although poems, in their brevity, are often the preferred text for this sort of exercise, my experience as a university teacher of literature has also taught me that this is the genre that many readers still find the most inaccessible and alienating; and my choice of two short stories – one by the Canadian author, Margaret Atwood, and the other by the Scottish author, Liz Lochhead – may thus be seen as an attempt to provide texts that would produce a less stressful reading encounter as well as still being reasonably quick to consume.[6] Apart from the context of their production (both Atwood and Lochhead are considered, though not unproblematically, 'feminist'

authors), both these texts focus on female experiences that I felt would produce a 'feminist' response from readers thus identified, and both, though
less obviously, dealt with issues of ethnicity and national identity on which
I hoped some readers might choose to reflect also. The two paintings which
formed the third 'text', meanwhile, are by the Montréal artist Prudence
Heward (1896–1947), and are studies of female subjects (*Rollande* and *Girl
at a Window*) carefully coded in terms of ethnicity and national identity
(although, admittedly, in a way that was far more obvious to my Canadian
than my British readers).[7] All three, then, were selected by me as texts which
I felt provided the basis for a feminist and ethnically aware engagement, as
well as being 'about' other aspects of female experience and open to a wide
range of interpretations and reading-events. Although restrictions of length
have meant that I have only been able to focus on the responses to *one* of
these texts – Margaret Atwood's 'Death by Landscape' – for the purposes of
this chapter, the other material has supported and informed my discussion
as a whole. Indeed, one of the reasons I was finally persuaded to focus on
the 'readings' of a single text was the realization that, as far as the *processes*
of reading are concerned, common factors appear to be at work whatever
the text. Were this project concerned with the international differences
between feminist reading communities *per se* then a full comparison and
evaluation of British and Canadian responses to the three texts would, of
course, have been vital. The fact that the focus is rather on the *structures*
that give rise to the differences makes it less so. I was sorry, however, not to
have been able to reflect more on the qualitative difference in the readers'
responses to literary and visual texts, although – once again – all the 'covert'
factors of interpretive community, audience and text–reader interaction
could be seen to be at work in strikingly similar ways. While never wishing
to collapse and undermine the specificities of reading literature and reading
visual images, one of the key things to have emerged out of the research I
have done for this book as a whole is, indeed, the (problematically?) trans-
generic nature of our 'structures of reading', and in particular the common
processes in which we appear to engage in in the production of the 'textual
other'.

Reading 'Atwood'

As I indicated in my opening comments to this chapter, my analysis of the
readers' responses to this text will follow the model employed in Chapter 7,
whereby discussion of our ostensible reasons for 'engaging' or not with a text
(broadly separable into 'aesthetic' and 'political' criteria) will be followed by
speculation on the more covert (or 'unspoken') factors at work in the reading process (namely, interpretive community, audience and text–reader interaction).

Despite what I had hoped was a clear suggestion to readers that they reflect upon their *engagement* by these particular texts as much as possible, it is striking how many individuals preferred to comment on their relationship to 'Atwood' in the abstract – as an *œuvre* – rather than comment on their relationship to this particular story. Consider the following observations:[8]

> Atwood is very over-loaded for me: I've spent too much time with her texts and I *expect* to be both irritated and impressed: which I was here. There is something very negative about her take on women and feminism . . . Atwood dispels myths about female friendships, women, etc. but there is a denial and a longing for something different . . . Atwood signifies Canada for me: her settings are familiar and this was certainly true in this story. (O, Halifax)

> Like most readerly Canadians, especially feminist ones, I've been responding to the themes and nuances of Atwood's texts and public personae . . . since forever. I approached this story expecting a familiar blend of amusement, irritation and a straining towards pathos. And so it was. (T, Halifax)

> I had most trouble with this text because not only have I taught Atwood short stories (not this) but have resisted studying her since I was an undergraduate. I felt she was too sensationalist as a writer at the same time as she captures Canadianness which irritated me. (L, Montréal)

> I do not feel particularly included in the Atwood voice – as a woman, as a feminist, or a North American – perhaps because I read her work as highly autobiographical. Not that she writes about her own life so much as she is, in a sense, a portraitist of feminine interiority. (U, Lancaster)

The declared *over*-familiarity of all these Canadian/North American readers with Atwood's writing is a clear obstacle to their engaging with this particular text on its own terms: what they have been asked to read and respond to is overlaid by so many expectations and preconceptions that the only parts of the story they attend to are the ones which correspond with previous reading experiences. Having learnt all the Atwood 'codes' – both textual and intertextual – and having sorted out their own relationship to her politics (feminist and otherwise), these readers are apparently reluctant to respond to a new text except through this prepared grid, and their comments have the tone of stubborn resistance. 'Atwood' is too reified and over-determined an icon ('feminist'/'Canadian') for them to relate to easily: the author's powerful inscription in her text silences the reader, forestalling and inhibiting any effective dialogic exchange.

It is clear, however, that there *is* very much a dialogue *between the readers* (both as individuals and as part of a North American/Canadian feminist reading community) and the author-function.[9] The resistance to Atwood is not simply one of over-familiarity or the canonization of her work, but is in part due to the apparently stultifying inscription of her identity on their own. The 'irritation' (referred to explicitly by three respondents) may thus be seen to derive from a mutual 'recognition': 'Atwood' is the literary 'mother' who must be resisted if the 'daughter' is ever to achieve her own feminist/'national' identity. For it is the conflation of femininity, feminism and 'Canadianness' that Atwood's writing has come to signify for these readers above all. As T (Halifax) observes:

> Lois's responses to Lucy remind (are meant to remind?) [us] of the Canadian/feminine desire to please through silence or assent. We pander; are polite. So one side of this story goes. On another level, Atwood suggests that neither landscape nor woman is what it/she seems. They live with each other quietly and tragically and above all mysteriously. Again: this picture is utterly familiar, but I do not 'identify' with it, either. Such codes bore and annoy me.

It is interesting to observe also the way in which this reader's resistance to the Atwood '*œuvre*' is displaced into a highly professionalized critical rhetoric. While always writing about Atwood generically, rather than about this particular story, she nevertheless proceeds to 'make a reading', thus exercising her own will-to-knowledge over both the text and the problematic author-function. This exercise of readerly authority very much echoes my own 'practice' in my earlier readings (see especially Chapter 3) and, indeed, the shift between the implicated and hermeneutic modes in many of the readings performed in Chapters 5 and 6.

Not surprisingly, the British readers' responses to 'Atwood' were qualitatively different from those. As academic and feminist readers, many were as familiar with her work and 'reputation' as their Canadian/North American counterparts, and expressed similar problems with her 'feminism' both inside and outside this particular text. In no instance did this impinge on the British readers' own feminine/feminist identities, however: 'Atwood' is 'always fascinating though problematic' (V, Sheffield), but the 'problems' are not experienced as personally threatening and/or undermining, and they certainly do not block the readers' responses to the text in the same way. One might observe that this is an instance of a national identity somehow 'fixing' a very particular gendered identity (see T's comment above): it is as though the particular brand of 'Canadian-feminine' associated with Atwood's heroines has become a stereotype by which they feel themselves to be involuntarily inscribed by.[10]

It should not be concluded, however, that *all* the Canadian participants involved in this project were prevented from engaging with the Atwood text through this over-determination of the Atwood author-function. As we shall see, other groups and individuals (notably those who were younger or had less literary-critical training) report a very interactive reading experience, as do a number of the British readers. The crucial inference to be drawn here is thus further acknowledgement of how it is our differential structural articulation within a text – the factors which enable us (or not) to discover within it a textual other with whom we can dialogize – that will mark most powerfully the nature of our reading experience. The fact that in my own former readings of Jeanette Winterson (see Chapter 6) the author-function ('Winterson') was adored rather than resisted does not alter the fact that for me, as for some of the 'Atwood' readers here, the extrapolation was similarly in lieu of a more implicated engagement of the text itself.

Frameworks of Meaning

As far as readers themselves are concerned, meanwhile (and I include myself: see again Chapters 5 and 6) the most obvious, or most easily articulated, *obstacles* to a more dialogic or interactive textual encounter are to be located in the aesthetic and political features of the text itself. Like many of the negative reviewers of *The Piano* in Chapter 7, a number of readers here – both Canadian and British – blame their lack of involvement in the text on specific narrative strategies, in particular its teasing and manipulation of the reader.[11] For example:

> This story also annoys me because I feel like I am being manipulated towards a *big* thematic revelation, but I never get there. (M, Halifax)

> I feel the death was a cheap strategy by Atwood and a 'cop-out' artistically. (L, Montréal)

> But the ending of the text is spelled out too much for my taste. It told me what I was already figuring out – as though Atwood doesn't trust me enough, doesn't think I'm smart enough to get it. (O, Toronto)

> Principal emotion was annoyance. Liked the title, but felt that the story was so teleological as to be redundant . . . Generally avoid short stories because they seem so calculating. I feel very driven and can't help racing – speeding up – as the story progresses . . . All in all very claustrophobic. Suppose could step back and this is what the story intends – asking me to question this – but feel that this is external to the story and not so aesthetically satisfying. (E, Lancaster)

It could be argued that, in their different ways, all these readers are criticizing the story or the *genre* to which it belongs, as the last respondent makes clear, for being too aesthetically contrived and controlling: the reader is not given enough freedom to enter the text and make her own interpretation. It is the hermeneutic over-determination of the text which is the obstacle, whether its 'secret' (what really happens to Lucy?) is seen to be too obscure or too obvious. These are, of course, sophisticated literary-critical objections to the text, and not the sort of 'resistance' that would be available to less trained readers.

The last reader quoted here, for example, is fully aware of the theoretically informed nature of her critique and the fact that she could see the text's manipulations as part of its 'success' ('this is what the story intends'), and that she could make another reading by 'stepping back': she rejects this possibility, however, and pushes responsibility back on the text by implying that this is asking the reader to work 'too hard', and that such a reading would be 'external to the text itself' and therefore not 'aesthetically satisfying'. The text is thus made to 'fail' on the basis of both its 'over'- and 'under'-control of the reader. It should also be noted that this is a complex manœuvre in terms of text–reader power (see my own practices in Chapter 2), since, although the greater power is ostensibly granted to the text (it is *made responsible* for its reader-positioning), this power is undermined by the reader's 'seeing through it', and by her refusal to engage with the text in this and other ways.

Resistance to the text is also channelled through a political dissatisfaction with its subject matter. Although, as we have already seen, much of the feminist criticism of the work is deflected onto an author whose own feminism has for many years been in dispute, readers less overwhelmed by the 'Atwood' persona have discovered a problematic politics within the text itself. For example, D, from Lancaster, is quickly alienated by the middle-classness of Atwood's narrator, and clearly resents the lack of a more positive/politically affirming character with whom she can relate:

> A cleaning lady only 2× a week – shame (is this writer trying to wind people up – purposefully alienate – is it a Brechtian strategy?) (D, Lancaster)

Although many literary critics may, indeed, choose to defend the 'unsympathetic' nature of the narrator in terms of the Brechtian strategies to which the reader alludes (emphasizing the distinction between 'author', 'text' and 'narrator'), D's rejection of the text – or, more precisely, her alienation by it on account of 'unlikeable' characters – should be familiar to all of us (see my own response to Winterson's bourgeois characters in Chapter 6). In this instance, the story seems to conjure up a world of privilege to which the reader is politically hostile ('Lost interest with stories of cheery girls. Enid Blyton here we come') and which obstructs any pro-feminist reading of the characters and their actions.

A superficial reading of a text's politics through its character representation is also the basis for a more positive engagement with the text, however, and is, as we shall see, the springboard for many of the more interactive responses. Several of the younger readers regarded either Lucy, or Lois, or both, as positive role-models for women, and deemed the text 'feminist' on this count. For example:

> As a feminist reader Atwood's story appeals to me because it is a story about young women and friendship. This story evokes memories of the important relationships I had with female friends and the continued importance of female companionship in my life. (C, Montréal)

> As a feminist I could relate to the roles women are expected to play –
> being stuck in the life you landed in and also the momentary escape
> from female destiny that girls at a summer camp might experience.
> (F, Montréal)

Although both these texts proceed to show their readers to be critically
aware of the class-specificity of the girls being represented, this is not an
obstacle to a feminist reading in the way that it is for D. It is clear, therefore,
that – as we saw in the previous chapter – a number of less obvious forces
are at work in the reader's political 'coding' of a text, since the manifest content, as here, can be variously appropriated. What is significant as far as the
reading experience is concerned is that readers can *perceive* a text's political
field to be the total explanation for their 'involvement' with it, or not.

Generally speaking, the response to the text's presentation of ethnic identity was less critical, with most readers regarding the text as a 'critique' of
colonialism and racism, rather than a collusive discourse:

> I feel her sense [i.e., Lois's] of haunting is justified as wilderness and
> First Peoples vanished like Lucy. (U, Montréal)

> The issue of stereotyping and appropriation was presented in a way I
> enjoyed, because it wasn't simplified and didactic. (P, Toronto)

Other responses are more ambiguous, however, suggesting that the readers
found the representation of 'Indians' less clearly framed. For example:

> The great outdoors and escaping to Canada has one pull, but the
> pseudo-'Indian' stuff makes me furious. (M, Lancaster)

> The Indian stuff made me think 'liberals'. (D, Lancaster)

Once again, then, we have a situation in which a text's politics is
approved or rejected (and, by extension, the text itself approved or
rejected) through an extrapolation of its author's intentions or perceived
ideological position (see my discussion of *The Piano* in Chapter 6). Even
critically trained readers (myself included), who are evidently aware that
they are at least *partly* responsible for 'making' the text's meaning, tend
to uphold this right to discrimination. Such 'objectification' of the text's
status is clearly easier for us to acknowledge and articulate than the complex *contextual* factors, such as audience and interpretive community,
that are also central to our evaluation.

'Community' Pressure

As we saw in the last chapter, virtually all the aesthetic and political evaluations of the text posited by its readers can be seen to derive from the various interpretive communities to which they belong. My particular interest in

such affiliations here, however, is not one of simple identification – it will already be obvious that my readers inhabit a fairly predictable spectrum of intellectual and cultural communities – but in assessing how 'membership' of such a community affects the total reading experience: in particular, how the community can both inhibit ('forbid') and promote a more implicated, interactive relationship to the text.

Before beginning this assessment, it is first important to distinguish between 'discourses' and 'communities' (see note 3). While the two are sometimes virtually indistinguishable (certain intellectual groupings might appear to be 'defined' by a particular theoretical and/or political line circulating in an academic community at a given time, such as the specific blend of feminism, Marxism and psychoanalysis associated with the Marxist Feminist Literature Collective in the the late 1970s), interpretive communities should, according to my own definition, also have a *physical* location in a country, an institution (or group of institutions), a friendship network or a cultural/intellectual 'application', as in university teaching, student learning or journalism (see Chapter 7).[12] Therefore, although it is clear that many of my respondents are 'interpellated' by the contemporary discourses of feminism, post-colonialism and poststructuralism, these inscriptions are not in themselves identical to their 'interpretive communities' which, as we will see, are better thought of as sites where a number of such discourses meet, cross and are validated.[13] The interpretive communities that I will be identifying here are, indeed, best thought of as the sites of social interaction, themselves profoundly power-inscribed, which cause – or even force – an individual to adopt a certain set of values and practices which then become endemic to his or her reading practice.

We have already seen, in the first part of this chapter, the way in which several of my North American/Canadian participants read Atwood's story through the author-function rather than engaging with the specifics of the text in hand. Regarded with the hindsight of my own practices in Chapters 5 and 6, it seems clear to me that for these respondents the reading experience was certainly *not* a 'process': what their texts signal is an instant, almost knee-jerk reaction to the signifier 'Atwood' which then prompts a 'prepared' reading of her *œuvre*. This reading may refer, in passing, to 'Death in the Landscape', but the significant 'other' with whom the reader is in dialogue is, for the most part, not 'the words on the page'.

What I now want to suggest, however, is that – contrary to my previous argument based on the manifest content of the readers' returns – this 'other' is also *more* than 'Atwood', the author-function. It is, to hypothesize bluntly, '"Atwood" as she has been produced (and circulated) by a particular interpretive community': i.e., 'Atwood' + her interpretive community.

So how do we define such a community, and how does membership of it impact upon the reading process? As I indicated above, all interpretive communities need a physically conceived location, even if, paradoxically, it is conceived as an 'imagined' one.[14] The community that has spawned these readings of 'Atwood' has, I would suggest, a specific *national location* (there is a definite Canadian – or possibly, by extension, North American – parameter to the interpretations), but is also defined (*within* those boundaries) by the *communication channels* through which its discourses are spread. If we think of the first characterization as the geographical space of the country 'Canada' therefore, we might envisage the second as the domestic railway system that traverses it, connecting, at least potentially, all the members of its far-flung community. What was distinctive in my survey, certainly, was the way in which certain members of all three of my Canadian groups produced readings which were themselves nationally situated (both they and 'Atwood' were constrained by the same 'Canadian-feminine' identity), and which implied a certain – unspecified – 'knowledge' about 'Atwood's' feminism which, I would suggest, has the quality of 'gossip'. This 'knowledge' may be likened to a Chinese-whisper which has spread, over the years, through various academic and friendship networks; which is, in part, supported by the conclusions of academic scholarship and journalism (see Chapter 7), but which mixes more 'official' evaluations of Atwood and her work with urban myth and legend. I was amazed, for example, at the number of women I met in Canada who had 'known' Atwood at some stage in their lives, or had, at least, met with her or 'grown up' in the same places. Two of my respondents here, indeed, have drawn attention to these very personal associations, with O (from Halifax) observing how 'her settings are familiar . . . I can fill in the blanks – the city is Toronto – I can fill in *her* [my emphasis] details' whilst U (from Lancaster) states how her attitude to 'Atwood' changed after she had interviewed the author:

> I once interviewed Atwood and was slightly horrified by her in person, which I am sure influences my response to her work. I was quite a fan of her writing before then – because of its irony and almost cruel insightfulness. (U, Lancaster)

These personal encounters with the author, and shared 'experience' of her spaces and places, have clearly criss-crossed Canada and its intellectual/feminist communities like a rail network, supplementing the ever-proliferating academic and media representations of Atwood and her work.[15] Although some of my Canadian respondents expressed retrospective 'surprise' at how similar their responses to the Atwood text were (see discussion above), the wildfire spread of any discourse operating within this sort of 'grapevine' suggests that they should not have done.

If we turn now from a characterization of the 'Atwood' interpretive community to what it means to 'belong' to such a group, we may observe that it grants its members defensive protection (when asked about 'Atwood' and her status as Canada's leading 'feminist' writer, they have something to say); but, as we have seen, they are also likely to be silenced in their response to the texts themselves. A certain intellectual machismo may be seen to account for both these situations: membership of this sort of interpretive community (as we also witnessed in the community of 'Arts Journalism' discussed in the previous chapter) is concomitant with the rules of 'connoisseurship': in such company (even if it is 'imagined', and the participants are not *consciously* aware that they are thinking along the same lines as others) it is 'undignified' and 'tasteless' to admit your 'involvement' with a text. It – or its signifier (for example, 'Atwood') – has to be held at a distance and criticized in *disinterested* terms. One of the privileges of belonging to an interpretive community, after all, is the gift of a received set of criteria for judging a work, a set of frameworks, as we saw in Chapter 7, to prevent one soiling one's own critical hands. Even though they might proclaim their relationship with 'Atwood' complex and difficult, many of my respondents were able to dispatch her work and its significance with apparent nonchalance. Consider again the *tone* of the following extract, which ironizes the reader's relationship to 'Atwood' in a style characteristic of much of my own past work on Pre-Raphaelite art (see Chapter 2, pp. 43–4):

> Like most readerly Canadians, especially feminist ones, I've been responding to the themes and nuances of Atwood's texts and public personae . . . since forever. I approached this story expecting a familiar blend of amusement, irritation, and a straining towards pathos. And so it was. (T, Halifax)

By making 'Atwood' an objectified point of reference, as discussed above, and with the support and validation of other 'readerly Canadians', this reader is able to sum up her 'response' to 'Atwood' in two words: 'amusement' and 'irritation'. She thus makes clearly visible her own power and authority over the text and its author-function, while avoiding comment on her own role, as reader, in its meaning-production. Her imagined community of fellow-readers has suggested to her what to say, and she has repeated it: a positioning of the reading self somewhere *between* the text and one's interpretive community that will be familiar to many of us working within academia.

But although the interpretive community can thus be seen to afford its members a relatively simple and effective protection against enquiries such as my own (all Canadian feminists will be expected to have an 'opinion' on Atwood), this is clearly at the cost of *articulating* a more personal engagement with individual texts – which is not to imply that such interactions might not nevertheless take place 'off the record'. At the risk of over-dramatizing the scenario, the 'Atwood' reader may thus be seen to be both permanently protected and constantly threatened by members of her community. The only way she can displace her 'official' reading of an Atwood text with a more complex engagement is to defy her community and lose its protection.

It should also be noted, however, that interpretive communities *can* work to promote a more positive and interactive text–reader relationship, although simultaneously raising again the question of whether an implicated reading mediated by another is really 'implicated' in the sense that I have previously defined it. As I have already indicated in Chapter 7, it is debatable whether, in such cases, the reader's relationship is with an other in the text or with her mediating agent. Or is her dialogue effectively with both? (a proposition that breaks down what is, after all, a problematic polarization of text and context within the reading process).[16] These questions are certainly germane to the readings produced by my group of readers from Montréal, who appear to represent a strikingly homogeneous interpretive community (with the exception of one group member, who came from another institution) on the basis of their inscription by a set of shared theoretical and political discourses, supported and promoted by their university department. In this instance, the students' 'training' as readers has clearly encouraged a dialogic and self-reflexive reading practice, and these young women consequently come closest of all my respondents to integrating their 'personal' relationship to the text with their political and theoretical assessment of it. Here are just two examples:

> I felt alienated by Atwood's story in one particular respect. Her narrative seemed only to speak of white Anglo-Saxon young women who came from middle- or upper-middle class homes. As a first-generation Canadian of Eastern European background, I felt that this story has excluded the Canadian immigrant who is not a descendent of British stock. (C, Montréal)

> These stories are not about immigrants but about those who are established – the British in Britain and their descendants in a colonized Canada. Half my family fits this bill, so I feel very much in touch with the characters in these stories even though my personal experience is not so much like theirs. (F, Montréal)

These readers' interpretive community may thus be seen to actively promote a personal involvement and 'implication', in the same way that membership of the 'Atwood' club prevents (or 'protects') its readers from this. In conclusion, then, it seems important to keep distinct the ideological and the structural role of interpretive communities within the reading process. Whereas one interpretive community might incline a reader to 'love' 'Atwood', and another to 'hate' her, for example, I would argue that, in terms of *models* of reading, *all* such communities work to make themselves, and not the text, the real focus of the reader's attention, notwithstanding the complex, almost paradoxical instance cited above, where the community leads the reader back to the text through its own mediation. Since no readers exist entirely outside of such communities, it may consequently be best to argue that implicated readings ultimately take place only *by permission* of interpretive communities which do not seek to usurp/displace the text or textual other in question: where the community is present without being a *presence*.

Audience Pressure

As exemplified by the 'Atwood' club, the reader's interpretive community also functions as one of her *audiences*; and this is another key ingredient in the reading process. Indeed, as the above discussion (and that in Chapter 7) will have begun to make clear, the interpretive community is a profoundly dialogic site, a station on the rail network at which the reader both receives information and passes it on, her words constrained and (sometimes) policed by the fact that her (exogamous) addressees share the same platform as her 'community' mentors. It is important to remember, however, that although this internalized, discursive audience undoubtedly puts pressure on the reader and is active in determining her total reading experience, other, named and identifiable interlocutors are also instrumental in this process. In Chapter 7, for example, I distinguished between the journalists' interpretive community and the specific, overt and covert audiences which they were addressing in their newspapers. These interlocutors may share the same values as the reader's dominant interpretive community; but if they do not, the reader might find herself 'taking on' their anticipated response – *as well* as that of her community – when she 'makes her reading' or engages with the text. In one respect this might at first appear like another sort of readerly policing, though it would often seem to be experienced by readers as a more positive challenge: defining one's own response to a text *against* that of another may be experienced as a complex pleasure. Our reading might thus become a dialogic event, in which our engagements with the text are quickly translated into a conversation with an extratextual 'other' whom we wish both to share the experience with and to persuade of our point of view.

Although these audiences to our readings will not always become *actual* audiences, even though they are consciously present in our minds as particular individuals or groups of individuals, this exercise provided participants with two very obvious audiences that they could not escape: myself, as researcher, and the fellow members of their group (see the discussion above). And because it was clear from the start that their readings *of* the texts were quickly to become writings *about* them, we must assume that these audiences were, themselves, a fundamental *condition* of the reading process: all the reading 'about' was simultaneously a 'reading to'.

This model of split address within the reading process, constituted here as a relationship between the reader and the text and the reader and an extratextual interlocutor, is usefully annotated by reference back to Voloshinov's work on *intonation*.[17] Although the concept has traditionally been employed in order to help distinguish the mixture of address within individual utterances, the notion that any utterance always faces in at least *two directions* is also helpful in explaining the complex interaction between the reader and the text and the reader and her audience, and in sorting out the complex power-dynamics that must always appertain both within and between the relationships. As Don Bialostosky has usefully summed up: 'Every instance of intonation is oriented *in two directions*: with respect to the listener as ally or witness, and with respect to the object of the utterance as the third, living participant whom the intonation scolds or caresses, denigrates or magnifies.'[18] Shifted to the arena of the reading process, this invites us to attend to the way in which the reader's relationship to the text (and its 'object of utterance') expresses itself in her relationship to her audience and vice versa, and to recognize that her preference for, or intimacy with, the one might not extend to the other, thus producing a strained and extremely volatile reading event. A reader might realize the *possibility* of becoming very intimately and emotionally bound up with a certain text, for example, but, knowing that a prospective interlocutor to her reading will feel very differently about it, may be pushed towards a more defensive engagement (as is evident in my, and others', trauma in speaking publicly about *The Piano*). Alternatively, the prospect of a sympathetic audience, one whom she knows to think and feel similarly to herself, might *encourage* her to open herself up to the text even more. Both of these scenarios can, I think, be identified in the responses of my participants here as they seek to negotiate their own relationship with both text and audience.

To deal with the last of these first, it was very noticeable that those readers who demonstrated a more intimate, consensual relationship with their audience or interlocutor were also those most likely to have experienced a more implicated and interactive relationship with the text. They were also, in most cases, the undergraduate readers, and in particular those who belonged to an established and supportive intellectual forum, itself commensurate with a well-defined intepretive community – for example, my Montréal group (see also the discussion above concerning the interpretive community). The ease with which this particular group engaged with the texts, openly exploring their relationships to them, will be demonstrated in the next section of this chapter, but it is worth observing in passing how reader–text and reader–audience intimacy reproduce one another. For example:

> The story was very Ontario, very waspy – a place I know well. Lois's attitude, her quiet solitude, I also feel that I know – she reminded me a great deal of my grandmother. She who absorbs all (much like landscape) and yet seems/feels empty. This, like 'Quelque Fleurs' [Liz Lockhead's short story] was very white, purebred nationhood. These stories are not about immigrants but about those who are established – the British in Britain and their descendants in Canada. Half of my family fits this bill, so I feel very much in touch with the characters in these stories even though my personal existence is not so much like theirs. (F, Montréal)

> This story evokes memories of the important relationships I had with female friends and the continued importance of female companionship

in my life. I cannot completely identify with this story because I never went to a sleep-away camp, though I do remember the many stories my female friends spoke of, concerning their sleep-away camp adventures and mischief. (C, Montréal)

In both these extracts, the readers' easy movement between a professional 'reading' of the text and its bearing on their own life-experience is clearly facilitated by their positioning of their audience (presumably myself and the other group members) as 'allies', who both recognize and will be interested in the connections they are making.[19] The mode of inscription here is most like a personal letter, and the narrativization of the reading experience (each reader has begun to incorporate a 'story' of herself and her own past life into her text) assumes the presence of a comfortable listener. This epistolary framework is even more explicit in the text of one of the Toronto group who, as we will see in the next section, also produces the most implicated of all the responses to Atwood's story. Although this participant was not personally known to me before the exercise, I am clearly positioned as a sympathetic respondent of her reading/memory:[20]

First, let me say that although I have read a great deal of Atwood's writing, I do not find her writing very emotionally engaging – her work generally does not *touch* me. This is true of 'Death by Landscape', though to a lesser extent than her other work – it did provide opportunities for me to engage with it, to *feel* in response to it . . . Reading of people being embodied in nature brought back, very vividly, the eerie feeling I've usually had when I've been in forests or other natural settings *by myself*. The feeling has often been one of presences watching me. In fact, I once became frightened of the entire city and surrounding area of Thunder Bay, Ontario, because it feels haunted . . . I wondered while reading, the same thing I often do – I wondered *why* I'm so afraid of 'nature' – and I also argued with myself a little about it – got a little bit annoyed because it seems such a silly thing to be afraid of aloneness in. (K, Toronto)

Both the phrasing of the opening sentence ('First let me say . . .') and the use of conversational connecting clauses throughout ('In fact'; 'So, as I read . . .'; 'and I also') gives this text the quality of a spoken dialogue. Although her comments are ostensibly *self-reflexive,* they clearly signal the presence of a sympathetic interlocutor, one who will not be censorious of the the the fact that the emotions she describes are, in one sense, 'silly'.

This willingness to lay oneself open to both text and audience is certainly not reproduced in the texts of all my respondents. Whilst a few of the older, postgraduate readers (many of them now working as university lecturers) attempt a more dialogic exchange with both text and audience, many of those belonging to this category demonstrate a somewhat strained and anxious relationship with their (immediate) audience which, in turn, impacts upon their engagement with the text itself. Unfortunately, ethical questions about the role of the researcher in using her analytic power and ('inside') knowledge of the groups, their members and the dynamics between them (both intellectual *and* personal) has made it virtually impossible for me to present 'evidence' of this here.[21] Reflecting upon my highly situated observations 'in the abstract', however, it seems clear to me that various stylistic features of the returns – such as an 'objectification' of the text, recourse to a highly professionalized rhetoric, and the invocation of certain external frameworks of taste and discrimination (see the extracts quoted in the 'Frameworks of Meaning' section, pp. 228–30) – point to major insecurities both about displaying one's own critical skills in public (and perhaps *especially* when one's audience is also one's colleagues) and about exposing one's own personal investments (both readerly and otherwise) through a more implicated reading of the text. In some instances this defensiveness and insecurity displayed itself through a certain theatricality of style (which made it very clear that the participants were acutely aware of the audience to whom their reading/writing would be publicly addressed); in others it did so through repeated disclaimers of competence directed both at me, as researcher, and the other group members, and summed up by the phrase 'I don't know if I've done this right'. What such over-determination of the audience adds up to on one level is, of course, a questioning of my research practice: was the implementation of the follow-up group discussion counter-productive? If the aim of the project was to investigate differences *within* the reading process, would not the prospect of a public discussion *inevitably* pressure the participants into dialogizing with members of the group rather than with an other within the text? The short answer to this hypothesis has to be 'yes', although, as has already been seen, the research procedure did not affect all the groups or participants in the same way and to the same extent, while the (interactive) 'pressure' of both interpretive community and audience in *all* the reading practices and processes I have explored in this book (including my own readings and those of the critics in Chapter 7) questions whether there can ever be such a thing as totally 'private', audience-free textual engagement. The variable factor, as I have already suggested in Chapter 7, is *to what extent* the 'third party' is present and whether their presence *permits* a more implicated relationship.

The Implicated Reader

I now move on to a discussion of the different forms of text–reader interaction that have been demonstrated in these responses to Atwood's story. For those who managed to evade or negotiate the polemical pressures of audience and interpretive community, who/what is seen to constitute the textual other? How does the text–reader relationship begin? How does it develop?

As I indicated in the previous section, a more interactive and implicated text–reader relationship is usually accompanied, first by the reader's acknowledgement of a sympathetic interlocutor of the 'reading' (actual or implicit), and second, by a narrativized and/or participatory engagement with the text (as opposed to an 'abstract'/distanced 'evaluation'). I wish to consider some of the most striking features of this aspect of the reading process by focusing on the text of one respondent in particular, although several aspects of her reading-experience have echoes, as I shall point out, in the returns of the other respondents. I shall begin by reproducing her text in full:

First, let me say that although I have read a great deal of Atwood's writing, I do not find her writing very emotionally engaging – her work generally does not *touch* me. This is true of 'Death by Landscape', though to a lesser extent than her other work – it did provide opportunities for me to engage with it, to *feel* in response to it.

My biggest reaction to this story comes as a response to the descriptions of the setting – Ontario's 'Near North' is familiar to me, and Atwood captured the feeling and fit of this landscape very well. So, I moved into memory mode as I read it. The last couple of pages, where Lois describes the trees' energy and identifies Lucy as alive in her Group of Seven paintings was a very close, very accurate painting of how I feel in the kind of forests those pictures portray. Though Lois is referring to the trees and landscape in the paintings, she is bringing to light how that landscape has made me feel in actuality. Reading of people being embodied in nature brought back, very vividly, the eerie feeling I've usually had when I've been in forests or other natural settings *by myself.* The feeling has often been one of presences watching me. In fact, I once became frightened of the entire city and surrounding area of Thunder Bay, Ontario, because I felt it to be haunted. That feeling still lingers when I imagine Thunder Bay. So, as I read, Thunder Bay came back to me, as did solitary walks in the wilderness, and time spent sitting alone on the dock. I wondered, while reading, the same thing I often do – I wondered *why* I'm so afraid of 'nature' – and I also argued with myself a little about it – got a little bit annoyed because it seems such a silly thing to be afraid of aloneness in. I thought also of the contradictory way I feel in wilderness alone – both eerie because I feel watched, and comfortable because I'm more truly alone than [I] ever can be at other times. Finally, I decided, I think – all of this was in disjointed terms, occurring as I read –, that maybe the reason for the eerie, watched sense is the profound solitude. Maybe, even, something in me can't deal with the idea that there is no-one watching (in a metaphorical sense), that I'm completely free.

Also, Atwood's descriptions of the dynamic that existed between Lois and Lucy sometimes made me smile in remembrance and a feeling of 'yeah, that's exactly how it is (as it was for me)' between girls at that age. And I identified, really, the most, with Lois's feelings of awe and desire to impress Lucy, because those are things I look on fondly and with some poignancy as the beginnings of a lesbian identity, for me. Also, it made me go off on a small tangent of thought about children and motherhood, which is something I've been thinking about a lot lately, for some reason. I felt, mostly, sad and apprehensive about two things. First, the idea of raising a kid and watching them go through pain, and second, at the idea, at the idea of having my kid die. This reaction was just a series of pangs, a lot like what I have when women about me describe their experience of motherhood. (K, Toronto)

Although many of the respondents demonstrate the way in which a literary text acts as a 'springboard' for their own thoughts and memories (as V from Sheffield writes: 'It's like a springboard for working against/through ideas about my own subjectivity and childhood, in particular, but also other peoples''), this reader's 'leap' is exceptional in both its length and detail. In a reflex similar to my own engagement with *The Piano* (see Chapter 5), this reader declares that it is the 'setting' of Atwood's story that is the source of her 'biggest reaction', not the characters or what happens to them. Indeed, rather like me, her primary move seems to be to 'clear' the text of all Atwood's own characters, and insert herself in their landscape: the descriptions of the Group of Seven paintings launch her into 'memory mode', and soon she is back in Thunder Bay, an area of Canada which epitomizes the Canadian wilderness experience for her. Although we, as readers of another's reading, cannot, of course, know exactly what form this reverie took, her text points to a clear third-person imagining of herself in that landscape (part Atwood's, part Thunder Bay): 'So as I read, Thunder Bay came back to me, as did solitary walks in the wilderness, and time spent sitting alone on the dock'. This reader has become her own heroine, and behind the images there are the clear seeds of a story, a narrative, every bit as curious as Lois's.

The reader's self-reflexivity also provides us with some clues as to how these personalized memories or reveries relate to the reading of the text itself: in an appropriately stumbling sentence she paints a picture of these thoughts and feelings coming to her in fragments, *as she read*, with the text, also, going in and out of focus: 'I decided, I think – all of this was in disjointed terms, occuring as I read –, that maybe the reason for the eerie, watched sense is the profound solitude'. This description corresponds with many of my own readerly experiences, as evidenced in Chapters 5 and 6, and also brings to mind Roland Barthes's description of the reading process in *The Pleasure of the Text*.[22] What has happened, here, indeed, is that the text has become overlaid with the reader's own *parallel story*: traces of the original show through in places, but as the reader lets go of the need 'to make a reading', another reading, which is also a writing, begins.

Signs of this process beginning are present in the texts of some of the other respondents, though they mostly represent the 'springboard' without jumping off it. The following readers, for example, are clearly reminded of close childhood friendships whilst reading the story, but their own narratives fall short of becoming a parallel or 'usurping' text:

> I identify with the speaker in that I was a dull, timid girl and had more exciting best friends, one of whom I broke up with at camp. (L, Montréal)

> The friendships of the two girls bring memories of my friendships – the intense closeness and sharing, the fondness that borders on infatuation/love. (U, Montréal)

> It reminded me of pre-adolescent childhood-tomboy days when I felt I could do anything boys could do. It reminded me of camps I went to with mixed feelings . . . Reminder of lost friendships from that age which are incredibly powerful – sense of loss. (L, Sheffield)

> Also, something which struck me at the end is the importance to me of early friendship; all of my school friendships haunt me. Even if I don't see these people I have their names in my address book and keep in contact with a lot of them, but they occupy a disproportionate space in the way I think about myself in relation to others. That type of relation is figured here. The loss of my school friend Louise still haunts me and I still think of trying to make contact again. (V, Sheffield)

> I enjoyed reading about how L and L pretended they were sisters – I pretended my next door neighbour and friend was my cousin when we were younger. (O, Toronto)

> I felt close to both Lucy and Lois, it reminded me of a friendship I had when I was young. I felt sad because I was not back in that time and space. (C, Halifax)

Although we may guess that each of these readers will have begun filling in the details of the stories connected with these early friendships in the course of their reading, they do not develop into the extended reverie of K's response. Indeed, it seems to me important to distinguish two quite separate aspects of the reading process here, since the parallel story or reverie uses personal experience in *dynamic interaction* with the text, whereas these records of 'recognition' or 'identification' may be seen as more typical of 'authentic realist' critical practice.[23] By this I mean that although these memories of past friendships might *constitute* the springboard for a reader-reverie, *in the context of these returns* they are used rather to authenticate and 'approve' the text: because the relationships described match the readers' own experiences they are deemed 'real', and thus facilitate textual engagement.

Characters, at least in fiction, undoubtedly represent the most common and most significant 'textual other' as far as the majority of readers are concerned. Whilst all of the above citations (including the latter part of K's entry) constitute that 'other' in terms of 'identification', however, a few respondents indicate the complementary pull of 'desire for'. As I noted in Chapter 5, in the discussion of my own relationship with the character of Lyndall in Schreiner's *The Story of an African Farm*, this is a less commonly recorded, but one suspects equally prevalent, reflex in the reading process, promoting as it does a complex and *unstable* range of reader-positionings and thus maximizing the reader's interaction with the text.[24] It is significant, for example, that the two texts from which the following citations are taken are amongst the lengthiest and 'most involved' responses:

> The part that struck me most was when Lois looks down from the cliff in awe of the distance they have travelled by canoe – the result of a female team's efforts. She takes pride in this achievement and affirms her strength. This small passage in the story evoked a sense of female empowerment and a sense of confident optimism in Lois's potential. As a reader I felt inspired by this passage which made me explore my own determination in realizing my capabilities and potential. (C, Montréal)

> My emotional response to the section about Lois's realization of how she'd canoed, was quite strong. I felt very happy that this young woman felt a sense of accomplishment from her activity – she loved her body not because it was skinny or pretty, but because it was strong. (P, Toronto)

Both these (young) female readers are moved to admiration for the textual characters: they represent what they would like to be rather than what they are, thus signifying a different order of textual engagement. At other points, however, the relationship is more obviously identificatory ('I enjoyed reading how L and L pretended they were sisters. I pretended my next door neighbour and best friend was my cousin'), confirming the peripatetic nature of the reader's relation to her textual other.

As we saw in Chapter 5, the reader's positive identification of a 'textual other' to whom she can relate – whether this be a character she 'identifies' with, one she 'admires', or some other, dis-embodied textual site – quickly becomes a responsibility she must 'defend' against other aspects of the text (or the text *as it is produced through the reading process*) that trouble her. I would therefore like to conclude this section on my readers' responses to Atwood's story by looking briefly at some of the ways in which their narratives betray the *stress* of trying to reconcile politically informed or 'epistemological' 'readings', with personalized, 'ontological' *reading events*. What we discover is that, for my readers as for myself, 'reading *as* a feminist' is not easily incorporated into the more implicated reader–text relations I have just described, although this is not to say that the reading process as a whole might not be ascribed that distinction (in as much as gender is always present).

If we return first to K's response (quoted above): it is clear that this reader's route into the text has not activated her feminist or racially aware consciousness. Although her reverie, like Atwood's story, is implicitly 'about' being a white, 'colonial' woman in the Canadian/Native American wilderness, she does not approach the experience in those terms. The dilemma she ponders – why she is afraid in unpeopled spaces/places – is construed in personal and existential rather than political terms. This seems to me to accord with my own reading practices in Chapters 5 and 6, where the personal and the political pull apart from each other *despite* the theory that tells me that they are inextricably linked: that all 'emotional' experiences occur within a social and political context. In this respect, there is also a distinct break in this text between the wilderness reverie and the final paragraph, focusing on female friendship and motherhood. Whilst certain aspects of the text have clearly functioned as a springboard here also, they do not cause the reader to 'enter' or 'supplant' it in the same way. Instead, she prefers to meditate on these issues (and their bearing on her own life) in more philosophical terms, and from a 'distance' which also permits the engagement of her political consciousness as a feminist and a lesbian. It should be noted, however, that these personally inflected politics are different again from the feminist and other 'readings' of the text made in response to the constraints/demands of a specific audience or interpretive community, and it is to the tension between such 'professional readings' and a more implicated 'reading event' that I now wish to turn in my concluding section of this chapter. Here I will seek to explain why so few of my readers were able to articulate their thoughts on how the text made them *feel* in relation to their own feminism, ethnicity and national identity.

Why the Personal is Not Political

It is significant, if unsurprising, that this project could be seen to have 'failed' in its attempt to get readers to reflect upon the role of *ethnicity* in the reading process, even though certain participants – the Canadians in particular – have shown themselves alert to the questions of *national identity* raised by 'Atwood' and her texts. Although my own interest in both these areas was clearly signalled in the guidelines to the questionnaire (see Appendix), the request that readers consider how the texts impacted upon them in terms of feminism *and* ethnicity *and* national identity was clearly in itself extremely demanding. What my discussion in the previous section has hopefully set in motion, however, is the hypothesis that what my participants found most difficult was *not* attending to three discursive positionings *per se*, but the problem of aligning *any* political reading of the text with an account of its 'emotional' impact on them. Even though my directions (such as 'To what extent did you feel included/excluded by each of the texts *vis-à-vis* ethnicity/national identity?') attempted to bring the two together, for the majority of the participants the aspects of the texts which 'involved' and 'alienated' them were clearly not *experienced* as overtly political positionings. Indeed, as we have already seen, the most common form of reading practice would seem to be one in which readers move between a professionalized and politically informed 'reading' of the text, to a more personalized engagement connecting it (though in different ways, and to a greater or lesser extent: see above) with their own life-experiences. Many of these points of (personal) connection strike me, with the hindsight of my own reading processes (see Chapters 5 and 6), to be expressly 'about' the readers' positioning in terms of their position as women or their ethnic/national identities, but the crucial fact is that the readers are not able to articulate their more implicated relationship to the text in these terms. As my own readings in Chapters 5 and 6 revealed, it is clearly very difficult – if not impossible – to make the 'reading self' a 'reading subject' in this way.

What interests me most in the context of this chapter, however, is how this theorization helps us to understand a little more about reading *as a process*: what *kind* of journeys readers are making as they read, and as they pass from one sort of engagement with the text to the next. I have therefore chosen to end the chapter by looking in some detail at one reader's response to the Atwood story, which exemplifies this passage from a professional, politically informed 'reading' of the text to a more personal, interactive and implicated engagement, observing on the way how it is these two models of reading, rather than any simple ideological blindspot, that has caused questions of ethnicity, especially, to be under-represented in these returns.

The text I have selected is that of a young Canadian student, and demonstrates clearly the movement between the different text–reader relations I have been describing, and their consequences as far as a politicized engagement of the text is concerned:

> I know that I have read this story before, because I own *Wilderness Tips*, but I didn't remember any of it, until the part where they talk about peeing in the woods – don't ask me why I remember that instead of the scariest part (the disappearance of Lucy).
>
> At first this story spoke to me about how a woman's life is put on hold while she mothers, while she is a wife. Lois is an artist in her talent to appreciate art, but it is her husband's money that allows her to collect art. I wonder why she never painted. The descriptions of her paintings (the ones she owns) drew me in because I recognized Group of Seven Artists, and because I could visually recall paintings of theirs I've seen in galleries, art books, on posters and postcards etc. It interested me how the paintings weren't peaceful to Lois; they were agitating – about being watched (an interesting commentary, I think, on the victim-position Atwood often uses for Canadians and specifically for

women: were Lucy and Lois being watched/followed/hunted prior to their disappearance?)

The section about camps also included me in the text because I'd been to an overnight camp when I was 9 and could relate to some of the experiences Lois and Lucy had. The animal names for the various levels of campers interested me: the way gender roles are encoded in the rankings: girls are prey – delicate birds; males are aggressors/predators (the dichotomy between hunted/hunter) .

The division between things American and things Canadian was clearly cut, but I'm not sure that growing up I was so aware of that line. The attitude of the know-all American (who isn't disturbed by what they don't know) did seem to match the the perception that I did develop as I met American campers later on.

I enjoyed reading about how L and L pretended they were sisters – I pretended my next door neighbour and best friend was my cousin, when we were younger. The description of the tender friendship and letter-writing – growing up and apart – sounded like a first love, a courting. And the rite of passage, burning the sanitary towel, was a delightful celebration of menstruation. The growing up theme was dealt with nicely – related to a sexual awareness, a realization of cheating and disappointment that rang true for me. The narrator looks back on the loons calling to each other and now realizes what as a child sounded like background, now smacks of grief – but it was a grief shared; the bitter-sweet sadness of growing up and losing innocence.

The issue of stereotyping and appropriation was presented in a way I enjoyed because it wasn't simplified and didactic. Although natives were stereotyped and reduced to costumes and rituals and language (no ideology, philosophy etc.), Cappie is presented as one who really thinks (ignorantly) that this is how an 'Indian' is. Where do we draw the line between stealing culture and making stereotypes, and appreciating or adopting parts of other cultures within the larger culture of what may be a Canadian identity? How do we educate children about the various cultures within a multicultural society, without becoming a token/holiday-/custom-/food-based system? How do we define culture?

My emotional response to the section about Lois's realization of how far she'd canoed was quite strong. I felt happy that this young woman felt a sense of accomplishment from her activity – she loved her body not because it was skinny or pretty, but because it was strong. Of course, being skinny or pretty can be nice, but it's not something we can all be at all times – but we can be strong and have good self-esteem and the ensuing sense that were are capable of doing anything – as Lois felt. (P, Toronto)

Whilst this is once again very much the account of a reading made within the parameters of this project (the reader is clearly self-consciously aware of both her immediate audience and the expectations of her interpretive community), the pressure to 'make a reading' does not entirely cause her to omit discussion of the processes involved.

The opening paragraph, which sets up an intimate and confiding relationship between the reader and her interlocutor(s), immediately registers her expectation to be 'involved' with the text. Although she admits to not remembering it immediately, her subsequent recollection of the 'peeing in the woods' is an acknowledgement of a somewhat embarrassing, but therefore all the more 'authentic', text–reader engagement. The opening line of the next paragraph ('At first this story spoke to me . . .') can thus be read as an expression of her continuing desire to foreground herself in this more recent reading; but this potential relationship is immediately undermined by the rest of the sentence (and the one that follows) which takes the form of a feminist 'interpretation' of the text rendered, apparently objectively, in the 'third person'. This professional/political analysis is then sustained for the rest of the paragraph (and marked, stylistically, by phrases such as 'It interested me'), with the exception of the sentence referring to the 'Group of Seven' paintings, in which her own extratextual experience is once again validated and pushed to the fore. Whilst this allusion, of course, points to the significance of another intepretive community ('middle-class culture') in the making of textual meaning, P nevertheless reveals herself to be *actively* negotiating her position between different frames of reference and bringing the text within the circuit of experiences that do not relate directly to her training as a literary critic. She observes, significantly, that it was this moment of connection between the textual and the extratextual that 'drew her into the text', enabled her to become more 'implicated'. Such a sentence, I would suggest, may be read as the representation of a springboard moment when P *might* have followed K and engaged in a narrative/reverie on her own experience of landscape or landscape art. Whilst outside her *written text* this may well, of course, have happened, what is recorded here, however, is the reader's rapid track back to the official, 'feminist' reading which she is supposed to be making. Although she records her own, individual point of connection with the story (in answer to my question 'how does the text include you?'), her own text presents it as an 'aside': a deviation from the work at hand which presents itself as a hiatus between the personal and the political.

This sort of hiatus is repeated throughout P's text, where it is marked stylistically by sentences that do not follow through from one another (see also my reading of *Written on the Body*, pp. 159–60 above). At the beginning of the next paragraph, for example, she states that the 'section about camps' included her, but does not force any particular connection between this 'involvement' and the subsequent feminist observation on the gendering of the animal names. Although this would be an obvious point for her to reflect on how the text has 'made her feel as a feminist reader', she dissociates her personal feelings (memories) from her feminism. Once again it is as though our personal implication in the text as readers cannot be brought within this political frame. An almost indentical dissociation occurs in the fifth paragraph, where the feminist analysis/evaluation of Atwood's presentation of female friendship and adolescence is juxtaposed to her memory of the best friend she made into a cousin without any attempt to intergrate the two. These records of more personal interaction thus take on the quality of parenthetical interludes within the reading process as a whole, and this, perhaps, is how we experience them (a moment of daydream *apparently* unrelated to the task in hand); although we should, of course, remember that, within the reading process as a whole, the interlude and the parallel story it produces may well be longer and more significant than any 'reading' we make of the text *per se* (witness my own readings in Chapters 5 and 6, and K's, cited above).

If the reader's difficulty in bringing herself and her relation to the text within a political frame is marked with respect to feminism, then the schism is even more marked in questions of ethnicity and national identity. Like the majority of the Canadian readers, this participant is obviously aware of the importance of these factors in any reading/interpretation/evaluation of the text; but, like myself in my readings of *The Piano* in Chapter 6, she clearly finds it harder to think about these issues in terms of her own identity as a white, colonizing subject. The depersonalization of these politics is signalled in the text by the fact that they are dealt with in two paragraphs separated off from the rest of the discussion: the first on the issue of Canadian *vs.* American identity, and the second on the role and representation of native 'Indians' within Canadian culture. Although in the first of these her own childhood experience is used to question the authenticity of Atwood's text (she asks herself whether she was really aware of the 'difference' between Americans and Canadians at that age), she does not consider how the text interrogates her *present* sense of national/ethnic identity. There is no reference, for example, to the way in which her identification with Lois and/or Lucy makes her feel proud/uncomfortable/confused about her identity as a white Canadian/North American. Like the majority of participants in this exercise, her emotional engagements with these 'textual others' remain broadly humanist (what she relates to most are the common experiences of childhood), and are separate from her politically informed discussions.

Apart from my own theory that this particular dissociation can be related to two types of reading practice (the implicated/interactive and the hermeneutic/proactive), it can, of course, be supplemented by the research which has shown the problems which white people have in both seeing and articulating their own ethnic identity.[25] While not wishing to appear to pick on this particular reader, since her practice is typical of many of my respondents and myself, it is clear that it is the 'Indians' that constitute the ethnic group under discussion in the text, and that *they* are 'the problem' – even if that problem is represented as 'our' responsibility (note the use of the first-person-plural pronoun in paragraph 6: 'Where do *we* draw the line between stealing culture and making stereotypes, and appreciating or adopting parts of other cultures within the larger framework of what may be a Canadian identity?'). With the hindsight of my own textual analyses, also, I would suggest that this 'white imperialism' ('we' are the invisible subjects, 'they' the visible objects) compounds the schism between the ontological and epistemological within the reading process. Although politically aware of the importance of ethnicity and national identity in this text, this reader addresses these issues with the voice of (and in anticipated response of) her interpretive community and not via a more self-reflexive implication in the text.[26]

Conclusion

What I feel we must observe in conclusion, then, is that differences in reading (both as an 'act of interpretation' and as an 'event') cannot be accounted for in purely ideological or discursive terms. It is not only the fact that the feminist reading community is characterized by a vast spectrum of political and theoretical affiliation, *but that these contending ideological standpoints (or, indeed, blindspots) are articulated through different models of text–reader interaction.* As the various responses to Atwood's story have so aptly demonstrated, the more personal/'emotional' engagements with the text, which might at first be accounted for simply in terms of readers moving from a feminist to a humanist framework of interpretation, need also to be thought about in terms of a whole range of *structural positionings* endemic to the reading process itself.

Within the specific context of this reader survey, this has meant that while the interpretive communities and audiences to which the readers refer have been hugely important in affecting their relationship to the text in the process of reading (and, indeed, in producing apparent *disagreements* between groups and readers), this is not so much because of their ideological prescriptions (for example, reasons why we should/should not enjoy 'Atwood') as because of the extent to which they have blocked ('forbidden') or facilitated ('permitted') the readers' dialogue with the text itself. For, as the readings across both Part II and Part III of this text will, I hope, have shown, what I have described as an 'implicated reading' is predicated not on the assumption that the reader is 'involved' in the text in terms of a simple reflex of 'recognition', but rather that s/he (inter)actively *engages* with it in a fully dialogic exchange. One of the conditions of implication, therefore, is that the text (or its representative 'textual others') becomes – if only temporarily and as matter of illusion – the reader's *primary* interlocutor, and in the process causes her to suspend her dialogue with all the extratextual 'others' who are also, of course, the source of her aesthetic and political 'judgement'. I am reminded here of Virginia Woolf's famous statement on 'perspective' in *To the Lighthouse*: 'So much depends upon whether people are near to you or far from you.'[27] In the reading process, certainly, it is clear that readers have problems in entertaining 'proximity' and 'distance' simultaneously: it is as though the 'I–thou', text–reader relation (when the reader is fully engaged and interactive with her textual other) produces a readerly myopia which excludes the possibility of seeing the text through a disinterested 'epistemological' frame – and vice versa.

The range of factors that will cause one reader to have a qualitatively different reading experience to another may therefore be thought of as far more structurally articulated than has hitherto been acknowledged. Consonant with my earlier discussions in Part II, my feeling is that an over-emphasis on the act of interpretation *per se* has caused theorists to overlook the complex dynamics of how readers actually engage with texts and, as a consequence, to fail to recognize that much of this engagement is *not* reducible to meaning-production. Indeed, what the findings of my own small reader-survey would seem to suggest is that, at a certain level, 'engagement' and 'interpretation' may be thought of as mutually exclusive, as readers, swept away by the blind intimacy of their 'I–thou' relation, lose the hermeneutic 'act of reading' in the experiential 'event'.

Notes

1 The Questionnaire is reproduced in the Appendix.
2 See Stanley Fish's essays in Part Two of *Is There a Text in This Class?* (n. 9, Ch. 1). Further page references to this volume will be given after quotations in the text. Fish's concept of the intepretive community and how it functions within literary critical practice is reproduced and developed in much of his subsequent work, and has been of abiding significance within the realm of reception theory; though it is interesting to observe how few scholars have made the obvious point of connection between Fish's account of how reading communities function, and a Marxist view of reader-positioning through ideology (see Preface to Part I) or a Foucauldian account of our inscription by and through discourse. Having made the connection, I feel it is none the less important to distinguish between the 'local' and materially specific constraints of what Fish intends by the concept of a 'reading community', and a more general theory of discursive positioning, as I attempt to make clear later in this chapter. The essence of Fish's hardline 'interpretive community' theorizing (which he subsequently moderates and modifies, in further attempts to transcend the polarization of text and reader in the creation of meaning) is to be seen in the essay, 'How to Recognise a Poem When You See One' (pp. 322–37).
3 This recognition of the researcher's material presence as a dialogic 'other' in ethnographic research has, of course, been brought to widespread consciousness in recent years. See, for example, the problematization of David Morley's early work (see Bibliography) in John Tulloch's *Television Drama: Agency, Audience and Myth* (London and New York: Routledge, 1990), pp. 200–1, and Beverley Skeggs's chapter, 'Theorising, Ethics and Representation in Feminist Ethnography', in *Feminist Cultural Theory: Process and Production*, ed. Beverley Skeggs (Manchester and New York: Manchester University Press, 1995). Although I refer to the recording-document used by my respondents as a

'questionnaire', moreover, its extreme openness, together with the upfront posi-tioning of myself as a 'correspondent', make it methodologically more in line with the epistolary model employed by researchers such as Ien Ang in *Watching Dallas* (n. 16, Ch. 1) and Jackie Stacey in *Star Gazing: Hollywood Cinema and Female Spectatorship* (n. 19, Ch. 1) than the more traditionally 'anonymous' questionnaire employed, for example, by Janice Radway in *Reading the Romance* (n. 16, Ch. 1).

4 See Jackie Stacey's chapter, 'Cinema History and Feminist Film Criticism' in *Feminist Cultural Theory: Process and Production*, ed. Beverley Skeggs (n. 3 above), pp. 113–15, for further discussion of the textuality of participants' responses within audience research.

5 This theorizing about the interrelatedness of reading and writing (of reading *as* writing) has also been informed by my many dialogues with Rowena Murray on the subject. For an exemplification of this theory in her own work, see *Ethical Dilemmas in Healthcare: A Practical Approach Through Medical Humanities* (London: Chapman and Hall, 1997).

6 For an example of a poem used in this sort of reader-survey, see Sara Mills's chapter 'Reading as/like a Feminist', in *Gendering the Reader* (see n. 24, Ch. 1), pp. 25–46. See also Margaret Atwood's story, 'Death by Landscape', in *Wilderness Tips* (London: Bloomsbury Press, 1991), and Liz Lochhead's 'Quleques Fleurs', in *Bagpipe Muzak* (Harmondsworth: Penguin, 1991). Further references to Atwood's text will be given after quotations in the the text.

7 Both these images are reproduced in *The Art and Expressions of Will: Prudence Heward* (Kingston, Ontario: exhibition catalogue, Agnes Etherington Art Centre, 1986).

8 I have protected the anonymity of my respondents by identifying them by initials, randomly selected, which are not their own. This is despite the fact that the vast majority of participants indicated that they were happy to be identified. Although I accept the methodological principle that the anonymization of the participants in ethnographic research can be seen as a reinforcement of the power-relations which situate the researcher as a privileged 'authority' (see Beverley Skeggs's essay in *Feminist Cultural Theory*, n. 3 above), I felt that, on balance, the arguments for concealing identity were, on this occasion, stronger. I would also emphasize once again the fact that I deal with these responses *as texts*, and not as the 'opinions' attached to named individuals.

9 'Author-function': see n. 30, Ch. 5.

10 'Canadian-feminine': this identity-category is comparable to (though to be dis-tinguished from!) Maxine Hong Kingston's concept of 'American-feminine' in her novel, *The Woman Warrior: Memoir of a Girlhood Amongst Ghosts* (New York: Knopf, 1977).

11 *The Piano* (1993), dir. Jane Campion (see n. 41, Ch. 1)

12 The Marxist-Feminist Literature Collective operated out of the University of Essex in the 1970s, and involved well-known literary critics such as Cora Kaplan and Helen Taylor. Their most celebrated piece of collective writing is the essay 'Women's Writing: *Jane Eyre, Shirley, Villette, Aurora Leigh*', first published in *Ideology and Consciousness*, 1(3) (Spring 1978). Some excellent work on the importance of friendship networks in reading women's painting in the context of its production has been done by art historians Deborah Cherry (see n. 14, Ch. 3) and Janice Helland, *The Studios of Frances and Margaret Macdonald* (Manchester and New York: Manchester University Press, 1996).

13 'Interpellated': see n. 25, Ch. 4.

14 See Benedict Anderson, *Imagined Communities: Reflections on the Origins and Spread of Nationalism* (London: Verso, 1983).

15 See Barbara Comisky's Ph.D. on Atwood ('Margaret Atwood: Fiction and Feminisms in Dialogue', Lancaster, 1996). Comisky offers an excellent account of the way in which 'Atwood' has been discursively produced by the different readers of her texts alongside the way in which the texts can themselves be seen to identify a wide range of interlocutors, feminist and otherwise.

16 I am indebted to Greg Kucich (University of Notre Dame) for prompting me to reconsider the relationship between text and context with respect to my theory of implicated reading. My position *vis-à-vis* the discussion here is that, although ostensibly contextual factors such as audience and interpretive community attend *every* reading-event, the extent to which they impact on the reader's dialogue with the text and its textual others will be variable and differently characterized (see Ch. 7 and discussion following).

17 For a full discussion of the role of intonation in dialogic theory, see my *Reading Dialogics* (n. 4, Ch. 1), pp. 77–9. The principal source of this theorizing in the work of the Bakhtin school is V. N. Voloshinov's essay, 'Discourse in Life and Discourse in Poetry' (1924–8) reproduced in the *Bakhtin School Papers*, ed. Ann Shukman (see n. 14, Ch. 4).

18 See Don Bialostosky, *Making Tales: The Poetics of Wordsworth's Narrative Experiments* (Chicago and London: University of Chicago Press, 1984), pp. 42–3.

19 This concept of interlocutors as 'allies' or 'adversaries' has its origins in Anne Herrmann's *The Dialogic and Difference* (n. 13, Ch. 4). For discussion of Herrmann's work on this point, see my *Reading Dialogics* (n. 4, Ch. 1), pp. 106–7.

20 See Jackie Stacey's article, 'Hollywood Memories', *Screen*, 35(4) (Winter, 1994), pp. 317–35.

21 I am very grateful to Jackie Stacey for her comments on an earlier draft of this chapter with respect to the ethics and responsibility of my role as researcher and commentator. See also Beverley Skeggs's chapter on these issues (n. 3 above).

22 See Roland Barthes, *The Pleasure of the Text* (n. 48, Ch. 1), pp. 10–12: 'Yet the most classical narrative (a novel by Zola or Balzac or Dickens or Tolstoy) bears within it a sort of diluted tmesis: we do not read everything with the same intensity of reading; a rhythm is established, casual, unconcerned with the *integrity* of the text: our very avidity for knowledge impels us to skim or skip certain passages . . .Thus what I enjoy in a narrative is not directly its content or even its structure, but rather the abrasions I impose upon the fine surface: I read on, I skip, I look up, I dip in again. Which has nothing to do with the deep laceration the text of bliss inflicts upon language itself, and not upon the simple temporality of its reading.'

23 'Authentic Realism': see n. 35, Ch. 1.

24 Olive Schreiner, *The Story of an African Farm* (see n. 1, Ch. 1).

25 See e.g. Richard Dyer's 'White', *Screen* (see n. 18, Ch. 7), Helen (charles)'s '"Whiteness"' (n. 27, Ch. 3), and Ruth Frankenberg, *White Women, Race Matters: The Social Construction of Whiteness* (London: Routledge, 1993).

26 While wishing to maintain my thesis that our problems in producing implicated and political (hermeneutic) readings simultaneously is a structural condition, I do, of course, acknowledge that a differently worded questionnaire might have yielded different responses here. We must also recognize that the anticipation of the feedback session will also have had a major impact on the way in which participants addressed this especially sensitive politcal issue (i.e., it is not surprising that their focus should be on their audience/community rather than their own articulation within the text).

27 Virginia Woolf, *To the Lighthouse* (see n. 12, Ch. 1), p. 258.

Conclusion

Here I argue that it is computer screens where we project ourselves into our own dramas, dramas in which we are producer, director and star. Some of these dramas are private, but increasingly we are able to draw in other people. Computer screens are the new location for our fantasies, both erotic and intellectual.

(Sherry Turkle, *Life on the Screen*, 1995)[1]

He took hold of her. They were both translucent, and she had an odd sensation of their quasi bodies intermingling like smoke and fog. She felt a momentary comfort in his ghostly embrace.

(Marge Piercy, *He, She and It*, 1991)[2]

Since each section of this book has been introduced by a Preface, summing up the main concerns of the chapters which follow and how these relate to the thesis of the book as a whole, it is unnecessary for me to repeat them here. Instead, I would like to project that thesis – and in particular, the epistemological and ontological consequences of our different models of reading – forwards in time, and speculate upon our lives as feminist readers in the twenty-first century.

Although several people with whom I have shared material from the central section of the book have already taken my description of implicated reading to be a *prescription* – a recommendation that we learn to open ourselves up to texts, to make our critical practice more emotive, personal and self-reflexive – this is most certainly *not* my intention. In the same way that I avoided, in the first instance at least, the overwhelming question of *why* we read, so too have I avoided the question of how we are *supposed to read*: a question which professional readers (students, critics) and political readers (such as feminists) must nevertheless address in the context of broader institutional and political debates. What I hope this project will have done is merely to open the doors a little further onto what happens to us *when we read*. In other words, it has proceeded from the assumption that it is only by being as honest as possible about the (unofficial) processes as well as the (professional) practices of reading that we can begin to manage the political and ethical implications of what we do each and every time we engage with a text – verbal, visual or otherwise.

It is, of course, the unavoidable evidence that texts are rapidly becoming 'otherwise' that must cause us to prepare ourselves for a major reconceptualization of reading and its politics as we move into the next century. The changes afoot are so major, so radically transformative, indeed, that a study like this one will soon be shelved – and who knows how soon? – as 'reader-archeology': an historical analysis of how people *used* to read; how textual analysis *used* to be performed. Because even those of us situated on the margins of the new cybernetic technology – whose knowledge of what is happening is as yet limited to newspaper articles, books like Sherry Turkle's (see the opening quotation), and a tentative dip into the waters of electronic mail and the Internet – cannot help but be aware that what we used to know as reading and writing (and, indeed, *the relation between them*) are in the process of being radically transformed. Not only is it clear that we now read for *different reasons* than we used to do (both personally and professionally), but also that we *are reading differently*. And even as the processes and practices are changing (with the process becoming, perhaps, a more explicit part of the practice), so will we experience different pleasures, frustrations and disappointments.

From our (my) position *in medias res*, and without the technological experience and expertise of someone like Turkle, it is impossible to speculate very clearly as to what form these new readerly experiences will take. In the same way that we enjoy and make sense of science fiction through a constant interplay of *heimlich/unheimlich* criteria, however, so too does this brave new world of what I shall call interactive textual engagement (hereafter ITE) help us to understand and critique our present (and 'retro') practices more clearly.[3] In the context of my project here, indeed, my sketchy and peripheral sense of the techno/texto-logical changes taking place have been most useful in helping me to (re)conceptualize the 'old reading' (the readerly community in which we still live).[4] In many instances, indeed, these visions of our ITE-future appear simply to make visible things about reading that have always appertained, not least, as in my thesis here, that it is predicated upon a *desire*, at least, for interactivity.[5] Placed alongside my own readerly adventures in Chapters 5 and 6, for instance, can we honestly say that Turkle's description of ITE in the quotation which heads this chapter is *really* a 'vision of the future'? Is this not rather an image of what reading has always been, but was never seen to be – because we were blind to the investments, other than hermeneutic ones, that attended our processes? What ITE has done, it seems to me, is simply bring our readerly/writerly desires to the fore through a belated acknowledgement of the *intensity* of the experience. Something of what I mean by this is illustrated in another extract from Piercy's science-fiction novel, *He, She and It*:

She ran quickly to the terminal. It was not the enhanced one they had always used. It was a minimal terminal, set to run the house, take messages, answer simple questions, control a cleaning robot. It was the caretaker type that lacked even a protect function. She felt as if her chest were filling with cold mud. She felt heavy, formless, chilled through. What was going on? She sank into the chair before the terminal and identified herself.

Josh's face appeared on the screen, his lips drawn thin . . .

She sat stunned. Then she ran upstairs to Ari's room . . . Then she flung herself at the terminal and replayed Josh's message.

'You really took revenge on me. You really did,' she said to his face frozen on the screen at the message's end. She went on sitting there while the room darkened. (p. 15)

While this extract concerns a techno/textual interaction between two materially identified subjects, rather than between the entities we have been used to thinking about as 'text' and 'reader', I feel that it nevertheless dramatizes superbly the readerly frustrations I describe in Chapter 6 when the textual other exerts power over us by *refusing* interaction and rendering us notionally passive, impotent and without control. Shira's wild and desperate response here, of 'flinging herself at the terminal', sums up perfectly what for me is the *worst* of 'reading': the sense that our text/textual other cannot be *made* to respond to us. In this instance, then, the highly advanced expectations of interactivity towards which our network practices are leading us help make visible what has, I feel, *always* been been a key component in the reading process. We read, it seems to me, in the hope/expectation that we will be *spoken to*; and it is the weight of that expectation, and the knowledge that it will frequently *not* be met, that has made it such a fraught, as well as a potentially pleasurable, activity. And placed in the context of how the new technology is, inevitably, increasing our desire for and expectation of an ITE, it certainly helps to explain why we – and here I speak for myself in a major way – are finding reading (in the old sense) increasingly difficult, unappealing. It helps to explain, in other words, the irony of the fact that I have written a book 'about reading' (and about reading literary and cultural texts intended for entertainment, stimulation, pleasure) at a time in my life/career when I am increasingly disinclined to do so: when I wander through bookstores, avoid films and art galleries, through an aversion to what I characterize as 'passive consumption'. Thus, when I try to explain this to my friends and colleagues by saying that 'these days I would rather write than read', I assume that what I mean is that I am craving a more interactive textual experience. And where once I (we) were prepared to put in the readerly labour to get this interaction from textual products, now we are more attracted to *textual processes* (such as electronic mail, MUDs and other interactive art forms) where our textual others are more readily responsive.[6]

But there are dangers with the promise/realization of such ITEs as well, of course, and it is here that our politics – our residual desire, perhaps, to remain 'feminist readers' – once again comes to the fore. In the same way that my demonstrations of implicated reading in Chapters 5 and 6 begged the question of how a satisfying engagement with a textual other could, at the very least, *obscure* the political (and emphatically *gendered*) context in which that engagement is made, so too might our newly interactive textual opportunities blind us to the *practices* that frame the *processes*. Far from being a call for process over practice, then, or for the pursuit of implicated reading at the expense of hermeneutic textual interpretation, I see an urgent need for us to find a way of keeping the material contexts of our ITEs in mind. The materialist feminist's erstwhile struggle to keep her theories of textuality, of reading, of theory and criticism *grounded* in 'the real world' is now in danger of being considered an absurd impossibility. As books like Turkle's articulate only too clearly, large swathes of the population have already given up on the concept of Real Life (RL) completely, believing that the virtual worlds they can inhabit have as much claim on 'reality' as the former. Whether this might be the experience of the (privileged) few or the many, however, it of course ignores the social and economic contexts in which those communications, and the technologies that support them, are being produced and consumed. In the same way that literary criticism was once guilty of a dangerous reification of 'the text', so, now, are we in danger of doing the same to the 'intertext' – forgetting that the relationship between 'readers' (however construed) does not incorporate the context in which those readers operate.

So difficult is it to keep this particular (inter)text and context in mind simultaneously, however, that it will require great effort and imagination to continue to 'read on behalf of feminism'. The reason such honourable intentions cannot support us as we move into the twenty-first century is that the hermeneutic project of reading is crumbling before our eyes. As we come to realize the full implication of living in a world where texts 'speak back to us' with so little effort on our part, how can we, as textual critics especially, ever again assume enough authority to make a text *mean* anything, let alone cause it to be applied – to serve – a broader political mission? Our only way forward, as I see it, is to confront the changes head-on: to remind ourselves again and again (and I forced myself to do so throughout the writing of this book) that every engagement of a textual other is always already gendered, and socially marked in other ways, even though the intimacy of the I–Thou relation serves to make us blind to that fact (see the conclusion to Chapter 8). In this respect, indeed, I see my romance trope serving one final and rather unexpected purpose. Far from *encouraging* us to surrender to the pleasures of textual engagement (as do most of the other theories that have seen reading as a metaphorical/literal expression of 'desire' in some way), I now hold up my own model of implicated reading as a *warning*. What my readings do, it seems, is show us all too readily how our enchantment by a textual other – however airy, unspecified or non-human – may blind us to the contexts (gendered, raced, classed, sexualized) in which those relations operate. It may cause us to forget that every nuance of the power-dynamic in which we are engaged – and which *seems* such an intimate, private and unique thing – will have its end in some material chain of power relations, even if that materialism is itself rendered 'invisible' through the anti-matter of discourse. For as we get more and more adept at living with the ambiguity and *apparent* intransitivity of the (hyper)textual universe, even the *possibility* that all relations are connected, however tangentially, to what we used to know as Real Life will trouble us less and less. What the stories of readerly enchantment I have told here should nevertheless do, however, is warn us against such hubris – if only because of the role of *narratives* (in particular, the romance narrative) in producing, sustaining and *controlling* those relations. My own feeling is, indeed, that the narratives which structure our cultures and psyches are fair set to survive any possible reconfiguration of 'RL' as we know it, and that the discourses around desire, and romance in particular, are likely to keep our reading processes (no matter how interactive) as hungry they have ever been. It is a scenario, surely, in which the more our interactive textual needs are met, the more we will crave. And while such uncontainable desire is not in itself the 'problem', the increased intensity of the techno-textual interaction will, I fear, make the political contextualization of both our practices and processes increasingly difficult. Would I ever be able to think 'about' reading again if, for example, Lyndall, the heroine of Schreiner's *Story of an African Farm*, had stepped out of her textual frame, and spoken to me as I, in my old-fashioned, implicated reading, had wanted her to?[7]

Notes

1 Sherry Turkle, *Life on the Screen: Identity in the Age of the Internet* (New York: Simon and Schuster, 1995). Page references to this volume are given after quotations in the text.

2 Marge Piercy, *He, She and It* (1991; New York: Ballantine Books, 1993). Page references to this volume are given after quotations in the text. (This book is published in the UK under the alternative title of *Body of Glass*.)

3 *Unheimlich*: see n. 24, Ch. 5.

4 See Lucie Armitt, *Theorizing the Fantastic* (London: Arnold, 1996): 'Long before the advent or virtual reality, reading enabled us to "enjoy virtual relationships, virtual sex or virtual reunions without leaving our homes". All novels, plays, poems and stories are simulations of the "real" . . .' (p. 74).

5 See Kingsley Amis, *New Maps of Hell: A Survey of Science Fiction* (New York: Harcourt, 1960). Amis writes: 'Science fiction's most important use . . . is a means of dramatising social enquiry' (p. 54).

6 MUDs: the acronym for Multi-User Domains. See Turkle (n. 1), pp. 11–14.

7 Olive Schreiner, *Story of an African Farm* (see n. 1, Ch 1). See Ch. 5, pp. 112–13.

Appendix

Feminist Reading Survey: The Role of Ethnicity/National Identity in the Reading Process

Section A

Context of the Research

Many thanks for agreeing to participate in my research on how ethnicity and national identity impact upon the reading process.

This research is for a chapter of my forthcoming book, *Feminism and the Politics of Reading* (Arnold, London) and will complement work I am currently engaged in on the 'emotional politics' of reading and the role of memory in the reading process.

For the ethnicity/national identity chapter I am hoping to solicit the participation of between five and six groups of 'feminist readers' in Britain and Canada. The bilateral nature of this study will enable me to assess similarities and differences in reader-response that are dependent upon the participants' own sense of ethnic/national identity and also establish whether there are substantive trans-Atlantic differences in political awareness *vis-à-vis* these issues.

Composition of the Reading Groups

The 'groups' that I am hoping to work with will consist of between four and six individuals from five/six regional locations. These are: (Canada) Montréal, Toronto, Halifax and (UK) Lancaster, Glasgow, Sheffield.

According to the reader-theorist Stanley Fish's formulation, these groups all belong to a single 'interpretive community' in as much as the participants are all feminists associated in some way with Higher Education. In so far as the groups (and the individuals within the groups) will represent feminists from very different backgrounds, and at different stages in their academic careers, I am, however, confident that the responses will be far from monolithic. Indeed, one of the major objectives of this research is to explore the significant differences that exist *within* the feminist community in its reception of feminist texts.

While some of the groups will consist of individuals who have been working together for some time (such as my own research group at Lancaster, for instance) others will have come together purely for the purposes of this survey. In so far as the substance of my analysis will be based upon *individual responses* to the selected texts this is not, I feel, a significant variable; although it will undoubtedly affect the 'follow-up' report that I am asking you to participate in (see below).

For the most part, then, the 5/6 groups are principally geographical/institutional affiliations of feminists. Further attempts to homogenize the groups in terms of age/level of educational attainment would have been difficult to achieve and counter to my principal objective, which is to explore the differences rather than the similarities betwen feminist readers.

Nature of the Participation

I should also explain that my decision to base my analysis on written rather than verbal responses to the different texts is not merely logistical. Most recent reader/spectator theory acknowledges the impossibility of gaining access to the 'authentic' (i.e., 'spontaneous', 'original') responses of readers in so much as all reading is 'always already' mediated by previous textual and theoretical experiences. By soliciting your own responses in written form, I am hoping to foreground the highly *contextual* nature of the enterprise we are all engaged in. I will not, ultimately, be analysing your response as the authentic experience of a 'real reader' but as another text on reading.

This relates, too, to my decision *not* to request your reponse to the selected texts in the form of a subdivided questionnaire. While I do, as you will see, request limited personal information in this form, I decided that it would be restrictive, and ultimately reductive, to structure your responses according to this sort of formula. In terms of my subsequent analysis I will be as interested in seeing what participants have felt *unable to say*, for example, as in what they do say, and the *narrativization* of your engagement – the order in which you deal with particular issues – will also be significant. Do not, however, feel that you have to provide me with an elegantly styled composition! Responses in the form of notes are equally acceptable, and you are of course free to write as little (or as much!) as you like.

I trust that this 'textualization' of your role within the project will not put you off participating in it! I am extremely grateful for your help and everyone will be duly named and acknowledged (unless they request otherwise) in the final publication.

Relationship between Researcher and Participant

From what I have seen of other ethnographic reader-surveys this presentation of my own rationale to participants is, itself, relatively new. While I realize that it is possible largely because I am working with groups that will be familiar with the terms of my theoretical discourse, my purpose has been to foreground the 'dialogic' nature of such work. As audience-researchers like Janice Radway, Ien Ang and Jackie Stacey have acknowledged, this type of survey is profoundly affected by the nature of the relationship between the researcher and the participant: in particular, the participant's *perception* of the role of researcher and what she is after. By laying my own objectives and speculations on the line in this way, I am hoping to make dialogue an explicit rather than an implicit aspect of the exercise.

For each of the groups the survey will take the following form:

1. Preliminary meeting with participants to explain purpose of survey and the nature of their participation.
2. Participants to read selected texts and record their responses.
3. Participants to meet again as a group and discuss responses in follow-up meeting.
4. Participants to record their impressions of what was discussed in follow-up meeting.
5. Participants to mail their responses back to me.

With many thanks for your involvement in this project. I am extremely grateful.

Section B

Personal Details

(a) Name:
  (Please indicate if you would prefer *not* to be identified)
(b) Address (permanent residence):
(c) Nationality:
(d) Ethnic Group:
(e) Present Occupation:
(f) Institutional Affiliation (University, College, etc.):
(g) Level of Educational Attainment (High School, BA, MA, PhD etc.):
(h) Feminist Affiliations:
  Please specify in terms of the following *if appropriate*:
  (i) Political (e.g., liberal feminist, Marxist feminist, radical feminist etc.)
  (ii) Educational (e.g., Women's Studies Teacher/Undergraduate/ Research Student/ Member of Feminist Study Group)

(iii) Community Groups (e.g., race awareness, gay/lesbian, rape crisis etc.)

(iv) Any other affiliation which you think helps to define your feminism.

Section C

Responding to the Texts: Guidelines

The three texts I am inviting you to consider for the purpose of this survey are:

1. The Canadian writer Margaret Atwood's short story, 'Death by Landscape' (1991)
2. The Scottish writer Liz Lochhead's dramatic monologue, 'Quelques Fleurs' (1991)
3. Two paintings by the Canadian artist Prudence Heward:
   (a) *Rollande* (1929) Oil on canvas. 139.9 × 101.7cm
   (b) *Girl at a Window* (1941) Oil on canvas. 86.4 × 91.5cm

What I would like you to do is try and describe how each of these texts impacts on *you*, first as a *feminist* reader, and then in terms of their representations of ethnicity/national identity.

In line with my own work on the 'emotional politics' of reading I would be very interested to hear about your engagement with the texts in these terms. To what extent did you feel included/excluded by each of the texts *vis-à-vis* ethnicity/national identity? What aspects of the texts involved you as a reader/viewer, what aspects alienated you? And did you feel these emotional responses to the text sometimes contradicted your intellectual and/or political response?

These suggestions are not prescriptions, however, and I will be glad to read whatever you have to say about the texts concerned. The important thing to remember is that *this is an invitation for you to explore YOUR RESPONSES to the text as a feminist reader*: it is not an exercise in literary criticism! I don't want to hear what you think the texts are saying, but how what they are saying and doing makes *you* think and feel.

TEXT 1: 'Death by Landscape' by Margaret Atwood

Atwood is now officially recognized by the literary establishment as Canada's most celebrated writer, male or female – though to what extent she should be viewed a 'feminist writer' is constantly up for review! During my first month in Canada I searched for a short story by a less well-known

Canadian woman writer that I thought would promote interesting discussion in terms of ethnicity/national identity, but although I found several which were very articulate on the subject, none of them promised to involve you – as readers – as well as this one. Please offer your responses in the space below and use the other side of the sheet if necessary.

[The questionnaire also included notes on the Lochhead and Heward texts which I do not reproduce here since they are not part of the discussion in Chapter 8.]

Section D

Follow-up Group Discussion

Please use this space to make a note of what struck you as most interesting about your follow-up discussion with the other members of your group *vis-à-vis* these three texts. What do you see to be the most significant points of difference between yourself and the other participants, for example?

May I once again thank you all for participation in this survey. I hope you enjoyed reading the texts and that reflection upon your response proved an interesting experience.

Lynne Pearce
Montréal 1995

Select Bibliography

Since full references to all works cited are supplied in the chapter notes, this bibliography restricts itself to those texts which were central to the development of my thesis. It does not include journal articles which, once again, are given full citation in the individual chapters.

Abelove, Henry *et al.*, *Gay and Lesbian Studies Reader* (London and New York: Routledge, 1992).

Althusser, Louis, *Lenin and Philosophy and Other Essays*, trans. Ben Brewster (London: New Left Books, 1971).

Anderson, Benedict, *Imagined Communities: Reflections on the Origins and Spread of Nationalism* (London: Verso, 1983).

Ang, Ien, *Watching Dallas: Soap Opera and the Melodramatic Imagination* (London and New York: Methuen, 1985).

Appleyard, J. A., *Becoming a Reader: The Experience of Fiction from Childhood to Adulthood* (Cambridge: Cambridge University Press, 1990).

Armitt, Lucie, *Theorizing the Fantastic* (London: Arnold, 'Interrogating Texts' Series, 1996).

Atwood, Margaret, *The Handmaid's Tale* (London: Jonathan Cape, 1986).

—— *Wilderness Tips* (London: Bloomsbury Press, 1991).

Bakhtin, Mikhail / V. N. Voloshinov, *Marxism and the Philosophy of Language*, trans. Ladislaw Matejka and I. R. Titunik (1929; Cambridge, MA: Harvard University Press, 1986).

Bakhtin, Mikhail, *Problems of Dostoevsky's Poetics*, ed. and trans. Caryl Emerson (1929; Manchester: Manchester University Press, 1984).

—— *The Dialogic Imagination*, ed. Michael Holquist, trans. Caryl Emerson and Michael Holquist (1941; Austin, TX: Austin University Press, 1981).

Barthes, Roland, *S/Z*, trans. Richard Miller (New York: Hill and Wang, 1974).

—— *The Pleasure of the Text*, trans. Richard Miller (New York: Hill and Wang, 1975).

—— *A Lover's Discourse: Fragments*, trans. Richard Howard (Harmondsworth: Penguin, 1978).

Bauer, Dale (ed.), *Feminist Dialogics: A Theory of Failed Community* (New York: State University of New York Press, 1989).

—— *Feminism, Bakhtin and the Dialogic* (Albany, NY: State University of New York Press, 1991).

Belsey, Catherine, *Critical Practice* (London: Methuen, 1980).

—— *John Milton: Language, Gender, Power* (Oxford: Basil Blackwell, 1988).

—— *Desire: Love Stories in Western Culture* (Oxford: Basil Blackwell, 1994).

Betterton, Rosemary (ed.), *Looking On: Images of Femininity in the Visual Arts and Media* (London: Pandora, 1987).

Bialostosky, Don, *Making Tales: The Poetics of Wordsworth's Narrative Experiments* (Chicago and London: University of Chicago Press, 1984).

Booth, Wayne, *The Rhetoric of Fiction* (Chicago: University of Chicago Press, 1961).

Bouchard, Donald F. (ed.), *Language, Counter-Memory, Practice*, trans. Donald F. Bouchard and Sherry Simon (Ithaca, NY: Cornell University Press, 1977).

Bourdieu, Pierre, *Distinction: A Social Critique of the Judgement of Taste*, trans. R. Nice (Cambridge, MA: Harvard University Press, 1984).

Brittain, Vera, *Chronicle of Youth: The War Diary 1913–1917* (New York: Morrow, 1982).

Brontë, Charlotte, *Villette* (Oxford: Clarendon Press, 1984).

Brontë, Emily, *Wuthering Heights* (Harmondsworth: Penguin, 1965).

Butler, Judith, *Gender Trouble: Feminism and the Subversion of Identity* (London: Routledge, 1990).

—— *Bodies that Matter* (London and New York: Routledge, 1993).

Campion, Jane, and Kate Pullinger, *The Piano* (New York: Hyperion, 1994).

Campion, Jane (dir.), *The Piano* (Mirimax Pictures, 1993).

Chatman, Seymour, *Story and Discourse* (Ithaca, NY: Cornell University Press, 1978).

Cherry, Deborah, *Painting Women: Victorian Women Artists* (London and New York: Routledge, 1993).

Clark, Katarina, and Michael Holquist, *Mikhail Bakhtin* (Cambridge, MA: Harvard University Press, 1984).

Culler, Jonathan, *On Deconstruction: Theory and Criticism after Structuralism* (Ithaca, NY: Cornell University Press, 1982).

de Lauretis, Teresa, *Alice Doesn't: Feminism, Semiotics, Cinema* (London: Macmillan, 1984).

Derrida, Jacques, *The Truth in Painting* (Chicago: University of Chicago Press, 1987).

Dixon-Hunt, John, *The Pre-Raphaelite Imagination* (London: Routledge and Kegan Paul, 1968).

Doane, Mary Ann, *The Desire to Desire: The Woman's Film of the 1940s* (Bloomington and Indianapolis: Indiana University Press, 1987).

—— *Femmes Fatales: Feminism, Film Theory and Psychoanalysis* (London and New York: 1991).

Dostoevsky, Fyodor, *Notes from the Underground* (1864; New York: Bantam, 1981).

Eagleton, Terry, *Literary Theory* (Oxford: Basil Blackwell, 1983).

—— *The Rape of Clarissa: Writing, Sexuality and Class Struggle in Samuel Richardson* (Oxford: Basil Blackwell, 1986).

—— *Against the Grain: Essays 1975–1985* (London: Verso, 1986).

—— *Raymond Williams: Critical Perspectives* (London: Polity Press, 1989).

—— *Ideology: An Introduction* (London: Verso, 1991).

Faderman, Lilian, *Surpassing the Love of Men* (London: Women's Press, 1981; repr. 1985).

Feagin, Susan, *Reading with Feeling: The Aesthetics of Appreciation* (Ithaca and London: Cornell University Press, 1996).

Fetterley, Judith, *The Resisting Reader: A Feminist Approach to American Fiction* (Bloomington: Indiana University Press, 1978).

Fish, Stanley, *Is there a Text in this Class? The Authority of Interpretive Communities* (Cambridge, MA and London: Harvard University Press, 1980).

Elizabeth A. Flynn and Patrocinio Schweickart (eds.), *Gender and Reading: Essays on Readers, Texts and Contexts* (Baltimore and London: Johns Hopkins University Press, 1986).

Fowler, Bridget, *The Alienated Reader: Women and Popular Romantic Literature in the Twentieth Century* (Hemel Hempstead: Harvester-Wheatsheaf, 1991).

Frankenberg, Ruth, *White Women, Race Matters: The Social Construction of Whiteness* (London: Routledge, 1993).

Freud, Sigmund, *Standard Edition of the Complete Psychological Works of Sigmund Freud*, trans. and ed. by James Strachey (London: Hogarth Press and the Institute of Psychoanalysis, 1953–73).

Freund, Elizabeth, *The Return of the Reader: Reader-Response Criticism* (London and New York: Methuen, 1987).

Gagnon, Paulette, *Angela Grauerholz*, exhibition catalogue (Musée d'Art Contemporain et Les Publications du Quebec, 1995).

Galloway, Janice, *Foreign Parts* (London: Jonathan Cape, 1995).

Gamman, Lorraine, and Margaret Marshment (eds.), *The Female Gaze: Women as Viewers of Popular Culture* (London: Women's Press, 1986).

Godard, Barbara, 'Becoming my Hero, Becoming Myself: Notes Towards a Feminist Theory of Reading', in *Language in Her Eye*, ed. Mary Schreiner *et al.* (Toronto: Coach House, 1990).

Gray, Ann, *Video Playtime: The Gendering of a Leisure Technology* (London: Routledge, 1992).

Greer, Germaine, *The Obstacle Race* (London: Picador, 1981).

Hall, Stuart (ed.), *Culture/Media/Language* (London: Hutchinson, 1980).

Hawkes, Terence, *Structuralism and Semiotics* (London: Methuen, New Accents, 1978).

Helland, Janice, *The Studios of Frances and Margaret Macdonald* (Manchester and New York: Manchester University Press, 1996).

Herrmann, Anne, *The Dialogic and Difference: 'An/Other Woman' in Virginia Woolf and Christa Wolf* (New York: Columbia University Press, 1989).

Hinds, Hilary, Ann Phoenix and Jackie Stacey, *Working Out: New Directions for Women's Studies* (London: Falmer, 1992).

Hirsch, Marianne, and Evelyn Fox Keller, *Conflicts in Feminism* (London: Routledge, 1990).

Hirschkop, Ken, *Bakhtin and Cultural Theory* (Manchester and New York: Manchester University Press, 1989).

Holland, Norman, *The Dynamics of Literary Response* (New York: Oxford University Press, 1968).

Holquist, Michael, *Dialogism: Bakhtin and His World* (London and New York: Routledge, 1990).

Hutcheon, Linda, *Irony's Edge: The Theory and Politics of Irony* (London and New York: Routledge, 1994).

Iser, Wolfgang, *The Act of Reading: A Theory of Aesthetic Response* (Baltimore and London: Johns Hopkins University Press, 1978).

Jay, Karla, and Joanne Glasgow, *Lesbian Texts and Contexts* (New York and London: New York University Press, 1990).

Jordanova, Ludmilla, *Sexual Visions: Images of Gender in Science and Medicine between the Eighteenth and Twentieth Centuries* (Hemel Hempstead: Harvester-Wheatsheaf, 1990).

Juhasz, Suzanne, *Reading from the Heart: Women, Literature and the Search for True Love* (London and New York: Viking, 1994).

Kaplan, E. Ann, *Regarding Television: Critical Approaches – An Anthology* (Frederick, MD: University Publications of America Inc., 1983).

Kaplan, Cora, *Sea Changes: Culture and Feminism* (London: Verso, 1986).

Kellein, T., *Cindy Sherman* (Basle: Edition Cantz, 1991).

Kennedy, Alan, *Reading Resistance Value: Deconstructive Practice and the Politics of Literary Encounters* (New York: St. Martin's Press, 1990).

Kuhn, Annette, *Women's Pictures: Feminism and Cinema* (2nd edn; London and New York: Verso, 1994).

—— *Family Secrets: Acts of Memory and Imagination* (London: Verso, 1995).

Lochhead, Liz, 'Quelques Fleurs', in *Bagpipe Muzak* (Harmondsworth: Penguin, 1991).

Lodge, David, *After Bakhtin: Essays in Fiction and Criticism* (London and New York: Routledge, 1990).

Macherey, Pierre, *Theory of Literary Production,* trans. Geoffrey Wall (London: Routledge, 1978).

Mailloux, Steven, *Interpretive Communities: The Reader in the Study of American Fiction* (Ithaca and London: Cornell University Press, 1982).

Marcus, Steven, *The Other Victorians: A Study of Pornography and Sexuality in Mid-Nineteenth-Century England* (London: Weidenfeld and Nicolson, 1966).

Marsh, Jan, *The Pre-Raphaelite Sisterhood* (London: Quartet, 1984).

Miller, Jane, *Seductions: Studies in Reading and Culture* (London: Virago Press, 1990).

Millett, Kate, *Sexual Politics* (1969; London: Virago, 1977).

Mills, Sara (ed.), *Gendering the Reader* (Hemel Hempstead: Harvester-Wheatsheaf, 1994).

—— and Lynne Pearce, *Feminist Readings/Feminists Reading* (2nd edn; Hemel Hempstead: Harvester-Wheatsheaf, 1996).

Mills, Sara, *Discourses of Difference: Women's Travel Writing and Colonialism* (London: Routledge, 1991).

—— *Language and Gender* (Harlow: Longman, 1995).

Modleski, Tania, *Loving with a Vengeance: Mass-Produced Fantasies for Women* (London: Methuen, 1982).

Moi, Toril, *Sexual/Textual Politics* (London: Methuen, 1985).

Montgomery, Martin *et al.*, *Ways of Reading* (London: Routledge, 1992).

Morley, David, *The 'Nationwide' Audience: Structure and Decoding* (London: British Film Institute, 1980).

—— *Family Television: Cultural Power and Domestic Leisure* (London: Comedia, 1986).

Morrison, Toni, *Beloved* (London: Picador, 1988).

Mulvey, Laura, *Visual and Other Pleasures* (London: Macmillan, 1989).

Murray, Rowena, *Ethical Dilemmas in Healthcare: A Practical Approach through Medical Humanities* (London: Chapman and Hall, 1997).

Nardocchio, Elaine F. (ed.), *Reader-Response Literature: The Empirical Dimension* (Berlin and New York: Mouton de Gruyter, 1992).

Nead, Lynda, *The Female Nude: Art, Obscenity, and Sexuality* (London and New York: Routledge, 1992).

Pearce, Lynne, *Woman/Image/Text: Readings in Pre-Raphaelite Art and Literature* (Hemel Hempstead: Harvester-Wheatsheaf, 1991).

—— 'Dialogic Theory and Women's Writing', in *Working Out: New Directions for Women's Studies*, ed. Hilary Hinds, Ann Phoenix and Jackie Stacey (Brighton: Falmer Press, 1992).

—— '"I" the Reader: Text, Context and the Balance of Power', in *Feminist Subjects, Multi-Media: New Approaches to Criticism and Creativity*, ed. Penny Florence and Dee Reynolds (Manchester: Manchester University Press, 1994).

—— 'Pre-Raphaelite Painting and the Female Spectator: Sexual/Textual Positioning in Dante Gabriel Rossetti's *The Beloved*', in *Gendering the Reader*, ed. Sara Mills (Hemel Hempstead: Harvester-Wheatsheaf, 1994).

—— *Reading Dialogics* (London: Edward Arnold, 1994).

—— and Jackie Stacey, *Romance Revisited* (London: Lawrence and Wishart, 1995).

—— '"Written on Tablets of Stone"? Roland Barthes, Jeanette Winterson and the Discourse of Romantic Love', in *Volcanoes and Pearl Divers: Essays in Lesbian Feminist Studies,* ed. Suzanne Raitt (London: Onlywomen Press, 1995).

—— 'Another Time/Another Place: The Chronotope of Romantic Love in Contemporary Feminist Fiction', in *Fatal Attractions and Cultural Subversions: Re-scripting Romance in Contemporary Literature and Film,* ed. Lynne Pearce and Gina Wisker (London: Pluto Press, forthcoming).

Piercy, Marge, *Small Changes* (Garden City, NY: Doubleday, 1973).

—— *He, She and It* (1991; New York: Ballantine Books, 1993).

Pollock, Griselda, *Vision and Difference: Femininity, Feminism and the Histories of Art* (London and New York: Routledge, 1988).

Pribram, E. Deirdre (ed.), *Female Spectators: Looking at Film and Television* (London and New York: Verso, 1988).

Probyn, Elspeth, *Sexing the Self: Gendered Positions in Cultural Studies* (London and New York: Routledge, 1993).

Radway, Janice, *Reading the Romance: Women, Patriarchy and Popular Literature* (Chapel Hill and London: University of North Carolina Press, 1984).

Richards, I. A., *Principles of Literary Criticism* (New York: Harcourt, Brace and Co., 1926).

Roberts, Michèle, *A Piece of the Night* (London: Women's Press, 1978).

Rosenblum, Barbara, 'Cancer in Two Voices', in *An Intimate Wilderness: Lesbian Writers on Sexuality,* ed. Judith Barrington (Portland, OR: Eighth Mountain Press).

Rule, Jane, *This is Not for You* (London: Pandora Press, 1982; repr. 1987).

Schreiner, Olive, *The Story of an African Farm* (1899; New York: Bantam, 1993).

Schwartz, Lynne Sharon, *Ruined by Reading: A Life in Books* (Boston: Beacon Press, 1996).

Showalter, Elaine (ed.), *The New Feminist Criticism* (London: Virago, 1987).

Shukman, Ann (ed.), *The Bakhtin School Papers* (Oxford: RPT Publications, 1983).

Shumaker, Wayne, *Literature and the Irrational* (Englewood Cliffs, NJ: Prentice Hall, 1960).

Skeggs, Beverley (ed.), *Feminist Cultural Theory: Process and Production* (Manchester and New York: Manchester University Press, 1995).

Smith, Murray, *Engaging Characters: Fiction, Emotion and the Cinema* (Oxford: Oxford University Press, 1995).

Stacey, Jackie, *Star Gazing: Hollywood Cinema and Female Spectatorship* (London and New York: Routledge, 1994).

—— *Teratologies: A Cultural Study of Cancer* (London and New York: Routledge, 1997).

Suleiman, Susan and Inge Crossman (eds.), *The Reader in the Text: Essays on Audience and Interpretation* (Princeton: Princeton University Press, 1980).

Surtees, Virginia, *The Paintings and Drawings of Dante Gabriel Rossetti (1828–1832): A Catalogue Raissoné* (2 vols., Oxford: Oxford University Press, 1971).

Tompkins, Jane P., *Reader-Response Criticism: From Formalism to Poststructuralism* (Baltimore and London: Johns Hopkins University Press, 1980).

Tulloch, John, *Television Drama: Agency, Audience and Myth* (London and New York: Routledge, 1990).

Turkle, Sherry, *Life on the Screen: Identity in the Age of the Internet* (New York: Simon and Schuster, 1995).

Walker, Alice, *The Color Purple* (London: Women's Press, 1983).

Williams, Raymond, *Politics and Letters* (London: Verso, 1979).

Williamson, Judith, *Decoding Advertisements: Ideology and Meaning in Advertising* (London: Marion Boyars, 1978).

Wimsatt, William K. and Monroe C. Beardsley, *The Verbal Icon: Studies in the Meaning of Poetry* (1954; London: Methuen, 1970).

Winterson, Jeanette, *Boating for Beginners* (London: Methuen, 1985).

—— *Oranges are not the Only Fruit* (London: Pandora Press, 1985).

—— *The Passion* (Harmondsworth: Penguin, 1987).

—— *Sexing the Cherry* (London: Bloomsbury, 1989).

—— *Written on the Body* (London: Jonathan Cape, 1992).

Wolf, Christa, *The Quest for Christa T.,* trans. Christopher Middleton (1968; London: Virago, 1982).

Woolf, Janet, *Resident Alien: Feminist Cultural Criticism* (New Haven and London: Yale University Press, 1995).

Woolf, Virginia, *To the Lighthouse* (1927; Oxford: Oxford University Press, World's Classics Series, 1992).

Wright, Elizabeth, *Feminism and Psychoanalysis: A Critical Dictionary* (Oxford: Basil Blackwell, 1992).

Index